WEBSTER'S
LARGE PRINT
CROSSWORD PUZZLE DICTIONARY

COMPILED BY PATRICIA FOX-SHEINWOLD

LARGE
PRINT
REFERENCE

To my son, John,
who has a way with words

Special thanks to Evelyn Lee Jones,
Barbara Lea, and Jeanne Schapiro

HOW TO USE THIS DICTIONARY

This handy book for the avid crossword puzzler is not meant to replace your standard dictionary, but in many instances it may lead you to the correct word. For example: **file** row, enter, cabinet. All three answers are accurate though different definitions. So, if the word you are seeking does not fit into the *row* category, then switch your thinking to the *cabinet* definition. The entries include prepositions, pronouns and adverbs along with antonyms, prefixes, suffixes, slang and combined forms. Sometimes it may be necessary to look up more than one word for the definition. For example, if you do not find *at odds* under *odds*, then check under *at*. A defined word that is derived from the main entry appears with a hyphen followed by the additional letter or suffix. For example:

wall parapet, barrier
  -ed town burg

There is a heavy concentration on historical names, book titles, authors, musicians, mythology and heraldry and poetic and musical references—you know, the ones that are so difficult to find. The more you use this book, the more elusive words and odd definitions you will find. Plus, the Quick Reference List contains concise information that usually takes hours to track down if you don't happen to have it filed away in your memory bank. If you do not find what you are looking for in the Quick Reference List, go back and check the entries.

Good luck—and happy word hunting.

Patricia Fox-Sheinwold

CONTENTS

A-Z 1–337

Quick Reference List 339
  Foreign Alphabets 340
  Foreign Days of the Week 341
  Foreign Months 341
  Foreign Numbers 342
  Jewish Calendar 342
  Jewish Holidays 342
  Native Tribes 343
  Birth Flowers and Stones 347
  Zodiac Signs 347
  Presidents of the United States 348
  Thirteen Original States 350
  State Facts 351
  Academy Awards 361
  Nobel Prizes 369
  Olympic Game Locations 373
  The Super Bowl 374
  National Basketball Association Championships 375
  World Series 376

ABBREVIATIONS USED IN THIS DICTIONARY

abbrev. abbreviation
A.F.C. American Football Conference
Afr. African
Am. American
A.L. American League
Ar. Arabic
Austral. Australian
Brit. British
colloq. colloquial
comb. form combining form
Dut. Dutch
E. Eastern Conference
Eng. English
Eur. European
Fr. French
Ger. German
Gr. Greek
Haw. Hawaiian
Heb. Hebrew
instr. instrument
It. Italian

Jp. Japanese
Lat. Latin
Mex. Mexican
myth. mythology
mus. music
N. North
N.A. North American
N.F.C. National Football Conference
N.L. National League
pert. to pertaining to
pl. plural
poet. poetic
Russ. Russian
S. South
S.A. South American
S. Afr. South African
Scot. Scottish
sl. slang
Sp. Spanish
W. Western Conference

A

a an, ay, one, per, each
aa lava
aal, al mulberry
  dye morindin
aalii tree, wood
Aaron
  associate Hur
  brother Moses
  burial place Hor
  daughter Ithamar
  father Amram
  rod mullein
  sister Miriam
  son Nadab, Abihu
Aaronic Levitical
aba robe, cloth, garment
abaca hemp, lupis, linaga
abactor cattle thief
abaculus tile, tessera
abacus slab, stone, calculator
Abaddon hell, abyss, Satan
  angel Apollyon
Abadite, Ibidite Muslim
abaft aft, astern, rearward
abalone ear, ormer, mollusk
abandon cede, flee, yield, discard
abandonment
  instrument waiver
abase avale, lower, shame
abash cow, shame, confound
abate ebb, allay, assuage, slacken
abatis obstacle, barricade
abb wool, yarn
abba title, father

abbé cleric, priest, ecclesiastic
  domain abbacy, monastery
abbess amma, prelatess
  domain convent, nunnery
abbot abbas, coarb, hegumen
  assistant prior
  hero Rollo
abbreviate cut, prune, curtail, shorten,
  truncate
abdicate cede, quit, expel, forego
abdomen pleon, paunch, venter
abduct kidnap, snatch, shanghai
Abdul the Bul Bul Amir
abecederium book, primer
Abel
  brother Cain, Seth
  father Adam
  mother Eve
Abelard
  love (H)Eloise
abele pine, poplar
aberrant wild, abnormal
abet aid, egg, boost, incite
abettor fautor, promoter, accessory, auxiliary, confederate, accomplice
abeyance pause, respite, interval, cessation
Abi
  father Zechariah
  husband Ahaz
  mother Hezekiah
Abiah
  father Samuel
  husband Herzon
  son Ashur

abide bear, last, stay, brook, endure
Abiel
  grandson Abner, Saul
  son Kish, Ne
abies firs, evergreens
Abigail maid
  husband David, Nabal
  son Amasa
Abital
  husband David
  son Shephatiah
abject base, pitiful, servile
abjectly afraid craven, chicken
ablation surgery
ablaze afire, aglow, burning
able apt, keen, alert, facile
ablegate envoy
abluent soap, detergent
ablution bath, lotion, baptism
abnegate deny, abjure, disclaim
Abner
  cousin Saul
  father Ner
  slayer Joab
aboard onto, athwart
abode hut, cell, bower, residence
  animal zoo menagerie
  of the dead Dar, Aaru, Hades, Orcus, Sheol
  of gods Meru, Asgard(th), Olympus
abolish end, annul, quash, revoke
aboma boa, bom, serpent
abominable vile, odious, loathsome
Abominable Snowman Bigfoot, yeti
aboriginal first, natal, primitive, indigenous
aborigine native, autochthon
abortion failure, feticide, misconception
abound flow, swarm, exuberate
abounding rife, flush, abundant, plentiful
  comb. form poly, acity
  with plants braky
about re, near, anent, circa, nearly, circiter, approximately
above atop, supra, overhead
  board open, legit
  the ear epiotic

poetic o'er
reproach pure, innocent
abra pass, defile
abracadabra spell, incantation
abrade rub, bark, file, rasp, chafe, grind, irritate, excoriate
abrading
  tool file, rasp
  material sand(paper), emery, corundum
Abraham
  birthplace Ur
  bosom Zion, Canaan, heaven, paradise
  brother Nahor
  concubine Hagar
  father Terah
  grandfather Nahor
  grandson Esau
  maid Hagar
  nephew Lot
  son Isaac, Medan, Shuah, Midian, Zimran, Ishmael
  wife Sara(h), Sarai, Keturah
abramis carp, fish, bream
abrasion scar, bruise, attrition
abraxas gem, charm, stone
abret bread, wafer
abri shed, cavity, dugout
abridge cut, brief, limit, curtail
abrini Abrus, licorice
abrogate annul, quash, revoke, nullify
abrupt curt, blunt, terse, craggy, unceremonious
Abruzzi
  city Atri
Absalom favorite son
  cousin/captain Amasa
  father David
  slayer Joab
  sister Tamar
abscess moro, ulcer, lesion, gathering
  on gums gumboil
abscond flee, escape, decamp, levant
absence
  leave of exit, furlough
  of feeling numbness, insensate
  of hair acomia, alopecia

of motion rest, inertia
of shame brazen
of taste ageusia
absent off, away, gone, missing
without leave AWOL
absentee truant, malingerer
absentminded bemused, faraway, distrait
absinthe genipi, liqueur, wormwood
absolute mear, plat, total, plenary, explicit, unconditional
independence alod
rule autarchy
absolve free, acquit, shrive, dispense, exculpate
in law vested
in sin shrive
absorb sop, unite, occupy, engross, occlude
absorbent fomes, bibulous
material sponge, blotter
absquatulate elope
abstain deny, spurn, eschew, for(e)bear, teetotal
from eating fast
abstemious ascetic, temperate
absterge wipe, purge, rinse
abstract cull, brief, detach, excerpt
being ens, esse, entia (pl.)
abstruse deep, mystic, recondite, acroamatic
absurd balmy, comic, inane, foolish
abundance flow, plenty, foison, amplitude, exuberance
abuse mar, tax, defile, vilify, yatter, traduce, invective
abut join, rest, border, project
abutment pier, alette
abysmal deep, dreary, profound, wretched
abyss pit, gulf, chasm, gehenna
Babylonian mythology Apsu
below Hades tartarus
Abyssinia, Abyssinian Kaffa, Ethiopian
coin talari
drink mese, bousa
fly zimb
herb ramtil
weight aket, kasm, natr, alada

acacia gum, babul, siris, arabic
academy USMA, USNA, lyceum, Annapolis, West Point
Academy Awards see Quick Reference List
Acadian Cajun
acaleph jellyfish, sea nettle
acantha fin, spine, prickle
acarus mite, tick, insect
acaudal bobbed, anurous, ecaudate, tailless
accede let, allow, yield, comply, acquiesce
accelerate rev, urge, impel, hasten, forward
accented marcato, stressed
syllable arsis
accept agree, honor, espouse, acknowledge
access adit, entry, accost, portal, paroxysm, passageway,
accession consent, addition, entrance, inaugural, enlargement
accessorius nerve
accessory tool, extra, helper, addition
accidental odd, fluky, chance, random, unmeant
acclaim cry, clap, hail, eclat, exalt, extol, plaudit, applause
acclimate inure, season, accustom
acclivity bank, hill, slope, incline
accolade sign, award, token, symbol
accommodate aid, favor, humor, oblige
accompaniment descant, obligato
accomplice ally, crony, confederate
accord deal, fuse, jibe, agree, concur
accordant even, attuned, suitable, harmonious
according to by, à la (Fr.), alter, compared
Hoyle fair, correct
rule conformity
accost hail, greet, halloo, approach
accouter rig, arrn, gird, equip, furnish
accredit vouch, depute, certify
accretion gain, deposit, increase, enlargement
accrue earn, ensue, mature, acquire, increase
accumulate hive, mass, store, muster
accurate leal, exact, proper, correct
accursed fey, damned, doomed, execrable

accustom haft, enure, train, season
ace jot, pip, hero, adept, basto, topnotcher
acerb tart, harsh, severe, caustic
acetic sour, sharp
  acid vinegar
  salt acetate
acetylene gas, tolan, ethin(e)
Achates
  companion Aeneas
ache hurt, lust, smart, throb, twinge
Achilles
  adviser Nestor
  captive Briseis
  father Peleus
  friend Patroclus
  horse Xanthus
  mother Thetis
  slayer Paris
  soldiers Myrmidons
  teacher Chiron
  victim Hector
  vulnerable part heel
achiote tree, arnatta(o)
achira canna, handless
achromatic substance linin
Achsah
  father Caleb
  husband Othniel
acid keen, amino, ulmic, oleate
  comb. form oxy, acer
  etching mordant
  nicotinic niacin
  or base indicator litmus
  slang LSD
  tanning catechin
acinus raspberry
Acis
  lover Galatea
  slayer Polyphemus
acle ironwood
acme cap, apex, apogee, zenith, pinnacle
acolyte helper, altar boy/girl, satellite
  garb cotta
acomia baldness
aconite bik(h), remedy, wolfsbane

acor acidity
acorn nut, mast, orest
  barnacle scuta
  cup valonia
  dried camata
  edible ballote, bellote
  shaped balanoid
acouchi elemi, resin, protium
acoustic
  equipment sirene
  vase echea
acquaint know, verse, inform, apprise
acquiesce bow, cime, agree, accede
acquit act, bear, free, absolve, comport
acre arpent, farmhold
  1/4 of rood
  1/100 of hectare
acrobat zany, gymnast, schoenobatist
  garment leotard, fleshings (tights)
  high wire aerialist
  net trampoline
  of India nat
acrogen fern
acrolith statue, caryatid
acropolis hill, cadmea, Larissa
act actu, deed, emote, bestir
  according to rules conform
  (ing) by turns altern
  like ape, imitate, simulate
  of prudence caution
  silly clown
  up priss
  with exaggeration ham
action fray, work, doing, process, conflict
  comb. form cin(o), kin(o), praxia
  field of bowl, arena, stage, stadium
  legal res, suit, actus
  painting tachism
  pert. to practical
  put out of KO, disable
  to recover property trover, replevin
activation kinesis
active apry, pert, alert, nimble, vigorous
actor player, protean, thespian
  aid prompter, teleprompter

assignment lead, part, role
cast dramatis personae
cue hint, prompt
group Afra, Aftra, troop, troupe
part role, function
poor ham, barnstormer
(s) in a play cast
supporting bit, cameo, super
actual true, posit, genuine, concrete
actuate stir, impel, arouse, galvanize
acuity wit, edge, keenness, sharpness
acute keen, quick, snell, intense
Adah
  husband Esau, Lamech
  son Jabal, Jubal
Adam plant, puttyroot
  ale water
  grandson Enos
  needle yucca
  other wife Lilith
  rib Eve
  son Abel, Cain, Seth
  teacher Raisel
Adam and Eve puttyroot
adamantine firm, stone, immovable
  pert. to boric
Adam Bede
  author Eliot
Adam's apple larynx
adda skink, lizard
adder snake, viper, whorl
ad design logo
addict fan, buff, hound, lover, junkie, zealot
addition and, ell, also, rider, adjunct, codicil
  number addend, summand
  prefix super
addled asea, putrid, rotten, confused
address aim, level, apply, appeal, consign
adeps fat, lard
Adhem Abou
adherent votary, disciple
adherents ists, ites, sequelae
adhesive gum, paste, tacky, mucilage

adhibit use, admit, attach
ad interim acting, pro tem, temporary
adipose fat, pursy, squab
adjudicate act, try, hear, judge
adjunct ally, helper, auxiliary
ad lib offhand, improvise
Admetus
  father Pheres
  wife Alcestis
admiral officer, flagship, butterfly, nymphalida
  American Byrd, Sims, Dewey, Halsey, Nimitz, Farragut
  English Nelson, Rodney, Vernon, Mountbatten
admixture alloy, blend, tinge
admonish chide, scold, censure, reprove
admonisher monitor
Adonijah
  brother Ammon, Absalom, Chileab
  father David
  mother Haggith
  slayer Benaiah
Adonis
  beloved Venus, Aphrodite
  mother Myrrh(a)
  slayer Ares
  slayer of boar
adorn deck, grace, enrich, decorate
ad patres dead
Adriana
  servant Luce
Adriatic
  city Venice
  island Bua, Eso, Lagosta (ovo)
  peninsula Istria
  port Pola, Rimini, Trieste
  resort Lido
  river Po, Reno, Kerka
  wind bora
adroit deft, handy, sharp, skillful
adult grown, grown-up
  insect imago
  pike luce
  steer beeve

aduncuous bent, hooked
advance aid, pay, gain, better, progress
  guard vanguard
  military anabasis
  slowly inch, creep
adventitious casual, episodic
adverb
  ending ly
adversary foe, rival, opponent
advice rede, avis, lore
  contain mentorial
adytum shrine, sanctuary
Aeacus
  father Zeus
  son Peleus, Telamon
Aeetes
  daughter Medea
Aegean Sea
  ancient people Psara, Samian, Leleges
  arm of Saros
  islands Nio, Ilos, Paros, Samos, Thera, Rhodes
  port Enos
  river Struma, Vardar, Marista
  rock Aex
Aegeon
  wife Aemilia
aeger ill, sick, excuse
Aegir
  wife Ran
aegis ward, shield, auspice, patronage
Aegisthus
  cousin Agamemnon
  daughter Erigone
  father Thyestes
  killed by Orestes
  mother Pelopia
  seduced Clytemnestra
Aello Harpy
aelurophile cat lover
Aeneas
  beloved Dido
  father Anchises
  follower Achates
  grandfather Capys
  great-grandson Brut

  mother Aphrodite
  rival Turnus
  son Iulus, Ascanius
  wife Creusa, Lavinia
Aeneid
  author Virgil
  hero Aeneas
  first word arma
  second word virumque
  third word cano
Aeolian lyricist Sappho
Aeolus
  daughter Halcyone
aeonian eternal, infinite, lasting
aerolite meteorite
Aerope
  husband Atreus
  lover Thyestes
  son Menelaus, Agamemnon
aerose brassy, copper
aerugo rust, patina, verdigris
Aesculapius
  daughter Hygeia, Panacea
  father Apollo
  mother Coronis
  slayer Zeus, Jupiter
  son Machaon, Podalirus
  teacher Chiron
  wife Epione
Aeson
  son Jason
Aesop work fables
Aeta Ita, Filipino
Aether
  father Erebus
Aetolian prince Xydeus
afar off, away, saho, hamite
affeer assess, confirm
affray melee, battle, combat
affy trust, betroth, confide
Afghan, Afghanistan Pathan, Durani
  coin anania, pul
  language Pashto, Pushto
  prince amir, ameer
  rug cover(let), blanket
  tribe safi, ulus

aforesaid ditto, prior, antecedent
Africa, African black, Negro
  ancient name Libya
  animal arui, civet, okapi, zoril
  antelope gnu, tora, impala, okapi
  Arab tribe Battakhin
  assembly read
  bat hammerhead
  boss baas
  buffalo niare
  bushman Qung
  camp boma, lager
  chief kaid
  coin akey, pesa, rupie
  dance juba
  garment haik, tobe
  hemp ife, sisal
  hill Kop
  Hottentot Nama
  house tembe
  language taal, bantu, swahili
  measure doti, curba
  Negro egba
  peasant Kopi
  secret society poro, Mau-Mau
aftermath rowen, result, eagrass
aftersong epode
Ag silver
Agag
  slayer of Samuel
agalite talc
agalloch wood, garoo
agama guana, iguana, lizard
Agamemnon
  brother Menelaus
  daughter Electra, Iphigenia
  father Atreus
  son Orestes
  wife Clytemnestra
agar-agar gelose
agaric fungus
agave aloe, datil, mescal
  fiber pita, istle, sisal
age eon, olam, ripen, mature
  grow old senesce
  pert. to senile, geriatric

  same as coeval
  study of nostology
agendum slate, ritual, liturgy
Agenor
  daughter Europa
  father Antenor
  son Cadmus
agent doer, means, facient
  act through an medium
agglomerate heap, lump, mass
aggrandize lift, boost, exalt
aglet tag, lace, spangle
agnate akin, allied, cognate
Agni Kali
agnomen name, alias, epithet
agnus dei, lamb
Agra tomb Taj (Mahal)
agrestic rural, bucolic, unpolished
Agrippina
  son Nero
Ahab
  wife Jezebel
Ahasuerus
  minister Haman
  wife Vashti
Ahaz
  son Hezekiah
  wife Abi
Ahaziah
  sister Jehosheba(th)
Ahiam
  father Sacar
Ahinoam
  husband Saul, David
  son Amnon
Ahira
  son Enan
Aholibamah
  husband Esau
Ahriman's angel/spirit div, deev, deva
ahu heap, mound, gazelle
ahuehuete cedar, sabino, cypress
ai sloth, edentate
Aida
  composer Verdi
  father Amonasro

lover Radames
rival Amneris
Ailie Helen
aine elder, senior
air sky, aria, mien, pose
  component argon, oxygen, nitrogen
  current thermal
  filled with aerate
  fresh ozone
  open alfresco
  passage flue, vent
  spirit sylph
  tight hermetic
  upper ether
  warm oam
airplane jet, aero, gyro
  carrier flattop
  marker pylon
  part wing, cabin, aileron, cockpit, fusilage
  runway strip, tarmac
  vapor contrail
airn iron
airy gay, rare, ethereal
aiseweed goutweed
ait oat, eyot, holm, isle
aith oath
aitu god, demon, spirit
aizle ember, spark
ajaja bird, jabiru, spoonbill
Ajax
  father Telamon
  tale about myth
ajonjoli sesame
ajuga herb, bugloss
akia poison
akin sib, allied, germane
aku victorfish
Alabama see Quick Reference List
alabarch magistrate
alabaster gypsum
Aladdin's spirit genie, genii, jinni
Alamo fort, tree, battle, shrine, cottonwood
  hero Bowie, Crockett
alan dog, wolfhound
alar pteric, winged
alas ach, heu, oime(e), ochone
  poetic ay

Alaska, Alaskan see Quick Reference List; Aleut, Eskimo, Dene
  garment parka
  glacier Muir
  purchaser Seward
  river Yukon
alate ant, aphid, insect, winged
alb camisia, vestment
Albania, Albanian cham, gheg, tosk
  coin lek, qintar
  dialect tosk, gheghish
  soldier palikar
albertin coin
Albion Anglia, England
albula fish, chiro
alburnum sapwood
Alcestis
  father Pelias
  husband Admetus
  rescuer Hercules
alchemy magic, thaumaturgy
  god Hermes
  iron Mars
alcidine bird auk, muree, puffin, murrelet
Alcimedon
  daughter Philao
  father Laerces
Alcinous
  daughter Nausicaa
  wife Arete
Alcmaeon
  brother Amphilochus
  father Amphiaraus
  mother Eriphyle
  son Acarnan, Amphoterus
  wife Arsinoe, Callirrhoe
Alcmaon
  father Thestor
  slayer Sarpedon
  victim Glaucus
Alcmene
  husband Amphitryon
  son Hercules
alcohol ethyl, vinic, liquor, methyl
  basis ethyl
  crystalline guaiol, talitol

desire for dipsomania
from idose idite, iditol
liquid farnesol
radical al
solid sterin, sterol
standard proof
suffix ol
Alcoran Koran
Alcott heroine Jo, Amy, Meg, Beth
aldehyde derivative acetal
comb. form ald(o)
imino aldime
sugar aldose
radical al, amyl, bornyl
alder arn, bush, sagerose
genus alnus
tree arn (Scot.)
ale mum, bock, flip, stout, porter
mug toby, stein
sweet mixture bragget
Alea light, Athena
alee ahead
opposed to stoss
alembic cup, retort, vessel
alencon
product lace
aleppo berea, haleb
fabric agabanee
stone eye, gem, agate
alette wing, doorjamb
Aleus
daughter Auge
Aleut Atka, Unalaska
Aleutian Island Attu, Kiska, Kodiak
Alewife fish, herring, pompano, walleye
Alexander
born Pella
horse Bucephalus
kingdom Macedonia
mistress Campaspe
victory Issus, Arbela
Alexandrian
bishop Athanasius
clover berseem
laurel shrub, poon tree
magistrate alabarch
patriarch papa

pleiad Homer, Apollonius, Theocritus
theologian Arius
alfa esparto
alfalfa hay, fodder, lucern(e)
alforja bag, pouch, wallet
alga nori, nostoc, seaweed
envelope ceramidium
flower nostol
freshwater desmid
genus dasya, alaria, padina
one-cell diatom
study algology
algarroba tree, carob, calden
Algeria, Algerian
cavalryman spahi, spahee
city Boba, Oran, Media, Constantine
commune setif
governor dey
grass diss, esparto
measure pik, tavri
monastery ribat
mountain Atlas
people Arabs, Berbers, Kabyles
river Shelif
Roman name Pomaria
ruler bey, dey
ship xebec
tirailleur turco
weight rotl
Algiers
natives' quarters Casbah
Alhambra site Granada
Ali
descendant Fatmid
wife Fatima
Ali Baba
brother Cassim
word sesame
alias else, title, epithet, sobriquet
Alice in Wonderland
author Carroll
character Queen, Walrus, Mad Hatter, Cheshire Cat, White Rabbit
alidade diopter
alien deed, remote, adverse, foreign
in Hebrew territory ger
aliform winglike, wing-shaped

alike akin, same, uniform, congruent
  comb. form iso
alkali lye, reh, soda, usar
alkaloid caffein(e), atropine
  calabar bean eserine
  hemlock conin(e)
  mustard sinapin(e)
  poison curare
all sum, total, whole, everyone, thoroughly
  comb. form pan, omni
  in weary
  -knowing omniscient
  Lat. toto
  right OK, yes, okay, agreed
  there sane
allan gull
allanite cerine, silicate
alleged force od, odyl
allegiance duty, honor, fealty
  violation of treason
allegory myth, tale, fable
  religious parable
alleviate aid, ease, pacify, relieve,
  palliate
alley lane, byway, chare, tewer
  back slum
allice shad
alligator cayman (S.A.), lagarto
  pear avocado, aguacate
allium leek, onion, garlic
allowance fee, dole, edge, share, bounty
  short ration
  traveling mileage, per diem
  weight tare, scalage
allowing for that if
alloy mix, garble, amalgamate
  black copper niello
  carbon + iron steel
  copper + tin bronze
  copper + zinc brass
  gold + silver asem
  nickel + silver alfenide
  nonferrous tula
  pewter bidri
  yellow aich

allspice tree pimento
alluvial
  clay adobe
  deposit mud, silt, drift
  fan delta
  matter geest
allyene propyne
almandine garnet, spinel
almond nut, amygdala
  emulsion orgeat
  liqueur ratafia
  oil amarin(e)
alms dole, bounty, charity
  box arca, reliquary
  -house poorhouse
  -man pauper, beggar
almuce hood, tippet
alnus tree, alder, birch
aloe pita, agave, maguey
  derivative aloin
  extract orcin
alone lorn, apart, unaided
  comb. form soli
  on stage sola, solo, solus
alongside close, abreast, parallel
  prefix para
Alonso
  son Ferdinand
alopecia baldness
alopecoid foxlike, vulpine
alouatte monkey
alpaca paco, llama
  -like guanaco
alphabet order, letters, see also Quick
  Reference List
  early/old rune
  Hindu Sarada
  teacher of abecedarian
Alpine hat, stick
  dance gavot
  dwelling chalet
  pass col
  shepherd senn
  wind bora
already e'en, now, before

alsike clover
also eke, too, likewise
  ran loser, losing candidate
altar ara, autere, shrine
  area apse
  boy/girl acolyte
  carpet pedale
  cloth coster
  curtain riddel
  enclosure bema
  hanging dorsal, dossel
  ledge retable
  platform predella
  screen reredos
  top mensa
  vessel pyx
alter ego self, agent, friend
althaea mallow
Althaea
  husband Oeneus
altiloquence bombast, pomposity
altitude apex, height, elevation, loftiness
  measuring device orometer, altimeter
  sickness soroche
altruism generosity, philanthropy
alture height
aludel pot
alula wing, lobe
alum styptic, astringent
  rock alunite
alumina argil
aluminum
  discoverers Davy, Wohler
  oxide alumina
  sulphate alum
alveary beehive
alveolate pitted, honeycombed
ama cup, diver, vessel
Amadis
  beloved Oriana
amadou punk, tinder
Amalekite king Agag
Amalthaea goat
  horn cornucopia
  nursling Zeus

amanuensis scribe, typist, recorder
amara beetle
amaryllis girl, lily, agave
Amasa
  father Jether
amate tree, daunt, match
amative fond, loving, passionate
Amazon river, warrior
  cetacean inia
  discoverer Orellana
  estuary Para
  lily eucharis
  mat yapa
  queen Calafia, Hippolyta, Penthesileia
  rain forest selva, silvas
  sex female
  tributary Apa, Ica, Napo
ambari hemp, fiber
ambassador envoy, nuncio, diplomat
  pert. to legatine
amber gris, resin, electrum
  colored resinous
amber fish medregal
ambiance milieu
ambit limit, scope
ambo desk, pulpit
Amboina
  button yaws
  pine galagala
Ambos incus
ambrosia honey, nectar
  genus ragweed
ambry niche, closet, pantry
Amen-Ra
  wife Mut
ament idiot, catkin, imbecile
amerce fine, punish
America, American New World, continent, Yankee
  apple Roxbury
  ash rowan
  balsam tolu
  bear musquaw
  bird rhea, condor, tanager
  butterfly viceroy

buzzard buteo, vulture
deer wapiti
discoverer Cabot, Votan, Ericson
elk wapiti
elm ulmus
first child Virginia Dare
flag Old Glory
grape catawba
holly assi
imaginary town Podunk
lion puma, cougar
Mexican gringo
monkey titi
moth io
plains pampas, prairie
shrub majo, guava, wahoo
soldier G.I., Sammy, doughboy
star mullet
tree fir, lin, oak, pine, maple, walnut,
    sequoia
volcano Lassen, Shasta
wind pampero
Amerind Eskimo, Indian, native
  clan symbol totem
  memorial post xat
Amfortas
  father Titurel
amice cape, hood, vestment
amino
  acid protein
  compound diamide, triamine
amit lose
amm mother, abbess
ammonia hartshorn, refrigerant
  derivative amin(e), anilid(e)
  plant oshac
ammoniac plant oshac
Ammonite king Hanun, Uzziah
ammunition arms, bombs, shell, bullet,
    materiel, artillery
  case bandolier
  depot arsenal
  holder gun, belt, tray
  wagon caisson
amnesia lapse, blackout

amnesty pardon
amnion sac, membrane
amoeba olm, porteus, protozoan
amole salt, soap, plant
Amon
  son Josiah
among in, amid, midst
  prefix epi
amora rabbi
Amorc member Rosicrucian
Amorite king 0g, Sihon
amorphous vague, shapeless
amort dejected, inanimate
amount gob, feck, ream, total, whole,
    quantity
  fixed rate
  indefinite any, some
  made lot, batch
  relative ratio, degree
  smallest jot, iota, whit, grain
ampere unit volt, watt
amphibian eft, olm, newt, proteus
  extinct eryop
  young tadpole
Amphion
  father Zeus, Iasus
  mother Antiope
  twin brother Zethus
  wife Niobe
Amphitrite
  father Nereus
  husband Poseidon
  mother Doris
Amphitryon
  wife Alcmene
amphora jar, urn, cadus
amplify pad, swell, expand
  factor mu
ampyx plate, fillet, headdress
amula ama
amulet gem, mojo, scroll, token, periapt
Amulius
  brother Numitor
Amycus
  enemy Lycus

father Poseidon
friend Hercules
mother Melie
amygdala almond, tonsil
amyl starch, pentyl, alcohol
radical al, amyl
anabasis expedition
Anacreon
birthplace Teos
anadem crown, wreath
anagogic occult, abstruse
analgesic opium, codein(e), aspirin
ananas pineapple
Ananias liar
wife Sapphira
anaqua tree, anama
anarchist rebel, nihilist
anathema ban, oath, curse
Anatolia Armenia
goddess Ma, Cybele
rug tuzla
anatomy body, skeleton
animal zootomy
microscopic histology
quick vivisection
Anaximander's principle apeiron
ancestor sire, elder, stock
common sept
remote atavus
ancestral avital
spirits lares, manes
anchor bind, moor, affix, support
hoist cat, capstan
position atrip
ring tore
anchorite monk, hermit
anchovy sprat
sauce alec
ancient eld, old, hoary, primal, archaic
comb. form arche, paleo
country Gaul, Canaan
flute tiba
sign rune
weight mina
ancilla helper, servant

ancon elbow, console
Andes, Andean Peru, Peruvian
animal llama
bird condor
deer pudu, vanada
grass ichu
tribe anti, campa
android robot
Andromache
husband Hector
Andromeda heath, plant
father Cepheus
husband Perseus
mother Cassiopeia
anecdote joke, tale, sketch
collection ana
anele bless, anoint, shrive
anemia surra(h)
anemone buttercup, windflower
aneroid barometer
angel deva, backer, seraph
biblical Gabriel, Raphael
bottomless pit abaddon, apollyon
fallen Eblis, Satan, Lucifer
of death Azrael, Sammuel
of resurrection Israfil
Paradise Lost Uriel, Belial, Ariocha
Persian mah
worship dulia
angle fish, fork, scheme
acute akimbo
forty-five degree octant
having none agonic
of stem axil
Anglo-Saxon
armor hauberk
coin ora, sceat, mancus
freeman thane
slave esne
tax geld
Angola coin macuta, angolar
aniline dye benzol(e), magenta
animal brute, carnal, creature
anatomy of zootomy
body of soma

carrying young marsupial
crossbred mule, hybrid
fat lard, suet, tallow
footless apod(a)
myth faun, dragon, griffin, unicorn
pert. to zoic
plant life biota
anion ion
opposed to cation
Anius
daughter Elais
ankle coot, hock, talus, tarsus
comb. form tar(so)
pert. to tarsal, talaric
ann stipend
anna coin, hoa(c)tzin
Annam
boat gayyou
measure con, dam, ngu, sao, vai, phan
money quan
tribe Moi
weight li, can, hao, yen, binh
Annapolis
student plebe, middy
annatto dye, urucu, salmon
derivative orellin
annelid worm
freshwater naid
marine lurg
anniversary fete, mass, annual
1st paper
5th wooden
10th tin
15th crystal
20th china
25th silver
30th pearl
40th ruby, emerald
50th gold
announcer of coming events seer, herald, prophet
annual yearly
income rentes (Fr.)
winds etesian
annuity income, pension
form of tontine
annular round, circular

die dod
reinforcement hoop, sput
ant mine, emmet, pismire, termite
bear aardvark
comb. form myrmec(o)
cero aphid
nest formicary
nonworker drone
stinging kelep
white anai, termite
worker ergate (comb. form)
Antaeus
enemy Heracles, Hercules
father Poseidon
mother Gaea
Antarctic
bird skua, penguin
explorer Byrd, Cook, Ross
icebreaker Atka
mountain Siple
sea Ross
anteater manis, pangolin
antelope gnu, sus, poku, yakin, gazelle
ancient addax
female doe
forest bongo
genus oryx
golden impala
-like bovid
male buck
myth yale
royal ipete
tawny oribi
young kid
antenna palp, aerial, feeler
insect clava
radar scanner
anthelion halo, nimbus, anti-sun
anther tip, stamen
Anthony Adverse
author Allen
Anthozoan coryl, polyp
anthracite coal
inferior culm
Antigone
mother Jocasta
sister Ismene

Antilles
　god Zeme
　native Ineri
　pearl Cuba
antimony kohl, metal, paradox
　pert. to stibial
antiseptic eupad, salol, cresol, iodine
　acid boric
　mercury egol, Metaphen
antler horn
　stag's rack, attire
　unbranched dag, spike
Anvil City Nome
any all, some, part
　dialect oni
　of stars Deneb
　one an
ape mimic, orang, monkey, simian, primate
　long-tailed (India) kra
　man alalus
apetalous flower trema, cactus
apex acme, apogee, zenith
　belonging to apical
　covering epi
　elbow ancon
Aphareus
　brother Lynceus
　son Idas
aphasia alalia
Aphrodite Venus, Urania
　father Zeus
　got apple from Paris
　love of Adonis
　mother Dione
　son Eros
　temple site Paphos
apiaceous herb/plant anise, nondo, celery, parsley,
aplomb ease, poise, coolness
apocalypse oracle, vision, prophecy
apocarp etaerio, strawberry
apocryphal sham, false, wrong, unreal
　book Tobit, Baruck, Esdras
apodal footless
apode eel, moray
Apollo Mercury
　birthplace Delos

instrument bow, lute
mother Leto, Latonia
son Ion
twin Diana, Artemis
apollyon devil, fiend, diablo, Old Nick
apologue myth, fable, parable
apoplexy esca, plant, stroke
apostle disciple, follower, apprentice
　of the English Augustine
　of the Gentiles Paul
　of Germany Boniface
　of Indies Xavier
　of Ireland Patrick
　of Native Americans John Eliot
　pert. to petrine
　teaching of didache
　to Franks Remi
　to Gauls Denis
　to Goths Ulfilas
apothegm maxim, dictum, saying
appetite greed, gusto, taste, orexis
　morbid pica, bulimia
　want of asitia
applause eclat, salvo, acclaim, plaudits
　reaching for captation, esurience
apple pome, tree, fruit
　acid malic
　crushed pomace
　genus malus
　immature codlin(g)
　love tomato
　tree sorb
　wild crab, deucin
apricot mebo(s), fruit
　cordial persico(t)
　disease blight
　Jp. ume
　Korean ansu, anzu
apteryx moa, bird, kiwi
aquamarine blue, beryl
Aquinas' work Summa
Arab, Arabian gamin, nomad, Semite, wanderer
　abode dar, tent
　ancient country Sheba (Saha)
　cloak aba
　coin carat, dinar, kabik

people of Omani
measure den, ardeb, covid(o)
script neski
state of bliss kef
teacher ulema
title sidi
wind simoon
Arabic acid arabin
arachnid mite, tick, spider
  trap web
Aram
  children Uz, Hul, Mash, Gether
Arawakan
  language Taino
  tribe Guana
arboreal dendral
  animal ai, lemur, sloth, dasyure
arc bow, curve, orbit
  chord sine
Arcadian rural, rustic, bucolic
  god Ladon
  king Lycaon
  princess Auge
arch coy, sly, prime, cunning
  angel Satan, Uriel, Gabriel
  of heaven cope
  pointed ogee, ogive
  Roman alette
archery target clout
architectural
  order Greek, Ionic, Noric, Roman,
    Gothic, Modern, Norman,
    Corinthian
  pier anta
Arctic north, polar, frigid
  base Etah
  dog samoyed
  gull genus xema
  jacket parka, anorak
  plain tundra
  transportation sled, kayak,
    umiak
arctoid ursine, bearlike
areca nut, palm, betel
arenose sandy
Ares Mars
  father Zeus

mother Enyo
sister Eris
Argentina, Argentine
  coin peso, centavo, argentino
  measure sino, vara, cuadra
  plain(s) pampa(s)
  tree tala
  weight grano, quintal
argillaceous slaty, spongy, clayey
Argonaut Jason, Acastus
  ship Argo
arhat monk, lohan, saint
Arikara Ree, Indian
Aristotle
  birthplace Thrace, Stagira
  school lyceum
  teacher Plato
Arizona see Quick Reference List
Arkansas see Quick Reference List
arm limb, wing, equip, fiord
  bone ulna, radius
  comb. form brachi(o)
  part wrist, elbow, ares
  pert. to brachial
  pit ala, oxter, axilla
  sleeve hole mail, scye
armadillo peva, poyou, mulita
  extinct animal-like glyptodon
  giant tatu, peludo
  small peba
Armenia, Armenian Minni, Anatolia
  cap calpac
  cumin caraway
  lake Van, Urumiyah
  mountain Ararat, Taurus
  people Gomer
  river Kur, Cyrus, Tigris, Euphrates
armful yaffle
armhole mail, scye
armor egis, plate, defense
  bearer squire
  head sconce
  leg jamb(e), tuille
  shoulder ailette
  thigh cuish
armpit ala, oxter, axilla
  pert. to axillar

army host, array, force, legion
  ant driver
  base camp, depot
  car jeep
  commission brevet
  follower sutler
  mascot mule
  meal chow, rations
  pert. to martial, military
  school OCS, OTS, academy, West
    Point
aroid taro, tanier
aromatic balmy, spicy, odorous
  fruit nutmeg
  gum myrrh
  herb anise, clary
  medicinal leaves buchu
around near, about, circa
  comb. form peri
arpeggio sweep, roulade
arquebus support croc
arrange plat, align, scheme
  in layers tiered, stratose
  side by side appose
arras drapery, tapestry
arris peen, angle
arriviste snob, parvenu
arrogate claim, seize, usurp
arrow bolt, dart, shaft, missile
  end nock
  feathered vire
  handle stele
  maker bowyer, fletcher
  -shaped beloid
arrowroot pia, musa, canna, ararao
arsenic
  comb. form arseno
  mixture speiss
  of copper erinite
  symbol As
Artemis Upis, Delia, Phoebe
  twin Apollo
  victim Orion
artery road, vessel, conduit
  large aorta
  neck carotid
  pulse of ictus

arthropoda crab, phyla, spider
Arthur king
  capital Camelot
  father Uther
  foster brother Kay
  lady Enid, Elaine
  sword Excalibur
article an, the, item, thing, clause, object
  Ar. al
  Fr. la, le, un, des, les, une(s)
  Ger. das, der, ein
  Sp. el, la, las, los
artificial language Ro, Ido, Esperanto
artistic strewing seme
arum taro, plant, cuckoopint
  water calla
Aryan Mede, Slav, Caucasian
  deity Ormazd
  fire god Ayni
  Indian God Hindu
as qua, like, since, while
  far as to
  it stands/written sic, sta (mus.)
  usual solito
Asa
  father Abia
asafetida hing, laser, ferula
ascetic nun, yogi, friar, stoic, austere
  ancient essene
Asher
  daughter Serah, Beriah
  father Jacob
  son Usui, Jimnah
Asia, Asian
  ancient region Aria, Canaan, Babylon
  bird myna, pitta
  blizzard buran
  carnivore panda
  cattle zobo
  Christian Uniat
  comb. form Indo
  country Iran, Iraq, Laos, Siam, China,
    India, Korea, Syria, Tibet, Malaya,
    Turkey, Siberia, Vietnam, Cambodia
  cow zo(h), zobo
  deer roe, axis
  desert Gobi

evergreen bago
fiber hemp, ramie
monkey rhesus
native Shan
ox yak
sea Aral, Caspian
tree acle, asok
weight tael, catty
aspect mien, guise, feature
general facies
asperity ire, severity, bitterness
ass dolt, fool, burro, donkey
comb. form ono
wild kulan, onager
Assam
Mongol Naga
shrub tea, tche
silkworm eri(a)
tribesman ao, aka, Garo
assay try, prove, analysis
vessel of cup, cupel
asse fox, caama
assembly hui, mass, unite, gather, muster
ecclesiastical coetus
full plena
hall kiva
place agora
asseverate aver, swear, declare
association guild, union, cartel
merchants' hanse
secret cabal, lodge
assonance pun, rhyme, paragram
Assyria, Assyrian Ashur, Assur
king Pul
queen Semiramis (myth.)
river Zab
sky anat
weight cola
Asterius argonaut, minotaur
father Hyperasius
mother Pasiphae
wife Europa
asteroid
first Ceres
nearest Earth Eros
Astolat, Lily Maid Elaine

Astrakhan city, apple, cloth, caracul, karakul
astral lamp, starry
fluid od, odyl(e)
astrological belief siderism
astronomy, astronomical far, huge, uranic, distant, science
cloud nebula
cycle saros
measure apsis
muse Urania
at ab, al, to, the, atlen
all ava, any
any time ever
home in, tea, chez (Fr.), here
last finally, ultimately
no time ne'er (poet.)
odds out
same age coeval
ates sweetsop
Athamas
daughter Helle
son Phrixos, Learchus
wife Ino
Athens, Athenian Attic(a), Greece
assembly pnyx, boule
clan obe
coin chalcus
founder Cecrops
harbor Piraeus
hill Acropolis
of
America Boston
Ireland Belfast
the North Edinburgh
Switzerland Zurich
the West Cordoba
pert. to Attic
rival Sparta
sculptor Phidias
temple Nike, Zeus
Atlantides Pleiades, Hesperides
atlas book, maps, titan
Atlas
daughter Calypso, Electra
mother Clymene
atmosphere aura, mood, nimbus, welkin

gas argon, oxygen, nitrogen
phenomenon aurora, lightning
prefix atmo(s)
pressure barometric
atom, atomic ion, iota, monad, shade, minute, particle, molecular
  machine betatron, rheotron
  part proton, neutron, electron
  physicist Buhr, Rabi, Pauli, Compton
  pile reactor
  theorist Dalton
Atreus
  brother Thyestes
  father Pelops
  mother Hippodamia
  slayer Aegisthus
  son Menelaus, Agamemnon, Pleisthenes
  wife Aerope
atrocha larva
Atropos Fate
atrous ebon, black
Attica
  legendary king Ogyges
  resident metic
  subdivision deme
  valley Icaria
Attila Hun, Etzel
attire array, cloth(e), dress, outfit
  in armor panoply
atua being, demon, spirit
Au gold
auction roup, sale, vendue
  famous for Christy's, Parke-Bernet
  hammer gavel
  platform block
  price bid, upset
au fait expert, proper
auric acid salt aurate
Augie March
  creator Bellow
Augustus' death place Nola
auk loom, lemot, puffin
  family alcidae
  genus alca, alle
  razorbill falk, murre
aunt tia (Sp.), bawd, tante (Fr.), gossip
aural appendage ear

aurochs tur, urus, bison, wisent
Aurora Eos, dawn
Australia, Australian Aussie
  apple colane
  bag dilli
  bear koala
  bird emu, lory, bittern
  boomerang kiley, kilie
  cake damper
  call cooey
  cat dasyure
  coin dump
  countryman Billijim
  dog dingo, kelpie
  duckbill platypus
  fruit nonda
  gum tree kari, touart
  hut mimi, miamia
  kangaroo joey
  kiwi roa
  language yabber
  measure saum
  no baal, bale
  ostrich emu, emeu
  parrot lory, corella
  petrel titi
  pond billabong
  settler Cook
  shark mako
  spear womerah, wommala
  toy weet-weet
  tree belah, gidya, beefwood
  tulip waratah
  war club waddy
  wilderness outback
Austria, Austrian
  amphibian olm
  coin ducat, krune, gulden
  measure fass, muth
  weight unze
  writer Kafka
austringer falconer
auto race drag, derby
Avalon isle, island
  tomb Arthur
avellane nut, hazel, filbert
avens herb, geum

Avesta
  division Yasna, Gathas
  translation of Zend
avocet bird, godwit
away
  prefix aph, apo
aweto weri, caterpillar
awl punch, broach, needle
ax, axe adze, hatchet, poleax, cleaver
  blade bit
  butt poll
  handle helve
  pickaxe gurlet
axillary alar
axoloti newt, salamander
ay champagne
aye-aye lemur
Azores
  port Horta
  volcano Pico
Aztec
  god Xipe, Meztli
  hero Natu
  language Nahautl
  temple Teopan, Teocalli
  wife Nana
azym(e) bread
  opposed to enzyme

B

baa bleat
baahling lamb
Baal (sun) god, idol, deity
  consort Baltis
  Baalist idolater
baba baby, male, child
  au rhum rum cake
babacoote lemur
babassu oil, palm, soap
babbitt Philistine, businessman, materialist
babblative garrulous, talkative, loquacious
babble chat, prate, tumult
babel tower, tumult, confusion
babiche thong(s), lacing

babillard bird, whitethroat
baboon ape, drill, chaema
babul gum, acacia
  pod garad
babushka scarf, grandmother
baby doll, bairn (Scot.), moppet
  carriage pram
  outfit layette
  shoe bootie
Babylonia, Babylonian Shinar, Shinor
  abode of the dead Aralu
  Adam Adapa
  chief god Anu, Enki
  chief goddess Is(h)tar
  city Akkad, Calneh, Cunaxa
  foe Elamite
  king Nebuchadnezzar
  mountain Ararat
  people Sumerian
  priest En
  priestess Entum
  sea Nina
  waters Apsu
  weight mina
bacalao murre, grouper
bacca berry
baccarat game
  player punter
  term banco
  variety of chemin-de-fer
bacchanal orgy, devotee, reveler, carouser
  cry of evoe, evohe
bacchante menad, maenad, Thyiad, priestess
Bacchus god, Dionysus
  devotee carouser, Bacchante
  son Comus
bacillus germ, microbe
back aid, fro, rat, abet, hind, nata, again, dorsum, posterior
  and fill zigzag
  at the abaft, astern
  backbite slander
  backbone grit, pluck, spine, mettle, spirit, courage
  call revoke
  comb. form notus

country hinterland
down, out withdraw
entrance postern
flow ebb, recede
lower loin
lying on supine
off ebb, recede
out funk, crawfish
pain lumbago
pert. to dorsal, lumbar, tergal
prefix re, retro
scratcher toady
talk lip (colloq.), sass, insolence
toward aft, astern, dorsad
backlog reserve, surplus, accumulation
Back Street
  author Hurst
backward lax, arrear, dilatory, unfavorable
backwater ebb, bayou, retract
backwort comfrey
bacon pork, prize, rustic
  bring home the win, succeed
  fat speck
  side flitch, gammon
  slice collop, rasher
  strip lardon, lardoon
Bacon work Novum Organum
bacteria germ, aerobe, fungus, microbe, bacillus
  chain towla
  culture (-)agar
  dissolver Lysin
  free from harmful asepsis, aseptic
  vaccine bacterin
bactrian Asian, camel
bad lewd, qued, vile, nasty, rotten
  comb. form dys, mal, caco
  debt default
  habit vice
  luck ambsace
  prefix mal, mis
badak rhino
badderlocks murlin, seaweed, honeyware
badge pin, token, symbol
  infamy stigma
  policeman star, busser, shield
badgerweed pasqueflower

badinage banter, raillery, trifling
baff bang, beat, blow, strike, worthless
baft astern
bag pod, sac, poke, womb, bouge, bulse, purse, seize, udder, woman (sl.), alforja, capture, reticule, gladstone, portmanteau
  botanic sac, asci, ascus, spore
  canvas musette
  fishing net bunt, fyke
  floating balloon
  for books, papers, etc. briefcase
  grain sack
  hop sarpler
  kind of duffel
  -making material flax, hemp, jute, burlap, sacking
  muslin tillot
  sleeping sack
  toilette musette
  with perfumed powder sachet
  traveling luggage
bagatelle trifle
baggage gear, minx, harlot, valises, satchels, viaticals
  car/wagon fourgon
  carrier ham(m)al, porter, redcap
baggie belly, stomach
Baghdad merchant Sinbad
bagman tramp, salesman, collector
bagnio bagne, cabana, prison, brothel, hothouse, bathhouse
Bagnold Enid
bagpipe drone, musette, zampogne, doodelsack, sordellina
  drone bourdon
  flute chanter
  mouthpiece muse
  music pibroch
  pipe drones, chanter
  play skirl
  player piper, doodler
  tune port
Bahama Islands Abaco, Andros, Bimini, Eleuthera
  capital Nassau
  premier Pindling
Bahia bay, (Sao) Salvador

baikie stick
bail bond, ring, vouch
bailiff reeve, tipstaff
  farm hind
bain near, direct, supple
bairn child
bait chum, lure, hector, fulcrum, gudgeon
  artificial fly, hackle
  bird-enticing shrap(e)
  drop dap, dip
  fish chum, lure
  salmon-fishing baker
  take bite
baize cloth, drape, domett, fabric, drapery
baked clay/dishes/pot olla, tile,
  crockery
baker
  itch rash, psoriasis
  kneading trough brake
  sheet pan
  shovel/tool peel
  workshop yale, bakery
baker bird hornero
baker's dozen thirteen
bakie trough, vessel
baking
  chamber kiln, oast, oven
  dish cocotte, ramekin, scallop, remequin,
    casserole
  pit imu (Haw.)
  soda saleratus, bicarbonate
Bakongo's goddess Nyambe, Nzambe
baksheesh tip, alms, gratuity
bal masque, tabarin
Balaam's beast ass, donkey
balance even, offset, equilibrium
  crossbar of beam
  of sales atry
  state of equipoise
  weighing steelyard
balancing weight ballast
balata gum chicle
balate trepang
balcony piazza, sollar, mirador, brattice
  church singer cantoria
  projecting gazabo, gazebo

bald bare, frank, glabrous, hairless
  -headed man pilgarlic
baldachin canopy, brocade
balderdash rot, drivel, jargon
baldicoot coot, monk
baldmoney gentian, spicknel
baldness acomia, alopecia
baldric, baldrick belt, zodiac, support,
  necklace
Baldur
  father Odin
  giant, victim of Loke, Loki
  mother Frigg
  murder weapon mistletoe
  slayer Loke, Loki, Hoth(r)
  son Forsete
  wife Nanna
bale woe, evil, bundle
  of wool sarpler
Balearic Island Iviza, Cabrera, Majorca,
  Menorca, Minorca, Formentera
  capital Palma
  language Catalan
  measure palmo, quarta
  weight artal, corta, rotel
baleen whale, whalebone
baleise flog
baler tier, bundler, hay press
Bali (Indonesia)
  dance ardja, kriss, ketjak, djanger
  holy day njepi
  musical instrument gamelan(g)
  religion Hinduism
  rice field sawaii
balk shy, omit, waver, mistake
Balkan Serb, Slav, Albanian, Rumanian,
  Yugoslav
  bandit haiduk
  coin novcic
  instrument gusla
Balkh Bactria
ball orb, dance, globe, ivory
  hit for practice fungo
  metal, athletics hammer, shotput
  of electrical discharge corposant
  of meat/rice pinda

of perfume mixture pomander
of yarn/thread clew
tiny globule
wooden knur
ballad lolt, derry, canzone
ballet dance, masque
leap jete
movement brise, glissade
posture arabesque
skirt tutu
ballista catapult
ballistic missile
launching blastoff
storage place silo
warhead payload
balloon bag, gasbag, aerostat
altitude controller ballast
basket car, gondola, nacelle
covering envelope
gas helium, hydrogen
mooring line dragrope
pilot aeronaut
shape of round, sausage
trial test, feeler
vine heartseed
balm bito, soothe, anodyne, comfort
horse citronella
of Gilead balsam
Balmoral cap, castle, petticoat
balneal bathing
balneary bathhouse
baloney bunk, hooey
balsa raft, wood
-like wood bongo
balsam tolu, resin, copaiba
gum resin storax
Swiss riga
tree tolu
Balt Yod, Esth, Lett, Estonian, Lithuanian
balteus belt, baldric
Baltic
barge praam
city Riga, Danzig
gulf Riga
island Dago, Faro, Os(s)el, Alsen, Oesel, Oland

language Lettic
river Oder
seaport Kiel, Riga, Memel, Reval, Talinn, Rostock, Stettin
balustrade barrier, railing
Balzac character Nana, Goriot
bam hoax, sham, wheedle
Bambi deer
author Salten
bambino baby, infant
bamboo cane, reed, tree, tonkin
shoots pickle
sprouts achar
stalk reed
sugar tabasheer
woven sawaii
bamboozle dupe, cheat, buffalo
Bana
conqueror Krishna
daughter Usha
banana fei, musa, ensete, pesang, platano (Sp.), plantain
bunch hand, stem
disease mosaic
family musa, pesang, musaceae
fish albula, ladyfish
leaf frond
of the musaceous
oil nonsense (sl.), softsoap
Philippine saging, latundan
plant musa, pesang
wild fei
band tie, cord, gang, cohort, fillet, hyphen, cincture
armed posse
armor tonlet
brain ligula(e)
clothes fastener patte
narrow tape, stria
small bandelet(te)
bandicoot rat, marsupial
bandikai okra
Bani
son Uel, Amzi, Amram
bank bar, dike, ridge, depend
clerk teller

examiner accountant
fish cod
martin swallow
note bill
river ripa
thistle musk
bankroll wad, bills
bankrupt sap, broke, busted
banquet fete, feast, junket, repast, carousal
room cenacula (pl.), cenaculum
banshee fay, fairy, sidhe, goblin
bant diet, fast, reduce
bantam cock, chicken, diminutive
breed Sebright
banteng ox, tsine
Bantu Baya, Gogo, Jaga, Zulu, Swahili
dialect Chwana
banxring tana, tupaia
banyan bur(r), tree, banian
banzai cry, attack
baobab tree, tebeldi
baptism dip, immersion
font basin, spring
robe Chrisom
vessel font, laver, piscina
bar ban, band, hinder
acrobat trapeze
bullion ingot
legally estop
millstone rynd
resistance strut
supporting fid, rod
barb awn, hook, bristle
anchor flue
feather herl, ramus
Barbados
capital Bridgetown
liquor rum
native Bim
barbarian Hun, Goth, brute, vandal, Philistine
North African Berber
barbarous fell, cruel, inhuman
Barbary ape, magot, simian
sheep aoudad
states Tunis, Algiers, Morocco, Tripoli

barber's itch ringworm
bard poet, scop, druid
India bhat
Bard of Avon Shakespeare
bardy bold, defiant, audacious
bare buff, bleak
-faced impudent
poles spars
bargain deal, pact, haggle, good buy, negotiate
for expect
barge tow, lunge, thrust
bargeman pug, huffler
bark bay, boat, husk, shout
aromatic sintoc, canella, sassafras
beetle boree
canoe cascara
cloth tap(p)a, mulberry
exterior ross
medicinal coto, madar, quinine
pert. to cortical
up the wrong tree err, stray
barley grain
ground tsamba
pert. to hordeaceous
steep malt
variety big, bere, bigg
barmy filly, foamy, yeasty
barnacle
genus Lepas
plate terga (pl.), tergum
barn mew, stall, cowshed
dance hoedown
dance official caller
grass ankee, millet
owl lulu, tyto
storage area bag, loft
-yard golf horseshoes
barnstorm tour
barometric line isobar
baronet sir, commoner
barraclade blanket
barracuda spet, pelon, picuda, guanchepelon
barras gal(l)ipot
barrator bully, rowdy, fighter
barrel keg, cask, runlet, hogshead, kilderkin

herring cade
maker cooper
part hoop, side, stave
raising device parbuckle
stopper bung
support hoop, gantry, gauntry
barren dry, gaunt, meager
barren oak blackjack
barren privet alatern, houseleek
barrette (small) bar, clasp, ornament
Barrie character Wendy, Peter
barrier bar, gate, limit
moveable door, blind, shutter(s)
barrio slum, ghetto, village
Bartered Bride
composer Smetana
bartizan turret, lookout
basalt marble, navite, pottery
base low, snide, paltry, alkaline, scullion, ignominious
architectural socle, plinth
attached by sessile
structural plinth
baseball
field diamond
founder Doubleday (Abner)
hit bunt, double, single
on balls pass, walk
team nine
Bashemath's husband Esau
Bashkir
capital Ufa
basil herb, plant, royal, fetter
basilica canopy, church, temple, Lateran
part of apse
basin ewer, stoup, marina, aspersorium
geological tala
basket fan, kipe, scull, dorser, hanaper
coal mine corf
eel buck
fig caba, frail, tapnet
fire grate, cresset
fish pot, cawl, maund, gabion
fruit pottle, punnet
material otate
twig wattle

watertight wattape
work caba(s), slath, slarth
basque waist, Iberian
cap beret
dance auresca, zortzico
game pelota
language Uskara, Euskara
people Euscaro
petticoat basquine
province Alava, Biscay
bas-relief plaquette
bassinet basket, cradle
basswood lin, bast, tilia, linden
bast flax, piassava
basta stop, enough
bastion
defensive fort
shoulder epaule
Bataan
bay Subic
city Balanga
Batavia (D)Jakarta
batfish diablo
bath
comb. form balneo
pert. to balneal
public piscine
river Avon
sponge loofah
bathos comedown, anticlimax
Bathsheba
husband Uriah
son Solomon
batrachian frog, toad
battery
floating praam, artillery
plate grid
battle fray, conflict
area arena, field, sector
formation herse, deploy
line front
site Shiloh, Bull Run, Manassas
Battle Hymn of the Republic
author Howe
battologize repeat, iterate
bauxite derivative aluminum

Bavaria, Bavarian
  community Passau
  measure fass, rute, metze, morgen
  weight gran, quentchen
bay cove, roan, fiord, oriel
  bird snipe, curlew, godwit, plover
  camphor laurin
bayardly blind, stupid
beacon mark, sign, signal
  light cresset, lantern
Beaconsfield Disraeli (Brit. prime minister)
beadle macer, herald, servitor
beadsman, bedesman beggar, hermit,
  petitioner
beak bill, prow, lorum, master
  ship's bow, ram, prow
  without erostrate
beaker cup, tass, bouse
bean urd, caster, noggin, thrash
  Asian gram, mungo
  climbing lima, pole
  cluster guar
  eye hila, hilum
  locust carob
  lubricant ben
  Mexican frejol, frijol(e)
  poisonous loco, castor, calabar
Bean Town Boston
bear
  bane wolfsbane
  bush inkberry
  cat paud, binturong
  -shaped ursiform
beard barb, defy, front, Vandyke
  grain awn
bearing air, mien, orient, gestation
  fine belair
  heraldic ente, orle, pheon
beast bete (Fr.), monster, quadriped
  myth ogre, Rahu, Apepi, giant, hydra,
    Geryon, Kraken, scylla, triton,
    centaur, figfaun, griffin, bucentaur,
    chichevache
  pert. to leonine
beat cob, bash, cane, thump, accent, cudgel
  back repulse
  into plate/leaf malleate

beau geste favor
beau monde fashion, society
beaut lulu (sl.)
beautiful
  comb. form bel, calo, calli
beaver hat, coin, castor, rodent
  cloth kersey
  eater wolverine
  skin plew
because of that thereby, therefore
bechance befall, chance
beck vat, becon, brook
becken cymbals
becloud darken, obscure, overcast
becoming right, farrant
becuna barracuda
bed cot, bunk, doss, matrix, pallet, plancher
  feather tye
  small pallet, truckle, bassinet
  stay slat
  straw shakedown
bedbug cimex, chinch, cimice (pl.), conenose
bedizen daub, adorn, overdress
Bedouin Arab, Moor, nomad
  bead cord agal
  official cadi, sheik
  tribe Harb
bedrock nadir, bottom
bedroll bindle
bee dor, apis, dingar, hymenoptera
  colony of swarm, yeast
  comb. form api
  family apina, apidae
  female queen
  house covering hackle
  male drone
  nose lora (pl.), lorum
  pollen brush scopa, scopae (pl.),
    sarothrum
beech buck, tree, myrtle
  genus fagus
beef meat, complain
  dried bucan, vivda, charqui
  pickled bully
  salted junk
beekeeper apiarist, skeppist
beer mum, grog, kvass, lager

barley chang
cask butt
ingredient hops, malt
maize chic(h)a
unfermented wort
vessel mug, seidel, schooner
beeswax substitute ceresin
beet chard, mangel
  genus beta
Beethoven
  birthplace Bonn, Germany
  composer of Egmont, Eroica, Fidelio
    (opera), Kreutzer, Missa Solemnis
beetle bug, goga, gogo, hispa, scarab,
  battledore
  bark borer
  bright ladybug
  family elateridae, clavicornes
  fire cucuyo
  genus fidia
  grain cadelle
  ground amara
  mustard blackjack
  rhinoceros uang
  wing cover scarab
beetle-browed morose, scowling
beflum deceive
before afore, avant (Fr.), coram (Lat.), prior
  long anon
  now ere, over
  prefix pre, pro, ante, prae
befuddle besot, confuse, stupefy
beggar randy, almsman, mendicant,
  panhandler
  saint Giles
  speech cant
Beggar's Opera
  author Gay
behemoth huge, beast, hippo
behoof profit, advantage
being ens, entity, mortal
  abstract ens, entia
  actual esse
  in front anteal
  physiological bion
  science of ontology
  suffix ure

Bel
  -esprit wit, intellectual
  father Ea
  wife Belit(is)
Bela
  father Beor, Benjamin
  son Ard, Iri, Uzzi, Ezbon
Belait Europe
belaying pin kevel, bollard
Belgium, Belgian Fleming, Walloon
  coin belga, franc, centime
  endive witloof
  Gaul tribe Remi, Nervii
  horse Brabanco
  marble rance
  measure vat, aune, pied, perche
  province Spa, Liege, Namur, Flanders
  river Lys, Maas, Senne, Ourthe
Belgrade native Serb
Belial devil, Satan
believer ist
  in all religions omnist
  in God deist, theist
  in reality of matter Cartesian
belittle dwarf, slight, denigrate
bell gong, codon, knell, bellow, corolla
  alarm tocsin
  axle-bearing cod
  clapper tongue
  kind of cow, jingle, electric
  pert. to campanular
  ringer tolier, carilloneur
  room belfry
  sound ding, dong, toll, knell, tinkle
  tower belfry, campanile
belladonna dwale, narcotic, nightshade
  extract atropin(e)
bellbird shrike, arapunga
bell, book, candle excommunication
bell-bottoms trousers
bell ear cannon
bellerophon
  father Glaucus
  spring Pelrene
belles-lettres literature
Bell for Adano
  author Hersey

bellicose irate, hostile, militant
Bellini
  opera Norma, I Puritani, La Sonnambula
  sleepwalker Amina
Bellow
  character Herzog, Sammler, Augie March
bellware kelp
bellweed knapweed
bellwether pilot, sheep, leader
belly gut, tummy, paunch
  comb. form gastro, ventro
belongings goods, traps, effects, chattels
below next, under, nether
  comb. form infero
  prefix sub, infra
belt band, blow, cest(us), gird, zone, region
  celestial zodiac
  comb. form zon(o)
  conveyor apron
  ecclesiastical balt(h)eus
  non-Mohammedan zonar
  sword baldric
Belus
  brother Agenor
  daughter Dido
  father Neptune, Poseidon
  mother Libya
  son Danaus, Phineus
belvedere alcove, gazebo, pagoda
bema pace, step, chancel
bemired oozy, muddy, claggy
bemoan rue, wail, lament, deplore
bemuse daze, addle, confuse, distract
bench bar, banc, stool, settee
  church pew
  outdoor exedra
  upholstered banquette
bench hook clamp
bend ply, sag, flex, crimp
  backward retort
  in timber sny
bender toot, binge, blast, spree, sixpence
benedict eggs, monk, benign, kindly

Benedictine monk, liqueur
  title dom
benefice feu, curacy, kindness
  first fruit annat(e)
benefit aid, boon, gain, deserve
Bengal
  boat batel, baulea(h)
  capital Dacca
  caste member baidya
  cotton adati, adaty
  district Dacca, Nadia
  gentlemen baboo
  grass millet
  hemp sunn
  measure cotta(h), chattack
  native Ebo(e), Kol, Banian
  quince b(a)el, bhel
  root cassumunar
  singer baul
  town Dacca, Madras, Barisal, Rangoon, Calcutta, Tittacarh
  tree bola
benign kind, mild, clement
benison blessing, invocation
Benjamin
  descendant Aher
  grandson Iri
  son Ehi, Gera, Rosh
benne sesame
bent set, gift, flair, curved, stooped
  comb. form cyrt, ancyl(o), campto
benthonic plant enalid
benthos fauna, flora
benzine derivative phenol
Beor
  son Bela, Balaam
Beowulf epic, poem
Berber Moor, Hamite, Kabyle, Haratin
  chief caid, qaid
  dialect Tuareg
  tribe Daza, Riff, Tibu, Tuareg
Berea Aleppo
  grit sandstone
Berechiah
  son Zechariah

bereft orb, lost, forlorn
beret cap, tam, biretta
berg ice, floe, eminence
bergamot bose, mint, pear, essence
Bergen
   dummy Snerd, McCarthy
bergstock alpenstock
Beriah
   father Asher, Shimei, Ephraim
beriberi kakke
Berkshire
   racecourse Ascot
berm bank, edge, path, terrace
Bermuda
   arrowroot aruru, ararao
   barracuda spet
   berry soapberry
   capital Hamilton
   catfish coelho
   ceremony gombay
   grass doob
Bernice
   brother Agrippa
   father Herod
   husband Polemo
   lover Titu, Vespasian
berry dew, haw, fruit, whortle
   comb. form bacci
   disease bluestem
   medicinal cubeb
   oil olive
berth bed, job, bunk, dock, slip
Bertha
   son Orlando
berrylike baccate
bertha cape, collar, cannon
beryl gem, jewel, emerald, aquamarine
   green davidsonite
   yellow heliodor
beryx alfonsin
beseeching begging, precative
beside by, bar, hear, opposite
   comb. form para, juxta
besmear, besmirch ray, balm, soil, sully, taint

besom man, broom, sweep, heather
best
   comb. form arist(o)
bet ante, risk, hedge, stake
   broker bookie
   fail to pay off welch
   faro slepper
bete silly, beast
betel ikmo, itmo, siri
   leaf pan, buyo
betelgeuse star
   constellation Orion
betel palm areca
   extract catechu
   masticatory pan, buyo
   seed betel nut
bête noir hate, dread, terror
Beth
   sister Jo, Amy, Meg
Bethesda pool, chapel
Bethlehemite Boaz
Bethuel
   daughter Rebekah
   father Nahor
   mother Milcah
   son Laban
   uncle Abraham
betise folly, silliness, stupidity
betting
   adviser tout
   figures odds
   odds price
Betty dessert
between amid, betwixt
   law mesne
   prefix dia, meta, inter
between the lines latent, secret
bevel edge, miter, slant, incline
   corners splay
   end of timber snape
   out ream
beverage ade, pop, soda, lager, posset
   extract kola
   malted wheat zythem, zythum
   mixed negus, punch, smash, bishop

mulberry and honey morat
Oriental rak(ee), sake, arrack
pepper kava
South American mate
bewitch charm, fasci, grigri
Beyle
penname Stendhal
beyond yon, free, over, ultra
comb. form preter
prefix sur, meta
bezel, basil rim, seal, chaton
bezezteen bazaar
bezzle drink, waste, plunder
bhalu bear
bhandar store, library
bhut ghost, goblin
Bhutan
disease dha
pine kail
religion shamanism
robe bakkhu
bibelot curio, bauble, whatnot
Bible, biblical
angel Micah, Raphael
animal reem, daman, hydrax, behemoth
ascetic order Essene
giant Anak, Emim, Goliath
hunter Nimrod
money beka(h), shekel
ornament urim, thummin
pool Siloam
region Enon, Ophir, Perea, Bashan
spice myrrh, stacte, frankincense
stone ezel, ligure
weed tare
witch's home Endor
biddy hen, chicken
bifid forked
bifurcation wye, fork, split
Big Bertha
birthplace Essen
Big Dipper
constellation Ursa Major
star Alcor, Dubhe, Merak, Mizar
bigener mule, hybrid
Bigfoot Omah, Sasquatch
bigot racist, zealot, fanatic

big toe hallux
bilbie refuge, shelter
bill act, beak, note
anchor pee
five-dollar fin, vee
one-dollar buck, frogskin
ten-dollar sawbuck
billingsgate abuse, ribaldry
billionaire nabob
billycock derby, bowler
bin box, crib, hutch, container
fish kench
for coal bunker
bind jam, confine
comb. form desmo
tightly frap
to secrecy tile, tyle
up in absorb
binding cord, valid, webbing
comb. form desis
limp yapp
bindle stiff hobo, tramp
Binnui
father Henedad
son Noadiah
biographer
American Weems, Freeman, Sandburg
English Morley, Walton, Boswell
French Maurois
German Ludwig
Greek Plutarch
Italian Vasari
Roman Suetonius
biography life, memoir, history
biological class genus, species
factor id, gene, idant
biose disaccharid(e)
biotite mica, anomite
bird
adjutant stork, argala, hurgila, marabou
Afr. taha, umbrette
Am. sora, robin, vireo, darter, fulmar, turkey, grackle, tanager, cardinal, bufflehead
Antarctic skua, penguin
aquatic duck, swan, goose, grebe, penguin
aquiline eagle

Arabian Nights roc
Arctic auk, fulmar
Asiatic mine, hill tit, brambling
Attic nightingale
Austral. emu, boobook, lorikeet
black ani, merle, jackdaw
Central Am. daw, magpie, jacamar
cranelike wader, chunga
crying ramage, limpkin
diving auk
dressing of feathers preen
emulike cassowaries
extinct moa, kiwi, offbird
finchlike chewink, tanager
fish-catching osprey, cormorant
larklike pipit
of paradise manucode
oldest known archaeopteryx
parts of body neb, mala, prectn, syrinx
pert. to avian, avine, ornithic, volucrine
predatory owl, yager, shrike
red-tailed koae
sacred ibis
S.A. guan, mynah, boatbill
tropical koae, barbet
web-footed duck, avocet
birdcage pinjira, volary
bird crest tuft
bird nest aery, eyry
bird's-eye view apercu
biri cigarette
birl spin, rattle
birma calaba
birse temper, bristle
birsle broil, toast
birth bear, nascency
  after postnatal
  before prenatal
  goddess Parca
  help with accouche
  nobleness eugeny
birth-control leader Sanger
birth flower see Quick Reference List
birthmark mole, nevus, spiloma
  pert. to naevoid
birthright legacy, heritage
birthstone see Quick Reference List

bishop pope, pontiff
  apron gremial
  assistant verger, coadjutor
  buskin caliga
  cap hura, mitre, biretta
  district diocese
  robe chimer(e)
  staff crosier
  throne apse
  title abba
  vestment alb, chimer, tunicle
bishop's weed ammi, goutweed
bismar steelyard
bison bovine, aurochs
bisulcate cloven
bit iota, morsel, smidge(o)n
  by bit gradually
  horse's curb pelham
  Irish traneen
  part walk-on
biting dragon tarragon
biting of nails phaneromania
bito balm, tree
  oil zachun
bitter bask, acrid, caustic
  apple colocynth
  bush snakeroot
  gentian baldmoney
  grass colicroot
  oak cerris
  spar dolomite
  vetch ers, vicia
bitters amer (Fr.), tonic
  pert. to amaroidal
bitterwort felwort, dandelion
bituman tar, pitch, asphalt
bivalve clam, mollusk, pandora, scallop
  genus pinna, toheroa
bivouac etape, encamp
biwa loquat
Bizet opera Carmen
blab blart, clack, tattle
black calo, inky, atrous
  amoor black, Negro
  and blue livid
    spot bruise, shiner, ecchymosis
  and white clear-cut, chiaroscuro

art alchemy, necromancy
berry agawam, dewberry
bird ani, merl, ouzel, jackdaw
cap gull, titmouse, raspberry
cod beshow
comb. form atra, atro, mela(n)
damp chokedamp
diamond coal, hematite
earth mold, chernozem
-eyed Susan ketmia, coneflower
fin fish, cisco, sesis
fish whale, tautog, nigrescent
grunt tripletail
head comedo
horn haw, sloe
leg scab, gambler, strikebreaker
school grind
sheep deviate, reprobate
smith gow, shoer, farrier
shop anvil, smithy
snake whip, racer, quirt
blackball pill, ballot, exclude
Black Forest
  city Baden-Baden
  peak Feldberg
  river Rhine, Danube
Black Muslim
  founder Farad
black prince Edward, Othello
Black Sea
  city Batum, Odessa
  old name Euxine
  peninsula Crimea
  pert. to Pontic
  river Bug, Don, Prut, Danube
blackshirt fascist
bladder sac, blister, inflate, vesicle
  comb. form asco
blae blo, bleak, sunless
blague lie, humbug, raillery
blain sore, bulla, pustule
blake wan, pale, yellow, colorless
Blake
  symbol Zoas
blame twit, revile, inculpate
  blameless innocent, spotless
  deserving culpable

blanche fade, scald, wince, whiten
Blancheflor
  beloved Flores, Floris
blandish con, coax, flatter, wheedle
blanket wrap, layer, throw, coverlet
  cowboy s(o)ugan
  goat's hair cumbly
  horse manta
  Native American stroud
  Spanish sarape, serape
blasé bored, sated, weary
blaspheme abuse, curse, revile
blast furnace
  lower part bosh
  nozzle tuyere
blat bleat, blurt
blate dull, prate, sheepish
blaubok etaac, antelope
blazon deck, adorn, shield, declare
bleaching vat keir, kier
bleb blob, bubble, vesicle
bleeding heart dicentra
blemish mar, mulct, taint, stigma
  wood mote
  wound scar, cicatrix, cicatrice
blench foil, quail, shake, recoil
blended fondu, merged
blesbok nunni, antelope, blesbuck
blind ante, dunch, obscure, insensate
  as a hawk seel
  alley dead end, impasse, cul-de-sac
  god Hoder, Hoth(r)
  part of slat
  pig dive, saloon
  printing for braille
  spot hang-up, bigotry
  staggers gid, vertigo
  worm orvet
blindness bisson, ablepsia, ignorance
  color achromatopsia, monochromatism
  day hemeralopia
  partial meropia, cecutiency
  snow chiona-blepsia
blip box, slap, censor, expurgate
bliss joy, ecstasy, felicity
  place of Eden, Utopia, Elysium, Paradise

blithe gay, boon, jolly, winsome
blob lip, blot, mark, globule
block bar, check, hamper
  architectural dentil, mutule
  electrically insulated taplet
  football clip
  for shaping metal objects ame
  ice cube, serac
  mechanical pulley
  metal type quad, quod
  nautical deadeye
  perforated nut
  small tessera
blockhead ass, dolt, dope, tomfool, grouthead
blood sap, fluid, lineage
  comb. form hema, h(a)emo
  deficiency an(a)emia
  disease leukemia
  fluid part serum, plasma, opsonin
  of the gods ic(h)or
  particle in embolus
  poisoning pyemia, toxemia, septicemia
  stagnation clot, cruor, grume, stasis
  strain race, stock, family
  testing instrument hemabarometer
bloodhound lyam, lyme
  money cro, breaghe
  pudding sausage
  root puccoon, tetterwort
  stone chalcedony
blood vessel vein, hemad
  comb. form vas
  rupture rhexis
blooper error, roseate
blossom bud, blob
  small floweret
blow bop, cob, jab, conk, impel, depart
  -by-blow minute, detailed
  in enter, arrive
  mock feint
  out bash, shindig
  over end, pass
  to treat
  up rage, fume, seethe, explode
blowze trull, wench, hoyden
blowzed red, ruddy, flushed

blubber cry, foam, swollen
  remove flense
  whale fenks, speck, muktuk
blue low, aqua, perse, indigo
  asbestos crocidolite
  boneset mistflower
  bonnet cap, Scot, cornflower
  catalpa paulownia
  dandelion chicory
  dye herb woad
  fish bass, tuna, saury, weakfish
  gill sunfish
  gray merle, pearl, slate, cesious
  green bice, teal, beryl, calamine
  gum tree, eucalyptus
  -pencil edit, delete, redact, revise
  peter coot, flag, gallinule
  red smalt, mallow, gridelin, mazarine, gris-de-lin
  rocket monkshood
  sheep bharal
  throat warbler
Bluebeard's wife Fatima
Blue Boy
  painter Gainsborough
Blue Grotto
  site Capri, Italy
bluepoint oyster
bluer anil
bluestocking woman, intellectual
bluet plant, bluebottle, farkleberry
Bluff King Hal Henry
blunt bald, dull, flat, deaden
  mentally hebitate
bo, boh chief, leader, captain
boa scarf, snake, anaconda
  constrictor giboia
Boacidea
  people Iceni
boar hog, aper, swine
  head hure
  wound gore, ganch
boat ark, scor, scow, ship, barge, cutter, garvey, watercraft
  coal cargo collier
  comb. form scapo
  deck poop, orlop

engine-driven sampan
fishing bracozzo
flat-bottomed bac, punt, scow
garbage hopper
harbor tug, barge, bumboat
joint jerl
merchant argosy, holcad
ornamental navicella
power tug
round gufa, goofa(h)
boatswain bosun, serang
whistle pipe
Boaz
son Obed
wife Ruth
bobac marmot
bobbin reel, braid, spool, ratchet
frame ereel
pin spindle
Boccaccio work Decameron, Life of Dante
bodkin awl, needle, stiletto
body bulk, rupa, corpus
anterior part of prosoma
armor tace, corium
away from center distal
cavity sinus, coelom(e)
comb. form soma(to)
fluid blood, lymph, serum
heavenly sun, moon, star, planet, asteroid
joint hip, knee, elbow, wrist, shoulder
motion gesture
of men posse, authorized
of persons corps, posse
of water bay, sea, gulf, lake, pond, pool, ocean, lagoon, sealet, reservoir
path orbit
pert. to somal, systemic
wall paries, septum
bodyguard thane, trabant
Boeotia
capital Thebes
region Ionia
Boer dialect Taal
bogey hag, goblin, bugaboo
Bohemian arty, gypsy
dance redowa
residence village

boil sty, botch, seethe, simmer, inflame
almost scald
down decoct
bole dose, trunk, opening
Bolero
composer Ravel (Maurice)
bolide meteor, missile
Bolivia, Bolivian
animal vicuna
city La Paz, Oruro, Potosi
coin tomin, bolivar, centavo
district Elbeni, Colinas, Santa Cruz
dried mutton chalone
Indian Uro, Moxo, Charca
lake Poepo, Allagas, Rogagua, Titicaca, Desaguader
measure league, celemin
mountain Andes, Cuzco
plateau Altiplano
river Beni, Orton, Guapore
weight libra, macro
boll weevil picudo
bolus cud, lump, pill
bomb dud, egg, shell, pineapple
guide fin
hole crater
Bombay
arrowroot tikor
fabric rumal
hemp sunn, ambary
native Parsi, Parsee
vessel patamar
bombyx eri(a), moth, silkworm
bonasus ox, boson, aurochs
bond
chemical diene, valence
bone os, rib, fillet, radius, humerus
anvil incus, incudes (pl.)
breast sterna (pl.), sternum
cartilage ossein
comb. form os, osteo
elbow ulna
girdle sphenethmoid
pert. to osteal, osseous
scraper xyster
boneset comfrey, hempweed, thoroughwort
boniface landlord, innkeeper

Bonjour Tristesse
  author Sagan (Francoise)
bonnet hat, decoy, slouch
  brim poke
  monkey zati, munga
  string bride
boo hoot, jeer, decry
boob ass, goony, neddy
boobook owl, cuckoo
boojum snark
book opus, diary, catalog
  accounts bilan, ledger
  alphabet abecedary
  Apocrypha Tobit
  back spine
  binding material cloth, canvas, buckram
  church music hymnal
  cover ornamentation tooling
  dealer bonguiniste
  design format, layout
  destroyer biblioclast
  Islam Kitab, Koran
  lover bibliophile
  of masses missal
  part leaf, cover, spine, chapter, section, binding
  school primer, textbook
  title page rubric
  translation pony
  words of opera libretto
  Zoroastrian Avesta
bookcase forel(l)
boondocks sticks, backwoods
boondoggle trifle, goldbrick
boor oaf, Boer, churl, yahoo
boot pac, shoe, eject, benefit
  half buskin, cocker
  heavy stogy, brogan
  high-water wader
  loose-topped Wellington
  riding jemmy, gambado
  small bottine, bottekin
bootlick fawn, toady, flatter
borax tincal
border hem, dado, line, braid, forel, margin
  fluted frill

  ornamental dado
  wall dado, ogee, cornice
Border States (Civil War) Arkansas, Delaware, Kentucky, Maryland, Missouri, Virginia, Tennessee, North Carolina
Boreas wind, norther
  son Butes, Calais
boredom ennui, tedium
boric acid salt borate
boring tool bit, auger, drill, gimlet, wimble
born nee (Fr.), innate, nascent, natural, delivered
  dead stillborn
  prematurely abortive
  well free, noble, eugenic
  borne by the wind eolian
Borneo
  ape orang, orangutan
  city Bruni
  island near Java
  measure ganta(ng)
  mountain Kini-Balu
  native D(a)yak, Iban
  pepper plant ara
  pirates bajau
  snake boiga
  timbertree billian
  weight para, chapah
boron borax, boric, ulexite
borracho drunk(ard)
bosc pear
boscage wood, grove, thicket
Bosnian native Slav, Croat
boss pad, bully, headman
  logging camp bully
  political cacique
  shield umbo
Boston game, waltz
  leader Brahmin
  district hub
bot fly, larva
botany
  angle axil
  cell spore
  depression fovea, variole

both bo, two, equally
  -handed ambidextrous
  prefix bi, ambi
bothy cot, lodge, barracks
bottle vial, cruet, carage, preserve
  sealer capper
  size pint, pipe, fifth, quart, magnum, jeroboam
  small ampul, phial, costrel
boulder rock, stone
  monument megalith
  transported by ice erratic
bound dap, leap, stend, costive, confined
  back carom, bounce, resile
  by a vow votary
boundary ahu, dool, meer, verge, barrier
  comb. form ori
bounder cad, roué, snob
Bounty captain Bligh
  actor Laughton
bourgeois common, mediocre
bow arc, beck, archer, depress, rainbow
  facing sea atry
  of ship beak, prow, stem
  oriental salam, salaam
  toward afore
  wood for yew
  -shaped arcate
bowfin amia, lawyer, mudfish
bowling tenpins, duckpins, candlepins
  division frame
  pin ninepin, skittle
  place alley
  score spare, strike
box bin, till, crate, carton, fostell, container
  alms arca
  ammunition caisson, bandoleer
  sleigh pung
  tea canister
boxer
  hand covering cesti, glove
boxing
  blow KO, jab, TKO, feint, punch
  contest bout, match
  pert. to fistic, pugilistic
brachyuran crab, crustacean
brack crag, brine, crack

bract glume, palea, palet, spadix
Bragi
  wife Idun, Ithunn
Brahma Hindu, creator
  first woman created by Ahalya
Brahman zebu, Hindu, Bostonian
  land grant sasan
  precept sutra, sutta
  title aya
braid cue, tress, sennet, deceitful
  gold and silver orris
  hemp tagal
  knotted lacet
brain bean, utac, genius
  box pan, skull, cranium
  comb. form cerebro
  layer obex, cortex
  membrane tela, meninges
  operate on trepan
  orifice lura
  part aula, cerebrum, encephalon, pericranium
  passage iter
  pert. to cerebral
  white matter pia, alba, dura
brainstorm contemplate
bran treat, cereal, chisel
branch arm, bow, rame, shoot, vimen
  angle of axil
  of nerves rami (pl.), ramus
  pert. to ramal, remeal
  -like ramose
branchia gill
brand birn, flaw, character
  on stolen cattle duff
  sheep smit
brandy
  and soda peg
  mastic raki
  plum slivovitz
brank caper, mumps, pillory
brassica cole, rape, turnip
Brave New World
  author Huxley
Brazil, Brazilian
  ant tucandera
  bird ara, soco, macaw, tiriba

coffee plantation fazenda
coin reis, conto, dobra, milreis, cruziero
dance samba, maxixe
discoverer Cabral
drink assai
duck muscovy
estuary Para
fiber imbe
Indian Anta, Arana, Carib, Tariana, Botocudo
mammal tapir
measure pe, pipa, fanga, covado, tarefa, quartilho
monkey sai, miriki, belzebuth
palm jara, inaja, babassu
plant imbe, para, yage, caroa, ayapana, seringa, jaborandi
rubber (h)ule, Para, Caucho
tree apa, brauna, gomavel, barbatimao
weight bag, onca, libra, oitava, arratel, quilate, tonelada
wood embuia, kingwood
breach gap, flaw, schism, violation
of etiquette gaffe, solecism
pin tige
bread bun, aliment, sustenance
boiled cush, panada
browned toast, sippet, crouton
communion azym(e)
crust rind
leavened kisra, cocket
pert. to panary
unleavened azym(e), matzoh, matzos, bannock
break bust, rive, frush, hiatus, fissure, interval, penetrate
down debacle, failure, collapse, cataclysm, catabolism
in slip, stave, blunder, initiate, interrupt
out rash, erupt, escape
up split, disband, disperse, separate
breakbone fever dengue
breakwater cob, dike, quay, jetty
bream tai, fish, scup, broom, sunfish
sea shad, sargus
breast crop, bosom, brace, chest, thorax, encounter

-bone sternum, xiphoid
pert. to sternal, pectoral
breastplate urim, armor, lorica
ecclesiastical urim
breathing gasping, respiration
difficult dyspnea
harsh rale
smooth lene
sound pant, rale, snore, stridor
breeding origin, gestation
science eugenics
breeze aura, flow, pirr, rumor, zephyr, quarrel, whisper, disturbance
land terral
brevet confer, promotion, commission
brewer
grain rye, corn, malt, barley
vat tun
yeast barm, leaven
briar saw, pipe
brick tile, quarl(e)
handler baker, mason
oven kiln
sunbaked hat, adobe
tray hod
vitrified clinker
wood nog, dook, scutch
bridge game, span, trestle
forerunner whist, auction
lever bascule
of mus. instruments magas, ponticello
part deck, pier, cable, pylon
support pier, truss
type of auction, (game) rubber, contract, duplicate
briery sharp, spiny
brine sea, pickle
preserve in corn, cure, salt
shrimp artemia
brioche roll, stitch, cushion, pudding, savarin
Briseis
lover Achilles
British Columbia
Native American Haida, Shuswap
river Nicola
Britomartis Artemis, Dictynna
mother Carme

Brittany
  ancient name Armorica
  canvas vandelas
  king ban
  native Breton
  poetry soniou
  saint Anne
broad ample, coarse, obvious, tolerant
  comb. form late
  -footed platypod
  -minded lenient
broadbill bird, gaya, scaup, shoveler, swordfish
brobdingnagian huge, giant, colossal
brocard gibe, rule, maxim, sarcasm, principle
brocket deer, pita, spitter
brolly umbrella
Brontë Anne, Emily, Charlotte
  hero Rochester, Heathcliff
  heroine Jane Eyre
  pen name Bell
bronze tan, bust, brown, statue
  film patina, patine
  gilded ormolu
  nickel cupronickel
  pert. to aeneous
broom fray, besom, sweep
  plant hirse, heather, deerweed
brown dun, cook, sepia, bronze, russet, halfpenny
  and white roan
  Bess musket
  Betty pudding, coneflower
  dark burnet
  dark reddish cuba, henna, khaki
  light ecru, fawn, beige
  study absorption, abstraction
  thrasher bird, thrush
brume fog, vapor
Brython
  god Dea, Ler, Lludd
  goddess Don, Rhiannon, Arianrhod
bubal topi, antelope
buck fob, ram, deer, wash, dollar (sl.), oppose
  first year fawn
  fourth year sore

Buddha Fo(h), Gautama, Shakyamuni
  cause of infinite existence nidana, nirvana
  center Lhasa
  church Tera
  column lat
  disciple Ananda
  evil spirit Mara
  fate karma
  fertility spirit Yaksha, Yakshi
  festival bon
  god deva
  greater Mahayana
  hell Naraka
  language Pali
  prayer mani
  scripture sutra
  throne asana
  tree pipal, botree
buffalo ox, buff, bison, caribou
  gourd calabazilla
  large arna, arni, arnee
  meat biltong
  tree rabbitwood
  wild seladang
bufflehead duck, clown, merrywing
bug
  June dor
  lightning firefly
  needle ranatra
bugbane herb, hellebore, rattleroot
bugle bead, horn, buffalo, clarion
  blare tantara
  call taps, sennet, tattoo, retreat, reveille
  note not
  yellow iva
build
  nest nidify
  up enhance, strengthen
builder erector, tectonic
  labyrinth Daedalus
  of wooden horse Epe(i)us
bulbul bird, kala
Bulgaria, Bulgarian Slav, Churash
  coin lev, lew, stotinka
  measure oka, oke, krine, lekha
  weight oka, oke, tovar

bull apis, jest, quadruped
  angry gorer
  castrated stot, steer, bullock
  half man Minotaur
  hornless doddy, doddie
  -like taurine
  pert. to taurine
  young stirk, bullock
bulla bleb, seal, blain, vesicle
bullfinch alp, monk, hedge
bullion bar, ingot, metal, billot
Bull Run
  battle Manassas
  hero Lee
bumblebee dor, insect
bunch set, fagot, thump, quantity
  of grapes bob
  pert. to comal
buncombe rot, bunk, drivel, nonsense,
  poppycock
bundle wad, sheaf, bindle, parcel,
  collection
  maker baler
  arrows sheaf
  firewood bavin
  grain sheaf
  sticks fag(g)ot
  straw bolt
bung cork, spile, tampeon, bankrupt
Bunyan see Paul Bunyan
bunyip sham, imposter
buoy dan, elate, sustain
  mooring dolphin
  trawling marker dan
burbot cod, ling, eelpout
burden bearer Amos, Atlas
burgess citizen, commoner
burgoo, burgout soup, gruel, picnic,
  porridge
burial internment, deposition
  case box, casket, coffin
  litter bier
  mound barrow, tumulus
  pile pyre
  place tomb, grave, cemetery, Golgotha
  preparation for cere, pollincture
burin tool, graver

burl knot, pimple
  in mahogany roe
Burma, Burmese
  canopy tazaung
  chief bo(h), wun, woon
  dagger dah, dout
  deer thamin, thameng
  demon nat
  garment tamein
  girl mina
  headhunter Naga
  knife dah, dow
  measure dha, byee, dain, teng, palgat
  mus. instrument turr
  robber dacoit
  sash tubbeck
  spirit nat
  tree acle, yamani
  tribesman Lai
  weight mat, vis, kait, ticul
burning bush wahoo
burnoose, burnous cloak, garment,
  albornoz
burnt work pyrography
burse case, bazaar, exchange
burst pop, rend, erupt, salvo
  forth erupt, sally, blasted
  inward implode
bus jitney, vehicle, charabanc
bustle ado, fuss, to-do, tumult
  woman's bishop
but lo, ma (It.), sed (Lat.), yet, mere, still,
  unless
butcher cut, kill, bungle, vendor, pigstick
  hook gambrel
  rabbi shochtim (pl.)
  tool saw, knife, steel, cleaver
butcher-bird shrike
butte hill, picacho, mountain
butter shea, spread, blarney
  comb. form butyro
  pert. to butyric
  shea galam, bambuk
  tree shea, fulwa, phulwa
  tub firkin
butterbur eldin, plant
butterfish blenny, gunnel

butterfly kiho, idalya, viceroy, cecropia
  expert lepidopterist
  fish blenny
  genus melitaea, heliconius
  larva caterpillar
  lily sego, mariposa
  peacock io
butterwort steepweed
buy shop, trade, acquire, purchase
  cheaply snup
  to sell at a profit regrate
buying and selling nundination
by ago, per, near, close, beside
  -gone yore
  means of from, with, through
  mouth oral
  pass shun, avoid
Byron
  character Inez, Lara, Don Juan
byssin flax, linen
byssoid cottony, fiberlike, byssaceous
byword saw, axiom, proverb, catchword
Byzantine
  coin bezant
  scepter ferula
  works of art icons

C

C hundred
  -note 100-dollar bill (sl.)
Caaba shrine
  site Mecca
caama fox, asse, hartebeest
cabal plot, group, secret, faction, tradition
  pert. to factional
cabala mystery, occultism
cabbage chou, bowkail, colewort
  broth kale
  daisy globeflower
  family brassicaceae
  fermented sauerkraut
  salad slaw, coleslaw
  seed colza
  soup kale (Scot.)

  tree yaba, angelim
  variety red, cale, colza, celery
  worm looper, cutworm
caber beam, pole
cable boom, wire, ganger
  car telfer, telpher
  lifter wildcat
  post bitt
cabotin actor, charlatan
cacao bean, chocolate
  seed powder broma
cachalot sperm, whale, physeter
cache bury, hide, screen, conceal
cachet mark, seal, stamp, wafer, status, feature
cacholong opal
cachou catechu, lozenge
cacoëthes itch, desire, mania
cacography misspelling
cactus nopal, cholla
  drug peyote
  fruit fig, cochal
  plant tuna
  plantation nopalry
  plant process spine
cadaver body, stiff, corpse, carcass
caddis fly bait
caddisworm cadew
caddle fuss, confuse, disarray
Caddo Ree, Pawnee
caddow quilt, jackdaw, coverlet
caddy box, boy, can, chest
cade keg, pet, lamb, indulge, juniper
cadence beat, lilt, rate, meter, sound, rhythm, measure
cadet plebe, embryo, midshipman
cadge beg, tie, carry, frame, sponge
Cadmus
  daughter Ino, Agave, Semele, Autonoe
  father Agenor
  sister Europa
  wife Harmonia
cadre core, frame, group, scheme
Caen stone limestone
Caesar Sid, salad, tyrant, emperor
  assassin Brutus, Cassius
  augur who warned Spurinna
  capital Roma

colleague Bibulus
country conquered by Gaul
fatal day Ides
love of Servilia
mistress Cleo(patra), Eunoe
place of victory Actium
river crossed by Rubicon
sister Atia
site of famous message Zela
wife Cornelia, Calpurnia
cafard bigot, apathy, hypocrite
cage box, pen, prison, confine, platform,
  enclosure
  for hawk mew, meute
caiman jacare, alligator
Cain murderer, fratricide
  brother Pur, Abel, Seth
  descendant Jubal, Lamech
  father Adam
  land Nod
  mother Eve
  nephew Enos
  son Enoch
caique rowboat, sailboat
cairn pile, mound, landmark, monument
cairngorm quartz
caisson case, cheat, wagon, ponton
  disease bends, seizure
caitiff vile, wicked, cowardly
cajeput laurel
cake bun, wig, nacket, bannock
  almond macaroon
  boiled in honey teiglech (pl.)
  corn pone, fritter
  custard eclair, macaroon
  dough batter
  filled flan
  fish patty
  fried cruller, doughnut
  oatmeal bannock
  plum baba
  seed wig
  small tart, jumble
  tea scone
  unleavened matzo(h), damper,
    tortilla (Sp.)
cakewalk easy, cinch, dance, strut, prance

calaba tree, birma
calabash pipe, gourd, shell, curuba
caladium taro
calamanco manco, fabric, garment
calamus pen, cane, quill, sweetflag
calcar oven, spur
calcite animal, mineral, skeleton
  deposit spar, tatar
  soil with marl
calcium tufa
  crust sinter
  oxide quicklime
  sulphate gypsum, plaster
calculus (gall)stone, course, gravel
Calcutta
  hemp jute
  river Hugli, Hooghly
  state West Bengal
  weight pank, raik, hubba
Caleb
  companion Joshua
  daughter Achsah
  descendant Shobal, Ithrites
  son Hur, Iru, Elah, Mesha
  wife Ephah, Maacah
Caledonia, Caledonian Pict, Scot, Scotland
calefy heat, warm
calendar diary, register, ephemeris
  church ordo
  deficiency epact
  former Julian
calenture fire, ardor, fever
calf boy, dolt, bovine, fatling
  cry bleat
  front shin
  leather elk
  meat veal
  motherless dogy, dogie, maverick
  muscle plantaris
  pert. to sural
  skin parchment vellum
  suckling bob
  unbranded maverick
Caliban beast, slave
  adversary Prospero
  deity Setebos
  witch mother Sycorax

caliber bore, rank, virtue, ability, quality
calibrate set, measure, standardize
calico girl, goldfish, multicolored
  horse pinto
  pigment canarin(e)
  printing teer, fondu
California see Quick Reference List
  bay Monterey
  bulrush tule
  dam Shasta
  desert Mohave
  fan palm erythea
  fish reina, sprat
  fort Ord
  gold rusher argonaut
  grape picker bracero
  Indian Hupa, Seri, Yurok, Weitspekan
  island Alcatraz, Catalina, Treasure
  lake Tahoe, Salton
  laurel cajeput
  oak roble, encina
  observatory Lick, Palomar, Mt. Wilson
  pass Donner, Sonora
  peak Lassen, Shasta
  plant tarweed
  river Eel, Merced, Salmon, Russian
  sea Cortez
  shrub salal, chamiso, tarbush, chamisal, chaparral, manzanita
  town Napa, Fresno, Arcadia
  tree torrey, redwood, sequoia
  wine area Napa
Caligula bootikin
  horse Incitatus
  mother Agrippina
Caliph, Calif Abu, Ali, Bekr, Iman
  descendant Alide, Fatamid
  fourth Ali
calix cup, chalice
call bid, page, rouse, summon
  back revoke, retrieve
  creditor's dun
  distress SOS, May Day
  down scold, rebuke
  for page, exact, demand, require

  forth evoke, elicit, summon
  in question impugn
  off end, cancel
  prayer Adan, Azan
  to hail, address
  to attention hop, remind
  to mind cite, recall, remember
  theatrical curtain
callant lad, chap, fellow, customer
Calliope muse
  son Orpheus
Callisto nymph, constellation
  son Arcas
Call of the Wild
  author London (Jack)
calomel powder, cathartic
calorie, calory therm(e)
calotte coif, summit
calumet pipe
calyx leaf, sepal
  helmet-shaped galea
  of flower perianth
cam askew, trippet
  wheel projection lobe
camail hood, guard
Cambodia
  ancient capital Angkor
  capital Pnom-Penh
  native Khmer
  river Mekong
  ruins Angkor
  skirt samport
cambogia (gum) resin
cambric linen, batiste
Cambridge
  boat races Lent
  college official don, bedell, beadle
  council caput
  honor examination tripos
  student sizar, spoon, optime
camel mehari, dromedary
  driver sarwan, cameleer
  fermented milk kumiss, koumiss
  garment aba
  hair aba, cloth

hair cloth aba, cashmere
hair robe aba
load fardel
Camelot
  king Arthur
  magician Merlin
cameo gem, carving, phalera
  cutting tool spade
  stone onyx, sardonyx
camera box, chamber, instrument
  dark obscura
  eye retention
  part body, lens, finder, bellows, shutter
  platform dolly, tripod
  shot snap, flash, still
  small Brownie
Cameroon
  capital Yaounda
  inhabitant Sara
  largest city Douala
  monetary unit franc
  river Shari
Camilla
  father Metabus
  slayer Aruns
Camille
  creator Dumas
camion bus, dray, truck
camlet fabric, poncho
Camorra Mafia
campanero araponga, bellbird
camphol borneol
camphor asaron(e), menthol
campus quad, yard, field,
  building gym, dorm
Camus
  work Rebel, Stranger
Canada, Canadian Canuck
  city Banff, Ottawa, Calgary, Toronto
  court decree arret
  emblem maple
  fur company employee voyageur
  goose brant, honker
  measure ton, minot, arpent
  mountain Logan, Cascade, Rockies

  peninsula Gaspe
  policeman mountie
  province Quebec, Alberta, Manitoba
  river Back, Leaf, Trent, Mackenzie
  rodent lemming
  settler sourdough
  squaw mahala
  territory Yukon, Northwest
  town president reeve
canadine alkaloid
canaille mob, rabble
canal duct, drain
  bank berm(e)
  dredging machine couloir
  ear scala, scala media
  footpath towpath
  from mouth to anus enteron, alimentary
  lock gate sluice gate
Canal Zone
  city Balboa
  lake Gatun
canard hoax, fabrication
canary broom genista
Canary Islands Roca, Ferro, La Palma
  city Santa Cruz de Tenerife, Las Palmas
  commune Icod
  measure fanegada
  mountain El Cumbre, Tenerif(f)e
canary yellow meline
Candia Crete, seaport, Herakleion
candle dip, light, taper, chandelle
  holder sconce, candelabra, candlestick
  light dusk, twilight, nightfall
  lighter spill, acolyte
  material wax, wick, tallow, carnauba
  part wick, snaste
  place of keeping chandlery
  wax taper, bougie
candy lolly, sweet, comfit, flatter, sweet-
  meat
  base fondant
  pulled sugar taffy
candytuft plant, flower, iberis, mustard
cane rod, flog, reed
  dense growth canebrake

knife machete
like a ferulaceous
metal cap shoe, ferrule
part ferrule
strip splint
sugar sucrose
walking malacca
canfield Klondike, solitaire
cangle dispute, wrangle
canguelike device pillory
canine laniary
caning rattan, beating
Canis Major greater dog
  star Sirius
Canis Minor lesser dog
  star Procyon
cannabis hemp, marijuana
  drug bhang, hashish, marijuana
Cannery Row
  author Steinbeck (John)
cannibal savage, man-eater, carnivore
  human food long pig
cannikin can, pail
cannon gun, thief, mortar
  breech-end knob cascabel
  fire barrage
  firing stick linstock
  handle anse
  muzzle plug tampion
  old aspic, drake, falcon, culverin
  part bore, breech, muzzle, rimbase
  shot ball, grape
canoe pahi, kayak, pitpan
  bark cascara
  large bungo
  war prau, proa
canon law, code, rule, standard, criterion
  enigmatical nodi (pl.), nodus
  resident stagiary
canonical accepted, orthodox, conforming
  hour laud, matins, vespers
canopy hood, celure, pavilion, baldachin,
  baldacchino
  altar ciborium(a), baldachin(o)
  bed tester, sparver
canorous clear, sonorous
cantabank singer, chanter

cantata motet, serenata
canter pace
Canterbury
  archbishop Odo, Lang, Anselm, Becket,
  Cranmer
Canterbury Tales
  author Chaucer
  inn Tabard
cantharides irritant, stimulant
cantilena legato, graceful
cantina bag, pouch, saloon, canteen
canting pious
canto air, verse, division
cantoria balcony, gallery
cantrip charm, spell, trick
canvas duck, scrim
  like fabric wigan
  waterproof tarpaulin
canvass poll, hawk, debate, examine,
  inspect, solicit, investigate
canyon cajón, chasm, gorge, gulch
  mouth abra, jaws
  small cañada
  wall cliff
caoba quira, mahogany
caoutchouc rubber
  source ule, caucho
cap fez, lid, Eton, excel, outdo, beanie
  brimless tam, pileus, tarboosh
  child's mutch, toque, biggin
  close-fitting toque, cloche
  covering havelock
  ecclesiastical barret, biretta, galerum,
  berretta
  hunter's montero
  Jewish high priest's miter, mitre
  knitted thrum
  part bill, peak, visor
  sheepskin calpac(k)
  skull pileus, yarmulke
  slang lid
  steel cerveliere
  winter toque, tuque
capa cloak, mantle
capable apt, fit, competent
  of being cut sectile, scissile
  of being defended tenable

of being heard audible
of endurance wiry, tough
of extension tensile
capacitate qualify
Capaneus
  father Hipponous
  mother Astynome
  son Sthenelus
  wife Evadne
capataz boss, overseer
cape ras, writ, cloak, sagum
  cod food fish cero
  crocheted sontag
  ecclesiastical cope, amice
  hanging part tippet
  hooded amice, almuce, moz(z)etta
  lace fichu, bertha
Cape Dutch Afrikaans
Cape elk eland
cape jasmine gardenia
Cape polecat zoril, muishond
capelin smelt
caper lark, antic, shrub, cavort, gambol, seasoning
Cape Verde
  capital Praia
  island Sal, Fago
  native Brava, Serer
capias writ, process
capillus hair
capilotade stew, sauce, ragout
capital cash, city, seat, assets, letter, wealth, excellent, principal
  impairment of deficit
  provide back, angel, finance
Capitol Hill
  group House, Senate
  sound aye, nay
caporal foreman, tobacco, corporal (Fr.)
capote capa, hood, cloak, bonnet, topper
capper blind, decoy, shill, informer, by-bidder (sl.)
Capricorn
  planet Saturn
  symbol goat
caprylate acid, salt, ester
capuche cowl, hood

Capuchin friar, monkey, pigeon
capybara rodent
car box, coach, hutch, vehicle
  aerial cable telfer, telpher
  barn depot
caracara hawk
carafe bottle
carapace crust, shell, lorica
caravan van, trek, convoy
  slave coffle
caravansary inn, serai, imaret
carbon coal, coke, graphite
  copy (colloq.) (spitting) image, look-alike
  deposit soot
  point crayon
Carborundum emery, abrasive
carcajou wolverine
carcanet chain, collar, headband, necklace
carcel jail
carcoon clerk, manager
card map, menu, fiche, ticket
  jack pam
  spot pip
  widow skat
  wild joker
  wool comb, rove
cardialgia heartburn
cardinal bird, basic, cleric
  assembly at Rome college
  meeting room conclave
  office hat, datary
  skullcap zucchetto
  vestment dalmatic
care mind, auspice, direction, watchfulness
  for tend, foster
  requiring fragile
  under another's ward, protégé
Carew
  love Celia
careworn lined, haggard
cargador porter, carrier, stevedore
cargo bulk, load, shipment
  discarded jetsam
  hot contraband
  loader stevedore
  space in ship hold

stabilizer ballast
take on lade, load
wrecked ship flotsam
Caribbean
  bird tody
  gulf Darien
  island Cuba, Nassau
caribe fish, piranha
caribou deer, reindeer
  male stag
caricature ape, skit, squib, burlesque
caries decay, ulceration, saprodontia
cark worry, annoy
Carmelite monk, friar
  barefoot Teresian
carmen poem, song, opera, incantation
Carmen
  composer Bizet
carminative seeds caraway
carnauba palm
  product wax
carnelian sard, chalcedony
carnival gala, festival
  character shill, barker
  gambling operator grifter
carnose fleshy
carob pod, tree, locust, algar(r)oba
Caroline Islands Yap, Palu, Truk, Ponape
Carolinian tarheel
carotid artery
carp fish, cavil, criticize
  Jp. koi
  -like fish ide, dace, rudd, goldfish
carpal joint knee
carpel achene, carpophyl(l)
carpenter ant, framer, woodworker
  machine lathe, planer, shaper
  ship chips
  tool adz(e), awl, saw, level, plane, gimlet, hammer, square
carpet rug, tapete, covering
  city Agra, Tournai
  material drugget, moquette
carpus wrist
  bone carpal(e)
carrag(h)een alga, moss, seaweed
carriage air, buggy, landau, conduct

baby pram, stroller
covered landau, ricksha(w)
for hire fiacre
hood capote
one-horse fly, gig, sulky
open dos-a-dos
portable sedan
three-horse troika
carrion vile, rotten, corrupt
Carroll see Alice in Wonderland
carrot root, plant, daucus
  deadly drias
  family daucus
  genus carota
  oil tube vitta
  wild laceflower, Queen Anne's Lace
carry bear, cart, poise, convey
  away steal, remove
  on rant, perform
  out effect, sustain
  over tide, postpone
cart dray, haul, trundle
  farmer morfrey
  freight carreta
  racing sulky
  two-wheeled gig, tonga
Carthage, Carthaginian
  citadel Bursa, Byrsa
  conqueror Hannibal
  destroyer Romans, under Scipio
  foe Cato
  founder Dido
  god Moloch
  goddess Tanit(h)
  language, pert. to Punic
  queen Dido
cartilage tissue, gristle
  ossified bone
cartridge holder clip
carving
  in stone cameo, intaglio, engrailing
  pert. to glyphic, glyptic
  relief cameo
carya pecan, pignut, bitternut
Casanova cad, beau, lech, rake, roué, lover
casco barge, lighter
case box, deed, crate, lawsuit, instance

book holder for(r)el
cigar humidor
document hanaper
explosive shell, petard
small etui, bulla
cask keg, foist, barrel, cardel, puncheon
  oil rier
  rim chimb, chime
  stave lag
Caspian Sea
  ancient region Parthia
  harbor Baku
  river to Kura, Ural, Terek, Volga
Cassandra prophet, seeress
  father Priam
cassava aipi, juca, tapioca
cassena yaupon
cassia drug, herb
  bark cinnamon
Cassiopeia
  daughter Andromeda
  husband Cepheus
cassock gown, gippo, soutane
cassowary emu, bird, emeu, murup
caste rank, breed, class, order, degree
  group varna
  merchant banian, banyan
  priestly magi (pl.), magus
caster vial, wheel, pitcher
Castile
  hero Cid
  province Avila, Soria
  river Ebro, Esla, Douro, Duero
casting
  mold die, cast, matrix
  rough pig
castle morro, citadel, bastille
  part bawn, moat, drawbridge, portcullis
  tower keep
  wall bailey
  warden disdar, dizdar
Castor Gemini, Dioscuri
  father Zeus, Tyndareus
  horse Cyllaros
  mother Leda
  slayer Idas
  twin brother Pollux

castor-bean poison ricin
casus case, event, occasion
cat flog, whip, feline, mawkin
  breed Manx, Angora, Maltese, Persian, Siamese
  castrated gib(bed)
  civetlike genet, zibet(h)
  comb. form aelur(o)
  epithet baudrons
  female grimalkin
  genus Felis, Felidae (pl.)
  musk-yielding civet
  ring-tailed serval
catafalque bier, coffin
cataian thief, sharper, scoundrel
Catalonia
  dance Sardana
  famous person Casals
  marble brocatel(le)
catamount lynx, puma, cougar
cataplasm poultice
catarrh cold, rheum, inflammation
catbird mimidae
cate food, viands, provisions
catena link, chain, series
caterpillar muga, aweto, crawler, tractor
caterwaul cry, wail, miaul
cathedral dom, church
  passage slype
catkin ament, spike
catmint nep, nip, herb
Catoism austerity, harshness
Catreus
  daughter Aerope, Clymene, Apemosyne
  father Minos
  mother Pasiphae
cat's cradle ribwort
cattle cows, bulls, beasts, steers, bovines, bullocks
  assemblage herd, drove
  brand duff, buist
  call sook
  dehorned mul(l)ey
  genus Bos
  goddess Bubona
  plague rinderpest

shelter barn, byre, barth
yard cancha
Caucasia
  goat tur
  ibex zac
  language Laz, Udi, Avar, Semitic
  race Aryan, Osset(e)
  rug kub, baku, chila
  tribe Kurd, Lazi, Svan, Kubachi
caudal rear, posterior
  appendage tail
caudata newt, snake, salamander
caul cap, web, veil, network
caulking material tar, oakum
cauma heat, fever
caustic lye, tart, biting, bitter, severe, mordant, critical, scathing, vitriolic
  agent cautery, erodent
caution heed, advice, counsel, warning, wariness, alertness, vigilance, admonition, discretion, watchfulness, circumspection
cavalier gay, curt, escort, knight, gallant, haughty, horseman
cavalry horses, mounted troops
  horse lancer
  weapon lance, saber
cavalryman spahi, jaeger, lancer, courier, dragoon, chasseur
cave den, weem, grotto, spelunk
  dweller troglodyte
  researcher spelunker, speleologist
caveat beware, caution, warning
cavetto molding
caviar, caviare egg, ova, roe, ikra(y), delicacy
  source sterlet, sturgeon
cavity pit, vein, lumen, antrum, hollow
  anatomical fossa, sinus, antrum
  brain coelia
  heart auricle, ventricle
  pert. to sinal, atrial, geodic
  skull aula, fossa, sinus
cavy paca, pony, guinea pig
cawl trug, basket
caxi fish, snapper
cayuse cavy, pony, bronco

cecidium gall
cedar toon, tree, savin, waxwing
  camphor cedrol
  green cedre (Fr.), color
  moss hornwort
cedrat citron
ceilidh call, visit, conversation, entertainment
ceiling lining
  covering paint, calcimine, kalsomine
  division trave
  mine astel
  wooden plancher
Celebes
  bovine ox, anoa
  people tora(d)ja
celery
  family ammiaceae
  wild smallage
celestial holy, uranic, ethereal
  being angel, cherub, seraph
  body sun, star, comet, meteor, planet
  elevation of mind anagoge
  matter nebula
cell egg, jail, vault
  coloring endochrome
  colorless achroacyte, lymphocyte
  connecting heterocyst
  division spireme
  group ceptor, blastema
  layer blastula, blastoderm
  pert. to cytoid
  substance linin
cella naos
Celtic Erse, Scotch, Scottish
  abbot coarb
  chariot essed
  chieftain tanist
  foot soldier kern
  god Ler, Leir, Llyr
  peasant kern
  priest Druid
cenchrus grass, millet
cenobite nun, monk, monastic
censer thurible
centaur
  bull's head bucentaur

father Ixion
  killed by Hercules Nessus
centerpiece epergne
centipede veri, golach
Central America
  agave sisal
  ant kelep
  canoe pitpan
  Indian Maya, Carib
  measure cantaro, manzana
  monkey mono
  village boma
  weight libra
centripetal afferent
century plant aloe, agave, maguey
  fiber pita(o)
ceramics tiles, pottery, stoneware
  oven kiln
  sieve laun
cere wax, sere, embalm
cereal rye, oats, spelt, wheat, barley, porridge
  coating bran
  seed kernel
  spike ear
cerebrospinal axis cord, brain, spine
ceremonial fuss panjandrum
Ceres Demeter
  mother Ops
cernuous nodding, drooping
certificate bond, diploma, voucher, credential
  cargo navicert
  debt IOU, debenture
  medical, for ill student aegrotat
certiorari writ, review
cespitose matted, tufted, tangled
cess bog, duty, slope, impost
cessation letup, truce
  of being desition
cesspool sump, cistern
cest belt, cestus, girdle
cetacean orc, whale, dolphin, grampus
  blind susu
  genus Inia
Ceylon
  aborigine Toda, Vedda(h)
  coin cent

garment sarong
governor disawa
language Pali, Tamil
measure para(h)
monkey maha, langur, wanderoock
oak kusam
skirt reddha
soldier peon
tree doon, tala, talipot
chabutra dais, terrace, platform
chack bite, clack, wheatear
chacra farm, milpa, ranch
chaeta seta, spine, bristle
chaffinch robinet
chain guy, tew, bind, catena, manacle
  cable boom
  collar torque
  grab wildcat
  key chatelaine
  -like catenate
  of quotations catena
  of rocks reef
  of set precious stones sautoir
  pert. to catenary
chair seat, office
  back splat
  bishop's official cathedra
  cover tidy, antimacassar
  folding faldstool
chaise gig, shay, curicle, carriage
chaitya shrine, monument
Chalcodon
  father Abas
  son Elephenor
Chaldea
  astronomical cycle saros
  city Ur
  measure cane, makuk, ghalva
chalky silicate talc
chamber cell, atrium, lochlus
  bombproof casemate
  private adyta (pl.), sanctum
  underwater construction caisson
chambray cloth, fabric, gingham
chameleon anole, anoli, lizard
chamois skin, cloth, antelope
  male gemsbok

chamomile, camomile mayweed
champerty contest, rivalry, conspiracy
chancel
  part bema, altar
  screen jube
  seat sedile
chandelier pharos, fixture
chandelle lob, climb, candle
chang beer, noise, uproar
change move, adapt, amend, mutate,
  deviate
  appearance obvert
  back return, revert
  character of denature
  color allochromous
  music muta
  pattern kaleidoscopic
channel gat, vein, canal, arroyo, sluice
  artificial canal, drain, flume
  brain iter
  formed by cutting scarf
  marker buoy
  narrow furrow, strait
  vital artery
Channel Island Sark, Jersey, Guernsey
  measure cade, cabot
  seaweed vraic
channels media, striae
chantage extortion, blackmailing
chaos, Chaos mess, mixup, jumble
  Babylonian Apsu
  daughter Nox, Nyx
  Maori kore
  primeval fluid of Nu
  son Erebus
chap boy, man, bean, bully, crack (of skin),
  split, barter, shaver, customer (Brit. sl.)
  odd galoot
  old geezer, gaffer
chaparral buckthorn
chapel cage, shrine, sanctuary
  private oratory
  sailor's bethel
chaps jaws, breeches, overalls
charabanc bus, coach, vehicle
charact emblem
character bent, mold, mettle, quality

assumed role
group ethos
vein streak
word representing logogram, logograph
characteristic cast, mark, symbolic
  individual idiopathy
charco pool, puddle, spring
charcoal carbo, fusain, pencil
  animal boneblack
chard beet, thistle, artichoke
chariot car, esseda, carriage
  for carrying image of God rath(a)
  Gr. quadriga
  Roman essed(e), esseda
  two-horse biga
charivari babel, shivaree
chark cup, coal, noggin
Charlemagne
  brother Carloman
  conquest Avars
  father Pepin
  sword Joyeuse
Charlie Chan
  creator Biggers (Earl Derr)
Charlotte Corday
  victim Marat
charnel ghastly, cemetery, sepulchral
  house ossuary, mortuary
charpoy bed, cot
charqui beef, meat, jerky
Charybdis rock Scylla
chase hunt, score, engrave
  away rout, drive
  goddess Dian, Diana
chat mag, ament, babble, samara, small talk
chatelaine pin, clasp, mistress
chatta umbrella
chattels gear, goods, slaves
  distraint naam
  tenant's farleu, farley
  to recover detinue
chatter gab, prate, yammer, nashgob
  box jay, gossip
Chaucer
  inn Tabard
  pilgrim reeve
  title Dan

chauvinism jingoism, patriotism
chavel gnaw, mumble, nibble
chawbacon chaw, rustic, bumpkin
cheat do, con, dupe, weed, chisel, skelder, prestidigitator
checkers game, draughts
  move dyke, fife, huff, cross, bristol
  opening souter
  term king, jump, block, crown
checkerwork tessera(e) (pl.)
  inlay mosaic
checkrein curb, saccade
cheek gall, jowl, temerity
  bone malar, zygoma
  comb. form bucco
  muscle buccinator
  pert. to genal, malar, buccal
cheese feta, goat, gouda, Swiss, Mysost, cheddar, cottage, havarti, Sapsago, Stilton, American, provolone, mozzarella
  basis of casein
  cake dessert, photograph
  curdy trip
  drying frame hack
  maggot skipper
  milk whey ziega, zieger
  pert. to caseic, caseous
chela claw, slave
chelicera mandible, appendage
chemical acid, alkali
  agent catalyst
  catalyst reagent
  comb. capacity valence
  compound imin, azine, boride
  element See Quick Reference List
  measure dram, gram, liter, titer
  prefix oxa, aceto, amido, amino
  salt sal, borate
  substance linin
  suffix ane, ine, ose, olic
chemisette sham, guimpe
chequeen basket, sequin, zecchino
cherry duke, morel, oxheart
  acid cerasin
  color red, cerise
  disease blackknot

  extract cerasein
finch hawfinch
holly islay
laurel cerasus
orange kumquat
sour amarelle
sweet bing, lambert, oxheart
wild gean, choke, marasca, mazzard
chest box, arca, fund, bosom, thorax
  animal brisket
  cavity membrane pleura
  comb. form steth(o)
  located on the pectoral
  of sacred utensils cist
  sound rale
  vibration fremitus
chestnut mast, tree, horse, oldie
  colloquial joke, cliché
  tree chincapin, chinquapin
chevet apse, termination
chevisance booty, remedy, resource
chevrotain napu, deerlet, kanchil
chevy fret, hunt, chase
chew cud, gnaw, munch, ruminate
  inability to amasesis
chewing
  gum ingredient chicle, mastic
  gum tree sapodilla
  tobacco piece plug
chewink bird, finch, joree, towhee
Chicago Windy City
chicalote poppy
chick child, peeper, sheila
chicken fowl, biddy, manoc
  castrated capon
  chaser catchpole
  feed (sl.) cheap, coins, dimes, peanuts, piddling, negligible
  five-toed houdan
  pox varicella
  raising device brooder
  snake boba
  young chick, fryer, peeper, pullet
chicken out quit, renege
chickpea gram, herb, garbanzo
chickweed genus alsine
chicle gum, latex

chicory bunk, root
  family cichoriaceae
chief bo, aga, boss, main, titan
chigoe flea, chigger
chilblain kibe, sore
child imp, tad, baba, babe, tike, tyke, moppet, product
  advancement precocity
  bad-tempered changeling
  bastard by-blow
  bib dickey
  comb. form ped(o)
  homeless waif
  killer infanticide
  murder of filicide, prolicide
  of light and day, so-called Eros
  of the street arab, waif, gamin
  of the sun Inca
  patron saint Nicholas
  pert. to filial
  Scot. bairn
  unweaned suckling
childlike meek, docile, submissive
children progeny, offspring
  dislike of misopedia
  medical science pediatrics
  study pedology
  tender of amah, sitter, nursemaid
Chile, Chilean
  aborigine Inca
  beech tree roble
  coastal wind sures
  coin colon, escudo, centavo
  deer pudu
  measure vara, legua, linea, cuadra, fanega
  monetary unit escudo
  money condor
  national police carabineros
  rodent chinchilla
  saltpeter niter, nitre
  volcano Antuco, Calbuco
  weight grano, libra, quintal
  workman roto
chills and fever ague, malaria
chilver lamb
chimaera ratfish

chimera fancy, mirage
chin jaw, chat, mentum
  comb. form genio
  double fold, buccula
China, Chinese miao, seric, sinic, oriental
  aborigine Yao, Mans, Miao, Mantzu, Yao-min, Miaotse, Miaotze
  ancient name Tsao, Seres, Cathay
  aromatic root ginseng
  bamboo stick whangee
  bean soya, adzuki
  black tea oolong
  boat bark, junk, sampan, tongkang
  Buddha Fo, Foh
  Buddhist paradise Chingtu
  card game fan tan
  cloth sha, moxa, pulo, nankin
  coat mandarin
  coin pu, neu, sen, tael, lliang
  coin with hole cash
  dynasty, first Hsia
  dynasty, last Manchu
  festival Ching Ming
  god Ghos, Joss, Shen, Kuant
  idol joss, pagoda
  incense joss stick
  invention gunpowder
  mile li
  porcelain Celadon, Nankeen
  servant amah
  silkworm sina, tasar, tussah, ailanthus
  Sino, Sinic dynasty (comb. form) Fo, Ming, Tang
  spring Ch'un
  temple taa, pagoda
  treaty port Amoy, Shanghai
  wormwood moxa
chinch bedbug
Chinook wind, Indian, salmon, Flathead
  god Tamanoas
  lily/bulb quamash
  powwow wawa
  state Washington
chinse calk, seam, caulk, close
chip bit, nip, clip, flake, piece, scrap
  of stone spall, gallet

chipmunk chippy, trackee, squirrel
  cheek pouch alforja
chirk lively, cheerful
chirm din, croon
chiro (comb. form) hand
chiropter(a) bat, aliped
chisel cut, pare, gouge, broach, engrave
  ancient stone celt
  bar spudder
  broad-faced drove
  engraving scooper
  mason's pommel
  part tang
  stonemason's drove
chit note, shoot
  of a kind memo, voucher
chiton limpet, garment, mollusk
chlamys cloak, mantle
chloride salt, muriate
chlorophyll etiolin
chobdar usher, attendant
chocolate cocoa
  family sterculiaceae
  machine conche
  seed cacao
  tree cola, cacao
choir
  boy's collar Eton
  leader choragus
  vestment cotta, surplice
choke gag, quar, impede, throttle
choke coil reactor
chokedamp blackdamp
cholecyst (gall)bladder
choler bile, rage, wrath
cholla cactus
choosing, right of option
chop cut, hew, dice, mince
  down fell, raze
  eye of noisette
  off lop, prune
chopine shoe, pattern
chopping block hacklog
chord tone, triad
  harplike arpeggio
  musical major, minor
  succession cadence

Chorda filum sealace
chorister's garment cassock
choroid membrane tapetum
chorten stupa, monument
chose chattel
chough bird, crow
chowk bazaar, market
Christian, Christianity human, decent,
  Gentile, Nazarene
  abbrev. Xtian
  early Galilean
  Egyptian Copt
  love feast agape
  persecuted martyr
  pulpit ambo
  symbol cross, orant, lehthus
  unity irenics
Christian Science
  founder Eddy (Mary Baker)
Christmas Carol
  author Dickens
  character Tiny Tim, Scrooge
Christmas rose hellebore
chromium metal, element, mineral
  group element uranium, tungsten
  symbol Cr
chromosome load genes
chrysalis pupa, cocoon
chthonian infernal
chuff fat, cross, rustic
church sect, edifice, sanctuary,
  denomination
  altar end apse
  altar offerings altarage
  balcony cantoria
  basin font, lavabo
  bell ringer sexton
  bell tower belfry
  body of nave
  building ecclesia
  contribution to tithe
  cup chalice
  deputy vicar, curate
  doorkeeper ostiary
  law canon
  loft jube
  reader lector

seat for clergy sedilia
stand ambo
churchgoer member, communicant
churchyard parvis
churl cad, boor, hind, lout, miser
chute rush, flume, hopper
cibarious edible
cibol onion, shallot
ciborium cup, pyx, canopy
cicada locust
  vibrating membrane timbal
cicala locust, grasshopper
Cicero
  target Catiline
cicerone guide, pilot
cid Ruy, hero, Bivar, chief
  sword colada, tizona
cilium hair, eyelash
cimarron river, slave, maroon
cimbia
  band fillet
cimex bedbug, insect
cinch belt, snap, girth
cinchona bark, tree
  extract quinine
cinnabar ore, vermillion
  derivative quicksilver
cinnamon tree, spice, cassia
  apple sweetsop
  oak bluejack
  stone garnet, essonite
Cipango Japan, Nippon
cipo vine, liana
Circe siren, sorceress
  brother Aeetes
  father Helios
  island Aeaea
circle disk, hoop, swirl, spiral
  around sun or moon corona
  great equator
  heraldry annulet
circular
  motion eddy, gyre
  plate disc
circumference arc, border, limits
circumstantial exact, precise
circus arena, spectacle

arena wall spina
column meta
gear tent, rings, trapeze
cirrus cloud, tendril
cisco blackfin, whitefin
citadel arx, tower, fortification
citrine color, rhubarb
citrus fruit
  belt Florida, California
  disease buckskin
city
  celestial Zion
  eternal Rome
  holy Mecca, Medina, Jerusalem
  oldest inhabited Damascus
  pert. to civic, urban
  wicked Sodom, Gomorrah
City of
  Bells Strasbourg, Strassburg
  Bridges Bruges
  Brotherly Love Philadelphia
  Churches Brooklyn
  Kings Lima
  Lilies Florence
  Masts London
  Rams Canton
  Saints Montreal
  Seven Hills Rome
  Victory Cairo
civetlike animal genet
Civil War
  admiral Farragut
  battle Shiloh, Bull Run, Antietam, Gettysburg
  commander Lee, Pope, Ewell, Grant, Meade, Sykes, Forrest, Jackson, McClellan
  president of South Davis
civil wrong tort
civilian dress mufti
clabber mud, curdle
cladose ramose, branched
claggum taffy, molasses
clam base, hush, mollusk
  genus Mya
clan set, cult, horde
  pert. to tribal

clarinet reed, instrument
  mouthpiece birn
  snake charmer's been
class ilk, race, genus
  pert. to generic
classical pure, Attic, Greek, Latin, Roman
Claudia
  husband Pilate
claut hand, rake, scrape
clavecin harpsichord
claver prate, gossip
clavicle bone, collarbone
clay marl, earth, inanimate
  box saggar
  building adobe, tapia
  comb. form pel, argillo
  covered with lutose
  made of fictile
  pert. to bolar
clayey bolar, heavy, lutose
clear rid, open, acquit, candid
  as crystal evident, obvious
  away fey, dispel, remove
  out decamp, desert
  profit net
  the way! gangway
  to the mind palpable
  up solve, settle
clear-cut lucid, sharp
clearing
  in woods glade, tract
  of land sart, assart
clear-sighted discerning, perspicacious
cleat bitt, kevel, wedge
cleaver ax, axe, froe, frow
cleek club, crook
clef key, character
  bass eff
  treble gee
Cleite
  father Merops
  husband Cyzicus
Clemens
  pen name (Mark) Twain
Cleopatra
  attendant Iras, Charmian
  killer asp

  lover Antony, Caesar, Mark Antony
  needle obelisk
  river Nile
  sister Arsinoe
  son Caesarion
clepsydra clock, waterglass
clergyman/woman abbe, curate
  church-service vestment canonicals
  degree B.D., D.D.
  position/garment frock, cassock
  residence manse, rectory
  salary prebend
  with the military padre, chaplain
clerisy intellectuals
cleuch cleft, descent
clever adept, smart
  as a fox vulpine
  remark (sl.) crack, nifty
  retort sally, bon mot, ripost(e), repartee,
    witticism
clevis hake, copse, shackle
click beetle elater
cliff precipice
  debris talus
  edge brow
  fissure for climbing chimney
clinch hug, grip, fasten
  argument settle
  breaker referee
  nautical noose, clench
  sl. embrace
clingfish remora, testar
clique circle, faction
cloaca vent, privy, sewer
cloak garment, disguise
  blanketlike poncho, serape
  fur-lined pelisse
  hood cowl
cloam crockery
clock time(piece)
  face of dial
  part hand, chime, click, pallet, pendulum
  water clepsydra
clodpate fool, blockhead
close shut (in), finale, conclude
  conclusively clinch
  hermetically seal

in music coda
mouthed taciturn
poetic nigh, anear
to the wind luff
clot jell, coagulate
-preventing substance heparin
cloth goods, fabric
altar pall, vesperal
bark tapa
dealer draper, mercer
finisher beetler
measure ell, nail, yard
clothesmoth tinea
cloud haze, befog, stigma
comb. form nepho
morning velo
pert. to nebular
study of nephology
clour blow, dint
cloven cleft, split, bisulcate
cloven-footed fissiped
clown mime, zany, buffoon
garment motley
woman buffa
clubfoot talipes
clump mass, cluster
of bushes shaw
of earth clod
of ivy, etc. tod
of trees bosk, mott(e)
clupeid shad, herring, sardine
cluster bunch, clump
banana hand
fruits bunch
leaves fascicle
of seven stars Pleiades
Clytemnestra
husband Agamemnon
lover Aegisthus
mother Leda
son Orestes
cnemis shin, tibia, legging
coach tutor, carriage
for hire hack, fiacre
for state occasions caroche
coal fuel, carbon, cinder

agent fitter
bed seam
bin bunker
comb. form anthrac(o), bitumen
distillate tar
miner collier
wagon corb, tram
coalfish sey, parr, cuddy, podler
coarse low, raw, lewd, gross, blatant
coast bank, ripa, shore, border
dweller oarian
to coastal, orarian
coast guard
boat cutter
servicewoman Spar
coat jacket, garment
formal tails, cutaway
leather jack
neck george
of arms crest
sleeveless jack
coati nasua, animal, narica
coaxial conterminous
cobbler pie, snob, sheep, dessert, repairer
pitch code
cobia fish, bonito
cobra snake, viper
genus Naja
tree mamba
cochleate spiral
cock crow, rooster
-and-bull story hoax, yarn, fable, canard
fighting heeler
young cockerel
cockateel parrot
cockatrice serpent, basilisk
cockfight spar, derby
cocklebur burdock, ragweed
cockspur (haw)thorn
cocoa broma, chocolate
bean, crushed nibs
coconut palm
husk fiber coir
liquid milk
meat, dried copra(h)
cocoon pod, case, theca

fiber silk
in zoology follicle
silkworm clew
code law, salic
  church canon
  message in cryptogram
  moral ethics
  of a kind password
coelenterate hydra, acaleph(e), anemone, jellyfish
  larva planula
coercion duress, compulsion
coffee java, mocha
  beans nibs
  cup stand zarf
  plantation finca
  substitute chicory, succory
  tree chicot
coffer chest, strongbox
cogent valid, potent, telling, forceful, effective, believable, convincing
cognate akin, related
cognomen (sur)name, nickname
cogon grass
cohere fit, agree, cling, stick
cohort ally, band
  one-third of maniple
coil ado, clew, roll, whip, wind, twine, bustle, tumult, ringlet, trouble, disturbance
  electric teaser
coin cash, mint, money, shape, token, devise
  ancient obol, obolus
  box pyx, meter
  collector numismatist
  counterfeit brummagem
  front head, obverse
  new words neologize
  reverse side tail, verso
  weight shekel
coincide jibe, agree, tally, concur
col gap, pass
Colchis
  king Aeetes
  princess Medea
cold bleak, rheum
  -blooded callous

congeal freeze
extremely gelid
coleopter beetle, weevil
Coleridge
  poem Kubla Khan, Christabel
  sacred river Alph
Colette
  character Gigi, Cheri, Claudine
colewort kale, cabbage, collard
coliseum hall, stadium, theater, amphitheater
collapse cave, fail, fold, slump, crumble, debacle
collar neckware, capture
  bird's flange
  bone clavicle
  clerical rabato
  high fraise
collateral sub, side, related, parallel, security (loan), attendant, auxiliary, accompanying
collation tea, meal, repast, reading, collection
colleague aide, ally, unite, consort, associate
collection group, repertory
  anecdotes ana
  commentaries glossary
  essays symposium
  facts ana, data
  miscellaneous olio, fardel
  opinions symposium
  precious treasure
collector of
  art patron
  books bibliophile
  gems lapidary
  items curio, relic
  jokes Cerf
  plants herbalist
  shells conchologist
  stamps philatelist
colleen lass, belle, damsel
collegiate varsity
collet band, ring, collar, flange, socket
collide ram, hit, bump, crash, hurtle

collier boat, miner, vessel
  boy hodder
  lung disease anthracosis
colliery (coal) mine
  tunnel adit
collop piece, slice
collude plot, scheme, conspire
colly soot, grime, blacken
Cologne
  German spelling Köln
  king Caspar, Jaspar
Colombia, Colombian
  city Cali, Pasto, Bogota, Medellin
  coin peso, condor
  gulf Darien
  measure vara, celemin
  plant yocco
  province Cauca, Huila, Valle, Bolivar
  seaport Lorica, Cartagena
  volcano Huila, Pasto, Purace
  weight bag, saco, carga, libra, quintal
colonial teak flindosa
color dye, hue, ensign, distort, standard
  change iridesce, opalesce
  comb. form chrom(o), chromat(o)
  gradation shade
  light tint
  line of streak
  pale pastel
  primary red, blue, black, white, yellow
  quality tone
  secondary green, orange, purple
  unhealthy sallow
Colorado see Quick Reference List
colorant dye, anil, pigment
colored biased, warped, partisan, specious, deceptive, influenced
  partly pied, motley, variegated
color photography
  inventor Ives
colossus giant, statue
  sculptor Chares
colt gun, foal, pistol, youngster
Columbia River
  rapids Dalles

columbine aquilegia
Columbus, Christopher
  birthplace Genoa
  burial place Seville
  navigator of Pinzon
  son Diego
  starting point Palos
column shaft, pillar
  base plinth
  designating a Ionic, Doric
  figure, female caryatid
  figure, male Telamon, Atlantes
  ornament griffe
  support base, plinth, pedestal
coma tuft, bunch, sleep, stupor
comatose out, drowsy, torpid, lethargic
comb card, rake, sift, curry, smooth, caruncle
  comb. form cten(o)
  horse curry
combat war, bout, fight, repel, set-to, action, battle, contend, scuffle
  challenge to single cartel
  code duello
  place arena, field
combine add, wed, bloc, pool, merge, coalesce, compound, monopoly, alignment, amalgamate
combining form
  alike iso
  among inter
  bad cac(o), mal
  below infero
  between inter
  death necr(o)
  different heter(o)
  double dipl(o)
  end tel(o)
  far tele
  feet ped(e), pedi
  hatred mis(o)
  hundred hect(o), centi
  many poly
  people ethn(o)
  self auto
  small micr(o)

sun heli(o)
universe cosm(o)
water hydr(o)
weight baro
combust burn, consume, incinerate
come occur, appear, arrive, develop
  a cropper fail, fall
  across find, meet, contribute
  after ensue, follow, succeed
  again return
  along fare, improve
  apart break
  around revive
  back recur, return
  before precede, prevene
  between alienate, interpose
  by gain, obtain
  down land, alight
  down with catch, contract
  forth appear, emerge
  forward advance, volunteer
  into view loom
  of age mature
  out even draw, tie
  together meet, clash, collide
  to grips with tangle
  to a head climax
  to nothing end, cease
  to terms join, assent
  under subvene
  upon meet, chance
comedy drama, farce, movie, travesty
  character Pantaloon
  muse Thalia
  symbol sock
Comedy of Errors
  servant Luce
comely fair, pert, bonny, proper, seemly, becoming, pleasing
comensal inquiline
comet
  discoverer Biela, Encke, Swift, Halley, Olbers
  part coma
  tail streamer

comeuppance (sl.) punishment
comma mark, pause
  -shaped organism vibrio
command bid, rule, edict, govern, dictate
  supreme hegemony
Commandments, the Ten Decalogue
commedia 'dell Arte
commend pat, cite, laud, praise, bespeak, entrust
  highly extol, eulogize
  to favor ingratiate
comment remark, annotation
  adverse criticism
  at bottom of page footnote
  derisive jeer
  marginal margent
commentary memoir, account, glossary, explanation
comminate ban, curse
commingle mix, fuse, blend, mingle, combine
commit do, consign, entrust
  perjury forswear
  to mind memorize
common low, usual, public
  people masses
  people, of the grassroots
  saying saw, adage
  to both sexes epicene
commonly
  accepted popular, vulgate
  thought reputed, putative
commonplace prosaic, ordinary
Common Sense
  author Paine
commune mir, kibbutz, converse
communicate impart, transmit
communications
  satellite Telstar
  code word Alfa, Echo, Golf, Kilo, Lima, Mike, Papa, Xray, Zulu, Bravo, Delta, Hotel, India, Oscar, Romeo, Tango, Quebec, Sierra, Victor, Yankee, Charlie, Foxtrot, Juliett, Uniform, Whiskey, November

communion sharing
  cloth corporal
  cup ama
  Holy Eucharist, sacrament
  plate paten
  table credence
Communist
  curtain iron, bamboo
  party member comrade
  policy body Politburo
  youth league comsomol
commutator rheotrope
compact brief, solid, agreement
  between nations treaty
  mass wad
companion pal, comrade, associate
  colloq. sidekick
  constant shadow, alter ego
  of cease desist
company band, firm, society
  of hunters safari
  of ten soldiers decurion
  of travelers caravan
compare liken, contrast
  beyond peerless
  critically collate
compass scope, understand
  beam trammel
  case binnacle
  dial card
compend breviary
compendium digest, summary
compilation selection, collection
  of anecdotes memoirs
  of stories, poems anthology
complete full, entire, intact
  attendance plenary
  entity integer
  not partial
complex mixed-up, intricate
  kind of Oedipus, inferiority
complication mess, snag, nodus
compline hour, prayers, service
compo mortar, plaster
component part, unit, element, ingredient, constituent
  of atom proton

composition essay, theme
  for organ toccata
  for practice etude
  musical opus, suite
  operatic scena
  sacred motet
compound mix, combine, concoct, mixture
  carbon carbide
  of silica glass
  raceme panicle
  words, separation of parts tmesis
compound interest anatocism
comprehension grasp
  through intellect noesis
compulsion craze, mania, obsession
  petty thievery kleptomania
computer univac, machine
  information data, input, output
  inventor Babbage
  symbol system code
  type of IBM, analog, digital
conative state nisus
concatenate link(ed)
conceal hide, secrete
  goods cache, hoard
  in law eloin
concertina kin accordion
conclude end, close, deduce, finish
  a speech perorate
concoct hatch, devise, compound
concomitant attendant
concubinage hetaerism
concubine in harem odalisk, odalisque
concuss jar, jolt, force
condensed form
  moisture dew
condenser cric, aludel
condition if, status, provision
  contract proviso, stipulation
  of decline decadence
  of great vitality sthenia
  of oblivion limbo
  of stupor coma, narcosis
conditional surrender capitulation
conductor guide, maestro
  platform of podium

stick baton
woman quach
cone strobile
  -shaped conic(al), conoid, pineal, turbinate
  -shaped yarn roll cop
  spiral helix
conepate skunk
Confederacy
  banknote bluejack
  general Lee, Bragg, Jackson
  guerilla bushwacker
  president Davis
  soldier reb
conference confab, meeting
  site of 1943 Cairo, Teheran
  site of 1945 Yalta
confine limit, restrict
  to a place localize, quarantine
confined ill, bound, cloistered
  to select group esoteric
confluence crowd
confrere fellow, comrade, colleague
conge farewell, dismissal
congenital inborn, innate
  mark mole
Congo tea, dye, river
  language Bantu, Lingala, Swahili
congou tea
congress meeting, assembly, legislature
  attendant page
  time off recess
conjum hemlock
Connecticut see Quick Reference List
connective syndetic
  tissue fascia, tendon
connoisseur (a)esthete
  of art virtuoso
  of fine food/drinks epicure, go(u)rmand, gourmet
conscientious objector conchy
consciousness awareness
  loss of coma, apoplexy
consign send, deliver, entrust, relegate
  to hell damn, condemn
console cheer, comfort

-like bracket corbel
the bereaved condole
consonant
  aspirated fortis
  unaspirated lene
  voiceless atonic
constellation cluster, gathering
  altar ara
  brightest star cor
  cross crux
  dog canis
  equatorial cetus, orion
  stern puppis
  veil vela
constitution charter, basic law, structure
  addition to amendment
  composition of bylaws, articles, preamble
consuetude habit, usage
contagion pox, taint
container tin, crate, basket
  cardboard box, carton
  documents hanafer
  dose of medicine capsule
  glass jar, bottle, carboy
  wine ampulla
conte tale, short story
contest fight, dispute, tournament, competition
  endurance marathon
  in court litigation
  with lances tilt, joust
contiguous next, adjacent, touching
continent Asia, Africa, Europe, Australia, temperate, North America, South America
  icy Antarctica
  legendary Atlantis
continual constant, incessant
  movement flux
contort warp, twist, deform
contract incur, agreement
  illegal labor yellow-dog
  of agency mandate
  work indenture
contradiction denial, inconsistency
  in terms antilogy
contravene oppose

contrition remorse, penitence
controversial moot, debatable
  theorist Darwin
  theory evolution
controversialist eristic
contumacious unruly, riotous, stubborn, insubordinate
conundrum enigma, puzzle, riddle
convent nunnery, monastery
  dining hall refectory
  head superior
  member nun, monk, cenobite
  member, new neophyte
conversational
  comeback retort, riposte
  style/writing in causerie
convert turn, alter, proselytize
  fat into soap saponize
  into money realize, liquidate
  new novice, neophyte
convex
  curve camber
  molding tore, ovolo, torus, astragal
convey cede, carry, transmit
conveying
  away from center efferent
  toward center afferent
convict felon, condemn, prisoner
  privileged trusty
  sl. lifer, termer
convivial gay, jolly, sociable
  drinking bowl, wassail
convolute coil
convolvulus vine
cony das(sie), pika, daman, ganam, hyrax
cooing sound curr
cooking
  art cuisine, magirics
  odor nidor
cooled frappe
coolie changar
coom, coomb smut, soot, refuse
coop pen, cote, hutch
coorie cower, stoop, crouch
coot fowl, scoter, simpleton
copacetic fine, snappy

copaiba tree, balsam, oleoresin
copal resin, anime
copper coin, metal, element
  alloy aroide, tombac
  coating verd, patina, antique, verdigris
  comb. form chalco
  engraving mezzotint
  zinc alloy pinchbeck
coppice copse, thicket
copula band, link
copy ape, model, imitate
  closely mimic
  court record estreat
  of original replica
coquina limestone
cora gazelle
coral pink, skeleton, stalactite
  division aporosa
  formation palus
  island key, reef, atoll
cord rope, twine, string
  braided sennit
  drapery torsade
  rope end's marline
  trimming chenille
Cordelia
  father Lear
  sister Regan
cordelle tassel
corduroy fustian
  ridge wale
corf truck, basket
cork tap, plug, stopper
  barrel's bung
  -like suberose
corn grain, maize, kernel, papilloma
  bin crib
  husk shuck
  meal masa, samp, hominy
corner nook, trap, bight
  chimney/fireplace inglenook
  of building cant, quoin
cornice molding
  projection drip, corona
  support ancon
corolla ligule, petals

cup like part corona
heraldic galea
corpse body, cadaver, carcass
  animated zombi(e)
  dissection necrotomy
  embalmed mummy
  sl. stiff
corpuscle cell, leucocyte
  lack of red anemia
correspondent
  kind of pen pal, foreign, stringer
corrida cry olé
corroded carious
corrupt venal, infect, rotten
  morally putrid
  official grafter
cortex bark, rind
corvine bird crow, rook, raven
cosmic vast, grandiose
  cycle eon
  ray particle meson
cosset pet, lamb, pamper
costard head, apple
costrel dress, habit, getup
cot bed, charpoy
  poet. cottage
cotta surplice
cotton cloth, thread
  canvas like wigan
  measure lea, hank
  tuft lock
  twilled jean, chino, denim
  twisted rove
coulee lava, gulch, ravine
council board, junta
  chamber camarilla
  church synod
counterbalance equipoise
counterfeit sham, false, postiche
  coin slug
countersign password
countless myriad
country land, realm, region
  fellow corydon
  house villa, casino, cottage, hacienda
  in law pais

live in the rusticate
man rustic, compatriot
of the rural
poet. clime
-side, of the bucolic
coup blow, (master)stroke
  d'etat overthrow
  de grace death blow
  de grace dagger misericord(e)
  reporter's beat, scoop
couplet distich
courage nerve, mettle
  loss cold feet
  pretended bravado
  symbol bulldog
courian limpkin
court woo, bench, tribunal
  action suit
  case cause
  decree arret
  entrance atrium
  equity chancery
  hearing oyer
  jurisdiction soke
  messenger beadle
  minutes acta
  of law forum
  order extract estreat
  pert. to aulic
  writ oyer, summons, subpoena
cousin cos
cover top, roof, whelm
  detachable tarp, binder
  leg chaps, puttee, legging, chausses
  nipa thatch
  ornamental sham
  with feathers fledge
  with jewels begem
  with trappings caparison
covet envy, crave, desire
cow bully, daunt, bovine
  breed angus, kerry, jersey
  cud rumen
  fat suet, tallow
  genus Bos
  hornless mul(l)ey, polled

unbranded maverick
young calf, stirk, heifer
cowbird troupial
cowboy herder, wrangler, buckaroo
  Austral. ringer, stockman
  leggings chaps
  rope lasso, riata, lariat
  saddlebag alforja
  S.A. gaucho
cowfish toro, dugong, grampus, manatee
coxa hip
coyo avocado
coypu nutria, rodent
crab nag, shellfish
  apple scrab
  feeler antenna
  -like cancroid
crack joke, break, chink
  deep/glacier crevasse
  filler grout
  seal ca(u)lk
crackerjack nailer
cracklings scraps, greaves
crampfish torpedo
cranberry disease scald
crane heron, stork
  arm jib
  genus Grus
  pert. to gruine
  relative bustard
cranial nerve vagus
crappie sunfish
crater pit, cavity
  lunar linne
  one with volcano
cravat (neck)tie, ascot
  hangman's noose
crawler baby, worm, reptile
crayfish egg berry
creation cosmos, genesis, invention
crèche figure lamb, magi, Mary, infant,
  Joseph, shepherd
crecopia myth
credenza buffet
credit honor, rebate, believe, attribute
  for achievement kudos

credo creed, tenet, belief
creed
  Christian Nicene
  political ism, doxy
creeping repent, reptant
  charlie, for one weed
  plant bine, vine, liana
crenate notched, scalloped
creosol antiseptic
crescent demilune, meniscus, semilunar
  moons menisci
  of a horn, bicorn
  point of cusp
  -shaped lune, lunate
crest cap, top, acme, ridge
  mountain arete
  of bird/fowl comb, caruncle
  wave's comb
Crete
  city Candia
  mythical beast minotaur
cretonne toile
crew gang, team
  of ship complement
  relief relay
crier muezzin
crime sin, guilt, misdeed
  high treason
  major felony
  where committed venue
criminal felon, outlaw, convict,
  lawbreaker
  act job, crime
  habitual recidivist
crimson red, bloody, madder, carmine
crinoid sea lily
cripples halts
  patron saint (St.) Giles
crisper curler
critical exigent, captious
  analysis exegesis
  mark obelus
criticism review, descant
  abusive diatribe
  adverse (colloq.) pan
Croat Slav

cromlech tomb, monument
Cronus Titan, Saturn
  parent Gaea, Uranus
  sister Tethys
  son Zeus
crooked bent, askew, curved
  sl. cockeyed
cross rood, edgy, crucifix
  -bar rung
  -breed hybridize
  -current rip(tide)
  Egyptian Ankh
  in heraldry crux
  river ford
crossbill
  genus Loxia
crotchet hook, caprice
  half of a quaver
croton bug cockroach
crouton bread, sippet
crown top, crest, diadem
  bottle cap
  sl. conk
  small coronet
crucial severe, critical
  point crux, crisis
cruet vial, castor, ampulla
cruor gore, blood
crus shank
crush grind, bruise, squash
  to softness mash
  underfoot trample
  with mortar/pestle bruise
crustacean crab, isopod, lobster
  burrowing squilla, mantis crab
  eggs roe, coral
  segment somite, telson
  walking and swimming shrimp,
    amphipod, sand flea
crystalline pellucid
  biblical bdellium
  resin cannabin
  salt borax
Cuba, Cuban habanero
  bird tocororo
  castle Morro

coin peso
drink piña
tree culla
weight libra, tercio
cubeb berry, cigarette
cuckoopint arum
cucullate cowled, hooded
cucurbit flask, gourd
cudbear dye, lichen
cudgel club, drub, truncheon
cul-de-sac dead-end, blind alley
culex pipiens mosquito
cull glean, select, pick out
culmination acme, zenith
culpa fault, guilt
  "non mea" I am not guilty
culver dove, pigeon
culvert drain, waterway
  opening inlet
cumin anise
cumshaw tip, gratuity
cup mug, bowl, calix
  assaying test, cupel
  ceremonial ama
  drinking mug, cylix, stoup, goblet, tankard
  flower calyx
  holder zarf
  metal pannikin
cupbearer of the gods Hebe,
  Ganymede
Cupid Amor, Eros
  infant amorino, amoretto
  mother Venus
  sweetheart Psyche
  title Dan
cupola dome
  battleship's turret
cupric acid salt rutate
curbing inward adunc
curculio beetle
curdled milk clabber
curio(s) virtu, bibelot
current tide, going (on), stream
  air draft
  beneath surf undertow
  comb. form rheo

curse bane, damn, oath, anathema
  colloq. cuss
curt bluff, blunt, terse
  dismissal conge
curtain drape, screen, valance
  behind stage backdrop
  of gun fire barrage
  rod band cornice
curve arc, ogee, hyperbola
  double ess
  mark over vowel breve
  of a column entasis
  path of missile trajectory
  plane parabola
curved arched, arcuate, falcate
  in concave
  molding ogee
  out convex
  surface of arch extrados
  sword scimitar
curving inward adunc
custodian keeper, caretaker
  museum curator
customs mores
  charge duty, impost
  collector, biblical Matthew
  municipal octroi
  official surveyor
cut hew, saw, chop, snip, shear
  across transect, intersect
  down fell, mow, chop
  horse's tail bob, dock
  in half halve, bisect
  into lance, incise
  out elide, excise
  out disk trepan
cutter yacht, sleigh, vessel
  of precious stones lapidary
cutting keen, edged, incisive
  off last letter of word apocope
  off vowel elision
  part of tool bit, edge
cyanotype blueprint
cylinder tube, barrel
  part piston
  spiral helix

cylindrical terete, torose
cynic
  look of cold, sneer
  of sorts skeptic
cynosure lodestar, polestar, North Star
Czechoslovakia, Czechoslovakian
  Slovak, Bohemian, Moravian
  coin ducat, heller, koruna, kronen
  dance polka, redowa
  monetary unit koruna

D

D dee, delta
dabchick grebe
Dacian avar
dacoit, dakoit robber, criminal, murderer
dactyl toe, adonic, finger, piddock
dactylic hexameter epos
dactylogram fingerprint
dad beat, blow, hunk, papa, father, strike
dadaist Arp, Ray, Ball, Grosz, Tzara,
  Duchamp, Picabia, Schwitters
daddy longlegs stilt, curlew, spider, spinner
dado die, groove, solidum
daedal complex, skillful, ingenious, intricate, diversified
Daedalus architect, artificer
  construction labyrinth, wings
  father Metion
  son Icarus
  victim Talos, Perdix
daft gay, balmy, crazy, loon(e)y, merry,
  insane, simple, foolish, frolicsome
Dag
  father Delling
  horse Skinfaksi
  mother Nott
Dagda
  chief god of the Gaels, Irish
  kin Boann, Aengus, Brigit
dagger dirk, bayonet, poniard
  Burmese dah, dow
  handle hilt

Malay kris
Scot. dirk
short katar
stroke stab, stoccado
tapering anlace
Dahomey people Fon(g)
dairy lactarium
machine separator
daisy gowan, oxeye, morgan, shasta, gerbera
Daisy Miller
author James
dak post
Daksha
father Brahma
Dalai Lama monk, ruler, reincarnation
dale dell, glen, bottom, valley
dalles rapids
Dalmatia
channel Narenta
seaport Split, Spalato
Dalphon
father Haman
dam clog, mare, weir, impede, parent,
  obstruct
Arizona-Nevada Davis, Hoover
Australia Hume
California Shasta
Canal Zone Gatun
Egypt Aswan
Missouri Osage
S. Carolina Saluda
S. Dakota Oahe
Tennessee Norris
Virginia Kerr
dama gazelle
damage mar, loss, scathe, deterioration
pert. to noxal
daman hyrax
Damascus
king Aretas
people Syrian
river Abana(h), Barada, Pharpar
dame lady
correlative sire
Damien
island Molokai

Damkina
husband Ea
son Marduk
damnation perdition
Damon
friend Pythias
damourite mica, muscovite
damp fog, wet, dank, dull, soggy,
  vapor, deaden, steamy, depress,
  unenthusiastic
Dan
prince Ahiezer
town Elon
Danae
kin Zeus, Perseus, Acrisius
Danaus
brother Aegyptus
daughter Danaides
father Belus
founder Argos
grandfather Neptune, Poseidon
dance boh, tap, hoof, disco, stomp, twist,
  waltz, ballet, minuet
disco, minuet
art of orchesis
ceremonial areito
college hop, prom
country hay, auresca
Eng. althea, morris
Gr. belly
gypsy farruca, zingaresca
Hawaiian hula
Hebrew hora
masked ball, ridotto
muse Terpsichore
pert. to gestic
dancer gypsy, artist, hoofer
biblical Salome
clothing tutu, leotard, leg warmers
dandelion stalk scape
dandify spruce, adonize
dandiprat dwarf, pygmy, urchin
dandruff scurf
dandy fop, buck, dude, dildo, coxcomb,
  sailboat
female dandisette

Daniel
  American pioneer Boone
  father David
  mother Abigail
  statesman Webster
Danish
  hero Ogler
  king Christian, Frederick
  queen Margrethe
dank wet, damp, humid, moist, clammy
danta tapir
Dante
  birthplace Florence
  circle of hell Caina
  daughter Antonia
  love Beatrice
  party Guelph, Bianchi
  patron Scala
  place of death Ravenna
  teacher Latini
  verse form sestina
  wife Gemma
  work Convivo, Inferno, Commedia, Vita Nuova
Danton
  colleague Marat
Danube Ister
  fish huch(o), huchen
  town Ulm
Danzig
  coin gulden, pfennig
  liqueur ratafia
Daphne Mezereon
  father Ladon, Peneus
  form laurel tree
  mother Creusa
  pursuer Apollo
Daphnis
  lover Chloe
dapper neat, trim, natty, smart, foppish
dapple pied, spot, fleck, variegated
darbies manacles, handcuffs
Dardanelles Hellespont
dariole cup, shell, pastry
Darius
  father Ahasuerus
  prince Daniel

son Xerxes
  wife Atossa
dark dim, mum, ebon(y), black, cloud, unlit, dismal
  complexion swarthy
  horse candidate, contestant
darkness murk, umbra, ignorance
  place of Erebus, Po
  prince of devil, Satan, Ahriman
darnel tare, weed, grass, cockle
dart hurl, scud, arrow, missile
  shooter bow, Amor, Eros, Cupid
  -like spicular
D'Artagnan
  companion Athos, Aramis, Porthos
  creator Dumas
Dartmouth
  location Hanover
darts
  terms leg, bust, split, double, flight, treble
Darwin
  boat Beagle
  theory evolution
das badger, dassie
Das Kapital
  author Marx (Karl)
dasheen taro
dashes obeli
dashing gay, natty, impetuous, precipitate
  as of waves plangent
dastard coward, craven, milksop
dastardly base, foul, cowardly, sneaking
data facts, input, material, statistics, information
date era, day, fruit, tryst
  erroneous anachronism
  on coin exergue
Dathan
  father Eliab
daughter bint, filly, alumna(e)
  pert. to filial
  moon Nokomis
dauphin heir, guigo, prince, delphinium
daut, dawt caress, fondle
David
  captain Joab
  cave Adullam

commander Amasa
companion Hushai, Jonathan
daughter Tamar
employer Nabal
father Jesse
man of Ira, Igal
musician Asaph
prophet Nathan
scribe Shavsha
son Ammon, Absalom
David Copperfield
  author Dickens
  character Dora, Agnes, Micawber, Uriah Heep
davit spar, crane, hoist
Davy lamp
daw dawn, drab, fool, color, jackdaw, slattern, simpleton
dawdle lag, idle, dally, loiter, trifle
dawn dew, aurora, origin, sunrise, precursor
  comb. form eo
  goddess Eos, Aurora
  pert. to eoan, auroral
  symbol dew
  toward the eastward
dax spa
day time, epoch, period
  before eve
  father Erebus
  god Horus
  judgment doomsday
  pert. to ferial
days see also Quick Reference List
  fateful Ides
  fourteen fortnight
  of yore eld
daysman umpire, arbiter, mediator
daze fog, stun, dazzle, trance, confuse, stupefy, bewilder
dazzle blind, fulgo, eclipse, impress, brilliance
deacon adept, cleric, doctor, master
  stole orarion
  prayers ectene
dead amort, napoo, deceased, inactive, lifeless

abode Hades, Sheol
city Necropolis
house ossuary, mortuary, ossuarium
mass for black
relating mortuary
dead duck goner (sl.)
deadlock tie, draw, impasse, standstill
deadly fatal, lethal, malign, noxious
deadpan vacant, impassive, unemotional
Dead Sea
  city Sodom
  territory Moab
Dead Souls
  author Gogol
deaf dunch
  make surd
deaf and mute person surdomute
deafness amusia, baryecola
  cause stun
dealer agent, broker, monger, trader, merchant
  secondhand goods pawnbroker, flea marketer
dealing trading, business, exchanging, trafficking, apportioning
  shrewd deceit, chicanery
dean dell, vale, doyen
  pert. to decanal
dearth want, famine, paucity
death end, mort, demise
  angel Azrael
  aware of, portending fey
  black plague
  bringing funest
  eternal perdition
  goddess Hel, Dana, Danu
  march dirge, cortege
  mercy euthanasia
  notice obit
  rate mortality
  rattle rale
  rite funeral
  song elegy
  symbol orant
deave din, stun, bother, deafen, stupefy
debacle rout, smash, wreck, collapse, downfall

debar estop, hinder

debase mar, harm, sink, lower, impair, deprave, adulterate

debased vile, corrupt

debate moot, argue, rebut, argument
  pert. to forensic, quodlibetary
  stopping cloture

debating disputing, discussion, contentious, deliberation, consideration
  association lyceum

debauch orgy, spree, seduce, vilify, corrupt, pollute, intemperance

debauchee rake, roue, satyr, libertine

debilitated weak, seedy, weakened, enervated, enfeebled

debonair gay, airy, jaunty, carefree, gracious, sprightly

Deborah
  husband Lapidoth

debouche exit, issue, emerge, outlet, discharge

debris ruins, trash, waste, rubble, remains, rubbish, detritus, fragments

debt sin, fault, arrears, liability, obligation

debtless solvent

debtor
  note IOU
  proceed against excuss

debut opening, entrance, premiere

decade decennium

decadent effete, decaying, deteriorated

decamp bolt, flee, abscond, vamoose

decanter ewer, croft, carafe

decapod crab, prawn, squid, shrimp, lobster, crustacean
  crustacean genus Homarus

decay rot, conk, spoil, caries
  comb. form sapro
  in fruit blet
  process doty

decease die, demise, expire, succumb

deceitful wily, false, gaudy, hollow, tricky, deceptive, fallacious, fraudulent, misleading

deceive sile, bluff, cozen, hocus, mislead

decelerate slow, delay, slacken

decent apt, fit, fair, chaste, seemly, worthy, fitting, becoming, decorous, appropriate, respectable

deception dor, gyp, hoax, fraud, guile, trick, pretext, imposture, stratagem, treachery, subterfuge

decibels
  ten bel

decimal ten, tenth
  circulating repetend

decimate slay, destroy, slaughter

decipher read, decode, interpret, translate

decision end, fiat, canon, crisis, verdict, judgment
  maker judge, umpire, referee
  sudden whim

deck array, cards, enrich
  cards pack
  lower orlop
  post bitt
  raised border coaming
  ship main, poop, lower, orlop, promenade

deckhand gob, sailor, rouster, swabbie

deckle-edged erose

declaim rant, spout, utter, inveigh

declare bid, aver, deny, state, affirm, allege, assert, blazon, asservate
  in cards meld

declination bias, slope, bending, decline, refusal

decline dip, ebb, fade, hill, decay, lower, reject, weaken, dwindle, diminish, languish, degenerate

declivity grade, slope, descent

decoction dish, sapa, drink, extract
  decompose rot, decay, spoil, putrefy, separate, disintegrate

decorate (be)deck, adorn, scrimshaw
  garishly bedizen
  with letters miniate
  with raised patterns brocade

decorated cited, adorned, nielled
  wall part dado

decoration trim, niello, trophy
  metal ware tole
  military dsc, dsm, dso, medal, ribbon
  mineral purfle, tinsel
  pert. to medallic

decorous calm, prim, staid, demure, proper, ordered
decorticate flay, peel, skin, strip, debark
decorum propriety, convention
decoy lure, trap, snare, inveigle
  gambling shill, capper, ringer
decree canon, ordain, mandate
  imperial fiat, arret, irade, ukase
  papal bull
decuman huge, large
decussation chiasma, intersection
deer elk, moose, cervid
  antler bez, dag, horn, trestine
  axis chital
  cry bell
  fallow dama
  family cervidae
  genus Dama, Pudu, Rusa, Cervus
  grass rhexia
  male buck, hart, stag
  pert. to damine, cervine
  tail scut
  three-year-old sorrel
  track slot
  two-year-old brock(et)
  unbranched antler dag
  young fawn, pricket, spitter
Deerslayer
  author Cooper
  character Natty Bumppo
de facto really, actually, existing, genuinely
defect bug, flaw, want, foible
  in cloth scob, snag
  timber lag, knot
  without sound, perfect
defendant accused, appellee
  answer plea, nolo contendere
defense plea, alibi, bulwark
  in law answer
  making a salient angle ravelin
  means of abatis
  movement spar
  unit AAF, army, NATO, navy, SEATO, marines
deference honor, esteem, fealty
defile moil, taint, debauch, passage, tarnish, contaminate

Defoe
  character Moll, Xury, Crusoe, Friday
defray pay, expend, prepay, satisfy
degenerate rot, debase, degrade, deprave
degree rank, step, stage, extent
  conferral laureation
  equal as
  kind of nth, third
degust, degustate savor, taste, relish
dehisce gape, yawn, burst
dehort urge, dissuade
dehydrate dry, bake, parch, desiccate
Deianira
  brother Meleager
  father Oeneus
  husband Heracles, Hercules
  mother Althea
  victim Heracles, Hercules
Deidamia
  father Lycomedes
  husband Pirithous
  son Neoptolemus
deiform divine, godlike
deify exalt, honor, idolize, apotheosize
deign stoop, condescend
Deiphobus
  brother Paris, Hector
  father Priam
  mother Hecuba
  wife Helen
Deirdre
  beloved Noisi
  father Felim
deity deva, idol, muse, Almighty
  half-fish Ea, Oannes
  half-goat faun
  hawk-eyed Ra, Horus, Sokari(s)
  jackal-headed Anubis
  tutelary genie, lares, numen, Hershef, penates
dejeuner lunch, breakfast, collation
dekko look, peep
delate accuse, report, denounce
Delaware see Quick Reference List
delay daily, laten, linger, loiter
  law mora, continuance
  unjustifiable mora

dele blot, cancel, delete, remove
deletion
  last letter of word apocope
  restore stet
Delhi
  district Simla
Delian god Apollo
delibate sip, taste, dabble
Delibes
  ballet Sylvia, Coppelia, La Source
  opera Lakme
delicacy cate, tact, finesse
delict tort, crime, offense, violation
delight joy, glee, charm, revel, divert, rapture, transport, delectation, satisfaction
  in relish
Delilah
  paramour Samson
deliquesce melt, thaw, ramify, liquefy, dissolve
delitescent hidden, latent
dell glen, vale, ravine
Delphi oracle, shrine
  priestess Pythia
  modern name Kastri
delude bob, bilk, fool, cheat, deceive, mislead
delusion cheat, mirage, artifice, phantasm
  Buddhist Moha
  partner snare
delve dip, mine, plumb, elicit
demagogue orator, rouser, ochlocrat
demand ask, need, claim, exact, compel, mandate, require
demean abase, decry, lower, degrade
demeanor mien, port, habit, bearing, conduct, behavior, deportment
Demeter Ceres
  daughter Cora, Kore, Despoina, Persephone
  headdress polos
  mother Rhea
  shrine anaktoron
demigod hero, idol, satyr, godling
  pert. to satyric
demiss humble, dismiss
demit lower, resign, relinquish

demiurgic creative
demon imp, devil, fiend, daemon
  assembly Sabbat
  cunning imp, ogre, daedal
  female empusa, succubus
  Hebrew Asmodeus
  Iroquois otkon
  prince Beelzebub
  worship demonolatry
  Zoroastrian daeva
demos deme, people, district, populace
Demosthenes orator
  follower Bryan
  oration Philippic
demote bust, lower, reduce, degrade
demotic popular
demulcent balm, sedative, soothing
demur stay, delay, boggle, linger, object, suspend, hesitate
den dive, lair, retreat
  wild animal cavea (Roman)
denary ten, decimal
dendrophilous arboreal
dene dell, vale, mound
denizen cit, dweller, inhabitant
  of hell Satan, hellion
Denmark, Danish
  anatomist Steno
  animal aurochs
  astronomer Brahe
  author Bajer, Andersen
  chief jarl, yarl
  city A(a)lborg, Odense, Horsens, Copenhagen
  coin ore, fyrk, horse, krone
  comb. form Dano
  county Amt, Soro, A(a)lborg
  fjord ise
  island Oe, Als, Aero, Faroe, Samso, Seeland
  king Cnut(e), Knut, Christian
  measure fod, favn, fuder, linie, pflug, tomme, landmill
  mus. instr. lure
  parliament Rigsdag
  peninsula Jutland
  physicist Bohr

river Asa, Holm, Stor, Guden, Lonberg
sand ridge scaw, skagi
settlers Ostmen
speech stod
weight lod, ort, vog, pund, waag, kvint, quint, tonde, centner
dennet gig, carriage
denouement end, issue, solution
de novo again, newly, afresh
dental tool drill, scaler, forceps
dentil block
dentine ivory
denude bare, scalp, strip, devest
deodand forfeit
deodar tree, cedar
depilate pluck, shave, strip
depilatory rusma
deplore rue, sigh, wail, lament, regret
deploy spread, unfold, display
depone swear, attest, depose
deposit marl, ooze, cache, hoard, sediment
  alluvial delta, geest
  black soot
  black tissue melanosis
  clay marl
  geyser sinter
  gold-containing placer
  gravel apron
  ore vug
  roric dew
  teeth tartar, calculus
  wine cask tartar
depot base, dump, station, magazine, warehouse, storehouse
depravity vice, infamy, license, disgrace, iniquity
depression blues, cavity, trough
  between mountains col
  pert. to bathic
depth abyss, midst, acumen
deputation mission, delegation
depute send, allot, assign, appoint
deputies posse, agents
deracinate eradicate, extirpate
derange craze, upset, disturb, unhinge, disarrange

derelict tramp, castaway, forsaken
derf bold, daring
deride fleer, scoff, tease
de rigueur (Fr.) nice, decent, proper, fashionable
derma layer, corium, dermis, intestine
dermal filament hair
dern darl, dire, secret, somber
dernier (Fr.) last, final
dernier cri (Fr.) novelty, latest word, latest fashion
derrick rig, crane
  part gin, leg, boom
derring-do geste
dervish agib, yogi, fakir, ascetic, mendicant
  headgear taj
descendants litter, progeny
descended alit, fell, sank, stooped
  from same ancestor agnate, consanguineous
  source root, stirps
descent birth, lurch, origin, decline, lineage
  line(s) phyla, phylum
Desdemona
  husband Othello
  slanderer Iago
desecrate abuse, pollute, profane, violate
desert waste, barren, renege, abandon
  Afr. (el) Erg, Libyan, Sahara
  Asia Gobi
  group caravan
  hallucination mirage
  India Thar
  pert. to eremic, sere
  plant agave, alhagi, cactus
  region erg
  Russ. tundra
  watering spot oasis
  wind simoom, sirocco
desiccated arid, sere, dried, parched
design plot, decor, ettle, invent
  of scattered objects seme
  on skin tattoo
  perforated stencil
desipience folly, conceit, trifling

desire yen, itch, long, want, ardor, covet, crave, fancy, yearn, hunger, thirst, request, solicit, appetite
  want of inappetence
desist ho, halt, stop, cease
desman muskrat
desmanthus herb, acuan, shrub
desmid alga
desolate sad, lost, ruin, bleak, barren, desert, lonely, woeful, ravaged, wretched, miserable, woebegone, devastated, disconsolate
desolated area waste, desert
desperado bandit, ruffian, criminal
despite vex, insult, despise, notwithstanding
despiteous cruel, pitiless, malicious, contemptuous
despoil rob, booty, fleece, pillage, plunder
Despoina Kore
  mistress Persephone
  husband Hades
  realm underworld
despondency dumps, gloom, misery, despair, dejection
despot tsar, tyrant, autocrat, dictator
despumate foam, scum, skim, froth
destiny lot, fate, goal
  oriental Kismet
  goddess Fate, Norn, Atripos
destitute poor, needy, forlorn, indigent, deficient, penniless, necessitous, impoverished
destroyed kaput, ruined
destroying angel
  fungus amanita
  Mormon Danite
destruction tala, havoc, perdition
  god Siva
  goddess Ara
  of species genocide
desultory idle, hasty, loose, random, cursory
detain in wartime intern
detect espy, descry, discover
detecting device radar, sonar
detectives Sam Spade, The Saint, James Bond, Nero Wolfe, Perry Mason, Philo Vance, Charlie Chan, Ellery Queen,

Green Hornet, Simon Templar, Sherlock Holmes
detector tube (radio), crystal (radio), reagent
  defect troubleshooter
  storm sferics
deterge wash, wipe, purge, cleanse
detersion washing, ablution
dethrone depose, divest
detonator cap. exploder
detritus tuff, chaff, debris, garbage
Dev
  land Eire
deva angel, deity
Devaki
  son Krishna
develop grow, dilate, evolve
  rapidly boom
development
  full maturity
  incomplete aplasia
Devi
  beneficent Gauri
  consort Siva
  fierce Kali
  light Uma
  malignant Durga
  of parentage haimavati
  riding a tiger Chandi
deviate miss, warp, stray, diverge
  suddenly mutate
  vertically hade
device mot, tool, vehicle
  holding vise, clamp, tongs
devil demon, fiend, Lucifer
  Dante's Cagnazzo
  female demoness
  fish ray, manta, whale, octopus
  pert. to satanic
  printer's apprentice
  of bottomless pit Apollyon
  tree Dita, Abroma
devilkin imp
devil's bones dice, die
devious sly, artful, crafty, errant, secret, shifty, subtle, tricky, cunning, furtive, vagrant, indirect, involved, stealthy, tortuous, circuitous, roundabout, underhanded

devise plan, frame, weave, assign, design, invent, scheme, concoct, project, contrive, transmit, elaborate

devoir duty

Devonshire
  boat mumblebee
  river Exe

devotee fan, nun, monk, zealot, admirer, follower

devotion fealty, fervor, novena, adoration
  object of idol, fetish

devotional
  exercise Aves, worship
  period Lent, Novena

devouring vorant, edacious, voracious

dew bloom, moisten
  congealed rime, frost

dewlap fold, wattle

dexterity art, craft, skill, cunning, adroitness

dextrose sugar

dey pasha, ruler, governor

dhan cattle, wealth, property

diabetic remedy insulin, orinase

diablerie devilry, sorcery, demology, mischief

diacope wound, tmesis, incision

diadem crown, tiara, fillet

diagonal bias, virgule

diagram plan, chart, figure, sketch, scheme
  illustrative icon(ograph)

dialect argot, idiom, patois, speech, tongue

diameter bore, chord, width, module, breadth, caliber
  half radius, radii (pl.)

diametrically opposite antipodal

diamond gem, field, carbon
  blue Hope
  coarse bort
  crystal glassie
  cup for cutting dop
  face facet, bezel
  geometrical rhomb, lozenge
  holder dog, ring
  native carbon
  wheel skive
  with true luster of naif

Diana moon, Delia, Artemis, Cynthia

mother Latona

parent Latona, Jupiter

sacred grove Nemus

twin Apollo

diana monkey roloway

dianthus plumarius pink, flower, carnation

diaphragm midriff
  pert. to phrenic

diaskeuast editor, reviser, redactor

diaspora golah, galuth, dispersal

Diaz de Bivar
  title (El) Cid

dibs syrup

dice game, bones, cubes, reject
  cheater topper
  throw of six sice
  trick cog

dichotomy cleft, split, division

Dickens
  birthplace Portsmouth
  character Dora, Nell, Fagin, Dorritt, Tiny Tim, Uriah Heep
  pen name Boz
  work Hard Times, Bleak House, Oliver Twist, Barnaby Rudge, Tale of Two Cities, David Copperfield, Great Expectations, A Christmas Carol

dickey mate, collar, jacket

dictionary calepin, lexicon, vocabulary, onomasticon
  poet's gradus

dictum saw, adage, maxim, saying, opinion, apothegm

didactic preceptive, instructive

dido antic, caper, trick

Dido Elissa
  brother Pygmalion
  father Belus
  founder of Carthage
  husband Acerbas
  sister Anna
  wooer Aeneas

Dido and Aeneas
  composer Purcell

die coin, fade, mold, depart, expire, vanish
  loaded fulham
  symbol ace

diehard Tory
difficult
  prefix dys
difficulty cavil, trial, plight, dilemma
  pert. to spiny, crucial
  opposed to snap, easily
diffuse copious, pervade, disperse, circulate
diffusion (through membrane) osmosis
digestion eupepsia, absorption
  having good eupeptic
digging
  tool loy, pick, slick, spade, shovel,
    mattock
dight dab, rub, adorn, manage, repair
digit integer, phalange
  manual thumb, finger
  podal toe
diglot bilingual
dignify adorn, exalt, honor, ennoble
digraph AE, EA, OA, OE, SH, TH
digress veer, swerve, wander, deviate
dike bank, ditch, jetty, causeway
  military estacade
diked land polder
dilapidation ruin, decay, waste, debris,
  misuse, neglect
dilation expansion
dilatory slow, tardy, remiss
dilemma fix, node, quandary, question, difficulty, predicament
dill anet, herb, anise
diminish ebb, fade, abate, lessen, shrink,
  condense, dwindle, subside, contract,
  decrease
diminutive wee, puny, tiny, dwarf, runty,
  small, bantam, petite
  suffix el, et, cle, ita, ule, cula, ette
dimmet dusk, twilight
dindle ring, quiver, thrill, tingle, tremor,
  tremble, vibrate
ding dent, batter, reiterate, depression
dingle dale, dell, glen, valley
dining
  room cenade
  science of aristology
dinkum fair, truly, honest, square

dinner meal, feast, repast
  pert. to prandial
diocese center, bishopric, episcopate
Diomedes
  city founded by Arpi
  father Ares, Mars, Tydeus
  foe Aeness, Hector
  slayer Hercules
  victory Rhesus
Dione
  consort Zeus
  daughter Aphrodite
Dionysus Bacchus
  festival Agrania
  mother Semele
  pert. to Bromian
Dionyza
  husband Cleon
diopter level, alidade
Dioscuri twins, Anaces, Castor, Gemini,
  Pollux
  father Zeus
  mother Leda
  sister Helen
diplomat dean, consul, attaché
  corps head doyen
dipody syzygy
dipper piet, ladle, scoop, piggin
dipsacus plant teasel
diptera flies, gnats, mosquitoes
  lobe of wing alula
diphthong AE, OE, OU
dird blow, thump, buffeting
dirdum blame, rebuke, uproar, scolding
dire dern, evil, fatal, tragic, urgent, horrible
direction aim, course, bearing
  biblical selah
  line of range
  musical soli
  pole to pole axial
  printer stet
  without fixed astatic
dirigible blimp, airship
  famous Zeppelin, Hindenburg
  part fin, nacelle
dirk snee, sword, dagger

dirl ring, pierce, thrill
Dis Pluto
disaffected alienated
disaffirm deny, annul, reverse, contradict
disallow veto, forbid, reject, prohibit
disarm subdue
disarray mess, chaos, strip, caddle, undress, disorder, confusion
disavow deny, abjure, recant
disband sever, breakup, disperse, dissolve, release
disbeliever atheist, heretic
disburse pay, spend, defray, outlay, scatter, distribute
disc harrow, medallion
  plate paten
discalced unshod, barefoot
discarded shed, castoff
  place limbo
discernment acumen, insight, sagacity
disciple votary, apostle, scholar
  biblical John, James, Judas, Peter, Simon, Andrew, Philip, Thomas, Matthew, Thaddeus, Bartholomew
  chief Peter
disclaim deny, abjure, disown, refuse, reject, disavow, repudiate
discomfit foil, rout, abash, defeat, deject, confuse, scatter, frustrate
discolored molded, ustulate
disconcert faze, abash, daunt, baffle, ruffle, perplex, perturb, discompose
discord war, rancor, variance
  goddess Ate, Eris
discordant ajar, harsh, contrary
  musically scordato
  serenade charivari
Discordia Eris
discourse talk, confer, dissertation
  art of rhetoric
  long tirade, descant
discredit doubt, blemish, suspect, distrust, disrepute, disbelieve
discus disk, plate, quoit
  thrower Discobolus
discussion talk, conference

group class, forum, panel, seminar
open to moot
disdain tut, pride, scorn, spurn, contemn, despise, aversion, arrogance, contumely, haughtiness, contemptuousness, superciliousness
disease malady, illness, infirmity
  animals mange, nenta, surra, distemper
  declining state of catabasis
  diver's bends
  pert. to clinic, loimic
  producing zymotic
  science of classification nosology
  suffix oma, itis, osis
disembodiment soul, spirit
disembowel gut, remove, eviscerate
disembroil extricate, untangle
disfigure mar, blur, deface, deform, blemish
disgorge spew, vent, eject, yield, discharge
Dishan
  son Uz, Aran
dishevel muss, ruffle, tousle, disarray
dishonest corrupt, knavish, thievish, deceitful, fraudulent, perfidious, unscrupulous
dishonor abase, shame, stain, seduce, violate, disgrace, ignominy
disinclined shy, loath(e), averse, uneager, unwilling
disinfect cleanse, sterilize
disinterested fair, aloof, remote, unbiased, impartial
disjaskit jaded
disjune breakfast
disk dial, plate
  hockey puck
  -like discal, discoid
  metal tag
  solar aten
dislike odium, antipathy
  comb. form mis(o)
  object of anathema
dislocate splay, luxate, disjoint
dismantle raze, strip, divest
dismay fear, alarm, daunt, scare, appall, horrify, perturb, terrify, frighten, disconcert, intimidate

dismember maim, sever, dissect, mutilate

dismissal fire, conge, layoff, reject, release, removal, discharge

disorder mess, chaos, snafu, touse
  visual strabismus

disour jester, storyteller

disparage slur, abuse, slight, belittle, depreciate

disparate unlike, unequal, separate, different, divergent, dissimilar, inconsonant, incommensurable

dispatch rid, free, kill, speed, deliver, message

dispatch boat aviso, packet

dispel oust, eject, banish, scatter, disperse, dissipate

disperse sow, part, strew, spread, scatter, evanesce, broadcast, disappear, disseminate

dispirit cow, damp, depress, flatten, discourage, dishearten

display air, show, wear, evince, flaunt, unfold, exhibit, manifest

displeasure ire, anger, pique, dislike, offense, distaste, vexation, annoyance, disapproval, indignation, dissatisfaction
  show cry, pout, frown

dispone transfer, distribute

disport play, amuse, sport, frolic, gambol

disposition bent, spirit, proclivity
  toward work ergasia

dispossess oust, eject, strip, banish, divest

disputations sassy, eristic, quarrelsome

disquiet vex, fret, excite, anxiety, disturb, turmoil, uneasiness

dissemble hide, mask, feign, conceal

disseminate teach, diffuse, disperse

dissepiment septum, partition

dissenter heretic, nonconformist

dissever part, sever, cleave, sunder, separate

dissipate fray, spend, waste, vanish, scatter, disappear

dissolute fast, loose, corrupt
  person rake, roue, adventuress

dissolved
  substance solute

dissonant rude, harsh, jarring, discordant, incongruous

distal remote, distant
  angle axil
  opposite proximal

distant (a)far, away, aloof, remote, foreign
  comb. form tele

distasteful flat, odious, insipid, offensive

distended bloated, patulous

distich couplet

distilling device still, alembic
  tube matrass

distinctive
  air cachet
  mark badge

distort warp, alter, screw, twist, deform

distortion warp, twist, deformity, falsehood
  head to one side loxia

distraught mad, crazed, frantic, distracted, bewildered

distress need, dolor, agony, danger, misery, anguish, anxiety, trouble, hardship, adversity, tribulation
  call SOS

distribute deal, mete, allot

distributee heir

disturb vex, roil, rouse, hinder, molest, agitate, perplex, perturb, trouble, disorder, interrupt

disturbance bree, riot, storm, dustup, tumult, uproar, perturbation
  emotional neurosis
  ocean tsunami

disyllabic foot trochee

disyoke unteam

dit, ditt dot, poem, adage, saying, expression

ditch canal, relais, trench
  slope scarp

dithyramb ode, hymn, poetry

dithyrambic wild, boisterous

diurnal daily, butterfly, quotidian

divaricate forked, diverge, branching

dive crib, leap, swoop, resort
  kind back, swan, (half) gainer, jackknife

diver loon, pearler, plunger

comb. form dyta, dytes
disease bends
gear tank, flipper
divers many, sundry, several, various
  comb. form poly, vari(o), parti
diverse motley, unlike, varied, several, various, manifold, separate, divergent, dissimilar
  comb. form vari
divest bare, reft, spoil, strip, denude, deprive, uncover, unclothe, dismantle, dispossess
  of sham debunk
divide dole, sever, ration, sunder, alienate
  into feet scan
  into number of parts multisect
  in two parts halve, bisect
divider buntor, compass, partition
dividing wall(s) septa, septum, partition
divination omen, augury, presage, foretelling
  by dreams oneiromancy
  by figures geomancy
divine holy, predict
  communication oracle
  gift grace
  messenger apostle
  spirit numen
  word logos
  work theurgy
Divine Comedy
  author Dante
divinely inspired entheal
diving
  bird auk, loon, grebe
  hazard bends
division part, rift, schism, portion, segment
  house estre
  poem canto
  primary eogaea
  religious schism
  restricted meer
divot sod, clod, turf
Dixie
  composer Emmett
dizzard fool, jester

dizziness vertigo, giddiness
  pert. to dinic(al), vestibular
djebel hill
Dnieper tributary Bug, Psel, sula
do act, bilk, cheat, render
  mus. ut
  poet. didst
docent teacher, lecturer
dock pier, jetty, curtail
  post pile, bollard
  ship's slip, basin
  yard arsenal
Doctor of the Church Basil, Jerome, Ambrose, Gregory, Augustine, Athanaslus
doctor's oath Hippocratic
doctrine dogma, logic, principle
  pert. to dogmatical
  secret esotary
  single principle henism, monism
document deed, record, certificate
  file dossier
  provisional memo, note, draft, script
  true copy estreat
dod fit, huff, sulk
Dodecanese Island Coo, Cos, Kos, Rodi, Patmo(s), Rhodes
dodo
  genus Didus
doe roe, teg, faun, hind
doer
  suffix er, or, ast, eer, ier, ist, ator, euse, ster
dog cur, canine, rascal, shadow, mongrel
  Arctic husky, malamute
  comb. form cyn(o)
  duck-hunting toller, retriever
  extinct breed talbot
  fire andiron
  genus Canis
  India dhole
  -like animal wolf, hyena, jackal
  short-eared alan
  short-legged beagle
  star Sirius, Canicula
  tropical alco
  underworld Cerberus
  wild dingo (Austral.)

dogbane
  fruit aboli
  tree dita, apocynum
dog days canicule
doggery barroom, grogshop
dogma creed, tenet, dictum, doctrine,
  principle
  pert. to levitical
dogmatic saying dictum, levitism
Dogpatch
  cartoonist Al Capp
dog rose bucky, canker
  fruit hip
dog salmon Keta
dogwood tree, osier, sumac, cornus
  genus Cornus
dole lot, mete, mourn, share, ration, portion,
  dispense, pittance, allotment
dolent sorrowful
Doll's House
  character Nora
dolly car, cart, block, truck, mistress,
  locomotive
dolorous dismal, grievous
dolphin bouto, dorado, wreath
dolt oaf, idiot, simpleton
  -like genus Inia
Dombey and Son Cuttle
dome head, roof, cupola, tholus
domine lord, ruler, master
Dominican preacher, predicant
Dominican Republic
  capital Santo Domingo
  island Hispaniola
  measure ona
  monetary unit peso
  product cocoa, sugar, coffee, bauxite,
    tobacco
domino dice, amice, cloak
  spot on pip
domite trachyte
dompt cow, daunt, subdue
don wear, array, tutor, fellow, professor
Donalbain
  brother Malcolm
  father Duncan
Donar Thor

Don Camillo priest
Don Carlos
  author Schiller
  composer Verdi
  father Philip
Don Giovanni
  composer Mozart
Donizetti
  hero Roberto
  opera Lucia, Anna Bolena, La Favorite,
    Don Pasquale, Maria Stuarda
Don Juan rake, wolf, Romeo, masher, libertine
  drama The Stone Guest
  home Seville
  mother Inez
  poet Byron
donkey ass, ono, fool, auxiliary
  comb. form ono
  cry bray, heehaw
  engine yarder
  female jenny, jennet
donkey's years age, aeon, dog's age, blue
  moon, coon's age, eternity
donnybrook fray, brawl, melee, fracas
Don Quixote
  companion Sancho Panza
  steed Rosinante
doodlesack bagpipe
doolee litter
doomed fey, fatal
door gate, inlet, avenue
  back postern
  handle ansa, knob
  knocker risp
  part jam, rail, sill, mullion
doorpost durn, jamb, alette
dor(r) bee, joke, beetle, deceive
dorcas gazelle
Dorian festival Carne(i)a
doric rustic
  capital, part of Abacus
  fillet bottom of frieze taenia
  space between triglyphs metope
Doris
  brother Nereus
  daughters Nereids

father Oceanus
husband Nereus
king Aegimius
dormitory house, quarters
  monastery dorter
dormouse glis, lerot, rodent
  pert. to myoxine
dornick linen, boulder
dorp city, town, thorp(e), hamlet
dorsal nerve, notal, neural
  opposed to ventral
  pert. to notal, neural, tergal
dorsum back
doss tuft, sleep
dosseret abacus
dossil tent, spigot, pledget
dotard silly, senile, imbecile
dote rot, dove, love, bestow
dot over the letter i tittle
dotted pied, pinto, piebald
dotterel bird, dupe, morinel
Douay bible Aree
double dual, twofold, deceitful, substitute
  cross gyp, rat
  dagger diesis
  faced ancipital
  prefix di
  ripper bobsled
doubloon coin, onza
dough cash, duff, money, pasta
  fried spud
dove Inca, pigeon, tumbler
  genus Columbidae
  murmur coo
  ring cushat
dovekie auk, rotche, guillemot
  genus Alle
dovetail join, tenon, intersect
dowel peg, tenon, pinion
dowitcher fowl, snipe
down sad, fuzz, below, eider
  comb. form cat(a), cath
  facing prone, pronate, prostrate
  poet. adown
  prefix de
  wind leeward
  with a bas

dowry
  pert. to dotal
doxy opinion, paramour
doyen dean, senior
drachma coin, dram
  1/20 or 1/6 obol
Dracula demon, vampire
  home Bran, Risnov
draft plot, gully, sketch, current, protocol
  architectural epure
dragoman agent, guide
dragon ogre, duenna, musket
  Chinese lung
  -fly genus Odonata
  Norse myth Fafner
  of darkness Rahab
  two-legged, winged Wivern, Wyvern
dragon's teeth sower Cadmus
drama stage, masque, burletta, spectacle
  introduction protasis
  main action epitasis
  pert. to histrionic
  sudden reverse in peripetia
drapery baize, curtain
  on bed pand, canopy, tester
Dravidian Hindu, Tamil
  demon bhut
  language Kota, Toda, Tulu, Tamil
draw tug, draft, siphon, delineate
  away abduce, divert
  back wince, recoil, withdraw
  close steal, approach
  forth tug, derive, elicit
  out protract, attenuate
  fight bind, frap, pull
  together coul, frap, assemble
  up tuck
dray cart, wagon, sledge
dreadnaught, dreadnought tank, warship, fearless
dream scheme, fantasy, delusion
  day vision, reverie
  god Oniros
  pert. to oneiric, oneirotic
dregs faex, lees, dross, refuse, sordor
dress adorn, attire, apparel, bandage
  feathers preen

full armor panoply
looped part pouf
riding habit, breeches, jodhpurs
trimming gimp, lace, braid
dressmaker modiste
term godet, gusset
dried arid, sere, desiccated
out stale, effete
drink quaff, bracer, tipple, swallow
ancient morat
Christmas nog, wassail
habitually sot, tope
of the gods nectar
palm nipa
drinking
bowl mazer
cup facer, cyclix, tankard
horn rhyton
pledge toast, prosit, propine
drive urge, alley, avenue, direct, street, actuate
away dispel
back repel
in nail, tamp
public esplanade
drivel dote, fritter, slobber
driver club, jenu, whip, pilot, motorist
camel sarwan
of golden chariot Helios
droll odd, zany, funny, punch
saying gibe, jest, quip, taunt
dromedary camel, mehari
drooping alop
drop descent, globule, pendant, trickle
by drop guttatim
gently dap, flow
-like guttate
sudden plop, hance
dropsical puffy, hydropic
dropsy edema
dross trash, cinder, scoria
of iron sinter
drought need, dearth, aridity
plant guar, xerophyte
drowsiness torpor, lethargy

drugged bliss kef, kief
drugget mat, rug, cloth
Druid priest
lodge cove
priestess of opera Norma
stone sarsen
symbol mistletoe
drum beat, tabor, repeat
ear tympanum
oriental tomtom, anacara
roll at sunrise dian
tighten frap
drunkard sot, dipsomaniac
drunt pet, drawl, grumble
drupe plum, cherry, apricot
drupetum etaerio, raspberry
druplet grain, acinus
dry arid, brut, cynical, thirsty
as a narrative jejune
comb. form ser, xero
run try, rehearsal
shave cheat
dryad nymph
dual twin, binary
ducal noble
duck fowl, cloth, dodge, evade
bluebill scaup
brood team
dead goner
flock sord
freshwater teal
genus Anas, Aythya, Clangula
group sord, team, skein
hooked-bill merganser
lame congressman (not reelected)
large pato, Muscovy
-like coot, decoy
male drake
Muscovy pato
pert. to anatine
rare merse
ring-necked bunty
sitting decoy
small smew
wooden decoy

duckbill mammal, platypus
duckweed lemna
ductile soft, facile, pliant, plastic, tensile, malleable
ductless gland pineal, thymus, thyroid
dud failure
dude fop, dandy, coxcomb
  stage door Johnnie
dudeen pipe
duelist's aide second
duet duo, two, twosome
  upper part primo
duffer sham, cheat, hawker, useless, inferior, counterfeit, incompetent
dugong seacow
duke's realm duchy, dukedom
dull dim, dense, vapid, apathetic
  color dun, favel, khaki, terne
  finish mat(te)
  statement platitude
dulse seaweed
Dumas
  character Athos, Aramis, Porthos
  heroine Camille
dumping ground toom
dun ask, solicit
  color tan, ecru, grey, brown, khaki
dune bar, hill, mound, ridge, bark(h)an
dunker tumbler
dunlin bird, stib, sandpiper
dunt beat, blow, dizzy, thump, stupid
dupe ape, mug, coax, gull, trick, delude, sucker, duplicate
dupery ramp
durable stable, enduring
durance, vile jail, imprisonment
Durante
  byword Calabash
duration age, span, time, period
  note time, clock
  of ministerial charge pastorate
  without beginning or end eternity
D'Urberville lass Tess
durgah tomb, court
durra grain, millet, sorghum

dust dirt, pilm, stive, pollen
  reduce to mull
  speck mote
Dutch uncle oom
Dutchware blue delft
duty job, tax, role, task, charge, function, obligation, occupation, responsibility
  Hindu dharma
  on commodities excise, ad valorem
  shirking evasion, truancy, irresponsibility
  spell of shift, trick, watch
dux chief
dwarf elf, Galar, gnome, Pacolet, belittle, Cercopes
  king Alberich
  pert. to nanism
  race Nibelung(s)
dweller tenant, inhabitant
  cave troglodyte
  city urbanite
  earth tellurian
  desert Arab, nomad, sourdough
  fellow inmate
  formicary ant
  monastery cenobite
  temporary lodger, boarder
  underground mole, gnome
Dyak
  blowgun sumpitan
  knife parang
  sea iban
dye aal, kino, eosin, stain, tinge
  base aniline
  blue wad(e), anil, woad, indigo, cyanine
  blue-red orchal, orchil
  brown sumac(h)
  coal tar eosin(e)
  compound azo, diazin(e)
  gum kino
  indigo anil
  mulberry al
  purple murexide
  red-brown henna
  root pigment madder

source murex
violet archil
yellow weld, aruse, woald, annatto
dyeing
  apparatus ager
  chamber oven
dyewood tree tua
dynamite blast, explosive
  inventor Nobel
  kind dualin(e), fulgarite
dynamo motor, generator
  inventor Faraday
  part coil, limb, pulley
dynasty race, rule, realm, rulers, dominion,
  succession
  Chinese Fo, Yin, Isin, Ming
  Fr. Capet
dysphoria anxiety, disquiet
dysprosium
  symbol Dy
dzeren antelope
dzhugashvili Stalin

E

E epsilon
Ea
  daughter Nina
  god of wisdom
ea each, deity, inlet, river
each all, both, every
  for each per
  of each ana
eagle coin, harpy, bergut
  bald-headed sea ern(e), osprey
  biblical gier
  brood aerie
  comb. form aeto
  constellation/genus Aquila
  genus Haliaeetus
  male tercel
  N. American bald, golden
  nest eyry, eyrie
  relating to harpy, Jove's
eaglestone aetites

eaglewood aloes, agalloch
eagre bore, (tidal) wave
ear lug, knob, auricle, hearing
  anvil ambos, incus
  auricle pinna
  canal scala
  cavity meatus, cochlea
  comb. form ot(o), auri
  depression scapha
  lobe lug, pinna
  middle drum, tympanum
  part drum, anvil, canal, hammer, cochlea,
    stirrup, eustachian tube
  pert. to otic, aural, entotic
  science of otology
  section inner, outer, middle
  wax cerumen
earache otalgia
eared seal otary
earl lord, peer, noble, nobleman
  pert. to comital
earldom derby, territory, jurisdiction
earlier than before
  prefix pre, pro
Earl of Avon Eden
early soon, seasonable
  poet. rath(e), betimes
earnest grave, intent, diligent
  comb. form serio
  money aries, hansel
earnestness unction
earnings pay, wages, profits, stipend
earth orb, mold, soil, globe, terra, planet
  axis hinge
  born human, mortal, terrigenous
  comb. form geo, terra
  crust horst
  deposit marl, silt, loess
  god Geg, Keb, Seb, Dagan
  goddess Gaea, Ceres, Terra, Semele,
    Demeter
  layer clay, loam, soil, topsoil
  occur at surface epigene
  opposite side Antipodes
  pert. to geal, clayey, terrene, worldly,
    temporal
  poet. vale

ridge kame, rideau (Fr.)
satellite moon
surface crust, horst, epigene
volcanic lava, tuff, trass
earthdrake dragon
earthenware delft, pottery, crockery, porcelain
  cooking casserole
  maker potter
  -making material pug
  pert. to ceramic
earthflax asbestos, amianthus
earth hog aardvark
earthkin terella
earthling human, mortal
earthnut pod, chufa, tuber, peanut
earthquake tremor, temblor
  pert. to seismic
  point directly above epicenter
earthstar fungus, geaster
earthwork dike, fort, agger
earthworm ess, dew worm, angleworm, night crawler
earwig beetle, golach, goloch, insect, centipede
ease calm, abate, allay, peace, reduce, repose, soothe, comfort, relieve, calmness, serenity, alleviate, disburden, contentment, tranquillity, tranquillize
  at degagé, otiose, relaxed
  off ebb, slow, relax, slack
east Asia, Levant, Orient, sunrise
  pert. to eoan
East Africa, African see Africa
East Asia
  people Seres
  weight tras
East Indies, East India Indonesia
  agent gomashta
  animal tarsier
  arboreal mammal colugo
  bark lodh, niepa
  bead tree nim, neem(ba)
  bird baya
  bush sola
  cattle dhan, gaur
  civet musang

  coin cash
  dancing girl dasi
  disease lanas
  drink nipa
  fish dorab, gourami
  fruit durian, beeleric, cardamom
  garment sarong
  gateway toran(a)
  gulf Boni
  herb pia, rea, chay, sola, sesame, roselle, eggplant
  island Bali, Muna, Nias, Misal, Timor, Borneo, Celebes, Sumatra
  maid ayah
  market pasar
  measure kit, kos, depa, kilan, parah, tjenkal
  money bonk, duit
  musical instrument bina, vina
  nut ben, betel
  palm tal, nipa, jaggery, palmyra, tokopat
  poison bikh
  police chief darogah
  vehicle tonga
  vessel patamar
  weight singh
Easter
  feast of Pasch
  first Sunday after Quasimodo
  fruitcake Simnel
  Island Rapanui
  of paschal
  Sunday before Palm
  third Sunday after Jubilate
Eastern church
  bishop abba
  choir platform solea
  convent head hegumene
  festival day apodosis
  monk caloyer
  prayer ectene
easy glib, facile, lenient
  job snap, cinch, sinecure
eat feed, erode, devour, ingest
  between meals nosh, bever, snack
  greedily bolt, gorge, edacity, voracity

immoderately glut, sate
in gulps lab
regimentally diet
eave cornice
Ebal
    father Joktan, Shobal
Eban
    Israeli diplomat Abba
ebb abate, recede, decline
    and flow tide, (a)estus
Ebed
    son Gaal
Eber
    father Elpaal, Shashak
    son Joktan
Eblis Satan
    son Tir, Awar, Dasim, Zalabur
ebon dark, black, sable
eboulement landslide
ebullient boiling, bubbling, exuberant
ecaudate tailless
ecce lo, behold
eccentric odd, bizarre, irregular
    piece cam
ecclesiastic prelate, minister, religious
    court rota
    unit parish
ecclesiastical
    attendant acolyte
    banner labarum
    benefice glebe
    cap biretta, calotte, zucchetto
    council synod
    hood amice
    widow's office viduate
ecdysiast stripper, stripteaser
eche grow, enlarge, increase
echidna monster, anteater
    food ants
    three-toed nodiak
Echidna
    father Phorcys, Chrysaor
    mother Ceto, Calirrhoe
    offspring Hydra, dragon, Orthus, Sphink, Chim(a)era, Cerberus
echimyine cony, hutia
echinate spiny, bristly, prickly

echinoderm trepang, starfish, sea urchin
echo ring, sound, repeat, resound, response
Echo nymph
    beloved Narcissus
    loved by Pan
eciton ant
eclat praise, acclaim, splendor, reputation
eclectic liberal, inclusive, heterogeneous
eclipse cloud, obscure
    demon Rahu
    region penumbra
eclogue poem, idyl(l), pastoral
ecology bionomics
economical frugal, saving, prudent, sparing, thrifty, provident, parsimonious
economics
    term capital, Marxism, surplus, property, commodity, communism, inflation, Keynesian, recession, capitalism, competition, consumption, distribution, laissez-faire, mercantilism, gross national product
    theoretical plutology
economist
    American George, Hansen, Veblen, Walker, Weaver, Friedman, Laughlin, Galbraith, Samuelson, Schumpeter
    Canadian Leacock
    Dutch Tinbergen
    English Mill, Pigou, Keynes, Malthus, Ricardo, Marshall
    French Say, Turgot, Wairas, Quesnay
    German Marx, Weber, Schacht
    Italian Pareto
    Scottish Smith
    Swedish Myrdal
    Swiss Sismondi
economy saving, thrift, prudence, frugality, management
    practice scrape, scrimp
ecostate ribless
ecru beige, linen
ecstasy joy, bliss, frenzy, delight, rapture, transport, enthusiasm, exultation
ectad outer, exterior
    opposite entad
ectoparasite leech, remora

ecu coin, shield
Ecuador
  animal vicuña
  capital Quito
  city Loja, Banos, Tulcan, Zaruma, Salinas, Guayaquil
  coin sucre, condor
  conqueror Pizarro, Benalcazar, Huayna-Capal
  Indian Cara, Inca, Palta, Canelo, Jibaro
  island Mocha, Pinta, Tortuga, Santiago, Culpepper, Galapagos, Santa Cruz, Santa Maria, San Salvador
  measure libra, fanega, cuadra
  mountain Andes, Condor, Sangay, Cayambe, Cotopaxi, Antisana, Cotacachi, Pichincha
  province Loja, Azuay, Canar, Manabi
  tree balsa
  volcano Antisana
ecumenical council Lyon, Trent
eczema tetter, malanders (in horses)
edacious ravenous, devouring, voracious
edacity appetite, voracity
edaphic local, autochthonous
edda saga
eddaic god Odin
eddish arrish, edgrow, stubble
eddo taro root
eddy twirl, gyrate, vortex
edema tumor, dropsy, swelling
Eden garden, heaven, utopia, elysium, paradise
edental toothless
edentata
  group ai, sloth, aardvark, anteater
edentate
  genus Manis, Pangolin
Ederyn
  father Nudd
Edessa
  king Abgar
edge hem, lip, rim, arris, brink, verge, border, labrum, margin, keenness, advantage, sharpness
  run along skirt
  sharp beard

sloping basil, bezel
  uneven wane, wan(e)ly
edging lace, frill, border, rickrack
  loop picot
edgy sharp, angular, anxious, critical, impatient, irritable
edible eatable, esculent, palatable
  arum taro
  fungus morel
  gallingale chufa
  mollusk asi
  parts of fruit pulp
  rush chufa
  seaweed agar, dulse, laver, delisk
  seed pea, bean
  tuber root oca, uva, yam, beet, eddo, turnip
edict act, rule, mandate, ordinance
  papal bull(a)
edifice church, temple, building, structure
  kind palace, capitol, tabernacle
edify grow, teach, uplift, benefit, prosper, instruct
edile aedile, magistrate
Edinburgh Edina, capital
  part Leith
Edison, Thomas Alva inventor
edition kind, issue, print, source
  kind extra, reprint, revisal
editor redactor, diaskeuast
  room sanctum
Edom Esau, Idumaea
  chieftain Iram
  descendants Edomites
  district Teman
  king Hadad
  mountain Hor
educated taught, learned, cultured, literate
edulcorate sweeten
eel whip, congo, moray, conger
  fish for sniggle
  genus Conger
  sand launce
  young elver
eelboat schuit
eelpot trap
eelpout ling, burbot

eelworm nema
eemis, immis insecure
efface erase, obliterate
effect end, prey, force, fruit, issue, intent, result, outcome, validity, influence, consequence
  of past experience mneme
effects goods, baggage, chattels, moveables
effeminate soft, female, epicene, unmanly, womanly
effete spent, barren, sterile
efficacy impact, efficiency, effectiveness
efficient apt, able, potent, capable, feckful, skillful, competent, productive, proficient, crackerjack
effigy icon, likeness
  fate (sometimes) burned, hanged
effloresce flower, blossom-(out)
effluence issue, emanation
effluvium aura, flatus, exhalation
efflux outflow, effluence
effodient burrowing, fossorial
effort try, labor, strain, endeavor, exertion, striving, struggle, achievement, application
  single solo, trice
  violent burst
effulgence flare, luster, radiance
effuse gush, pour, fling, spread, dispense, disseminate
eft newt, lizard
  genus Triturus
egg ova, roe, ovum, embryo
  as food fried, omelet(te), poached, shirred, over easy, scrambled, hard-boiled, sunny-side up
  case shell, ovisac
  collector of bird's oologist
  comb. form oo, ovi
  feeding on ovivorous
  fertilized zoon, zygote, oosperm
  fish roe, berry
  nest clutch
  of insect nit
  on abet, goad, incite, provoke
  part yolk, shell, white, albumen, chalaza, latebra

  prefix oo
  shell shard, cascaron
  tester candler
  white glair, albumen
egger moth
egghead highbrow, intellectual
eggplant brinja(u)l
Egil
  brother Volund
Eglah
  husband David
  son Ithream
Eglantine
  father Pepin
  husband Valentine
Eglon
  king Debir
  slayer Ehud
ego id, self, atman, jivatma
egotistic selfish, conceited, self-centered
egregious gross, flagrant, precious
egress exit, vent
egret bird, heron, plume
egrimony sorrow
Egypt, Egyptian UAR, Arab, Copt, Gipsy, Nilot
  air god Shu
  animal fox, adda, genet, jerboa
  army chieftain sirdar
  astral body Ka
  beetle scarab
  bird sicsac
  boat baris, dahabeah
  body Ka, Sahu
  bottle doruck
  burial jar Canopus
  cap fez
  capital Cairo, Alexandria
  cat-headed goddess Bast, Pakht
  chaos Nu
  Christian Copt
  city No, Sais, Luxor, Armant, Thebes
  civilization Tasian
  cobra haje
  coin kees, para, fodda(h), girsh, purse, tallard, bedidlik
  concubine Hagar

cosmetic kohl
cotton sak, pima
cross of life ankh
crown atef
dancing girl alma
deity Hor, Mut, Anta, Sati, Hathor
descendant copt, fellah
desert Tih, Dakla, Scete, Skete, Sinai, Nubian, Sahara, Arabian
division lower, nubia, upper
dog saluki
drug nepenthe
evil spirit Set, Seth
gateway Pylon
god Set(h), Ptah, Nekenbet
goddess Bast, Isis, Pakht
governor Pasha
heaven Aaru
herb anise
isthmus Suez
jar canopic
judge of the dead Osiris
king Tut, Mena, Ram(e)ses, Ptolemy
language Coptic
lily calla, lotos, lotus
love goddess Hathor
maternity goddess Apet
measure theb, ardab, girba
monarch pharaoh
monument obelisk
mountain Sinai
native Copt, Nilot
negro Nubian
official mudir
peasant fellah
pharaoh's headdress pschent
plant cumin, lentil
queen Nofrete, Cleopatra
river Bahr, Nile
rulers Ptolemeis
sacred bird ibis
sacred bull apis
sea Red, Mediterranean
soul Ba
stone Rosetta
sun god Ra, Tem, (A)tum, Atmu
temple Idfu, Luxor, Abydos, Dendera

tomb mastaba
water bottle doruck
weight ket, oka, artal, uckia, drachma
wind duck, kamsin, kamseen, khamsin
Ehud Hebrew judge
son Naaman
victim Eglon
eident busy, careful, diligent
eider down, wamp, quilt
eidetic vivid
eidolon image, apparition
eight eta, card, VIII
comb. form octa, octo
days of feast utas
group of octet, octave, octette
set of octad, ogdoad
eighth
circle octant
day after nones ides
order octic
Einstein, Albert scientist
awarded Nobel Prize
birthplace Ulm
field physics
theory relativity, uranium fission
Eire Erin, Ireland, Hibernia
capital Tralee
legislature Dail
eireannach Irishman
ejaculation
mystic Om
el bend, elevated rail
Elah
father Uzzi, Caleb, Baasha
slayer Zimri
son Hoshea
Elaine
father Pelles
lover Lancelot
son Galahad
Elam
capital Susa, Sushan, Shushan
father Shem
king Chedorlaomer
élan vim, brio, dash, zeal, ardor, gusto
eland impofo, antelope
elanet kite

élan vital soul, anima, force, animus, psyche
elapine cobra, mamba
Elasah
  father Helez, Pashur, Shaphan
elasmobranch fish ray, shark, chimera, sawfish
elastic garter, pliant, spongy, ductile, stretchy
  fluid gas
  material from whales baleen
Elatha
  son Bres
Elatus
  daughter Caenis, Caeneus
Elbe
  tributary Eger, Iser
elbow push, angle, joint
  bend tope, drink, imbibe
  bone ulna(e)
  pert. to ulnar, anconeal
elbow grease work, force, muscle, exertion
elchee, elchi envoy, ambassador
elder dean, prior, ancestor
  shrub/tree sambucus
eldritch eerie, weird, ghastly
Eleanor
  husband Henry II
Eleazar
  brother Abihu, Nadab
  father Dodo, Aaron, Parosh, Abinadab
  son Phinehas
Electra Pleiad
  brother Orestes
  father Agamemnon
  husband Plyades
  mother Klytemnestra
  son Medon
electric
  atmosphere aura
  atom ion, electron
  circuit regulator booster
  coil tesla
  detective radar, sonar
  ion anion, cation
  terminal pole, electrode
  unit ohm, volt, ampere

electrode anode, cathode, terminal
electronic tube triode, vacuum, klystron
electrum amber
Electryon
  brother Mestor
  daughter Alcmene
  father Perseus
  king Mycenae
  mother Andromeda
  wife Anaxo
eleemosynary free, charitable, gratuitous
elegiac poem, funereal, plaintive
elegist Gray, poet, Milton, Propertius
element part, constituent
  chemical xenon, cobalt, iodine, silicon, uranium
  earth group erbium
  even valence artiad
  inert gas neon, xenon, helium
  nonvolatile barium
  of air argon, oxygen, nitrogen
  similar isotype
  white indium, silver, aluminum
elemi anime, resin, oleoresin
elenge dreary, remote, tedious
elephant mastodon, pachyderm
  cry barr, trumpet
  dentin ivory
  ear fern, taro
  extinct mammoth, mastodon
  group herd
  keeper mahout
  male bull
  pen kraal
  seat on howdah
  young calf
elephant boy Sabu
elevated
  ground mesa, rideau
elevation of mind anagoge
elf fay, nix, pixie, sprite
elfish sprite drac
elgin marbles sculptures
Eli Yale
  son Hophni, Phinehas
  successor Ahitub
Elia Charles Lamb, essayist

Eliab
- **brother** David
- **daughter** Abihail
- **father** Helon, Pallu
- **son** Abiram, Dathan

Eliada
- **father** David
- **son** Rezon

Eliakim
- **father** Josiah, Hilkiah

Eliam
- **daughter** Bathsheba

Elian Eretrian

Eliashib
- **father** Bani, Zattu, Elioenai

Eliatha
- **father** Heman

Eliel
- **father** Toah, Hebron, Shimhi

Eliezer
- **father** Harim, Moses, Becher, Zichri, Dodovah

Elijah prophet, Tishbite

Elimelech
- **wife** Naomi

Eliot, George
- **author of** Romola, Adam Bede, Middlemarch, Silas Marner, The Mill on the Floss
- **hero** Marner
- **heroine** Romola
- **real name** Mary Ann Evans

Eliphal
- **father** Ur

Eliphaz
- **father** Esau
- **mother** Adah
- **son** Teman

Elisabeth, Elizabeth
- **husband** Zacharias
- **son** John (the Baptist)

Elisha
- **father** Shaphat
- **home** Abelmeholah
- **servant** Gehazi

Elisheba
- **brother** Nahshon

father Amminadab
husband Aaron
- **son** Abihu, Nadab, Eleazar, Ithamar

elision syncope, haplology

elite best, type, cream, flower, oligarchy
- **gathering** galaxy

Eliud
- **father** Achim
- **son** Eleazar

elixir arcanum, panacea

Elizabeth I Bess, Oriana
- **advisor** Cecil, Burghley
- **brother** Edward the Sixth
- **father** Henry Tudor, Henry the Eighth
- **mother** Anne Boleyn
- **sister** Bloody Mary
- **victory over** Spanish Armada

Elizabeth II
- **daughter** Anne
- **father** George the Sixth
- **mother** Elizabeth
- **husband** Phillip Mountbatten
- **son** Andrew, Edward, Charles

elk deer, sambar, leather
- **bark** bay, magnolia

Elkanah
- **brother** Assir, Abiasaph
- **father** Joel, Korah, Mahath, Jeroham
- **son** Samuel
- **wife** Hannah, Peninnah

ell annex, measure

elliptical oval, ovoid, oblong

elm tree, ulme
- **borer** lamid
- **genus** Trema, Ulmus, Celtis, Planera

Elman, violinist Mischa

elocute declaim

elodian tortoise

eloign convey, remove, conceal

eloquence fluency, oratory, passion

El Salvador
- **capital** San Salvador
- **city** Cutuco, Libertad, Santa Ana, San Miguel
- **coin** peso, colon, centavo
- **conqueror** Alvarado
- **language** Spanish

measure vara, fanega, tercia
mountain Izalco
people Lenca, Pipil, Indian, Mangue, mestizo, Spanish, Matagalpa
religion Roman Catholic
river Jiboa, Lempa, de la Paz, Grande de San Miguel
weight caja, libra
elutriate decant, purify
elver eel, conger
Elysium Eden, bliss, paradise
emaciated lean, gaunt, wasted, tabetic
emanation(s) aura(e), niton, vapor, efflux, exhalation
flower aroma, scent
invisible aura, vapor
subtle aura
emasculate geld, soften, castrate
embale pack
embarrassment shame, caddle, chagrin, vexation, confusion, perplexity, discomposure
embattled creneled
embay shelter, encircle
ember ash, coal, brand, cinder
embezzle loot, steal, pilfer, peculate, misappropriate
emblem badge, token, symbol
of authority mace, star, stripe
of clan totem
of U.S. eagle
embodiment image, avatar, epitome
of Ptah Apis
embolus clot
embonpoint stoutness, corpulence
embossing celature, decoration
embrace hug, clip, adopt, cover, seize, twine, embody, enfold, espouse, welcome
embrocation arnica, liniment, poultice
embroider adorn, embellish
embroidery lace, brede, hedebo
figure etoile
frame hoop, taboret
hole eyelet
machine-made bonnaz
thread floss

embroil mire, jumble, perplex, implicate, complicate
embryo cell, germ
developed fetus
food endosperm
outer cells epiblast
membrane amnion
middle layer mesoderm, mesoblast
embusque shirker, slacker
eme uncle, friend, gossip, relative
emergent rising, arising, issuing, emerging
Emerson, Ralph Waldo
author of Fate, Brahma, Nature, Friendship, The Rhodora, Compensation, Self-Reliance, The Concord Hymn, The American Scholar
friend Thoreau
philosophy transcendentalism
emery abrasive, corundum
Emesh
brother Enten
father Enlil
emetic ipecac, mustard
Emilia
husband Iago, Palamon
slayer Iago
emmer spelt, wheat
emmet ant, pismire
emolument gain, salary, stipend
emotion envy, fear, hate, love, anger, pathos, feeling, passion
seat of liver, spleen
turn of caprice
emperor ruler, caesar, despot, autocrat
decree rescript
Ger. kaiser
Jp. tenno, mikado
sovereignty over empire, empery
empire realm, domain, commonwealth
Empire State New York
empiric faker, charlatan
empty barren, hollow, vacuous
comb. form ken(o)
empyreal airy, ethereal, celestial
empyrean sky, ether, firmament
emunctory skin, lungs, kidneys
emyd turtle, terrapin

enchantress Circe, siren, charmer
enchiridion handbook
enchorial native, popular
encomiast eulogist
encore over, again, recall
  anti boo, hiss, catcall
encumbrance burden
  in law lien, claim
  kind mortgage
end goal, close, design, expire, purpose
  mus. coda, fine
  result product
  tending to telic
endemic native, indigenous
endless eternal, limited, immortal
endocrine gland
  kind adrenal, thyroid, pituitary
endogamy inbreeding
endowment grant, largess(e)
Endymion shepherd
  lover Selene
energy force, might, power
  pert. to actinic
  potential ergal
  unit erg, ergon
enfilade rake, barrage
engine motor, machine, locomotive
  compressed air ramjet
  cylinder piston
  exhaust noise chug
  of war ram, onager, catapult, mangonel, trebuchet
England, English Albion, Anglican
  coin pence, florin, guinea, farthing
  emblem rose
  hills clee, wolds
  measure pin, cran
  order garter
  party Tory, Whig, Labo(u)r
  patron saint George
  race course Ascot, Epsom
  school Eton, Harrow
  weight tod, mast, stone
engrave etch, chisel, imprint
  by dots stipple
engraving print, carving
  act celature, xylography

coin, ancient carolus
  stone cameo, intaglio
  tool burin
engulf (over)whelm, swallow
enigma rebus, puzzle, mystery, conundrum
enigmatic obscure, baffling, inscrutable
  person sphinx
  saying parable
enisled alone, isolated
enkerchief drape
ennead ninefold
ennui tedium, boredom, fatigue
Enos
  father Seth
  grandmother Eve
  uncle Abel, Cain
ens being, entity, essence
ensiform bone, xiphoid
ensilage fodder, storage
ensorcel charm, bewitch
entablature
  part frieze, cornice, atlantes, architrave
  support atlas, column, atlantes
entad
  opposed to ectad
entellus monkey
entente pact, agreement
entertainment show, repast, recreation
  of strangers xenodochy
enthusiast fan, bigot, zealot, fanatic
enthymeme argument, syllogism
entire all, total, whole, complete, livelong
  comb. form holo
  prefix holo
  range gamut
entozoon hookworm, parasite, tapeworm
entrance adit, charm, portal, ingress, delight
  back postern
  court atrium
  hall foyer, lobby
  with evil intent entry
entrechat jump, leap
entrepot depot, warehouse
entresol mezzanine

enuresis urination
environment milieu, surroundings
  comb. form eco
envoy legate, nuncio, ambassador, plenipo-
  tentiary
enzyme olease, pepsin, diastase
  leather-making tannase
  opposed to azyme
eonic eral
Eos dawn, Aurora, goddess
eparch bishop, governor
eparchy diocese
ephemeris diary, almanac, calendar
epic epos, saga, narrative
  poem eneid, aeneid, epopee
epicarp husk, peel, rind
epicedium dirge
epicene neuter
epicrisis review, critique
Epictetus stoic
epicure glutton, gourmet, sybarite
epicurean hedonist, luxurious
epidermis bark, skin, cuticle
epigram mot, quip, adage, saying
  couplet distich
epilepsy fit, seizure, catalepsy
  attack grand mal, petit mal
Epimetheus Titan
  wife Pandora
epimyth moral
epinephrin(e) hormone, adrenaline
epiphyte moss, fungus, lichen, orchid
epistaxis nosebleed
epithet (by) name, oath, agnomen, misnomer
  Alexander (the) Great
  Clemenceau Tiger
  Eric (the) Red
  Ivan (the) Terrible
  Jackson Stonewall
  Pitt Ironside
epoch age, eon, era, period
epode (lyric) poem, aftersong
epopee epic (poem), epos
epoptic mystic
equable even, serene, tranquil
equal par, even, same, tantamount
  comb. form iso, pari

quantity ana, identic
sides isosceles
equanimity poise, composure, sangfroid
equilateral figure rhomb, triangle
equilibrist balancer, rope walker
equilibrium poise, balance, composure
  lack of astasia
equine horse, zebra, donkey
  water sprite kelpy
equiponderant balanced
equitable just, wise, impartial
  Roman law Bonitarian
equivocal vague, cryptic, dubious
eral epochal
ere prior, before, rather
Erebus Hades, darkness
  father Chaos
  offspring Day, Aether
  sister Nox, Night
eremite hermit, recluse
erewhile ago, once, heretofore
ergo hence, because, therefore
ergon erg, work
ergot fungus
  of rye spur
eri silkworm
erica heath
Erin Erie, Ierne, Old Sod, Ireland, Hibernia
eristic disputant, argumentative
Eritrea see Ethiopia
  measure cubi
Eros Amor, love, Cupid
  beloved Psyche
  father Hermes, Mercury
  mother Venus, Aphrodite
error(s) slip, boner, errata
  printing typo, erratum
ersatz substitute
Erse Irish, Gael(ic), Celt(ic)
erubescent reddish, blushing
erudition wisdom, knowledge, scholarship
erysipelas rose, disease (skin), wildfire
Esau Edom
  brother Jacob
  father Isaac
  wives Adah, Basemath
escarpment slope, fortification

eschatology subject death, immortality, resurrection
escheat confiscate
escolar fish, palu
escutcheon arms, crest
  band fess
  voided orle
Esdras Ezra, Nehemiah, Apocrypha
  angel Uriel
Eskimo Aleut, Alaskan
  Asian Yuit, Innuit
  boat bidar, kayak, umia(c)k
  garment parka, anorak, temiak
  house igloo, tupik
  knife ulu
esne serf, slave
esodic afferent
esophagus gula, gullet
esoteric arcane, occult, secret
  doctrine cabala
  knowledge gnosis
esparto grass alfa
Esperanto ido, language
  deviser Zamenhof
espy spy, view, descry
ess worm, curve, sigmoid
Essene mystic, ascetic
essential basic, vital, intrinsic, necessary
  element part
  oil essence
  part pith, member
  thing key
estafet courier
estate assets, degree, status, holdings
  manager steward, executor, guardian
ester ether, oleate, silicate
Esther Hadassah
  festival Purim
  husband Xerxes, Ahasuerus
esthetics arts
Est(h)onia, Esthonian Esth
  measure liin, suld
  weight nael, puud
estivate summer
  opposed to hibernate
estray waif, dogie
estuary creek, inlet, plata

estuate boil
esurient greedy, hungry
et al. others, elsewhere
etamine cloth, voile
etape encampment, storehouse
Eteocles
  brother Polynices
  father Oedipus
  kingdom Thebes
  mother Jocasta
Eternal City Rome
etesian annual, periodical
etheostomoid fish, darter
ether air, sky, space
  compound ester
  use solvent, anesthetic
Ethiopia, Ethiopian Seba, Abyssinia(n)
  coin besa, harf, girsh, kharaf, talari
  fly zimb
  measure tat, cuba, kuba, ardeb, berri
  plant (herb) teff
  primate abuna
  tree koso, cusso
  weight pek, rot, kasm, natr, oket, alada
ethnarch governor
ethos
  opposed to pathos
ethyl
  derivative ether
  hydride ethane
  hydroxide alcohol
  symbol et, eth
Etna lamp, volcano
Etruscan Tursenoi
  god Tinia
  goddess Menfra
ettle aim, intend
etui case, reticule, needlecase
etymon root, radix, radical
eucalypt yate, bloodwood
eucalyptus
  gum kino
  leaf deposit cerf
  secretion laap, larp
Eucharist
  box pix, pyx
  plate paten

vessel ama, amula
wafer host
wine krama
Euclid geometer, philosopher
  origin Megara
eudaemonia happiness
eugenic wellborn
  -s pioneer Galton
  subject races, breeds
eulogy tribute, encomium, panegyric
euouae trope
euphonium tuba
euphorbia plant, spurge
eureka aha, triumph
  red puce
euripus flow, strait
Europa
  father Ogenor
  lover Zeus
Europe and Asia Eurasia, Scythia
Europe, European Dane, Lapp, Lett, Slav
  ancient Celt
  ash sorb
  bat serotine
  central region Banat
  cherry gean
  coal basin Saar
  country (ancient) Dacia
  deer roe
  grape muscat
  hunting dog griffun
  language Ugric
  lavender aspic
  oak holm
  ox urus
  plain steppe
  rabbit con(e)y
  rodent erd
  squirrel sisel
  tree sorb
  worm sao
Eurydice
  husband Orpheus
eutectic fusible
Euterpe Muse
  son Rhesus

evanesce fade, vanish
evanescent fleeting, ephemeral, transient
even tied, level, plane, placid, equable, uniform
  if tho(ugh)
  -minded placid, equable
evening eve, dusk, twilight
  party soiree
  pert. to vesper, crepuscular
  song serena
  star Venus, hesper, Mercury
Everest
  mountain peak Lhotse
  site Nepal
evergreen pine, cedar, spruce, baretta
  cedarlike deodar
  genus Olax, Abies, Catha
  shrub toyon
everlasting ageless, eternal, constant
  plant orpine
everted turned, ectopic
evil(s) vice, malign, nefarious
  -doer felon, sinner, culprit
  prefix mal
  spirit bugan, demon, devil
eviscerate gut, devitalize, disembowel
evolution change, growth
  doctrine biogeny, cosmism
ewe keb, sheep, theave
  old crone
ewer jug, pitcher
exacerbate irk, annoy, embitter
exaggerated outre
  comedy farce
  pious feeling pietism
  praise puffery, flattery
examine try, test, explore, scrutinize
  accounts audit
  by touching palpate
excaudate tailless
excavation pit, shaft, cavity
  for ore mine, stope
except save, unless, besides
excerpt scrap, verse, choice
excessive ultra, undue, extravagant
  affection dotage
  comb. form hyper

in belief rabid
zeal fanaticism
exchange swap, bandy, trade, shuffle
premium agio
excise duty, levy, toll, expunge
exclamation ah(a), ow, bab, hey, hoy, tch, ahem, egad, phew
of disgust ugh, rats
of exhilaration evoe
excogitate devise, intent, contrive
excoriate flay, chafe, abrade, denounce
excresence lump, fungus, growth
exculpate clear, acquit, absolve, exonerate
excuse acquit, apology, pretext
for nonappearance plea, essoin
for sickness aeger
execrable bad, abominable, detestable
execution
by burning stake
by drowning noyade
by electricity electrocute
by hanging swing, halter, stretch
exequies wake, rites, ceremonies
exfoliate scale, desquamate
exhort urge, incite, preach
exhume dig, grub, disinter, disentomb
exigency pinch, crisis, urgency
exiguous small, meager, sparse, attenuated
existence ens, esse, being, status
beginning birth, nascent
having none null, void, defunct
exocoetoid fish ihi
exodus flight, hegira
exordium proem, prelude, preamble
exoteric public, popular, external
expatiate descant, enlarge, elaborate
expecting agog, atip, astir
expedient advisable, convenient
expedition speed, safari, crusade, dispatch
heroic quest
hunting safari
military anabasis
religious crusade
experience feel, know, endure, undergo
trying ordeal
expiate atone, repair, satisfy
explanation key, alibi, solution

marginal notes scholia, annotations
of a passage exegesis
expletive egad, oath, curse
explicit express, precise, definite
exploding
meteor bolide
star nova
explorer Rae, Byrd, Eric, Lewis, Perry, Balboa, Cortes, De Soto, Amundsen
explosive TNT, bomb, mine, dynamite
isometric mineral thorite
exponent ite, index, symbol
exposition fair, show, exhibition
expostulate object, protest, remonstrate
expression idiom, phrase, locution, utterance
hackneyed cliché
metaphorical figure
of assent placet
of contempt bah, fie, pooh
of sorrow alas
expunge erase, cancel, obliterate
expurgate purge, censor, purify, cleanse
exsanguine anemic
exscind cut, excise, extirpate
exsert thrust, protrude
exsiccate dry, parch, desiccate
extemporaneous offhand, impromptu
extension arm, ell, range
extenuate lessen, weaken, diminish
exterior alien, external, cortical, outside
covering hide, peel, pelt, siding, clothing
external outer, exterior, superficial
comb. form ect(o)
covering hide, pelt, coat
cover of flower perianth
world nonego
extinct bird auk, moa, roc, dodo, mamo
extirpate raze, erase, uproot
extra odd, spare, surplus, additional
actor super, supernumerary
pay bonus
extract pull, essence, excerpt, flavoring
from a book pericope
extraction descent, lineage, genealogy
extrasensory perception ESP

extreme ultra, drastic, radical
  limit outrance
  opposed to mean
  unction sacrament
  unction, give anele
extricate free, release
extrinsic alien, foreign, extraneous
exudate gum, tar, sudor, excretion
exuviate molt, cast off
eye view, optic, sight
  black pigment melanin
  cavity orbit
  dropper pipette
  film nebula
  membrane retina, conjunctiva
  opening pupil
  part iris, uvea, cornea, sclera
  pert. to optic
  symbolic uta
eyeball orb, globe
  covering cornea
eyebrow bree, supercilium
eyelash(es) cilia, cilium
  loss madarosis
eyelet grommet, ocellus, loophole
  making tool bodkin, stiletto
eyelid
  drop ptosis
  pert. to palpebral
eyetooth fang, canine, cuspid
eyot ait, isle(t)
eyra wildcat
eyre circuit, journey
Ezekiel
  father Buzi (Jeremiah)
Ezrahite Darda, Ethan, Heman

F

F ef, eff
fabaceous plant ers
fable myth, legend, fiction, allegory
  animal dragon, centaur, unicorn
  being ogre, dwarf, giant, troll
  bird roc, phoenix

  collection bestiary
  serpent basilisk
  teller fabulist, parabolist
fabled
  animal centaur, unicorn, basilisk
  being ogre, dwarf, giant, troll, mermaid
  fish mah
  serpent basilisk
fabric ras, web, felt
  calico sall(c)o
  coarse mat, crash
  corded rep, repp
  cotton susi, pique, wigan, buckram
  cotton knit balbriggan
  cotton mixture mashru, zanella
  cotton/worsted paramatta
  crinkled crape, crepe, seersucker
  curtain material leno, scrim, moreen, silesia
  dealer mercer
  design with wax coating batik
  figured moreen
  finisher beetle
  flag material bunting
  heavy denim, canvas
  lace val, alencon, mechlin
  linen ecru, carde, drabbet, sinelon
  lustrous poplin, sateen
  metallic lamé
  plaid tartan
  satin pekin, etoile
  sheer lawn, gauze, voile
  shiny sateen
  silk alma, caffa, ninon, chiffon, charmeuse
  silk imitation rayon, satinet
  silk-ribbed rep(p), faile, marocain
  silk yarn schappe
  striped susi, doria
  surface nap
  texture woof
  thin gossamer, tarlatan, grenadine
  towel huck, terry
  Turkish agaric, chekmak
  twilled serge, surah, corduroy, messaline
  unbleached beige
  waste material mungo

watered silk moire
waterproof Burberry
white coteline
wool tweed, droguet, frisado, gabardine
wool mixture delaine
worsted (light) etamine
woven lamé, twill, blanket
fabricate fake, form, mint, build, erect, forge, devise, concoct, manufacture
method of ornamenting fagoting
fabula story
fabulist liar, Aesop, Grimm, Andersen
  French La Fontaine
  Indian Bidpai, Pilpai
  Roman Phaedrus
  Russian Krylov
facade face, rear, facia
face pan, puss, facet, visage, physiognomy
  artery maxillary
  bone malar, zygoma, mandible
  covering mask, veil, domino, yashmak
  downward prone, prostrate
  false mask
  guard mask, beaver
  paint fard, parget
  -to-face vis-à-vis, tête-à-tête
  value par
  with masonry revet
face eastward orientate
facer bumper, defeat, dilemma, tankard
facet bezel, culet, aspect
  star pane
facetious droll, funny, witty, jocuse, amusing, comical, jesting, humorous
face value par
facia plate, tablet
facing
  down prone
  inward introse
  outward extrose
  up supine
fact deed, datum, actuality
faction bloc, side, cabal, party, clique, strife, dispute, intrigue, dissension
facto ipso
factory mill, plant, workshop, manufactory
  book bindery

factotum agent, servant
faculty wit, ease, knack, ability, aptitude
faddish ism, ismal
faddist neo, monomaniac
fadge fit, suit, agree, bundle, thrive, succeed
Faerie Queene
  author Spenser
  character Ate, Una, Talus, Amoret
Faeroes
  district manger foud
  island Ostero
  whirlwind oe
Fafnir
  brother Regin, Fasolt
  father Hreidmar
  form dragon
  slayer Sigurd, Sigurth, Siegfried
  victim Fasolt, Hreimar
fagot, faggot fadge, bundle
faik lessen
fain fond, glad, eager, gladly, content, obliged, pleased, willing, desirous, inclined, willingly, constrained
fainaigue cheat, shirk, renege, revoke, deceive, finagle
faineant idle, lazy, otiose
fair even, show, blond(e), bazaar, unbiased
  pert. to nundinal
fairy elf, fay, peri, pixie, sprite
  abode shee, sidhe
  air sylph
  ghost sprite
  king Oberon
  queen Mab, Una, Titania
  shoemaker leprechaun
  spirit of death banshee
  tricky Puck
fairylike elfin
fairy tale myth, fable, legend, fantasy
  author Wilde, Andersen, Perrault, Brothers Grimm
  character Gretel, Hansel, Emperor, Rapunzel, Snow White, Cinderella, Goldilocks, Thumbelina, Puss in Boots, Seven Dwarfs, Ugly Duckling, Sleeping Beauty

faith creed, dogma, tenet, trust, belief
  pert. to pistic
faithful leal, true, loyal, tried, devoted
  friend Achates
faitour fake, cheat, imposter
fake cheat, fraud, spurious
  comb. form pseud(o)
fakir monk, yogi, mendicant
falcon, falconry sorage, kestrel
  Arctic gyr
  bait lure
  blind seel
  genus Falco, Raptores
  male tercel
  pert. to accipter
  prairie lanner
  recorder Pliny, Martial
  ribbon or strap jess
  small besra, merlin
  unfledged bird eyas
falconer's summons wo
fall sag, drop, plop, slip, abate, occur, slope, season, topple, cascade, descend, subside, collapse
  back relapse, retreat
  in cave, agree, lapse, concur, collapse
  short shy, fail, lack, miss
fall guy butt, patsy, scapegoat
fallacious sly, untrue, delusive, deceptive, misleading, disappointing
fallal finery, geegaw
fallfish chub
falling cadent
  sickness epilepsy
fallout particles radiodust
false luke, sham, tale, bogus, untrue, unreliable
  comb. form pseud(o)
  form(s) of thinking idola, idolum
  items fakes, spurious
  wing alula
Falstaff
  companion Peto, Pistol, Bardolph
  composer Verdi
  creator Shakespeare
  follower Nym
  lieutenant and crony Pistol

  play Henry IV
  prince Hal
  tavern Boar's Head
Falstaffian fat, coarse, jovial, dissolute
familiar versant
  saying mot, saw, adage
family ilk, gens, line, tribe
  lineage tree, stemma, pedigree, genealogy
  famous It. Este
  pert. to nepotic
fan cool, foment, winnow, devotee
  form rooter, plicate
  Oriental swinging ogi, punka(h)
  palm genus Inodes
  stick brin, blade
fanatical rabid, energumen
fancy fad, whim, vagry, notion, caprice, capriccio, imagination, inclination
fandango ball, tune, dance
fane temple, sanctuary
fanfare pomp, show, array, display, panoply, flourish, publicity, advertising
  trumpet tucket
fanfaron bully, hector, swaggerer
fanfoot gecko, lizard
fang earn, tusk, grasp, seize, snare, tooth
fangle mode, dress, geegaw, fashion
fanion flag, banner
fanlike plaited, plicate
fanning device punka(h)
fanon cape, orale, maniple
fan palm talipot, palmetto
fantasy whim, dream, vision, whimsy, caprice, chimera, imagination, hallucination
fantoccini shows, puppets
fantod (sl.) pet, fuss, sulk
far afar, distant, progressed
  across wide
  comb. form tele
  down deep
farce mime, humor, comedy, mockery, drollery, forcemeat
farceur wag, joker
fardel lot, furl, bundle, burden, collection
farinaceous mealy, starchy

drink ptisan
meal sago, salep, farina, cereal
farm plow, ranch, cultivate
  building barn, byre, silo
  fee manor
  grazing ranch, station
  implement disk, plow, rake, harrow, header, seeder, tiller, combine, tractor
  tenant cotter, cropper
farming husbandry
farmyard barton
farnesol alcohol
faro game, monte
  bet sleeper
  card soda
  card combination split, cat-hop
  player punter
Faroe Island Bordo, Sando, Vaago, Ostero, Stromo
  duck eider, puffin
  fish char(r)
  whirlwind oe
farouche shy, wild, fierce, unsociable
farrago medley, mixture, hodgepodge
far-reaching deep, vast, intense, profound
farrow pig, litter
fascia band, fillet
fascicle group, cluster
fascinate charm, allure, attract, bewitch, intrigue
fascist Nazi, Hitler, Mussolini, totalitarian
fashion fad, way, mode, mo(u)ld, craze, vogue, custom, manner
fast diet, wild, apace, quick, speedy
  day Ember
  period Lent
fasten pin, glue, lace, link, moor, nail, tack, chain
  comb. form desmo
fastener peg, clamp, halter
fastigate conical, pointed
fat lipa, ester, obese
  animal lard, suet, adeps, tallow, lanolin
  butter oleo, caprin
  comb. form lip(o), pio, steat(o)
  constituent stearin, cholesterol
  geese axunge

liquid part olein(e), globule
pert. to adipic
true lipid
wool lanolin
fata morgana mirage
fatbird guacharo
fate lot, doom, kismet, destiny
  Buddhist Karma
  cuts thread of life Atropos (Morta)
  measures threads of life Lachesis
  Oriental Kismet
Fates
  Greek Moera(e), Moira, Clotho, Atropos, Lachesis
  Roman Nona, Decum, Morta, Parca(e)
fathead oaf, boob, dolt, fool, chump, sheephead
fatheaded dense, thick, stupid, doltish, nu(m)bskulled
father ama, dad, pop, abba, papa, pere (Fr.), sire, beget, padre, priest
  comb. form patr(o), patri
  of English learning Bede
  of geometry Euclid
  of gods and men Zeus
  of his country Cicero, Washington
  of history Herodotus
  of hydrogen bomb Teller
  of mankind Adam, Iapetus
  of medicine Hippocrates
  of modern surgery Pare
  of plenty Abiathar
  of the gods Amen, Amon
  of the symphony Haydn
  of waters Mississippi
  pert. to agnate, paternal
Fathers of the Oratory
  founder Neri
Father Time
  implement scythe
Fatima
  descendant Seid, Sayid
  husband Ali, Blubeard
  sister Anne
  stepbrother Ali
fatty greasy, adipose
  acid adipic, valeric, lanoceric

secretion oil, sebum
tumor lipoma
fatuous inane, silly, unreal, foolish, witless, illusory
faucet tap, cock, valve, spigot
faugh bah
faujasite zeolite
Faulkner, William
  author of The Bear, Absalom, Sartoris, Sanctuary, As I Lay Dying, Light in August, The Sound and the Fury
  character Caddy, Jason, Candace, Quentin, Benjamin
  family Compson
  fictional country Yoknapatawpha
fault crime, culpa, defect, imperfection
  find carp, cavil, censure
  in mining hade
faultfinder momus, grouch, sorehead, complainer
faun deity, satyr
  of Praxiteles marble
fauna animals
Faunus
  grandfather Saturn
  son Acis
Faust
  author Goethe, Marlowe
  beloved Gretchen
  composer Gounod
faux pas gaff, slip, boner, blunder, mistake, indiscretion
favonian mild
favor boon, gift, help, kindness, partiality
  pay woo, court
favoritism bias, nepotism, predilection
fawn doe, buck, deer, toady, kowtow
  skin nebris
fay elf, fairy, nisse, pixie, unite, sprite
Fe iron
fealty duty, homage, fidelity
fear awe, alarm, dread, panic, anxiety, suspect, solicitude
  of animals zoophobia
  of being alone monophobia
  of being buried alive taphephobia
  of cats aelurophobia

  of crowds ochlophobia
  of darkness nyctophobia
  of dirt mysophobia
  of drafts aerophobia
  of fire pyrophobia
  of great heights acrophobia
  of number 13 triakaidekaphobia
  of open spaces agoraphobia
  of pain algophobia
  of poisons toxiphobia
  of strangers xenophobia
  of thunder brontophobia
  of water hydrophobia
fearful
  comb. form dino
feast junket, regale, repast
  Christian agape, Eucharist
  comb. form mas
  funeral wake, arval
  Hawaiian luau
  January Epiphany
  of Lanterns Bon
  of Lights Hanukka(h), Chanukah
  of Lots Purim
  of Tabernacles Succoth
  of Weeks Schavout, Shabuoth, Pentecost
  Passover Seder
  Scottish foy
feasting epulation, celebrating
  companion convive
feather(s) down, sley, pinna
  barb harl, pinnula
  base of bird's wing alula
  bed tye
  comb. form ptile
  down dowl(e), plumage, plumule
  grass stipa
  quill aigret, covert
  scarf boa
  shaft scape
  shank boot
  slot spline
  yellow hulu
feathering endysis
featherless callow
feathers plumage

provide with fletch
shed mo(u)lt
feature mien, story, trait
  principal plot, motif
feaze unravel, untwist
febris fever
fecket vest, waistcoat
feckless weak, spiritless, ineffective
fecund fertile, creative, fruitful, prolific, productive
Federalist writer Jay, Madison, Hamilton
fedora hat
fee pay, tip, dues, charge, payment, stipend, gratuity, retainer
  minting brassage, seignorage
  wharf quayage, wharfage
feed dine, subsist, nourish
  animal hay, mash, oats, chops, grain, fodder
  pasture cattle agist
  to excess glut, agrote, pamper, surfeit
feeder tributary
  fire stoker, fireman
feeding, forced gavage
feed the kitty ante
feeler palpus, antenna, inquiry
feeling ardor, opinion, passion
  capable of sentient
  loss of analgesia, anesthesia
  show emote
feet
  having pedate
  pert. to podal, pedary
  six fathom
  two metric dipody
  verse of two dipody
  without apod, apodal
fegary whim, prank, finery, gewgaw
feign act, sham, pretend
  sickness malinger
feil neat, comfortable
feint ruse, trick, falsity, pretense
  in fencing appel
feist cur, dog, pup, mutt, mongrel
feldspar albite, leelite, odinite
  yield kaolin
felid cat, lion, ounce, tiger

felis
  Leo lion
  Pardus leopard
fellah peasant
Fellini, Frederico
  director of Amarcord, Casanova, La Strada, Satyricon, La Dolce Vita, Nights of Cabiria, Juliet of the Spirits
fellow egg, chap, mate, equal, companion
  awkward bub, oaf, gawk, booby, bumpkin
  brutish yahoo
  conceited dalteen
  craven coward
  dissolute rake, roue, debaucher
  fat glutton
  foolish goff
  idle footer, loafer, stocah
  ignorant dope, idiot, moron, gobbin
  mean cad, boor, bully
  old geezer, gleyde
  stupid clod, dolt, moron, foozle, bungler
  tricky knave, scamp, rascal, trickster
  vain fop
  worthless bum, cad, spalpeen, scoundrel
felly rim, craftily
felo-de-se suicide
felony arson, crime, murder, offense, burglary
feltlike pannose
feltwort herb, plant, mullein
female dame, lady, woman
  animal cow, doe, sow, mare, slut, bitch, jenny, sheder
  camel naga
  comb. form gyn(o), gyne
  figurine orant
  fish raun
  fox vixen
  principle Sakti
  red deer hind
  sandpiper reeve
  sheep ewe
  warrior Amazon
feminine name
  suffix ette
femme fatale siren, Lorelei
femoral crural

femur thigh(bone)
fen bog, sump, morass
  water sud(s)
fence bar, duel, rail, block, barrier, enclose,
    palisade
  crossing stile
  fish net, weir
  interwoven raddle
  movable glance, hurdle
  picket pale, paling
  steps over stile
  sunken aha
fencing
  attack reprise
  breastplate plastron
  cry sasa
  dummy pel
  hit punto
  maneuver appel
  movement volt
  parrying position seconde
  posture carte, guard, prime, sixte,
    octave, quarte, quinte, tierce, seconde,
    septime
  sword epee, foil, rapier
  thrust riposte
  weapon epee, foil, sabre, rapier
fenestra window, opening, aperture
fennel anis, plant, azorian
  genus Nigella
Fenrir
  chain Gleipnir
  chained by Gleipnir
  father Loki
  form wolf
  mother Angerboda
  slayer Vidar
  victim Odin
fent slit, opening
feral wild, deadly, savage
Ferber, Edna
  author of Giant, So Big, Cimarron, Show
    Boat, Ice Palace
fer-de-lance snake
Ferdinand
  beloved Miranda
  father Alonso

Ferdinand, King
  conquest Granada
  daughter Joanna
  wife Germaine, Isabella
feretory chapel, shrine
ferine rude, wild, savage, untamed
ferly marvel, wonder, amazement
fermail clasp, buckle
ferment yeast, leaven, seethe
  active principal enzyme
  agent to induce must
  revive stum
fermentative zymotic
fern tara, brake, nardoo, bracken
  climbing nito
  cluster sorus
  edible roi, tara
  genus Todea, Pteris, Osmunda,
    Polypody
  leaf frond
  -like plant acrogen
  male osmund
  patches sori
  rootstock roi
ferret
  female gill
  male hob
Ferrex
  brother Porrex
ferric oxide powder rouge
ferry bac, pont, carrier, traject
ferryman (of Hades) Charon
fertility god Frey(r)
fertilizer marl, guano, manure, nitrate,
    phosphate
ferule rod, ruler, fennel, punishment
fervent hot, keen, ardent, burning, glowing,
    intense
fess bar, band
  up own, avow, admit, confess
festival
  ancient Gr. Delia
  comb. form mas
  epiphany uphelya
  of Apollo Delia
festive gay, gala, jolly, merry, blithe,
    jocund, joyous

festivity mirth, revel, frolic, gaiety, splore, whoopee
  god Comus, Bacchus, Dionysus
festoon swag, garland, bucranium
fete gala, bazaar, fiesta
  rustic ale
fetid foul, olid, fusty, putrid, virose, odorous, stinking
fetter bind, bond, chain, anklet, confine, shackle
fettle trim, order, state, fitness, condition
fetus child, embryo
  human homunculus
  limbless ameli (pl.), amelus
feud fief, quarrel, vendetta
  blood vendetta
feudal
  domain fief
  Fr. feod
  land, right of feod, feud, fief
  lord liege
  opposed to al(l)odial
  service avera
  payment tac, tak
  pert. to banal
  tenant leud, vassal, socager
  tribute heriot
fever ardor, enecia
  affected with pyretic
  chills and ague
  intermittent malaria, quartan
  kind tap, octan, elodes
  reducer defervescent
  spot(s) petechia(e)
  tropical dengue, malaria
  without afebrile, apyretic
fever tree blue gum
few rare, scant, scarce
  comb. form olig(o), pauci
fey dead, dying, timid
fez cap, shako, turban, tarboosh
fiacre hack, coach
fiber eruc, hemp
  bark olona, terap
  century plant pita, clusters
  East Indian plant ramie
  hat datil

  knot nep
  palm agave, raffia
  wood bast, aralac
  wool nep, kemp, staple
fibril hair, filament
fibrin gluten, protein
fibula ouch, clasp, brooch
fickle giddy, mutable, capricious, inconstant
fico fig, snap, trifle
fictile molded, plastic
fictive imaginary
fiddle kit, crowd, scrape, violin
  medieval gigue, rebec
fiddle-faddle bosh, fudge, hooey, piffle, nonsense, triviality
fiddler crab uca
Fidelio
  composer Beethoven
  hero Florestan
  heroine Lenora, Leonora
fidelis semper
fidelity hold, piety, loyalty
  symbol topaz
fiducial firm, trusted, confident
fief fee, han, feud, tenure, benefice
field lea, area, grid
  Am. mouse vole
  athletic oval, ring, arena, course
  biblical ager, aner
  comb. form agro
  common share dale
  edge rand
  enclosed ager, court, croft
  god Pan, Faun
  goddess Fauna
  pert. to agrarian, campestral
  Roman ager
  stubble rowen
fieldbird plover
Fielding, Henry
  author of Amelia, Shamela, Tom Jones, Tom Thumb, Jonathan Wild, Joseph Andrews
field marshal
  Austrian Radetzky
  British Napier, Raglan, Wavell, Wilson,

Roberts, Wolseley, Kitchener, Montgomery
French Foch, Joffre, Petain
German Keitel, Paulus, Rommel, Rupert, Mackensen, Rundstedt, Waldersee, Kesselring
Japanese Sugiyama
Prussian Moltke
Russian Kutozov, Suvorov, Potemkin
field of blood Aceldama
fieldwork lunet(te), redan, exploration, fortification
fiend foe, demon, devil, enemy, Satan, trull, wizard
fiery hot, afire, fervid, glowing, intense, flashing, inflamed, sizzling, flammable
fiesta fete, feria, party, holiday
fifteen
  comb. form pentadec(a)
fifth
  comb. form quint(i)
fig(s) fico
  basket cabas
  crate seron
  dried carica
  genus Ficus
  It. fico
  -like caricous
  marigold samh
  not to care a fillip
  sacred pipal
  variety eleme, Smyrna
Figaro barber
fight row, fray, clash, set-to, combat, fracas, dispute
  against the gods theomachy
  street riot, brawl, rumble
fighting fish betta
figure image, motif, shape, effigy, symbol
  archeology telamon, caryatid
  earth geoid
  five-angled pentagon
  four-angled square, rhombus, tetragon, rectangle
  oval ellipse
  round circle

ten-sided decagon
three-angled triangle
figured adorned, faconne, computed
figure of speech pun, trope, simile, metaphor
figure out dope, solve, decipher, untangle
figure skating
  jump axel, loop, lutz, split, rocker, salchow
  spin sit, camel
figurine tanagra, statuette
Fiji
  chestnut rata
  drug tonga
  island Lau, Viti
  group Ra, Lau
filament fiber, strand, thread, tendril
  feather dowl(e)
  flax harl(e)
filbert nut, hazel
file row, enter, cabinet
  comb-maker's carlet
  finisher ender
  flat quannet
  half-round grail(le)
  rough rasp
filibeg kilt, skirt
Filipino see Philippine
fill pad, cram, gorge, occupy, fatiate, pervade, suffuse
  cracks ca(u)lk, shim
  with zeal enthuse
fillet orle, sola, ribbon
  bottom of frieze regula, taeina
  for hair band, snood
  jeweled tiara, diadem
  narrow listel, reglet
fill-in sub, alternate, surrogate, locum tenens
fill in clew, clue, post, warn, advise, apprise
filling
  dental inlay
  fabric weft, woof
fillip snap, tonic, excite
film haze, cinema, coating, membrane
  coated with patinate
  green/old patina
  thin brat, pellicle

filter sift, drain, purify, refine, strain
  sugar clay
fimbriate hem, hairy, fringe
fin
  spinous dorsal, acantha
  under ventral
final outcome issue, upshot
fin-footed animal pinniped
finch spink, siskin, redpoll
  Afr. fink, moro
  Am. junco, towhee, chewink
  canarylike serin
  copper chaffinch
  Eur. serin, tarin
  genus Fringillidae
  -like canary, tanager
find learn, detect, procure
  by keen search probe, ferret
  fault beef, carp, cavil
  law hold, ascertain, determine
fine tax, exact, small, penalty
  for killing cro, wergild
  for misdemeanor mulct
  law cro
  record estreat
Fingal
  cave island Staffa
  kingdom Morven
finger feel, handle, pointer
  cap cot, thimble
  comb. form digiti
  fore index
  guard stall, thimble
  inflammation felon, whitlow
  little pinky, minimus
  middle medius
  pert. to digital
  ring annular
fingerboard
  part fret
fingerlike dactyl
fingerling fish, parr, thimble
fingernail moon lunule
fingerprint arch, loop, whorl
finial epi, top, apex
finish die, cease, glaze, polish, coating, execute, fulfill

dull matte
glossy enamel
finishing line tape
finite bound(ed), defined, limited, measurable
fink spy, bird, scab, informer
Finland, Finnish Vod, Vote, Suomi
  bath sauna
  city Aba, Abo, Helsinki, Helsingfors
  coin penni, markka
  comb. form Fenno
  dialect karel
  division Ijore, Villipuri
  forest god Tapio
  god Jumala
  harp kantele
  island A(a)land
  isthmus Karelia
  lake and town Enare
  measure tunna, kannor
  pert. to Suomic, Suomish
  tribe Veps(e), Wote, Ugrian
Finlandia composer Sibelius
Finnegan's Wake
  author James Joyce
fin(n)ikin pigeon
fiord, fjord ise, inlet
fippenny bit fip
fir evergreen
  genus Abies
Firbolg queen Tailte
fire blaze, eject, arouse, animate, discharge, conflagration
  artillery barrage
  basket grate, cresset
  bullet tracer
  comb. form pyr(o), igni
  containing igneous
  drill chark
  fighter vamp
  military flak, salvo, barrage
  miss dud, snap
  particle arc, spark, cinder
  pert. to igneous
  sacrificial Agni
  worshipper pyrolater
fireback reredos, pheasant

fireboat palander
firecracker petard
firedog andiron, support
fireplace grate, ingle, hearth
   back reredos
   ledge hob, shelf, mantel
firestone flint
firewood bundle lena, fagot
firmament vault, sphere, heavens
firn ice, neve, snow
first star, maiden, primus, primordial
   comb. form proto
   day of Roman month Calends
   installment earnest, handsel
   year's revenue annat
firstborn heir, eigne, eldest, protegenist
first class top, A-one, capital, excellent
first dwellers aboriginals
first fruits annates
firsthand direct, primary, original,
   immediate
first man in space Gagarin
first U.S. state Delaware
firth arm, kyle, estuary
Firth of Clyde island Bute
fish dab, carp, hake, opah, peto, shad, angle,
   smelt
   Alaskan iconnu
   Atlantic Coast cod, tuna, porgy, bunker,
     alewife, bluefish, greentail
   Australian mado, gro(u)per
   basket caul, cawl, corf
   bat diablo
   bin for salting canch, kench
   bivalve clam, diatom, oyster, mollusk,
     pandora, scallop
   black swart, tautog
   bright-colored opah
   butter blenny, gunnel
   California re(i)na, rasher, garibaldi
   carp id(e), orf
   catch shack, string
   caviar-yielding sterlet, sturgeon
   chopped chum
   -colored opah, wrasse
   devil ray, manta
   eggs roe, caviar

   electric raad, torpedo
   European id(e), rud(d), boce, alose,
     barbel, picarel
   fabled, upholding world mah
   female raun, henfish
   flat (sand) dab, fluke, skate, turbot,
     halibut, flounder
   Florida grunt, atinga, salema, tomtate
   flying saury, gurnard
   food cod, eel, bass, carp, sole, tile,
     weever, snapper
   genus Amia, Lota, Mola, Elops, Perca,
     Apogon
   half-beak ihi
   Hawaiian aku(le), ulua, lania
   hook gaff, sproat
   imperfect thoke
   Jp. ayu, tai
   jew mero, grouper
   largest freshwater arapaima
   -like bib, hake, ling, gadus
   little smelt, minnow, sardine
   Mediterranean porgy, sargo, chivey,
     menominee
   New England hake
   newly hatched fry
   New Zealand ihi, hikus
   Nile erse, saide
   parasitic remora
   pen crawl
   pert. to finny, piscatory
   pilot remera
   raylike skate
   scale ganoid
   scaleless alepidote
   S. A. gogy, mapo, acara, almara, caribe
   snapper jocu
   spear-snouted gar
   voracious pike, shark, caribe, piranha,
     barracuda
   West Indies boga, cero, sier, chopa,
     Blanco, guapena
   young fry, parr, smolt, alevin
fisher bird, pekan, wejack
fisherman
   hat squam
fishes raiae

fishhook barb, angle
  attach to snell gange
  leader snell
fishing
  basket creel, slath, slarth
  gear fly, rod, hook, line, nets, reel, tackle
  pert. to halieutic
  smack dogger
fishlike ichthyic
  skin ichthyosis
fist neif, nieve
fitchew polecat
five
  books of Moses Pentateuch
  comb. form pent, penta
  -dollar bill fin, vee
  group of pentad
five-finger fish, oxlip, plant, cinquefoil
fivefold quintuple
Five Nations Cayugas, Mohawks,
  Oneidas, Senecas, Onondagas
  founder Hiawatha
five-year period pentad, lustrum
fixed firm, intent, stable
  routine rut
  star Vega
  time era, date, appointment
fizgig fireworks, whirligig
flag iris, droop, faint, bunting, pennant,
  streamer
  corner canton
  flower iris, calamus
  merchant vessel burgee
  military colors, fanion, guidon
  national ensign
  navy burgee
  pirate roger
  signal cornet
  yacht burgee
flagellant tail, whip, scourge
  religious alibi
flageolet pipe, flute, larigot
flambeau torch, cresset
flame ardor, blaze, gleed
  fire without punk
  movement dark, lick
Flaminia way, road

Flanders
  capital Ghent
flap fly, bangle, flutter
  furnished with lobed
  membranous loma
  of sails slat
flash blaze, spark, second, exhibit, dispatch,
  outburst
flashing gaudy, flange
flask carafe, flagon, canteen
  glass matrass
  leather olpe, girba, matara
  -shaped lageniform
flat level, prone, stale, smooth, insipid
  comb. form plani
  -nosed simous
flatboat ark, scow, barge
Flaubert
  heroine Emma
  novel Salammbo, Madame Bovary
flax lint, linen
  bundle head
  capsule boll
  comb card, hackle, hatchel
  disease rust
  dust pouce
  fiber tow
  filament harl
  genus Linum
  insect canker, dodder
  place for processing rettery
  seed linseed
  soak ret
  woody portion boon
flea flea, insect, pulicid
  genus Pulex
  water cyclops
Fleance
  father Banquo
fleche spire, broach, parapet
Fledermaus, Die bat
  character Adele, Falke, Frank, Alfred,
    Rosalinde, Eisenstein
  composer Strauss
fleer gibe, scoff, smirk, flaunt
Fleming, Ian
  hero James Bond

novel Dr. No, Goldfinger, Thunderball, Casino Royale, Diamonds Are Forever

flesh meat, pulp, stock, tissue
  -eating carnivorous, sarcophagic
  -like carnose
  pert. to sarcous

fleuret epee, sword, flower

flex bend, genuflect

flexion of a limb anaclasis

flight rout, volee, exodus, hegira
  of fancy sally
  of steps perron
  pert. to volar

flightless bird emu, kiwi, ratite
  genus Apteryx, Notornis

flint chert, stone, quartz
  impure chert

flittermouse bat

floating adrift, natant
  grass foxtail
  plant sudd, lotus, frogbit
  wreckage flotsam

flock mob, brood, covey, group, school
  pert. to gregal
  god Pan

floe berg

flogging toco, toko

flood sea, flow, excess, surplus, cataract
  gate clow, gool, sluice
  lights klieg
  tidal eagre

floor deck, playa, platform
  covering mat, rug, tapis, carpet, linoleum
  plank chess
  raised border coaming

flora and fauna biota

floral leaves perianth

Florence
  bridge Ponte Vecchio
  coin florin
  devotees neri
  family Medici
  museum Uffizi, Bargello
  river Arno

floret bracht palea, palet

florid ornate, flowery, rubicund, rhetorical
  style rococo

Florida see Quick Reference List
  fish tarpon
  region Everglades

Flotow opera Martha

flour
  and butter roux
  sifter bolter, sieve
  sprinkle with dredge
  unsorted ata, atta

flow gush, issue, spring, emanate
  out ooze, exude, issue, spill
  tide ebb, flux, neap

flower posy, bloom, unfold, develop
  algae genus Nostoc
  apetalus trema, cactus
  border floroon
  bud knot
  center eye
  cluster cyme, umbel, raceme, paniculate
  envelope perianth
  extract otto, attar
  forgetfulness lotus
  full bloom anthesis
  leaf bract, petal, sepal
  medicinal rue, aloe
  part spur, bract, petal, sepal, anther, carpel, pistil, stamen, corolla
  pistil, part of carpel
  seed ovule
  stalk stem, scape, petiole, peduncle
  grasses genus Stipa
  tree tulip, mimosa, catalpa

flowerless plant fern, moss, lichen, acrogen

flowerlike anthoid

Flowery Kingdom China

fluid juice, steam, liquid
  blood serum, plasma
  mythological blood ichor
  pert. to humoral
  without aneroid

fluosilicate of aluminum topaz

flute pipe, crimp, piccolo
  ancient tibia
  bagpipe chanter
  Hindu bin, pungi

player aulete, fl(a)utist
stop ventage
fly soar, aviate, insect, flutter
  as clouds scud
  block pulley
  catcher peewee, kingbird
  genus Musca
  small gnat, midge
  wings elytron, elytrum
flybane
  flyblow larva
  genus Silene
flycatcher
  bird tody, peewee, redstart
flying
  adder dragonfly
  body meteor
  expert ace
  fish saury, gurnard
  mammal bat
  pert. to aviatic
Flying Dutchman
  composer Wagner
  heroine Senta
Fo Buddha
fodder feed, stover, ensilage
  stalk stover
  storage place barn, silo
  trough manger
foederatus ally
fold bend, reef, flock, crease
  of skin plica
foliage
  mass spray, bouquet, leafage
foliated lobed, spathic
folletto imp, spirit, goblin
follicle crypt
Fomorian one-eyed giant Balor
font basin, laver, source
  holy water stoup
fontanel opening vacuity
food bit, chow, diet, cheer, viands
  comb. form sito, troph(o)
  excessive desire bulimia
  lacking desire asitia
  miracle manna
  pert. to cibarian

perverted desire pica
room for spence
semidigested chyme
soft pap
fool
  scepter bauble
  gold pyrites
  stitch tricot
foot
  and mouth disease murrain
  bone calcis, cuboid, scaphoid, astragalus
  comb. form ped(i), ped(o), pod(o)
  deformity planus, talipes
  -like part pes
  pert. to pedal, podal
  sans apod
  sole plantar
  three-syllable dactyl, anapaest
  two-syllable iambus, spondee, trochee
footed
  large megapod
footprint mold moulage
footrace
  double course diaulos
footstalk strig, pedicel
for pro, toward, because
  aye ever, always
  example e.g., vide
  fear that lest
  instance as, e.g.
  this case alone ad hoc
  this reason ergo, hence
foramen pore, aperture
Forbes hero (Johnny) Tremaine
Forbidden City Lhasa
force
  alleged od, elod
  brief and sudden brunt
  by amain
  down pack, tamp, detrude, trample
  out evict, expel
  unit dyne, staff
forced feeding gavage
Ford's folly Edsel
forearm antebrachium
  bone ulna, radius
  pert. to ulnar

forefoot paw
forehead brow, frons, sinciput
  pert. to metopic, sincipital
foreign alien, exotic, remote
  comb. form xeno
  quarter barrio, ghetto, enclave
  to dehors
foreshank shin
forest wood, grove, sylva
  -fire locater alidade
  glade camas(s)
  god Pan, Tapio, Faunus
  pert. to sylvan, nemoral
Forest City Portland, Savannah, Cleveland
Forester
  hero (Horatio) Hornblower
  novel African Queen
foretelling fatidic, prophetic
forfeit fine, mulct, penalty
  to God deodand
forfex shears
forge shape, falsify, fashion
  tongs tew
  waste dross, sprue
forgetfulness lethe, amnesia, oblivion
  fruit/tree lotus
  river of Lethe
form cast, mode, shape, invent, scheme, compose
  carved scrimsha, statuary
  into arc embow
  into ball conglobe
  into fabric knit, weave
  pert. to modal
  philosophy eidos
formation
  battle line, herse, column
  cell tissue
  flesh sarcosis
  sand dune
former die, old, late, prior, templet
  prefix ex
formicid ant
formless fluid, chaotic, shapeless
  comb. form amorph(o)
Formosa Taiwan
  capital Taipei

Forseti
  father Balder, Baldur
  palace Glitnir
fortification bastion, ravelin, redoubt, palisade
  slope talus
  work redan
Fortuna Tyche
  symbol wheel, rudder
Fortunate Islands Canaries
fortune hap, estate
  goddess Tyche
  teller seer, sibyl, oracle, palmist, prophetess
forty-five
  degree angle octant
  inches ell
forty-third asteroid Eros
For Whom the Bell Tolls
  author Hemingway
  character Maria, Pablo, Pilar, Jordan
fossil fogy, relic, stone
  egg ovulite
  footprint ichnite
  resin amber, retinite
  shell dolite, balanite
  toothlike conodont
founder metal yet(t)er
fountain fons, well, source
  god Fons
  nymph naiad, Egeria
  -of-youth site Bimini
four
  comb. form tetra
  -footed tetrapod, quadruped
  group of tetrad
  inches hand
fourgon car, van, tumbril
Four Horsemen War, Death, Famine, Pestilence
fourteen pounds stone
foveated pitted
fowl hen, bird, cock, chuck, pullet
  kinds malay, poult, snipe, bantam, Houdan, Sussex
fox
  female vixen

genus Vulpes
male stag
paw pad
foxglove popdock
leaf digitalis
Fra Diavolo
composer Auber
fragrant balmy, aromatic
ointment nard, valerian
wood aloe, cedar, mimosa
fram spear
framb(o)esia pian, yaws
frame bin, form, humor, invent
bar of soap sess
cloth-stretching tenter
glass-making drosser
skin-drying herse
supporting horse, trestle
France, French
ancient name Gaul, Gallia
art group Fauves
article see articles
assembly Senat
bacteriologist Pasteur
beast bete
decree arret
dialect patois
dry sec
friend ami(e)
god Dieu
house maison
inn hotel, auberge
maid bonne
measure kilo, minot, toise, kilaire, centiare
museum musee
noon midi
pancake crepe
priest abbe
pronoun il(s), tu, moi, nos, vos, elle(s), nous, vous, notre
railway station gare
saying dit
sister soeur
son fils
star etoile
street rue

water eau
weight gros, kilo, marc, once, livre, gramme
wood bois
Francesca
lover Paolo
Franciscan Capuchin, Minorite, Cordelier
nun Clare
francolin bird, titar, partridge
Frankenstein
author Mary Shelley
character Clerval, Justine, William, Elizabeth, The Monster, Robert Walton, Victor Frankenstein
Frankie
lover Johnny
frankincense gum, thus, incense, olibanum
Frankish hero Roland
Franklin, Benjamin
author of Poor Richard's Almanack
birthplace Boston
inventor of stove, bifocals, lightning rod
Franks, Frankish
hero Roland
king Clovis, Charlemagne
law salic
peasant liti, litus
pert. to salic
fratch dispute, quarrel
fraxinus ash, tree
fream roar
freckle spot, lentigo
remover adarce
Frederick the First (nickname) Barbarossa
Frederick the Great Old Fritz
free lax, liss, loose, slake, gratis, unbind
from bacteria sterile
from blame clear, exonerate
from discount net
-for-all melee
of charge buckshee
of dirt apinoid
time leisure, vacation
freebooter pirate, cateran, corsair
freedom
from fraud bona fides

from pain aponia
  of access entrée
freeholder yeoman
freemason templar
Free State Maryland
freight load, cargo, burden
  car six, gondola
frese bend, furl
freshet flood, spate, inundation
Freudian term id, ego, superego
Frey
  father Njord, Njorth
  sister Freya
  wife Gerd(a), Gerth
Freya
  brother Frey
  father Njord, Njorth
  husband Odin
friar monk, abbot, lister
  bird pimlico
  black Dominican
  gray Franciscan
  mendicant servite
  Robin Hood's Tuck
  white Carmelite
Friday
  rescuer Crusoe
friend pal, ally, crony, patron
  faithful dog, Achates
  false Judas, traitor
Friend Quaker
  church founder George Fox
friendly amicable, benevolent
  relations amity
  understanding entente
Friendly Island Tonga
Friendship author Cicero
frieze kelt (Scot.), adorn
  band taenia
frigate bird iwa
Frigg(a)
  husband Odin
  maid Fulla
  son Balder, Baldur
frill jabot, ruche, ruffle
frog polliwog, amphibian, hoarseness
  comb. form rani, batracho(s)

genus Hyla, Rana, Anura
  -like ranine
  pert. to batrachian
  tree genus Hyla
froise pancake
from fro
  head to foot capapied
  here hence
  that time thence
  the egg ab ovo
front dial, fore, mien, brass, facade
  extend the deploy
  in ahead, forne, anteal
  toward the anterior
frontiersman Cody, Boone, Carson
frontlet band, tiara, frontstall
fronton jai alai court
frostfish smelt, tomcod, scabbard, whitefish
frozen iced, gelid, frappe, congealed
  vapor rime, frost
fruit crop, berry, yield, outcome
  aggregate etaerio, magnolia, raspberry, strawberry
  blemish blet, spot
  comb. form carpo
  decay rot, blet
  dry nut, regma, achene, legume
  flesh pap, meat, pulp
  goddess Pomona
  hybrid pomato
  peddler coster
  pert. to pomonal, pomonic
  pulp pap
  refuse marc
  science carpology
  skin peel, rind, epicarp
  tree genus Olea
Fuegian Ona
fugue theme, tonal, Dorian, diatonic
  answer comes
  special passage stretta
  theme dux
fulcrum bait, prop, support
  oar lock, thole
full sated, mature, rotund, replete
  house SRO
  of cracks rimose

-sized ripe, adult
-size draft or plan epure
suffix ose, ous, itous
fuller
  earth bole
  herb teasel, teazel
fulmar bird, nelly, malduck
Fulton
  steamboat Clermont
fundamental basic, vital, primary, original, elementary
  trigonometry sine, cosine
funeral exequies, interment
  attendant mute
  bell mortbell
  oration elegy, encomium
  pile pyre
  song dirge, elegy, requiem
fungoid tissue trama
fungus mold, yeast, mildew, mushroom
  black ergot
  cells or sacs asci
  disease tinea, mycosis, framboesia
  edible cepe, morel, blewits, truffle, mushroom
  genus Tuber, Amanita, Boletus, Erysibe
  parasitic tinea, awetoergot
  plant uredo
fur coat, hair, pelt, vair, fitch, sable, nutria, pelage
  -bearing animal mink, seal, genet, otter, marten
  collection pelts
  regal ermine
  refuse kemp
furbelow finery, ruffle
Furies Dirae, Eumenides
  avenging Erinyes
  gracious Eumenides
  the three Alecto, Megaera, Tisiphone
furlana dance
fur-lined tippet amice
furnace kiln, stove, smelter
  flue pipe, tewel, chimney
  nozzle tuyere
  part bosh, grate
furniture style Empire, Regency, Colonial, Sheraton, Chippendale, Hepplewhite, Renaissance
furrow sulcus, trench, wrinkle
  having fluted, grooved, guttered
  in a plank rabbet
  minute stria
  notch score
furrowing mark feer, scratch
fur seal ursal
furze whin, gorse, plant
  genus Ulex
fuse melt, weld, solder, combine
  partially frit
fustanella petticoat
futurism
  founder Marinetti
  sculptor Boccioni
fyke net
fylfot cross, emblem, swastika

G

G gee
gab yap, mouth, prate, gibber, jabbler, prattle, chitchat
gabardine cloth, fabric
gabbard, gabbart scow, barge, lighter
gabbro rock, norite
gabel(le) tax, duty, excise, impost
gaberlunzie beggar
gabi taro
gabion cage, basket
Gabon Republic
  capital Libreville
  unit franc
Gabriel man of God, archangel
  instrument horn, trumpet
  spoke to Mary, Zacharias, Zechariah
gaby fool, dunce
gad roam, mooch, traipse
Gad
  brother Asher
  chieftain Ahi
  father Jacob
  mother Zilpah

son Eri, Ozni
tribe Erites
gadfly pest, oestrid, tabanid
Gadhelic Erse, Celtic, Gaelic
gadoid, a hake, codfish, haddock
gadus cod, fish
gadwall duck, fowl
Gaea Ge, Tellus
  husband Uranus
  offspring Giants, Pontus, Titans, Uranus,
    Erinyes
  parent Chaos
Gael, Gaelic Erse, Manx, Scot(ch), Irish,
  Scottish
  clan Sept
  hero Ossian
  John Ian
  land distribution rudale
  poem Duan
  spirit kelpy, banshee
  warrior Dagda, Fenian
gaff hoax, fraud, fleece
gag gegg, retch, throttle
Gaham
  father Nahor
  mother Reumah
Gaheris
  brother Gareth, Gawain
  father Lot
  uncle Arthur
  victim Margawse, Morgause
gain buy, earn, attain, realize
  ill-gotten pelf, graft, payola
gainsay deny, forbid, impugn
Gainsborough, Thomas
  artwork The Blue Boy, The Morning
    Walk, Peasant Girl Gathering Sticks
gait lope, shamble, carriage
  of a horse lope, pace, trot, canter, gallop
gaiter spat, puttee
gala fete, merry, festal
galago lemur, monkey
Galahad
  father La(u)ncelot
  mother Elaine
  quest Holy Grail
Galam Shea

Galatea
  father Nereus
  husband Pygmalion
  lover Acis
  mother Doris
galaxy nebula
Galba
  predecessor Nero
  successor Otho
gale gust, easter, declaim
galea helmet
Galen physician
  forte medicine
Galician river San, Styr
galilee porch, portico
Galilee
  ruler Herod
  town Cana, Nain, Nazareth, Tiberias
Galileo Galilei
  author of Dialogue, Discourses
  birthplace Pisa
  constructed telescope
  discovered Jupiter's satellites
  inventor of sector, thermometer
  nationality Italian
  studied motion, pendulum
galimatias gibberish
galingale root, sedge
galiot galley, merchant ship
galipot sap, resin, barras
gall vex, fret, annoy, harass, rancor
gallant brave, swain, escort, suitor
galled mad, sore, peeved
galleon boat, argosy, carrack
  cargo oro
gallery salon, museum, piazza
  open loggia
galliard hardy, lively, valiant
Gallic French
  chariot essed(e)
gallimaufry hash, medley, ragout, hodge-
    podge
gallinaceous rasorial
  bird quail, turkey, chicken, pheasant
gallinae grouse, quails, rasores, chickens,
    peafowls
  order rasores

gallinipper mosquito
gallinule hen, coot, rail
galliwasp lizard
galloon lace, trimming
gallows crap, frame, hanging
  bird villain, criminal
  pert. to patibulary
galluses braces, suspenders
gally worry, terrify, frighten
Galway island Aran
galyak fur, yak, cattle, hybrid
gam leg, pod, mouth, visit
Gambia
  capital Banjul
  monetary unit dalasi
gambit move, ruse, device, maneuver
gambler dicer, blackleg
  accomplice shill
  stake pot, pool
gambling
  cube(s) die, dice
  pert. to aleatory
gamboge tree family calaba
gambol hop, play, caper, prank, cavort
game fun, sport, strategy
  ball (tip)cat, tut, fives, pelota
  board keno, chess, halma, salta, checkers, cribbage, backgammon
  card hoc, loo, war, faro, fish, skat, poker, rummy, whist, euchre, bridge, hearts, old maid, reversi, solitaire, crazy eights
  carnival darts, hoopla
  child's tag, potsy, leapfrog, red rover, mother may I, green light/red light
  confidence bunko
  court rogue, pelota, tennis, croquet, jai alai, basketball
  dice ludo, craps, parchesi, trey-trip
  gambling beno, faro, boule, rondo, stuss, lottery, blackjack
  goal run, score, spare, tally, touchdown
  Gr. agon
  marbles taw
  rule maker Hoyle
  Scot. shinty
  small bird, fowl
  stewed in wine salmi, ragout

  using fingers mora
  war kriegspiel
  word crambo, anagram, acrostic, hangman
gamete egg, ovum, sperm, zygote, oosphere
gamic sexual
gamin imp, tad, monkey, urchin
  domain street
gamine hoyden, tomboy
gammon ham, dupe, humbug, deceive, mislead
gammy bad, lame, sore
gamp umbrella
gamut orbit, scale, extent, series
gamy rank, funky, spicy, lustful
ganch kill, impale, execute
gander goose, glance, stroll, wander
Gandhi
  name Bu, Aba, Abu, Abba, Abou, Bapu, India, Mahatma
  publication Harijan
gandul loafer
ganef ganov, thief, gonnif
Ganesa, Ganesh
  father S(h)iva
  head elephant
  mother Parvati
gang mob, set, pack, horde
Ganges River Benares
  dolphin susu
  efflorescence Reh
  goddess Gangadevi
  vessel puteli, putelee
ganglion tumor, nucleus
gangrel beggar
gangrene rot, decay, mortify, necrosis
gangster goon, hood, thug, mobster
  female companion moll
gangue matrix
gannet fowl, goose, solan
  family sula
ganoid fish gar, bowfin, sturgeon
Ganymede
  abductor Zeus, Jupiter
  brother Ilus
  father Tros
  function cupbearer
gaol brig, jail, prison

gap col, flaw, cleft, breach, lacuna
gape ope, gaze, rictus, rubberneck
gapes rictus
gapeseed starer
gaping open, ringent
  of plant capsule dehiscence
garand rifle
garb dress, getup, attire, vesture
  kind toga, mourning, sackcloth
garble bolt, sort, mangle, pervert
garboil confusion, turbulence
garçon boy, lad, waiter, bachelor
garden patch, Eden
  implement hoe, rake, mower, scythe,
    sickle, trowel, weeder
  kind herb, formal, botanical, vegetable
  of golden apples Hesperides
  protector Priapus
Garden City Chicago
Gareth
  brother Gawain, Gaheris
  father Lot
  mother Margawse, Morgause
  slayer La(u)ncelot
  uncle Arthur
  wife Liones
garfish snook, hornbeak
gargantuan huge, titanic, enormous
garibaldi blouse
garish loud, cheap, tawdry, dazzling
garland lei, crown, anadem, festoon
garlic ramp, chive
  root bulb, ramson
  segment clove
  wild moly
garment suit, wrap, dress, attire,
  vestment
  Afghan postin, pos(h)teen
  Afr. kaross, dashiki
  ancient toga, chlamys
  Arab aba, haik
  bishop's cope, chimer, rochet, gremial
  Brit. brat, mac(k)intosh
  Burmese tamein
  fitted reefer
  Gr. tunic, chiton
  Hindu sari, saree

  hooded (d)jellaba
  infant's woolly, bunting
  knight's mail, tabard
  Malay cabaya, sarong
  mourning weeds
  Muslim izar
  priest's alb, amice, stole
  rain poncho, slicker
  sleeveless cape, vest, mantle
  tuniclike tabard
  Turkish dolman
garnet red, jewel, pyrope
  berry currant
  black melanite
garret loft, attic
garrot fowl, tourniquet
garruline bird jay
garth yard, garden
garvey boat, scow
garvie fish, sprat
gas damp, fuel, fume, reek, vapor
  blue ozone
  charcoal oxan(e)
  charge with aerate
  colorless oxan(e), ethane, ketone
  comb. form aer, aero
  inert neon, argon, xenon
  marsh methane
  nonflammable helium
  poisonous arsine, stibine
gasconade boast, vaunt, bravado
gaseous thin, tenuous, aeriform
  element neon, radon, oxygen
  hydrocarbon ethane
gash cut, slit, witty, incision
gasket lute, ring, seal
gasp gape, pant, heave
Gaspar
  companion Melchoir, Balthazar
  gift frankincense
gast alarm, scare, frighten
gastropod slug, limpet
  ear-shaped abalone
  genus Harpa, Oliva, Nerita
  marine murex, tethys, aplysia
gat gun, pistol, channel, passage
gate entry, portal

flood sluice
rear postern
gatehouse bar, lodge
Gates of Hercules Gibralter
Gath
  giant Goliath
gather reap, muster, collect, convene
  and compare collate
gaucho cowboy
  knife bolo
  lariat bolas
  weapon machete
gaud adorn, bauble, finery, trinket, ornament
gaudy loud, showy, garish, tawdry
gauffer crimp, flute, pleat
gaufre wafer, waffle
gauge size, type, measure
  face dial
  pointer arm, hand
  rain udometer
Gauguin, Paul Eugène Henri
  artwork Nevermore, The Tahitians, The White Horse, The Yellow Christ, Be in Love and You'll Be Happy
  birthplace Paris
  island home Tahiti
Gaul France, Gallia (Lat.)
  ancient people Celt, Remi
  chariot esses, esseda
  city Alesia
  gods Esus (vegetation), Taranis (thunder)
  people Remi
  priest Druid
  river goddess Belisama
  seer vates
gaulding bird, egret, heron
gaum daub, heed, understand
gaunt bony, spare, hollow, meager
gauntlet cuff, glove, challenge
gauster brag, bully, gossip, bluster
Gautama Buddha, Siddhartha
  mother Maya
  son Rahula
  wife Ahalya
gauze film, leno, crepe, lisse

gavel mace, usury, hammer, mallet
gavial crocodile
Gawain
  brother Gaheris
  father Lot
  mother Margawise
  slayer Lancelot
  son Lovel, Florence, Gyngalyn
  uncle Arthur
  victim Uwayne, Lamerok
gawk oaf, lout, klutz, stare
gawky clumsy, gauche, awkward
gawn tub, pail
gay airy, keen, jovial, mirthful
Gay John, Enola
Gaza
  victor Allenby
gazabo guy, fellow, person
gaze eye, gape, moon, ogle, scan
gazebo alcove, pagoda, belvedere
gazelle dama, kudu, corinne
  Afr. admit, mohr
  Asian ahu
  four-horned chikara
  Tibetan goa
gazette paper, record, courant
geal ice, jelly, congeal
gean cherry
gear cam, cog, dress, aludel, matter
geason rare, scant, scarce
geaster earthstar
Geats
  king Hygelac
  prince Beowulf
Geb
  father Shu
  offspring Set, Isis, Osiris
  wife Nu, Nut
gecko lizard, tarente
Gedaliah
  father Ahikam, Pashhur, Jeduthun
  slayer Ishmael
Gehenna pit, hell, abyss, Sheol
gel set, gelate, harden, thicken
gelatin agar, jelly, collin
  plate (printing) bat
geld dry, spay, alter, prunegarble

gelid icy, cold, frozen, glacial
gell fun, spree, frolic, carousal
gem jewel, stone, bedeck, masterpiece
  carved cameo, intaglio
  changeable chatoyant
  face bezel, facet
  imitation glass, paste, strass
  imperfect loupe
  inlaying for crusta
  measure carat
  support setting
Gemariah
  brother Ahikam
  father Hilkiah, Shaphan
gemel twin
geminate double, paired, coupled
Gemini twins
  star Castor, Pollux
gemmation budding
gemmule bud, ovule
gemot court, meeting, assembly
gemsbok goat, oryx, chamois
gemutlich cozy, genial, agreeable
gendarme soldier, policeman
gender sex, instrument
  common to both epicene
gene factor, determiner
genealogy account, lineage, progeny
general wide, broad, vague
  Am. Meade, Custer, Patton, Powell, Marshall, Pershing, Eisenhower, Schwarzkopf
  Am. Revolutionary Knox, Ward, Greene, Washington
  aspect facies
  Austrian Wallenstein
  Brit. Gage, Howe, Clive, Wolfe, Cromwell, Wellington
  Carthaginian Hamilcar, Hannibal
  Chinese Ye, Feng, Chang
  Civil War Lee, Bragg, Grant, Meade, Sherman
  comb. form cen(o), caen(o), pano
  effect ensemble
  Fr. Foch, Petain, de Gaulle, Montcalm
  Ger. Jodl, Kleist, Rommel, Ludendorff
  Jp. Tojo, Koiso, Yasuda

  Mex. Zapata, Santa Anna
  Prussian Schamhorst
  Roman Sulla, Caesar, Fabius, Marius, Pompey
  Russ. Zhdanov, Yeremenko
  Sp. Alba, Alva, Franco
  Swedish Wrangel
general assembly plenum
generate make, beget, develop, produce
generation era, kind, posterity
  spontaneous abiogenesis
generic common, general, universal
generous kind, ample, lavish, profuse
genesis alpha, birth, origin, outset, nascency
genet berbe, horse
genetic hereditary
  material DNA, RNA, cistron, chromosome
  term synapsis, backcross
geniculate bent
genipap fruit
  tree dye lana
Genoa
  coin jane, genovino
  family Doria
  magistrate doge
genos clan, gens, family
genouillere kneelet, knee piece
gens clan, nomen, people
gentle tame, placid
  music direction amabile
  slope glacis
Gentlemen Prefer Blondes
  author Loos
genu flexure, bend
genuflect bend, kneel, curtsy
genus sort, type, class
  antelope Oryx
  bear Ursus
  bee Apis
  beech Fagus
  bivalve Pinna, Anomia
  cat Felis
  dog Canis
  duck Aix, Anas
  elm Ulmus, Celtis

fox Vulpes
frog Rana, Anura
goat Capra
hare Lepus
hog Sus
horse Equus
lizard Uta, Agama
monkey Cebus
oyster Ostrea
pigeon Goura, Columba
sheep Ovis
spider Agalena, Aranea
spider monkey Ateles
swan Olor
whale Inia
wolf Canis
geode voog, druse, nodule
geographer
  Am. Huntington
  Flemish Mercator
  Ger. Ratzel
  Gr. Strabo, Ptolemy
geological earth, science
  division eon, era, Lias, Trias
  epoch Miocene, Pliocene, Pleistocene
  era Cenozoic, Mesozoic, Paleozoic
  period Triassic, Jurassic, Cretaceous
  remains fossils
  stage riss
  vein angle hade
geomancy divination
geometrical
  body lune, prism, sphere
  figure solid, square, ellipse
  line(s) loci, locus
  point relating to curve acnode
  theory conics
geometry
  angle incidence
  coordinate abscissa(s)
  father Euclid
  figure cone, lune, prism, oblong, ellipse
  ratio pi
  rule theorem
  solid cone, cube, sphere
  surface nappe, torus
  term versor

geophagous pical
geoponic rural, rustic, bucolic
Georgia see Quick Reference List
Georgia (Caucasus) island Sapelo
  people Svan(e)
  queen Tamara
Gera
  father Bela
  grandfather Benjamin
  son Ehud, Shimei
Geraint
  wife Enid
gerefa reeve, bailiff
gerent ruler, manager
germ bug, spore, virus, bacteria (pl.)
  fermenting zyme
  freedom from asepsis
  seed chit
German, Germany Hun, Almain, Teuton
  about etwa
  article das, der, die, ein
  but aber
  child kind
  coin mark, albus, krone, thaler
  day tag
  dog hund
  foot fuss
  fruit obst
  god Donar, Wodan (Odin), Wotan
  hill berg
  lyric poems lieder
  measure aam, eimer, kette
  no nein
  pronoun ich, uns, du, sie
  valley tal, thal
  weight loth, tonne
  woman frau
Gershom, Gershon
  father Levi
  son Libni, Shimei
Gershwin Ira, George
  opera Porgy and Bess
Gertrude
  husband Claudius
  son Hamlet
Geryon
  dog Orthus

father Chrysaor
mother Callirrhoe
slayer Hercules
gesso chalk, gypsum, plaster
get take, secure, acquire, procure
  around cajole, circumvent
  away scat, shoo, escape
geum herb, avens, plant
gewgaw bauble, trifle, bibelot
geyser hot (spring)
  mouth crater
geyserite opal
ghee butter
Ghent
  river Lys, Schelde
ghost d(a)emon, haunt, spirit, lemures
  comb. form scio
  fish chiro
giant vast, jumbo, colossus, gargantua
  evil Loki, Jotun(n), Goliath
  god (Norse) Hymer, Hymir
  Gr. myth Gyges, Cottus, Cyclops
  Hindu Bana
  hundred eyes Argus
  land of Utgarthar
  Old Testament Anak, Goliath
  one-eyed Arges, Cyclops, Polyphemus
  race Anak
  sea demon Wade
  strong Titan
  thousand-armed Bana
giaour Christian, unbeliever
gibbet jib, gallows
gibbous convex, rounded
gibe scoff, heckle
Gibralter
  Cape Trafalgar
  founder Gebir
  point opposite Ceuta
gibus hat
gift bent, favor, talent, present, donation
  conciliatory sop
gila monster lizard
Gileadite judge Jair
gilsonite asphalt, uintaite
gimcrack toy, bauble, trifle
gimmer ewe, clasp

gin game, snare, liquor
  type sloe
ginger pep, spice, spirit
  genus Zingiber
  pine cedar
  wild asarum
gingerbread cake, money
  tree dum, doom
ginseng herb, plant, aralia
giraffe piano, spinet, camelopard
  -like animal okapi
girasol(e) opal, artichoke, sunflower
girdle obi, ring, sash
  pert. to zonal
  Roman cestus
  saddle cinch
  sash cummerband
girl chit, minx, damsel
  cover model
  graceful nymph, sylph
  lively filly, giglet
gist nub, heart, essence
give cede, waive, bestow, impart
  back remit, remise, restore
  forth emit, proclaim
  law devise, remise, bequeath
  up cede, devote, render, resign
gizz wig
glabrous bald, slick
glacial icy, gelid, frigid
  chasm crevasse
  deposit placer, moraine
  hill paha
  ice block serac
  ridge as(ar), os(ar), kame, eskar, esker
  snow firn, neve
  waste deposit drift
glacier
  erosion cirque, corrie
  facing stoss
  shafts moulins
glad fain, happy, blithe, elated, joyous
  tidings gospel, evangel
glade gap, vale, clearing
  comb. form nemo
gladiator fencer, athlete, battler,
  combatant

competitions ludi
trainer lanista
glairy slick, frosty, slippery
gland organ, adrenal, pituitary
  edible ris, noix, liver
  salivary parotid
  secretion saliva, hormone, insulin,
    adrenaline
glass lens, pane, goblet
  artificial gems paste, strass
  blue smalt
  bubble in ream, seed
  ingredient sand, potash, silica
  jar bocal, mason
  make into sheets platten
  molten parison
  mosaic tessera
  scum gall
  small pony, vial
  volcanic obsidian
glassmaking
  frame drosser
  material frit(t)
  oven lehr, tisar
glasswort jume, kali, plant
Glaucus
  father Sisyphus
  son Bellerophon
  wife Ione
glazier glassworker
  diamond emery, emeril
glazing machine calender
glebe sod, clod, soil, benefice
glebe bird kite
gleed coal, ember
gleeman minstrel
gleg keen, alert, sharp
gliadin glutin, protein, prolamin
gliding over labile, eliding
glioma tumor
globe earth, sphere
  fish diodon
  -like orbed, globular
glockenspiel lyra, carillon, xylophone
glonoin nitroglycerin
glory honor, kudos, aureola
  cloud of nimbus

glot
  comb. form languages
glottal stop stoss
glove mitt(en), gauntlet
  leather kid, napa
  shape trank
glucose honey, dextrose
glucoside root gein
glume husk, bract, chaff
glutin gelatin, gliadin
glutinous sizy, viscid, tenacious
gluttony greed, edacity, voracity
glycolaidehyde diose, sugar
gnede scanty, sparing, miserly
gnome imp, nis, dwarf, maxim, gremlin
  Ger. kobold
  N.A. owl
gnomic didactic, aphoristic
gnomon of a sundial pin, style
gnostic wise, clever
  representation abrasax, abraxas
  second-century sethite
gnu kokoon, antelope, wildebeast
go quit, sally, proceed
  about, nautical tack, wear
  astray err, diverge, aberrate
  away flee, scram, depart
  back return, revert
  forth fare, mosey, travel
goa gazelle
goal end, meta, tally, purpose
  distant reach, thule, destination
goat kid, billy, victim
  Angora chamal
  astronomy Capricorn
  cloth camlet, mohair
  genus Capra
  -like lewd, caprine, hircine
  male buck, billy
goatfish mullet
goatsucker potoo, nighthawk, whippoorwill
gobbet bit, lump, mass, chunk, fragment
goblet glass, tallboy
  constellation crater
  Eucharistic chalice
goby fish, mapo
god idol, deity

false Baal, idol, Baalim (pl.)
home Asgard, heaven, Olympus
god(s)
  Aztec Xipe, Eecati, Meztli
  Buddhist Deva
  Gr. Pan, Ares, Eros, Zeus, Pluto, Apollo,
    Hermes
    beauty Apollo, Helios
    dream Oniros
    hurricane Otus
    marriage Hymen
    underworld Python
    wine Bacchus
  Roman Lar, Pan, Faun, Mars, Cupid,
    Pales, Picus, Apollo, Boreas, Neptune
    death Mors
    fire Vulcan
    night Somnus
    sleep Somnus, Morpheus
goddess(es) Dea
  Egyptian Mut, Amen, Iris, Sekhet
    heavens Nut
    joy Hathor
    life Isis
    sky Nut
  Gr. Alea, Eris, Athena, Artemis, Nemesis,
    Aphrodite
    destiny Moera
    earth Ge, Gaea
    fire Hestia
    love Aphrodite
    moon Io, Diana, Selena, Selene,
    Artemis, Astarte
  Hawaiian
    fire Pele
  Peru
    fertility Mama
  Roman Nox, Nyx, Ceres, Diana, Vesta
    beauty Venus
    dawn Aurora
    death Proserpine
    earth Lua, Tellus
    fertility Fauna
    flowers Flora
    harvest Ops
    love Venus
    night Nox, Nyx

    plenty Ops
    war Vacuna, Minerva
goddess(es)
  classification
    air Aura, Hera
    arts Muse, Athena
    birth Parca, Lucina
    chase Diana, Artemis
    destiny Norn, Moera
    faith Fides, Clotho
    halcyon days Alcyone
    hope Spes
    justice Dice, Maat, Astraea
    life Isis
    memory Mnemosyne
gold au(rum), oro, cyme, wealth
  assaying cup cupel
  black oil
  coating gilt, gilding
  collar carcanet
  deposit lode, placer
  imitation ormolu, pinchbeck
  in alchemy sol
  -like aureate
  native nugget
  pert. to auric
  symbol Au
Gold Coast
  colony Togo
  language Twi, Akan, Fanti
  native Ga
golden auric, yellow, precious
  age Saturnian
goldeneye bird, whistler
golden fleece
  land Colchis
  seeker Jason
  ship Argo
goldenrod
  genus Solidago
golem booby, dunce, robot, automaton
goliard jester, minstrel
gombeen usury
gomeral dolt, fool, simpleton
gomuti ejoo, palm, areng
gonad ovary, testis, spermary
gonagra gout

Goneril
  father Lear
  sister Regan, Cordelia
gonfalon flag, banner, standard
good moral, valid, honest, genuine,
    palatable
  arrangement eutaxie
  -for-nothing ket, shotten
  -luck cap, newborn caul
  working order kilter
goods stock, effects
  admission of taking avowry
  cast overboard jetsam
  law bona
  movable chattels
  package box, bale, crate, carton
  sunk at sea lagan
goose dupe, fowl, gannet
  barnacle anatifer
  cry honk, cackle
  flock raft, gaggle
  genus Chen, Anser
  pert. to anserine
  wild barnacle
  young gosling
goosefoot blite, plant, shrub
gore stab, pierce
  of cloth gusset
Gorgon Medusa, Stheno, Euryale
  watchers for Enyo, Deino, Graeae,
    Pephredo
Gorki, novelist Maxim
gorse whin, furze
gossip cat, prate, rumor, babble, tattle,
    talebearer
  tattling piet
Gothic medieval, barbarous
  arch ogive
  bard runer
  vault's groin ogive
gourd flask, melon
  fruit pepo
  sponge loofa, luffa
government rule, sway, policy, regime
  by ten decarchy
  by women gynarchy, gynecocracy
  control regime, regimen

form polity
  without acracy, anarchy
gowan daisy, flower
gowk cuckoo, simpleton
Graces
  mother Aegle
  one Aglaia, Thalia, Euphrosyne
gracile slim, slender, sylphic
gradient slope, ascent, incline
gradus dictionary
graft cion, join, bribe, joint
  taker bribee
grafted heraldry ente
grail ama, cup, bowl, chalice, sangreal
  knight Bors, Galahad, Percivale
grain atom, iota, seed, particle
  black urd
  husk bran, glume
  measure moy, peck, grist, bushel
  pit silo
  refuse pug, chaff
  shelter barn, hutch
  to be ground grist
gramary magic
gramineous grassy
grammar
  logic and/or rhetoric trivia, trivium
grammatical
  arrangement syntax
  case dative
  construction synesis
  term parse, gender
grampus orc(a), whale, killer
grandchild oe, oy(e)
  great ieroe
grandfather atavus, ancestor, patriarch
  pert. to aval, avital
Grandma Moses Anna
grandmother beldam(e), granny, babushka
    (Russ.), matriarch
  Devil's Baba
granite
  constituent mica, quartz, feldspar,
    orthoclase
  porphyry elvan
grant admit, bestow, confer
  of rights deed, charter, franchise

grape berry, fruit
  bunch bob
  genus Vitis, Muscadinia
  -like berry uva
  wine disease erinose
grappling iron grapnel
grasp grip, hent, close, comprehend
grasping avid, miserly, rapacious
  adapted for prehensile, prehensive
grass sod, lawn, turf
  bamboolike reed
  blade leaf, spike, traneen
  bunch stipa
  devil's couch
  dried hay, fodder
  genus Poa, Coix, Avena, Stipa
  husk glume
  Kentucky blue poa
  rope-making mung
grasshopper grig, locust, katydid
gratinate cook, brown, crisp
gratis free, gratuitous
gratulation joy
graupel hail, sleet
gravamen complaint, grievance
grave tomb, carve, quiet
  cloth shroud, cerement
  mound barrow, tumulus
gravid pregnant
gray old, ashen, hoary, grizzled
  comb. form polio
  matter obex, brain, cortex, intellect
greasewood chico, shrub, chamiso
great huge, eminent, titanic
  artist master
  comb. form mega(lo), magni
greaves amor, cracknel, cracklings
grebe fowl, dabchick
gree goodwill
Greece, Greek Crete, Achaia, Helene
  abbess Amma
  assembly pnyx, agora
  clan Obe
  coin obol(us), mina, ducat, lepta, nomas,
    diobol(on), phenix, drachma
  column Doric, Ionic
  contest agon

  cupid Eros
  dance hormos, strophe
  drama mime
  drinking cup cotyle, holmos
  epic Iliad, Odyssey
  Furies Alecto, Erinyes, Megaera,
    Tisiphone
  garment chiton, peplos, chlamys
  headband taenia
  huntress Atalanta
  life bios
  marketplace agora
  measure bema, cados, dichas, hektos,
    stremma
  note, music nete
  pitcher olpe
  priest papa
  sacred place Abaton
  soothsayer Calchas
  theater odeon
  tunic chiton
  wine pitcher olpe
  word logos
green verd, unripe, unskilled
  -eyed jealous
  sand marl
greenfinch linnet, sparrow, grosbeak
greenheart wood, bebeeru
greenlet vireo, songbird
greenroom foyer, gossip
grego cloak, jacket
Gregorian doxology Euouae
gribble borer
gride rasp, scrape
grieve weep, lament, agonize
griffe spur, mulatto
griffin monster, vulture
grifter con man, swindler
  assistant shill
grilse fish, salmon
grimalkin cat, moll, woman
grinding
  stone mano, metate
  substance emery, abrasive,
    carborundum
gringo Americano, foreigner
gripple miserly, avaricious

Griqua mulatto
griskin loin
grit sand, pluck, gravel
grith peace, security, sanctuary
grivet tota, waag, monkey
grommet loop, ring, eyelet
groove rut, score, routine
  cut in barrel croze, rifle
  in masonry raggle
  minute/pilaster stria
grosbeak finch, sparrow, cardinal
grotto cave, grot, cavern
ground base, foundation, pulverized
  parcel plot, solum
  rising hurst, knoll
groundhog marmot, woodchuck
  day Candlemas
group band, squad, cluster, congregation
  of species genus, phylum
  together band, file, meet, cluster
grouse bird, grumble, complain
  gathering lek
  genus Bonasa
grout meal, dregs, mortar, grounds, sediment
grove tope, copse, thicket
  pert. to nemoral
grow wax, become, augment, develop,
   enlarge
  old age, ripen, senesce
  in couples binate
  out enate
growth corn, shoot, stubble, increase
  process of nascency development
  retarding paratonic
grue ice, snow
gruff blunt, short
grugru palm, larva
grume clot
grumous thick, clotted
grunt fish ronco, croaker
Grus crane, constellation
guachoncho fish pelon
guaiac seed, tonka bean
guanay cormorant
  droppings guano
guano manure, fertilizer
  source bats, guanay

guarapucu shrub, wahoo
guardian angel, warden, trustee
  church relics mystagogue
  subject ward
  watchful Argus
Guatemala, Guatemalan
  grass teosinte
  insect kelep
  money que(t)zal
  plain Peten
  volcano Fuego, Atitlan
gudgeon dupe, gull
guenon mona, grivet, monkey
guerdon prize, reward, recompense
guiding polar, dirigent
  star North, Cynosure, Lodestar
guidon flag, marker, streamer
Guido's scale
  highest note e la
  low note ut
  note ut, e la, e la mi
guile craft, fraud, wiles
guillemot auk, bird, quet
Guinea coin, fowl
  corn durra, millet
  fowl pintado
  native Susu, Fulani, Malinke
  pig, animal-like pika
  squash eggplant
guinea pig cavy, paca
  genus Cavia
  male boar
guitar tiple
  India vina
  Oriental sitar
  small uke, ukelele
guitguit bird, honey, creeper
gula cyma, gullet
gulf gap, pit, eddy, abysm
  weed sargasso
gull bird, dupe, larid
  -like skua, jaeger, teaser
  pert. to larine
gully ditch, gorge, arroyo
gum wax, tree, resin
  Ar. tree kikar
  astringent kino

boil abscess, parulis
plant ule, hule
white camphor
wood xylan
gumma tumor
gums uva
gun arm, rod, musket, weapon
  caliber bore
  chamber gomer
  handle stock
  lock part sear, catch
  pointer device
  sight bead
gunnel fish, blenny, gunwale
gunwale pin thole
gurgitation surging, whirling
gurnard fish, rochet
  genus Trigla
gusset gore, insert, bracket
gutta drop, spot, treenail
  percha balata
guttle gorge, gormandize
guttural gruff, husky, velar
gym feat kip(p)
gymnosophist nudist
gynoecium pistil(s)
gypsy nomad, wanderer
  fortune bahi
  girl chi, chai
  husband rom
  language Romany
  man chal
gyp con, scam, swindle
gyre eddy, ring, vortex
gyrene marine, leatherneck
gyves irons, fetters, shackles

H

H aitch
habergeon jacket, hauberk
habile apt, fit, handy, clever
habit garb, dress, usage, routine
  prefix eco
habitually silent reserved, taciturn

habituate drill, inure, frequent
  to weather/surroundings acclimate
hachure lines
hack ax, hoe, taxi, cough, stale
  driver cabbie
  literary devil, poetaster, scribbler
  worker jobber
hackbut arquebus, harquebus
hackney fly, fiacre
  driver jarvey
Hades pit, hell, aralu, orcus, Pluto, Sheol
  abyss below Tartarus
  guard Cerberus
  related to abyss, limbo
  river Styx, Lethe, Acheron
  wheel turner ixion
hadj pilgrimage
hagfish cyclostome
haha wall, fence, laugh
haiku poem
hair fur, nap, shag, tress, filament
  band fillet
  braid cue, pigtail
  coarse seta
  comb. form pil(o), chaet(o), tricho
  covered with lanate, pilose, shaggy
  disease mange, plica, xerasia
  falling out psilosis
  mass shock
  nostril vibrissa
  pigment melanin
  prefix crini
  tuft floccus
  unruly cowlick
hairiness pilosity, villosity
hairpin bodkin
Haiti, Haitian Hispaniola
  coin gourde
  evil spirit baka, bako
  sweet potato batata
  voodoo deity zombie
hake gadid, whiting
  kin cod
Hale, Nathan spy, patriot
half demi, hemi, semi, moiety, partial
  -baked amateurish, sophomoric
  -breed metis(se), mestee

brother half sib(ling)
man, half bull bucentaur
man, half dragon cecrops
man, half fish dagon, mermaid
man, half goat Pan, faunus
man, half horse centaur
mask loup, domino
-moon arc, lune, crescent
month fortnight
turn caracole
halibut butt, sole, flatfish
Halicarnassus' wonder mausoleum
halite (rock) salt
halitus aura, vapor, breath
hall dorm, salle, atrium, vestibule
  concert odeum
  heroes Valhalla
  round rotunda
halluces digits
hallux (big, great) toe
halogen iodine, bromine, chlorine
  compound halide
halting place inn, etape, oasis,
    caravansary
ham hock, meat, actor
  hog gammon
  slice rasher
Hamite Masai, Somal(i), Berber, Libyan
  language Numidian
Hamlet
  beloved Ophelia
  castle Elsinore
  country Denmark
  friend Horatio
  uncle Claudius
hammer bang, beat, maul, sledge,
    malleate
  auctioneer's gavel
  ear malleus
  head peen, poll
  part claw, head, peen
  striking part tup
hammerhead bat, bird, fish, shark
hamstring lame, maim, tendon, cripple
hanaper basket, hamper
hand aid, paw, pud, deal, help, manus,
    applause

by manual
cart barrow
clap to music tal
comb. form chiro
jurist learned
measure span
palm loaf, volar, thenar
handbill leaf, flyer, poser, throwaway
handle grip, hilt, wield, manage, operate
  boat tiller
  cup ear
  having ansate
  printing press raunce
  roughly paw, maul
  sword hilt
handrail (kind of) manrope, bannister
hands
  having two bimanous
  on hips akimbo
  pert. to manual
  without amanous
handsel token, present, earnest
handwriting fist, hand, script, penmanship
  bad cacography
  expert chirographer
  on the wall mene, tekel, graffiti
  pert. to graphic
  style character
handwritten
  document/will holograph
hangar shed, (aero)drome, shelter
  area apron
hangbird oriole
hanging pendant, pendent, pending,
    suspended, unsettled
  apparatus gibbet, gallows
  crookedly alop
  downward cernous
  noose of hangman halter
hangrail whitlow
hank coil, loop, skein
Hannibal
  conquered by Scipio
  father Hamilcar
  defeat Zama
  victory site Cannae
hanse guild, league

Hansen's disease leprosy
happen fare, occur, befall, transpire
  again recur
  in the end eventuate
  together concur, coincide
happening event, tiding, incident, occasion
  before due rath(e), premature
  by chance fortuitous
hara-kiri, hari-kari seppuku, suicide
harbor cove, haven, cherish, shelter
  boat tug
  laborer stevedore
  small marina
  wall jetty
hard dour, rigid, solid, stern, adamant
  bed pallet
  cash specie
  fat suet
  prefix dis
  rubber ebonite
hardhack rose, shrub, spirea
hardhead sculpin, menhaden
hardtack bread, wafer, pantile
hardwood ash, elm, oak, teak, ebony, maple, yakal, hickory, mahogany
hare cony, pika, malkin
  family leporid
  female doe
  genus Lepus
  male buck
  tail scut
  young leveret
harem serai, zenana, seraglio
  room oda
  slave odalisk, odalisque
haricot (kidney) bean, stew
harlot rahab, strumpet, prostitute
harmattan wind
harness rig, gear, draft, equip
  bull cup
  horse tackle, headgear
  men's bricole
  ring terret
  strap crupper
harrier dog, hawk, falcon
harsh stern, coarse, drastic, rasping

  critic slater
  sound roar, stridon
  sounding strident
  taste acerb, bitter
hart deer, stag
hartebeest asse, tora, lecama, antelope, bontebok
  kin sassaby
hartshorn antlers
hartstongue fern
haruspex priest, soothsayer
harvest crop, reap, yield
  bug tick, chigger
  feast Kirn
  festival Lammas
  man daddy-longlegs
hashish hemp, bhang, cannabis
hashmark stripe
hask dry, cold, harsh, coarse
hassock boss, pess, buffet, cushion
hasty pudding mush, supawn
hat cap, beret, toque, sconce, topper, headgear
  brimless fez, toque
  collapsible gibus
  crown poll
  ecclesiastic biretta
  medieval abacot, bycoket
  part band, brim, lining
  sl. lid
  trimming vouleau
  pert. to castorial
  pith topi, topee
  straw boater
hatchet ax(e), tomahawk
  handle helve
  stone mogo
  type claw, lathing
hate abhor, detest, malice, dislike
  comb. form mis(o)
hatred odium, enmity, phobia, animosity
  of change misoneism
  of children misopedia
  of foreigners xenophobia
  of mankind misanthropy
  of marriage misogamy
  of women misogyny
haulm hay, culm, stem, stalk, straw

hautboy oboe, strawberry
have own, hold, retain, possess
  effect tell
  feet pedate
  limits finite
  offensive smell olid, stink
  same origin cognate
  scruples demur
haver oat, babble, nonsense
Hawaii, Hawaiian Kanaka, Polynesian;
  see Quick Reference List
  basket ie
  canoe waapa
  chant mele
  cookout luau
  dance hula
  fiber pulu
  food poi, kalo, taro
  garment holoku, muumuu
  temple heiau
  woman wahine
hawk cry, sell, osprey, cheater, vulture
  bill pawl
  blind seel
  cage mew
  carrier cad
  claw talon
  falconry bater
  fish osprey
  genus Buteo, Accipiter
  male tercel
  nest aery
  small eyas, kite
  swoop souse
hay bed, net, fence, grass, hedge
  bundle bale, rick, wisp
  kind clover, alfalfa, timothy
  second cutting rowen
  spreader kicker, tedder
  storage mow, loft
haying job ted, pitch
haze fog, film, glin, vapor
  thin gauze
hazel nut, tree, wood, birch, shrub
head, hd. mind, pate, capita, (poll) chief
  and shoulders bust
  and shoulders cover nubia

  armor movion
  comb. form cephal(o)
  garland chaplet
  membrane covering caul, omentum
  shaved tonsure
headband agal, fillet, taenia
headdress wig, tiara, diadem
  bishop miter
  cobra uraeus
  military busby, shako
  nun cornet, wimple
headhunter dayak
headless etete, acephalous, leaderless
headlong rashly, pellmell, recklessly
  fall cropper
  flight lam
headspring origin, source, fountain
headstone stele, barrow
hearing oyer, trial, audition
  instrument audiometer, stethoscope
  keen hyperacusia
  organ ear, otocyst
  pert. to otic, aural
heart core, cardia, spirit, essence
  bleeding dicentra
  (largest) blood vessel aorta
  part auricle, ventricle
  point fess
heartburn envy, pyrosis, jealousy, water
  brash
hearth home, ling, fireside
  goddess Vesta, Hestia
heartsease pansy, wallflower
heat zeal, anger, calor, fever, intensity
  animal rut, estrus
  comb. form thermo, thermy
  decomposition by pyrolysis
  measuring device calorimeter,
    thermometer
  unit Btu, therm(e), calorie
heated hot, angry, inflamed
  white candent
  wine regus
heath moor, pipe, erica, azalea
  bird grouse, blackcock
heather ling, gorse, bilberry, crowberry
heaven zion, glory, elysium, firmament

comb. form urano
description uranology
belt zodiac
heavenly divine, ethereal, celestial
being angel, cherub, seraph(im)
body sun, moon, star, comet, meteor, planet
bread manna
path orbit
hebdomad week, seven
hebetate dull, blunt, stupid
Hebrew, Hebraic Semite, Israelite
ancestor Eber
Bible books nebiim
canonical book Talmud
coin gerah, shekel
festival Purim, Seder
horn shofar
measure hin, kab, kor
weight omer, gerah
universe olam
hecatomb sacrifice, slaughter
Hecuba
children Paris, Hector, Troilus, Cassandra
husband Priam
heddle caam
hedge boma, fence, waver, barrier
form a plash
part privet
trash brash
hedgehog urchin, porcupine
animal-like tenrec
spine quill
heel cad, tap, list, tilt, calyx, louse
bone fibula, calcaneus
comb. form talo
hegemonic ruling, leading
hegira exodus, flight, journey
destination Medina
hegumen abbot
height alt, top, apex, climax, summit, altitude
of great skyey
of play's action catastasis
Hejaz
holy cities Mecca, Medina
held gripped, detained

in music tenato
in trust fiduciary
Helen of Troy
abductor Paris
daughter Hermione
husband Menelaus
mother Leda
son Norus
suitor Ajax
helianthus sunflower
helico
comb. form spiral
Helios god, sun, Apollo
daughter Circe
father Hyperion
sister Artemis
heliotrope girasol, turnsole, sunflower, bloodstone
helix snail, spiral, mollusk
helmet hat, casque, morion, sallet
decoration panache
front ventail
lower part beaver
Roman Galea
visor armet
helminth worm (tape or round), parasite
helot esne, serf, slave
hem sew, edge, border, encircle
in crowd, fence, invest
stiffening cloth wigan
hemipterous insect lick, aphid, bedbug
hemlock kex, yew, weed, abies, poison
alkaloid conin(e)
poison bennet
hemp tow, pita, fiber, plant, ramie
Afr. ife
drug hashish
East Indies dunn
fiber tow, sisal
Gr. kannabis
leaves kef, bhany
shrub pua
source cannabis
hen layer, cackler
brooding setter, sitter
extinct heath
hawk redtail

house coop
mud rail
spayed poulard(e)
young pullet, chicken
henbane hyoscyamus, nightshade
  content hyoscin
henbit mint, plant
hence so, off, away, ergo, then, thus, therefore
henna dye, shrub, alcana
hepatic liverwort, liver-shaped
Hephaestus Vulcan
Hera
  husband Zeus, Jupiter
  mother Rhea
  of Romans Juno
  rival Io, Leda, Themis
  son Ares
heraldic bay, armorial
  band orle, fillet, tressure
  cross patte, patee
  design seme
  mastiff alan
  triangle giron
  shield
    border orle, bordure
    boss umbo
    division ente, canton
    horizontal band fess
    side segments flanch
    star estoile
    stripe pale
heraldry ente, armory
  bar, horizontal label
  bearing orle, saltire
  bend cotise
  bird martlet
  broken rompu
  chaplet orle
  colter aver
  creature lion, pard, bisse, cannet, griffon, martlet
  division pale, paly
  dog alant
  footless bird martlet
  factor gene
  five pean
  headless etete

pointed urde
standing statant
subject armory, genealogy, coat of arms
winged vol, aile
herb mint, grass, catnip
  aromatic anet, dill, mint, anise, basil, rosemary
  aromatic rout nondo
  aster family arnica
  bean family pea, lotus
  bitter rue, aloe, tansy, gentian
  carrot family dill, borage, eringo, fennel, parsley
  flowering hepatica
  forage sulla
  fragrant balm
  genus Geum, Ruta, Aletris
  laxative senna
  magic moly
  mustard family cress
  pea family lotus, mimosa
  perennial sego, sedum
  starchy pia
  strong-smelling rue, yarrow
  use food, medicine, seasoning
  woolly poly
herbivore tapir, vegetarian
Hercules strong man, constellation
  monster slain by Hydra
  parent Zeus, Alcmene
  victim Nessus
  wife Hebe, Deianira
herd crowd, flock, shoal, corral, shepherd
  animals together pod
  grass redtop, timothy
  of horses caviya, harras
  of whales gam, pod
herdsman cowboy, drover, gaucho, cowhand, vaquero, wrangler
  constellation bootes
  god Pales
  stick goad, crook
heredity line, inheritance
  factor DNA, RNA, gene
herl fly, barb
Hermes Mercury
  birthplace Cyllene

father Zeus
mother Maia
winged cap petasos, petasus
winged shoes talaria
hermit crab pagurian
hero ace, idol, demigod, topnotcher
  legendary Amadis, Roland, Paladin
  lover Leander
Herodias
  daughter Salome
  husband Herod, Antipas
heron rail, soco, crane, egret
herring raun, cisco, alewife, anchory, pilcher
  barrel cade, cran
  canned sardine
  catch tack
  family pilchard
  female raun
  genus Clupea
  young brit, sprat, sprot
hership loot, raid, foray
hery praise, glorify, worship
hesped eulogy, oration
Hesperia Italy, Spain, butterfly, Western land
Hesperus (evening) star, Venus
  father Astraeus
  fate wreck
  mother Eos
hessonite garnet
hest bid, pledge, promise, injunction
hetero
  comb. form (an)other, different
  opposed to homo
heterogynous insect ant, bee
hetman chief, ataman, headman
heu alas
hexad sextet
hexapod six-footed
hexastich poem, sestet, stanza, strophe
hexose sugar
Hezekiah
  kingdom Judah
  mother Abi
Hiawatha
  bark canoe
  grandmother Nokomis
  mother Wenonah

hickory pecan, butternut, shellbark
hidage tax
hidalgo nobleman
  state capital Pachuca
hide bury, skin, cloud, leather, hoodwink, suppress
  calf/lamb kip
  raw shagreen
  safe keeping cache
  undressed kip, pelt
  worker tanner
hiemal brumal, wintry
hiero
  comb. form holy, sacred
hieroglyphics key Rosetta stone
high tall, chief, sharp, exalted, important
  -and-mighty arrogant
  -brow egghead, intelligentsia
  comb. form alti
  crime treason
  flying Icarian, pretentious
  priest Eli
  sounding sonorous
  water flood
highest summa, upmost, supreme
  comb. form aero
  mountain Everest
  note (music) ela
  point apex, peak, zenith
  possible maximal, maximum
Highlander Gael, Scot, Tartan
  garment kilt
  pants trews
  pouch sporran
  sword claymore
highway road, avenue, freeway, turnpike, boulevard
  Alaska-Canada Alcan
  Ger. autobahn
  -man pad, rider, hijacker
  Roman iter, avian
hill heap, pile, mount, ascent, colline
  builder ant
  cone-shaped brae
  dugout abri
  flat-topped mesa
  glacial kame

on a plain butte
pointed tor
rounded knob, morro
sand dune
small mound
top brow, crest
hillock tump, hurst, knoll
  over grave tumulus
Himalaya, Himalayan Nepalese
  animal ounce, panda
  antelope goral, serow
  cedar deodar
  herb atis
  teu aucuba
hind doe, back, rear, peasant, posterior
  animal's leg ham
  brain cerebellum
hinddeck poop
Hindu, Hindustani Babu, Koli, Urdu,
  Tamil, Hindoo
  age of the world yuga
  ancestor manu
  bible Veda
  coin ana, pie, rupee
  drink soma
  ejaculation om, um
  garment sari, dhoti, saree
  guitar sitar
  hymn mantra
  paradise Nirvana
  philosophy yoga, tamas
  prayer rug asan, asana
  social division caste
  tunic jama(h)
  weight ser, tael, tola, maund
hinny mule, neigh, whinny
  parent horse, donkey
hip coxa, ilia, fruit, haunch
  bone pelvis, ilium
  boots waders
  joint disease coxalgia
  pert. to iliac, sciatic
hippo
  comb. form horse
Hippocrates
  birthplace Cos, Kos
  drug mecon (opium)

hippopotamus seacow, behemoth,
  pachyderm
hirple limp, hobble
hirsel herd, land, flock
hirsute hairy, rough, coarse, shaggy
hispid spiny, bristly, strigose
hiss sizz, whiz, assibitate
  sign of hatred, disapproval
hist hark, hush, shush
historical real, factual, authentic
  period era
  records annals, chronicles
  muse Clio
hit ace, bop, sock, pommel, pummel, success
  aloft lob
  direct bull's-eye
  hard slug
  lightly tap
  -or-miss casual, aimless
hitchpost picket
hitherto ago, yet, before, until, now
Hitler, Adolp(h)
  aerie Berchtesgaden
  chosen race Aryan
  follower Nazi
  occupation house painter
  rank corporal
  title Der fu(e)hrer
  wife Eva Braun
Hittite Syrian
  ancestor Heth
  capital Pteria
  storm god Teshub
hive box, gum, skep, swarm, apiary, multitude
hives uredo, allergy, urticaria
  cement for propolis
  remedy benadryl
ho! halt, long, stop, whoa, desist
hoarfrost rag, rime
hoarseness frog, coup, croup
hoactzin bird
hobbil dolt, clown, dunce, idiot
hobnail rustic
hobo bo, bum, tramp, vagrant, vagabond
  bedding/bundle bindle
  camp jungle
  food mulligan (stew)

Hobson's choice take it or leave it
hock ham, hox, pawn, wine, joint
  ailment of joint spavin
  of humans ankle
hockey game, bandy, shinny
  disk puck
  goal cage
  stick caman
  trophy Stanley (Cup)
hod soil, barrow, scuttle
hodgepodge ana, mess, stew, cento, medley, gallimaufry
hog pig, swine, grunter, shilling
  cholera rouget
  cured side flitch
  fat lard, adeps
  female sow, gilt
  food mash, grain, swill
  genus Sus
  male boar, barrow
  young shoat, shote
hogback ridge
hogfish porpoise, scorpene
hognose sand viper
hognut ouabe, pignut, earthnut
hogo taint, flavor, stench
hog peanut earthpea
hog plum amra
hogshead cask, barrel, vessel
  contents beer
hogtie clog, truss, fetter
hogwash draff, swill, refuse
hoiden tomboy
hoi polloi mob, masses, rabble, populace, commoners
hoist, hoisting cat, jack, lift, heave, raise, derrick
  anchor weigh
  device crane, winch
  -man engineman, bandsman
  off bottom atrip
  sail swig
hold bind, keep, grasp, adhere, clutch, occupy, retain
  a brief for defend
  attention interest
  back detain

  due to war intern
  fast grip
  forth offer
  off avert
  out endure
  over delay
  ship's hatch
  up rob, heist (sl.)
  water sound
holder haven, payee, tenant
  of a lease lessee, renter
holding asset, tenure, property
  adapted for prehensile
  device vise, clamp, tongs
hole bay, pit, cove, cavity, opening
  air spiracle
  animal's den, lair, burrow, warren
  cloth eyelet
  instr. for making awl, bore, drill, punch, stiletto
holes, full of perforated
holia fish, salmon
holiday fete, fiesta, outing, recess, festival, vacation
  kind Roman, Easter, weekend, Mardi Gras
Holland cloth, Dutch, The Netherlands
  coin doit, raps, florin, stiver
  dialect Frisian, Frunkish
  gin geneva, ochnapps
  merchant's league Hanse
  town hall stadhouse
  weight ons, lood, pond, koorel
hollow cave, hole, empty, gaunt, socket, sunken,
  boggy slak
  circular corrie
  comb. form coelo
  cylinder tube
  opposed to solid
  sound hoot
  title key
holly assi, holm, ilex, acebo, yapon
  pert. to ilicic
holm ait, oak, islet, bottoms
  oak ilex, holly
Holmes, Sherlock detective

alter ego Watson
creator Conan Doyle
expression elementary
holobaptist immersionist
holt hill, copse, grove, woods, willows
holy pious, devout, sacred, hallowed,
   inviolate, spiritual
   city Kiev, Rome, Zion, Mecca, Medina,
      Jerusalem
   comb. form hagio, hiero
   communion Eucharist
   cross rood
   Grail chalice, sangraal
   Grail finder Galahad
   land Palestine
   -land visitor palmer, pilgrim
   oil chrism
   picture icon
   -water container font, stoup
   -water sprinkling asperges
homage honor, eulogy, manrent, respect,
   tribute
   to saints dulia
homaloidal even, flat
homard lobster
home adobe, house, igloo, tepee, domicile,
   dwelling
   at chez (Fr.)
   animal's den, lair
   bird's nest, aerie
   for poor/sick hospice
   of gods Olympus
   wheeled trailer
Homer, Homeric Koz, epic(al), homerun
   birthplace Chios
   character Ajax, Nestor, Achilles,
      Odysseus
   enchantress Circe
   poem Iliad, Odyssey
homespun kelt (Scot.), plain, coarse,
   homely
   cloth russet
homestead toft, croft, onstead, messuage
   outbuildings steading
homesteader sooner, settler
homilist preacher
homily talk, adage, lecture, discourse

hominy corn, samp, grits
homo man, primate
   comb. form like, same, equal
   sapiens man, humankind
homonym synonym, namesake
homopterous insect aphid, cicada
homunculus dwarf, manikin
Honduras
   capital Tegucigalpa
   coin peso, centavo, lempira
   weight caja
honewort parsley
honey mel, dear, sweet, nectar, precious
   bear kinkajou
   bee apis, dingar, deseret
   comb. form melli
   fermented mead, metheglin
honeycombed favose, pitted, alveolar
honeysuckle vine, azalea, clover,
   widbin
Hong Kong
   bay Mirs
   coin cent, dollar, British/Hongkong/H.K.
      dollar
   peninsula Kowloon
honor fame, glory, esteem, homage
   mark laurel, chaplet
   pledge parole
honorarium fee, tip, reward, salary,
   gratuity
honorary military commission brevet
hood cap, biggin, bonnet, canopy, tippet
   academic liripipe, liripoop
   airplane's nacelle
   bird's calot(te), crest
   carriage/cloak capote
   monk's atis, cowl, amice
   part camail
hooded cowled, cucullate, capistrate
   garment cape, parka, anorak
   seal bladdernose
   snake adder, cobra, puffing adder
   woman's cloak capuchin
hoof paw, clee, foot, cloaf, dance
   paring tool butteris
   shaped ungulate
   sl. walk, tramp

hook gaff, hold, hitch, capture
  and loop gemel
  engine gab
  -like mark cedilla
  money larin
  part barb
  shaped uncinal
  stretcher tenter
hooka, hookah pipe, nargile, nargileh
hooked hamate, falcate, aquiline
hooklike hamate, falcate, uncinate
  process uncus
hooly slow, soft, wary
hooper cooper
Hoover dam, John, Herbert
  blankets newspapers
  flag (empty) pocket
  lake/dam Mead
hop leap, vine, bound, dance, gambol
  back vat
  -bush akeake
  kiln oast
  of ball/stone dap
  -o'-my-thumb dwarf
  plant lupulus
  stem bine
hope deem, wish, expect, prospect
  goddess Spes
  lack despair
  symbol opal
hophead addict
Hophni
  brother Phinehas
  father Eli
Hopi Indian Moki, Moqui
  god Kachina, Katc(h)ina
  room kiva
hoplite soldier
  weapon spear
hoppet yard, basket, bucket
hopple fetter, hobble, entangle
hoprine bine
hopscotch pallall
  stone potsy, peever
Horae Dike, hours, Eirene
horehound henbit
horizon rim, edge, goal, skyline

arc azimuth
  kind true, visible, celestial
horizontal flat, flush, level, plane, band
heraldic frieze
  position prone
hormigo quira, ant tree
horn scur, brass, siren, cornet, oliphant
  bell-like part flare
  bird's beak epithema
  comb. form kera
  deer's rack, tine, prong, antler
  drinking rhyton
  Hebrew shofar
  -like cornu
  of plenty cornucopia
  snail's tentacle
  tissue scur, keratin
  unbranched dag
hornbeam ironwood
hornbill bird, tock, homari
  genus Buceros
horned gored, corniculate
  animals gnu, ram, bull, deer, goat, ibex,
    stag, rhino, buffalo
  fabled animal unicorn
  toad lizard
  viper asp, cerastes
hornless polled, acerous
  cow mulley
horologe clock, watch, sundial, hourglass
  studier of horologist, watchmaker
horse gee, nay, beast, mount, steed,
  charger
  Achilles' Xanthus
  Alexander the Great's Bucephalus
  ankle hock
  armor bard(e)
  back of withers
  backward movement passade
  belly band girth
  blinder winker
  breastplate peytrel, poitrel
  breed Arab, Barb, Shire, hunter, Morgan,
    Belgian, harness, Suffolk, trotter,
    Shetland, Clydesdale
  brown bay, sorrel, chestnut
  calico pinto

comb. form hipp(o), kerat(o)
dappled roan, pinto, piebald
dark zain
female dam, mare, yaud, filly
foot frog, hoof, fetlock, pastern
forehead chanfrin
gait run, lope, pace, rack, trot, walk, canter, gallop, winding
genus Equus
golden palomino
gray schimmel
herd harras
lover hippophile
male colt, stud, steed, entire, gelding, stallion
mane crest
measure hand
pack bidet, drudge, sumpter
piebald pinto, calico
prehistoric eohippus
rearing pesade
saddle cob, mount, palfrey
small cob, nag, tit, foal, pony, genet, Shetland
winged Pegasus
horsefly cleg, botfly, gadfly, tabanid
horsehair mane, seton, snell
horseman rider, canter, cowboy, caballero, equestrian
armed cavalier
bullfighter's picador
horsemanship manege, equitation
pert. to equine
rearing pesade
sidewalk volt
turn caracole
horsemint monarda
horseshoe ringer
gripper/spur calk
one who applies farrier, blacksmith
point sponge
rim web
Horus Ra, Re, god, sun
brother Anubis
father Osiris
head hawk
mother Isis

Hosea Osse
wife Gomer
hospital spital, refuge, infirmary
attendant nurse, orderly
for foundlings crèche
for the poor lazarette
mobile ambulance
hospitality, to strangers xenodoehy
host army, bread, horde, throng
heavenly angels
receptacle pyx, paten, ciborium
hostel, hostelry inn, hotel, tavern
hot fiery, ardent, hectic, thermal
baths therme
cargo contraband
-rod race drag
spring geyser
wind sirocco
hothead raver, inciter, reactionary
hothouse bagnio, greenery, vivarium
hot-tempered iracund, choleric, irascible
Hottentut Nama, Negro, bushman
garment kaross
instr. gora(h)
village kraal
war club knobkerrie
hound dog, hunt, harry, addict, talbot
female brach
hunting basset, beagle, setter, pointer
tail stern
wolf alan, borzoi
hour matin
canonical none, sext
class period
lights out taps, curfew
houri nymph
house cot, hut, nest, hovel, manor, domicile, residence
bee hive
bird nest, aerie
cluster dorp, hamlet
comb. form eco
Eskimo igloo
fortified peel
Fr. maison
instant prefab
mud tembe

Newfoundland tilt
Oriental serai
outbuildings messuage
pert. to domal
pigeons cote
Russ. isba, dacha
Sp. casa
upper Senate
housefly pest, insect
  genus Musca, Fannia
  pert. to muscid
household meiny, common, menage
  gods Lares, Penates
  linen napery
  mallet beetle
  sprite kobold
housel Eucharist
houseleek sengreen
houses, buyer of old knacker
house site lot, toft
housing box, pad, cowl, cover, shelter
  engine nacelle
  horse barn, blanket, trappings
howe deep, empty, hollow
howling monkey araba
hoy barge
hoyden tomboy
hr., part of min., sec.
Hreidmar
  son Otter, Regin, Fafnir
huaca holy, idol, tomb, shrine
hub core, nave, center
  the Boston
hubris vanity, arrogance, insolence
huckle hip, haunch
huckleberry blueberry
  family ericaceae
Huckleberry Finn
  author Mark Twain (pen name), Samuel
    Clemens
hucklebone talus, hipbone, anklebone
hud hall, husk, shell
huff dod, pet, blow, puff, peeve
huffcap bully, heady, strong, blusterer
hug coll, clasp, cherish, embrace
  kind bear, bunny
  -me-tight vest

hugger-mugger sly, jumble, secret,
  confused
Hugo, Victor novelist
Huguenot Protestant
  leader Conde, Adrets
hui firm, guild, society
huisache wabi, aromo, shrub, cassie,
  popinac
huitain octave, stanza
huke cape, cloak, dress
hulled grain samp, groat
hulver holly
human man, biped, mortal, person,
  Adamite, primate
  body corpus, carcass
  -body model manikin, mannequin
  comb. form anthrop(o)
  soul psyche
  trunk torso
humble low, mean, meek, abase, plain,
  stoop
  pie crow, numbles
humbug bosh, dupe, flax, hoax, sham,
  fraud, cajole
humdinger lulu, (a)oner, corker
humect wet, moisten
humerus bone
humidity-measuring device hygrometer
humming brisk, brool, active
  bird ava, carib, froufrou, sheartail
    genus Sappho
  sound whir(r), chirm, drone
hummock hill, hump, knoll, mound
humor pet, wit, mood, whim
  bad tiff
  body bile
  quaint drollery
  sl. corn
humorist wag, wit, joker
  famous Cobb, Nash, Rogers, Benchley,
    Rabelais
hump bile, hunk, bulge, ridge
  animal with zebu, camel, dromedary
  -backed gibbous
  of a humpback kyphos
  the Himalayas
humus mold, soil, mulch

Hun savage, vandal, barbarian
  leader Etzel, Attila
Hunchback of Notre Dame Quasimodo
  actor/movie Lon Chaney
hundred centum, cantred, cantref
  comb. form centi, hecto
  division into centuriation
  dollar bill c-note (sl.)
  lacs crone
hundred-eyed-being Argus
hundredweight cwt, cental, quintal
Hundred Years' War battle Cressy
Hung Wu Ming
Hungary, Hungarian Magyar
  cavalryman Hussar
  chocolate party Dobos
  coin gara, balas, pengo, filler
  dance czardas
  dog puli
  dynasty Arpad
  gypsy tzigane
  measure ako, joch, antal, metze
  weight vamfont
  wine tokay
hunger yen, pine, starve
  abnormal bulimia, polyphagia
  greedy ravenous
hunks miser, tightwad
hunt seek, quest, trail, ferret
  god Ninip, Apollo
  goddess Diana, Artemis
  illegally poach
hunter yager, chaser, nimrod, trapper
  assistant gilly, jager
  bait decoy
  cap montero, deerstalker
  Golden Fleece Jason
  myth Orion
  patron saint Hubert
hunting
  art chase, venery
  bird falcon
  call toho, yoick, tallyhoo
  chase bake
  cry tongue
  dog hound, basset, beagle
  stance point, deadset

  pert. to venatic(al)
huntsman, changed into stag Actaeon
hurdies hips, rump, buttocks
hurds tow
hurlbat harpoon, javelin
Huron lake, grison, Indian
hurried sped, hasty, raced, urged
  music agitato
hurtful malefic
husband eke, rom, chap, mate, spouse,
  partner
  authority manus
  more than one polyandry
  one monagamy, monandry
husbandry thrift, economy, farming,
  geoponics
  god Faunus
husks chaff, bhoosa
hussar soldier, cavalryman
  headdress busby
  jacket dolman
  monkey patas
hussy doxy, minx, slut, tart, madam,
  sewing kit
hut cabin, hovel, lodge, shanty
  army Quonset
  fisherman skeo
  lean-to shed
  mining coe
  shepherd bothy
hyacinth stone, greggle, bluebell,
  harebell
  gem topaz, garnet, zircon
  wild camas
hyalite opal
hyaloid glassy, vitreous
hybrid
  bovine catalo
  citrus tree tangelo
  horse and ass mule, hinny
  horse and zebra zebrula, zebrinny
  language jargon
  zebra and donkey zebrass
hydra polyp, serpent, constellation
hydrocarbon butane, octane, retene,
  benzene
  compound imine

gaseous ethane, ethene
liquid toluene, kerosene
wax montan
hydromedusa jellyfish
hydromel mead (fermented), aloja
hydrometer spindle
  scale baume
hydrophobia lyssa, rabies
hydrous watery
  silicate talc
  wool fat lanolin
hymenopteron ant, bee, wasp, sawfly
hymn
  following psalm sticheron
  for the dead requiem
  funeral dirge
  of praise anthem
  victory epinicion
hyperbole elas, auxesis, exaggeration
hyperborean cold, gelid, frigid
Hyperion Titan
  daughter Eos, Selene
  parent Gaea, Uranus
  son Helios
hyperpnea panting
hypethral roofless
hypnotic
  condition coma, trance, lethargy
  compound amytal
  force od(yle)
hypnotism sleep, mesmerism
  founder Mesmer
hypnum moss
hypochondria hyp, megrim, anxiety, melancholy
  victim nosomania, valetudinarian
hypocrisy cant, deceit, pretense, simulation, pharisaism
hypocrite sham, Tartuf(f)e, pretender
hypostasis deposit, essence, sediment
hypostatic basic, elemental
hypotenuse slant
hypothesis ism, system, theory
hypothetical being ens, entity
hyrax cony, rabbit, hyracoid, procavia
Hyrtacus
  son Nisus

hyson tea
hyssop mint, thistle, aspergillum
hysteria fit, panic, frenzy, jitters, tarassis
  symptom aura, aerophagia
hystricomorphic animal cavy, rodent, agouti, porcupine

I

I ego, self
  am not to blame non mea culpa
  am to blame mea culpa
  do not wish to contend nolo contendere (Lat.)
  enlarged ego
  excessive use iotacism
  have found it eureka
  understand roger
Iago
  master Othello
  wife Emilia
iamb foot (metrical)
Iasi Jassy
  coin leu
Iasion
  father Zeus
Iberia Pict; see Spain
ibex tur, zac, goat, kail, walie
  habitat alps, Pyrenees, mountains
ibis heron, stork, jabiru
Icarian rash, daring, foolhardy
Icarius
  daughter Erigone, Penelope
Icarus
  father Daedalus
ICBM Atlas, weapon, missile
ice geal, chill, freeze, dessert, sherbet
  breaking up in water debacle
  coat rim
  floe pan, pack
  mass berg, serac, glacier
  pinnacle serac
icecap calotte
Iceland
  coin krona, aurar, eyrir

giant Atli
god Loki, Odin, Thor, Aesir
measure fet, alen, korntunna
weight pund, pound, tunna smjors
ichneumon fly, mongoose
ichnolite fossil, footprint
icicle shoggle
  limestone stalactite, stalagmite
icon, ikon image, figure, symbol
ictus fit, blew, attack, stroke
Idaho see Quick Reference List
  state gem garnet
idant chromosome
idea fancy, ideal, thought, archetype, impression
  comb. form ideo
  main motif
  worthless bilge, chimera
ideal state Eden, Oceana, Utopia, Erewhon
ideologist dreamer, theorist, visionary
idiocy anoesia, fatuity
idiosyncrasy way, idiasm, manner
idle talk rumor, gossip
Idmon
  father Apollo
  killer boar
  mother Cyrene
  ship Argo
idol icon, image, satyr, fetish
  Chinese Joss
  household Teraphim
  social lion
idolatrous pagan
idyl, idyll poem, eclogue
idyllic bucolic, pastoral
i.e. id est (Lat.), that is
Ieperen Ypres
if si (Fr., It., Lat.), granting, provided
  not else, nisi, unless
igneous rock trap, basalt, periodot
ignition cap fure, fuse
ignoble low, base, mean, humble
ignoramus dolt, dunce, nitwit
ignorance tamas, agnosy
Igorot, Igorrote Bontok, Nabaloi, Kankanai
  chief Apo

iguana lizard, tuatara
ihi fish, skipper, halfbeak
ikary caviar
ileus colic
  cause constipation
ilex oak, holly
Iliad epic, poem
  ascribed author Homer
  character Ajax, Priam, Hector, Achilles, Agamemnon, Cassandra
Ilium, Ilion Troy
ill evil, sick, ailing, adverse, noxious
  at ease awkward
  prefix mal
  smelling rank, fetid
  will spite, animus, enmity
illative word therefore
illegal foul, illicit, unlawful, contraband
  in boxing foul (blow), low blow
  liquor bootleg, moonshine
Illinois see Quick Reference List
illness colic, malady, disorder
  feign malinger
illude bilk, mock, cheat, deride
illuminant gas, ligroin(e), petroleum
illumination light, instruction
  device lamp, torch, candle, lantern, chandelier, flashlight
  in eclipse penumbra
  measure phot
  unit lux, lumen
illy badly
ilvaite yenite
image copy, form, effigy, likeness
  deceptive chimera
  destroyer iconoclast
  good luck alraun
  maker iconoplast
  mental idea, concept
  pert. to iconic, simulacral
  rainbowlike spectrum
  stone herma
  wooden tiki
  worship arati
imago bee
imam priest
  last Mahdi

imaret inn, serai, hospice
imbosom cherish, embrace, shelter
imbricate overlap
imbroglio plot, confusion, disagreement
imbrue wet, soak, steep, tinge
imidogen compound imid(e), imin(e)
imitation copy, echo, sham, bogus, counterfeit
  derisive mimicry, mockery
  fantastic travesty, caricature
  gem glass, paste
  gold oroide
  gold leaf clinquant
  of speech/behavior mimesis
  pearl olivet
immaterial spiritual, unimportant
immaturity
  period youth, non-age, infancy, pre-puberty
immersion baptism, dipping
immigrant alien, comeling, stranger
  illegal wetback
  Israel halutz, chalutz
  newly arrived griffin, greenhorn
immolate sacrifice
immortality athanasia, deathlessness
  Hindu amrita
immortelle everlasting
immunity freedom, exemption
  kind diplomatic, congressional
  method inoculation, vaccination
  -producing substance serum, toxoid, vaccine
Imogen
  mother Cymbeline
imp elf, brat, demon, scamp, sprite
impact hit, slam, force, whang, freeze
  main brunt
impala rooibok, rooyebok
impar odd, unequal
imparid fearless
imparting motion kinetic
impasse dead end, cul-de-sac (Fr.), deadlock, stalemate
impasto painting
impede clog, block, check, delay
  legally bar, debar, estop

impedimenta baggage, encumbrance
impelling force impetus, momentum
impend hang, loom, approach
impennate bird penguin
imperceptible unseen, invisible, unnoticeable
imperfect cull, poor, faulty, defective
  prefix mal, atelo
imperial regal, royal, kingly, august
  cap crown
  color purple
  decree rescript
  domain empery, empire
  officer palatine
imperial woodpecker ivorybill
imphee plant, sorghum
impi zulu, kaffir, soldiers, warriors
impignorate pawned, pledged
implement kit, gear, tool, fulfill, accomplish
  ancient celt, eolith
  baker's peel
  barbed harpoon
  enlarging reamer, dilator
  furcate fork
  hand-printing brayer, roller
  hay-spreading tedder, mulcher
  household appliance
  kitchen utensil
  lifting pry, lever, tongs
  logging tode, peevey
  pounding maul, pestle
  printer's biron, press
  threshing flail
  war petard
impone stake, wager
impose burden, entail, inflict
  by fraud foist
  upon fob, dupe
impost tax, duty, levy, tariff
  salt gabelle
imposture sham, fraud, artifice
impound poind, seize, store
impouring influx
imprecation oath, curse, blasphemy
impresa maxim, motto, device, proverb
impressed dearly graven

impression dent, mark, stamp, signet
  on coin mintage
  printing macule
  trial proof
imprest lent, loan, advance (cash)
imprevu unforeseen
imprimatur license, approval, sanction
improperly amiss, unduly
improvise devise, invent, contrive
  in mus. ride, vamp
  on stage ad lib, aside
impulse urge, motive, impetus
  characterized by sensory
  divine afflatus
  to steal kleptomania
  to travel wanderlust
in at, amid, nook, among, corner
  abeyance pending
  accord agreeing, en rapport
  accordance pursuant
  any event notwithstanding
  capacity of qua
  a chamber in camera
  concert together
  contact tangent, attingent
  existence extant
  fact de facto
  favor of pro
  a flutter pitapat
  a frenzy amuck
  great need straits
  manner of a la
  name only nominal, titular
  prefix en, il
  a row serial, aligned
  the same place ibid
  a series en suite
  a standing position statant
  truth certes, indeed
  a vertical line apeak
  the whole in toto
  the year of anno
inability impotence, incapacity
  to articulate anaudia
  to chew amasesis
  to read alexia
  to speak anepia

  to swallow aphagia
  to understand acatalepsia
    speech aphasia
Inachus
  daughter Io
inamorata beloved, mistress, sweetheart
inarch graft
inarm embrace
inasmuch as, for, since, because
inbeing essence
inborn innate, connate, natural
  desire conatus
inbreeding endogamy
Inca
  chief Atabalipa, Atahualpa
  empire Peru
  god Inti, Choun, Chasca
  priest Amauta
incarnadine red, rosy
incarnation advent, avatar, Christ
  of Vishnu Rama
incasement emboitement
incendiary goon, firebug, arsonist,
  flammable, pyromaniac
  bomb material thermit(e)
incense odor, anger, arouse, perfume
  burner censer, thurible
  Chinese joss stick
  spice balsam, stacte
  vessel censer, navette (Fr.)
inch uneia
  along worm
  forward edge
  one-thousandth mil
  three-quarters digit
inches
  eighteen cubit
  forty-five ell
  four hand
  nine span
  two and one-quarter nail
inchpin sweetbread
incidental odd, minor, chance, random
  music grace note
  opinion obiter dictum
incidentally byhand, obiter, apropos, by-
  the-by

incise cut, etch, rase, carve
   narrowly laciniate
incisor tooth, cutter, foretooth
inclusive generic
incognito disguised
income gain, rente, profit, revenue
   pert. to tontine
incondite crude, unpolished
incorporeal right patent, copyright
incorrect faulty, untrue, erroneous
   epithet/naming misnomer
increase wax, eche, swell, flourish
   comb. form auxo
   in sound crescendo
   possessions amass
incubus demon, burden, spirit
incunabulum, incunabula cocoon,
   cradle, origin, infancy
incus ambos, anvil
indefinite loose, vague, neutral
   amount any, some
   article an
   pronoun any, one
indehiscent fruit uva
index file, list, catalog(ue), exponent
India, Indian Tamil, Bharat,
   Hindustan(i)
   aborigine Bengali
   alcoholic drink arrack
   astrologer joshi
   attendant ayah, peon
   bazaar chawk
   bear baloo
   bearer sirdar
   bird balu, jacana
   British founder Clive
   buck sasin
   building mahal
   bush kanher
   canoe tanee
   carpet agra
   caste Jat, Mal, Gaddi, Rajput
   caste marke tilka
   cedar deodar
   cigarette biri
   coin anna, fels, hoon, pice, rupee
   comb. form Indo

condiment curcuma
dancing girl bayadeer
diamond, famous Kohinoor
falcon basara, shashin
festival dewali
garment dhoti, kurta, banian
greeting namaste
harem zenana
hat topi
headman patel
hemp drug hashish
hut bari
kingdom Nepal
laborer palli
lady begum, memsahib
lady's maid ayah
language Bihari, Bengali, Sanskrit
learned man pundit
litter bearer sirdar
low class bhat
master mian, sahib
measure of distance guz, kos
military caste rajput
Moslem Swat
mus. instr. vina, ruana, sitar
nurse amah, ayah, dhai
ox zebu
peasant ryot
pipe hookah
Punjabi caste Sansi
rainy season varsha, monsoon
rice boro
rule raj
silkworm eri
snake krait
song raga
turban seerband
vessel lota(h)
weight ser, pice, tola
wine shrab
Indian (see also Quick Reference List for
   Native Tribes) indic, redskin, aborigine
   arrow poison curare
   ax tomahawk
   baby papoose
   bead money wampum
   blanket stroud, mackinaw

brave, young tenderfoot
bread tuckahoe
ceremonial chamber kiva
  pipe calumet
ceremony powwow
chief sachem, sagamore
corn zea, samp, maize
daughter of moon Nakomis
female squaw, mahala
festival potlatch
game canute
Great Spirit manito(u)
guardian spirit totem
headdress topknot
man buck, brave, sannup
moccasin pac
pillar lat, xat
pony cayuse
prayer stick paho
sorcery obe, obi
village pueblo
white person paleface
Indiana see Quick Reference List
Indic dialect Pali
indicating marking, showing, signing
  chemical group azo
  literal transcript sic
  succession ordinal
indices files, tables, pointers
indigene native
indigent poor, needy, destitute
indigestion apepsy, dyspepsia
indign unworthy, disgraceful
indigo dye, anil, blue
  artificial source isatin
  bale seroon
  berry randia
  Chinese isatis
  derivative indol(e), ketole
  wild genus Baptisia
indigo bunting bird, finch
indirect devious, oblique, circular
  expense cost, overhead
  expression ambage, paraphrase
individual one, self, sole, unit
  biological development ontogeny
  comb. form indio

of compound animal zoon
performance solo
physiological bion
selfish egoist
smug prig
individuality oneness
  rare seity
Indo-Aryan Jat, Rajput
  god Indra
Indo-China
  dialect ao
  former kingdom Anam
  part Laos, Burma, Malaya, Vietnam,
    Cambodia, Thailand
  tree eng, mee
Indo-European Lett, Serb, Slav, Aryan,
  Croat, Czech
Indo-Portugese
  halfcaste Christian Topas(s), Topaz
Indonesia, Indonesian East Indies
  bird bulbul, peafowl
  coin rupiah
  Indian Ata
  law adat
  measure depa, depoh
  priest caste brahmana
  pyramid stupa
  shop toko
  weight soekoe
  wind brubu
Indra Sakka, Sakra
  dragon Vritra
  elephant Airavata
  food soma
indri lemur
inductance
  measure henry
inductile inflexible, unyielding
indulge pet, baby, coddle, cosset, pamper
  in antics skylark
  in fault-finding cavil
  in revelry roist
Indus river, constellation
  tribesman Gor
indweller denizen, sojourner
inearth bury, inter
inelastic limp, rigid, stiff

inert dull, lazy, stupid, torpid
inertia sloth, idleness
inesculant inedible
inexorability rigor
infant babe, bairn, chrisom, bantling
  doctor pediatrist, pediatrician
  in law minor
  murder infanticide
infanta princess
infante prince
infare housewarming
infection malady, plague, disease
  freedom from asepsis
infecund barren, sterile
inferal stygian
inferno fire, hell, Hades, Gehenna
  Hebrew Sheol
infest vex, haunt, torment
infix inset, engrave, instill
inflammation fire, itis, combustion
  bone osteitis
  bone marrow myelitis
  eyelid sty(e)
  intestinal colitis
  throat catarrh
inflated blew, turgid, bloated
  condition tympany
inflection tone, cadence
  of words paradigm
inflict deal, impose
  great pain torture
  vengeance wreak
inflorescence raceme, flowering
  axial circle of whorl
influence coax, impel, power, induce,
  wheedle
  by electricity induction
  by fixed ideas obsess
  by reward bribe
  region of orbit
inform tell, warn, alert, advise
  against delate, betray, denounce
  sl. rat, sing, squeal
information data, aviso, facts, notice
  bit item
  condensed digest
  detailed dossier

infortune Mars, Saturn, Mercury,
  misfortune
infusion tea, tincture, admixture
  malt wort
infusoria protozoa, vorticella
ingang porch, entrance, intestines
ingluvies craw, crop
ingot
  metal gad, pig, bullion
  silver sycee
  worker barman
  zinc spelter
ingredient element, compound
  baking alum, salt, soda, flour, yeast
  incense stacte
  ink tannin
  varnish lac, rosin
ingrowing nail acronyx
inhabitant ite, inmate, denizen, dweller
  desert nomad
  early aborigine
  foreign alien
  local native
  moon selenite
  suffix ese, ite
inhabiting
  caves spelean, troglodyte
  ground terricolous
  island nesiote
  lake lacustral
  sea pelagic
inhere stick, belong, cleave
inheritance legacy, bequest, parcenary
  by firstborn primogeniture
  law salic
  portion legitime
  restricted entailment
  seizer abator
inhume bury, inter, entomb
inimical averse, frosty, hostile
initial first, letter, elementary
  design monogram
  ornamental paraph
  payment ante, deposit
injure mar, harm, spoil, scathe
  by bruising contuse
  by scorching char, singe

injury ill, mar, loss, tort, wound, damage, trauma
  causing malefic, traumatic
  compensation damages, solatium
  pert. to noxal
  retaliation reprisal
  sense of umbrage
ink daub, color, blacken, millrynd
  berry pokeweed
  fish squid, cuttle
  ingredient tannin
  pad of printer dabber
  pert. to atramental
inkle tape, yarn, thread
inlaid bahl, mosaic, champleve
inlay adorn, insert, filling
  material tile, niello
inlet oe, cay, gio, zee, slew, fjord
  coastline bight, strait
inmate of harem oda
inn pub, fonda, tambo, hospice
  worker potboy, barmaid, tapster, bartender
inner ben, esoteric, interior
  bark bast
  comb. form ent(o), ental
  parts innards
  sole rand
Innisfail Eire, Erin, Ireland
Ino
  grandfather Agenor
innocence
  symbol diamond
inorganic mineral
insane daft, batty, manic, senseless
  asylum bedlam, madhouse
  to make dement, derange
  person lunatic
insanity
  temporary amentia
inscription rune, legend, epigram, graffito
  appropriate motto
  end of book colophon
  explanatory titulus
  on book envoy
  on coins sigla
  tomb epitaph

inscrutable secret, enigmatic, inexplorable
  expression deadpan, poker face
  one sphinx
insect ant, bug, mite, emmet
  adult imago
  antenna palp, feeler
  back of notum
  blood-sucking tick, bedbug, conenose
  burrow mine
  comb. form entomo
  egg nit
  female gyne
  genus Nepa, Acarus, Termes
  long-legged emesa
  limb prolog
  nest nidus
  order acarid, locust
  poison venom
  resin lac
  stinger dart
  wingless aptera
  young nit
insee foretell
inside inner, lining, secret, within
  comb. form intra
  out evert
  toward entad
insignificant minor, paltry, trivial, unimportant
  part bit, iota, tithe
  person snip, twirp, shrimp
insolation sunstroke
inspan yoke, harness
instar pupa, imago, larva, maggot
instruction order, advice, lesson
  art of pedagogy, didactics
  period term, year, quarter, session, semester
  place school, college, conservatoire
instrument deed, writ, means, medium, utensil
  altitude aba, altimeter
  copying Xerox, hectograph
  cutting knife, razor, scythe, scissors
  measuring octant, yardstick
  nautical sectant

sacred urim
surveying transit, theodolite
to study motion stroboscope
instruments
for all tutti
insulin
discoverer Best, Banting
disease used for diabetes
insurance guaranty, warranty
agent underwriter
computer actuary
contract policy
payee beneficiary
system tontine
intaglio die, gem, engrave
opposed to cameo
intarsia mosaic
integer whole, entity
odd gnomen
intellect nous, brain, inwit, reason
limited in moronic
of the noetic
intellectual ideal, mental, sophic,
egghead
identification empathy
liking palate
(s) collectively clerisy, intelligentsia
intemerate pure
inter bury, entomb, inhume
companion alia, alios
intercalary inserted
month Veadar
interconnection nexus
interest good, fetch, behalf, attract
exorbitant usury
in law right, title
lose bore, tire
rate yield
without jejeune
interfacing dineric
interference static
interferometer etalon
interlaced woven, complex
interlude truce, episode, interval
short verset
international pact, entente, worldwide
business cartel

exhibition exposition
language ro, ido, esperanto
organizations UN, NATO, SEATO,
UNESCO
sports Olympics
writers' group PEN
internecine deadly
interpret render, construe, explain
dreams rede
falsely gloss
interpretation gloss, sense, oracle
of science exegesis, hermeneutics
interrogation quiz, probe, query
mark eroteme
intersection secant, chiasma
interstice mesh, pore, space, areola,
cranny, crevice
pert. to areolar
interval gap, break, space, hiatus, lacuna,
interim
irregular sporadically
mus. fifth, ninth, sixth, tenth, third,
fourth, octave, second, seventh
intestinal enteric
intestine gut, inner, viscera, domestic
comb. form entero
part ile, ileum
pert. to enteric
into unto, among, until, inside
prefix en
that thereinto
intolerance misoneism
intort curl, twist
intracellular histonal
intrada prelude, introduction
intricate knotty, Gordian, Daedalian, difficult, complicated
intrinsically per se
introduction debut, intrada, preface,
exordium
of new word neology
to treatise isagoge
inulase enzyme
inunction ointment, anointing
pert. to aliptic
inundation alluvion, flooding
invader Hun, Pict, raider, vandal, intruder

inveigle coax, lure, snare, entrap
inventor creator, engineer, discoverer
  airplane Fokker, Wright, Langley
  baseball Doubleday
  cotton gin Whitney
  dynamite Nobel
  electric light Edison
  elevator Otis
  gun Maxim, Thornton, Hotchkiss
  motor Davenport
  photography Niepce, Talbot
  printing Gutenberg
  radio Marconi, de Forest
  right of patent
  sewing machine Howe, Lester
  steamboat Fitch, Fulton, Rumsey
  telegraph Morse
  telephone Bell
  television Nipkow
invertebrate worm, polyp, insect, sponge, mollusk
investigator P.I., prober, tracer, detective
  body of panel
investment list portfolio
Invisible Empire Klan
invitation initials R.S.V.P.
involucre whorl, rosette, envelope
Io
  father Inachus
  guard Argus
  son Epaphus
iodine
  comb. form iod(o)
  salt iodate
  source kelp
  substitute aristal
Iolcus king Pelias
ion
  negative anion
  positive cation, kation
Ion
  father Apollo
  mother Creusa
Ionia, Ionian
  city Myus, Teos
  coin obol(o)
  gulf Arta

island Corfu, Paxos, Zante, Ithaca
monk Aidan
iota ace, bit, jot, atom, whit
Iowa see Quick Reference List
ipecac
  genus Evea, Cephaelis
  substance emetine
Iphicles
  brother Hercules
  mother Alcmene
  son Iolaus
iracund choleric, irascible
Irak see Iraq
Iran, Iranian Lur, Kurd, Persia
  angel Mah
  bird bulbul
  caste magi
  chief Mir
  coin pal, cran, dinar, toman, rupee
  dynasty, founder of Agha (present), Cyrus (former)
  garment chedar
  hat fez, turban
  measure guz, mou, zar, zer, jerib, artaba
  nomad Luri
  saint Safari
  tent-maker Omar
  title mir, azam, shah
  vessel aftaba
  weight ser, dram, abbas, pinar
  writings Avesta
Iraq
  ancient Kish
  city Hilla, Mosul, Baghdad
  coin dinar
  district Basra
Ireland, Irish Celt, Eire, Erin, Irena, Innisfail
  accent blas, brogue
  basket skeough
  boat pook(h)aun
  cattle kerry
  church kil
  clan sept, siol, Cinel
  coin rap, real, turney
  dagger skean
  dance jig, rinkafadda

exclamation och, arra(h)
fairy sidhe, banshee, leprechaun
garment inar
goblin pooka
holiday Whitmonday
liquor pot(h)een
measure bandle
national emblem shamrock
no! sorra
pert. to Celtic, Gaelic
saint Aidan, Patrick
servant biddy
song rann
sweetheart gra
iridium
   pert. to iridic
   symbol Ir
iris lis, ixia, sedge, Florentine
   comb. form irid
   family tileroot
   part uvea, argola
   pert. to irian
iron hard, goose, fetter, robust, smooth, yetlin
   comb. form sidero
   compound steel
   magnet armature
   pert. to ferric
   sand iserin
   sulphate ilesite
   symbol Fe
Iron City Pittsburgh
ironwork ferament
   tool lifter
Iroquois see Quick Reference List
irrational number surd
irregular erose, ataxic, cursory, sporadic, anomalous
irreligious pagan, impious, profane
is exists, represents, personifies
is not nis, nys
Isaac
   kin Esau, Jacob, Abraham
isagoge intro(duction)
Iseult
   beloved Tristam, Tristan
   husband Mark
Ishmael rover, pariah, outcast

   kin Hagar, Abraham, Nebaioth
   son Kedar
Ishtar
   lover Tammuz
isinglass mica, kanten
Isis
   brother/husband Osiris
   mother Nut
   shrine Iseum
   son Sept
Islam see Mohammedan
island(s) oe, ait, cay, key, eyot, isle
   channel Sark, Jersey, Guernsey
   China Amoy, Quemoy, Taiwan
   comb. form neso
   coral atoll
   Cuba Pines
   enchanted Bali
   friendly Tonga
   Great Barrier Otea
   group Faroe, Samoa, Antilles, Caroline, Marshall, archipelago
   legendary/mythical Meru, Avalon, Utopia, Atlantis
   low key
   Mediterranean Gozo, Capri, Crete, Malta, Sicily
   pert. to insular
   snake-free Erin
Isle of Man
   city Peel, Ramsey, Douglas
   division Treen
   measure kishon
   part Ayre
   pert. to Manx
ism ology, tenet, belief, doctrine
   follower ist, ite
Isolde
   lover Tristan
isomeric hydrocarbon octane, terpene
isometric same, cubic, parallel
Israel, Israeli Sion, Zion, Jacob
   anthem Hatikva
   child sabra
   dance hora
   land of plenty Goshen
   lawgiver Moses

measure cor, hin, bath, omer, kaneh
settlement moshav, kibbutz
ist devotee, disciple, follower
Istanbul Byzantium, Constantinople
  foreign quarter Pera
  Gr. quarter Fanar
  inn imaret
isthmus land, neck, strait, peninsula
  Malay/Siam Kra
istle fiber pita, pito
isurus shark
Italy, Italian Oscan, Roman, Picene, Sabine, Volsci
  art center Sienna
  article et, il
  astronomer Galileo
  cathedral duomo
  coin lira, tari, paoli, ducato, zecchino, centisimo
  dance volta, rigoletto, tarantella
  diety faun
  food pasta, pizza, scampi, ravioli, spaghetti, zabaglione
  grape verdea
  holiday festa
  house casa, casino
  inlay work tarsia
  innkeeper/landlord padrone
  marble carrara
  measure orna, canna, palma, tavola, braccio
  monk padre
  opera Aida, Tosca, La Boheme
  opera house (La) Scala
  poetic name Ausonia
  policeman shirro, carabiniere
  pottery majolica
  priest fra
  secret society Mafia, Comorra
  song villanella
  soup minestrone
  street via, strada
  violin maker Amati, Stradivarius
  weight carat, libra, ottava
  wind sirocco
itch
  barber's sycosis

item bit, scrap, topic, detail
  curious ana
Ithaca king Odysseus
Ithunn
  husband Bragi
itineration eyre, tour, circuit
it may be haply
Ivanhoe
  author Scott
  character Tuck, Isaac, Cedric, Rowena, Beowulf, Rebecca
  clown Wamba
Ivan the Terrible czar, tsar
  wife Anastasia
ivories dice, keys (piano), teeth
ivorine white, smooth
ivory creamy, dentin, ribzuba
  bone black abaiser
  carving art toreutics
  dust/cement eburine
  Lat. ebur
  nut anta, tagua
  rasping scobs
  source tusk
  synthetic ivoride
ivy tod, gill, vine, laurel
  crowned with hederated
  ground hove, alehoof
  pert. to hederic
  poison genus Rhus
Ixion
  descendants Centaurs
ixtle pita, fiber, istle
Izmir Smyrna
izzat honor, credit, prestige

J

jaal goat, ibex, beden
jab hit, poke, lunge
Jabal
  brother Jubal
  father Lamech
  mother Adah
jabber jaw, yak, babble, prattle

jabberwocky tune, brillig, nonsense, rigmarole
  author Lewis Carroll
jabiru ibis, stork
jabot frill
jacamar bird
jacare caiman
jacent prone
jack toy, boor, coin, flag, lift, mule, pike, pump, tree, ensign, rabbit, carnation
  group of four quatorze
  in cards knave
  -in-the-pulpit herb, plant, figwort
  -of-all-trades tinker
  of clubs pam
  tree jaca
jackal kola, diebs
jackanapes ape, fop, beau, dandy, monkey, coxcomb
jackass dolt, fool, dunce, nitwit, blockhead
  comb. form ono
jackdaw coe, daw, kae, (black)bird, grackle
  genus Corvus
jacket bajo, grego, blazer, hietle, reefer, wampus
  Arctic parka, anorak, temiak
  armor acton
  knitted gans(e)y, sontag, cardigan, penelope
  short Eton, jerkin, spencer
  sleeveless vest, bolero
jackknife barlow, clasp knife
jackpot all, award, windfall
jackrabbit hare
jackstay rope, horse, staff
jackstones dibs
Jacob Israel (new name)
  brother Edom, Esau
  daughter Dinah
  descendant Levite, Israelite
  father-in-law Laban
  ladder phlox, flower
  parent Isaac, Rebekah
  retreat Haran
  son Dan, Gad, Levi, Asher, Judah, Joseph, Reuben, Simeon, Zebulum, Benjamin, Isaachar, Naphtali

vision Bethel
wife Leah, Bilhah, Rachel
wrestled with angel
jade ju, fag, nag, cloy, pall, plug, tire, green, hussy, weary, tremolite
jaded worn, blase, sated, glutted
jaeger bird, gull, skua, allan, shooi, hunter, diamond
Jael
  husband Heber
  victim Sisera
jag barb, load, prick, scrap, tooth, indent, quantity
Jagannath
  place of worship Puri
jagged erose, rough, hackly
jaguar car, cat, ounce, tiger, panther
jaguarundi cat, eyra
Jahaziah, Jahzeiah
  father Tikvah
Jahzeel, Jahziel
  father Naphtail
jai alai game, pelota
  basket racket cesta
  court fronton
jail can, jug, brig, stir, pokey, cooler, hoosgow, calaboose, penitentiary
  fever typhus
jailer caid, guard, gaoler, turnkey
Jair
  father Segub
  grandfather Hezron
  son Mordecai, Elhanan
Jairite Ira
jake fine, rube, greenhorn
jako parrot
Jalam
  father Esau
  mother Oholibama
jalousie blind, shutter
jam fix, bear, bind, crush, spread
Jamaica island
  bitter drug quassia
  capital Kingston
  dogwood barbasco
  export rum

ginger alcohol jake
hairstyle dreadlocks
monetary unit dollar
music reggae
nationalist Garvey
James
  brother Joh, Jesus, Joses
  cousin Jesus
  father Zebedee, Alphaeus
  mother Mary, Salome
James, Henry
  author Confidence, Daisy Miller, The American, The Europeans, The Bostonians, The Golden Bowl, The Tragic Muse
Jamshid Yima
  realm Persia
Jane Eyre
  author Charlotte Brontë
  lover Rochester
jangle ring, bicker, wrangle
jangling harsh, dissonant
janitor porter, charman, custodian
Janizarian chief dey
japan lacquer, varnish
Japan, Japanese Nip(p)on
  abacus soroban
  abalone awabi
  aborigine Aino, Ainu
  alcoholic beverage saki
  art design notan
  apricot ume, ansu
  baron daimio, daimyo
  battle cry banzai
  bay ise
  boxes inro
  Buddha Amida, Amita
  Buddhist festival Bon
  Buddhist sect Zen, Jodo-shu, Shin-shu
  button netsuke
  calisthenics judo, karate
  cherry fuji
  church tera
  city Kobe, Nara, Kyoto, Osaka, Sendai
  clan Satsuma
  clogs geta

coin rin, yen, koban, tempo, ichibu
court dairi
dancing girl geisha
deer sika
dish rice, sushi, tempura, sukiyaki
dog tanate
drama no(h)
drink mate, sake, saki
fan ogi
festival Bon, Matsuri
fish aya, tai, fugu
garment haori, kimono, mumpei
girdle obi
girl mousme(e)
god Ebisu, Hotei, Benten, Jurojin
goddess Amaterasu
harp koto
lacquer urushi
magnolia yulan
measure bu, jo, cho, hiro, tsubo
money mo, ro
outcast eta, ronin
pire matsu
plum kelsey
quince japonica
religion (early) Shinto
rice cake ame
ruler mikado, shogun
samurai ronin
seaweed nori
shoes geta, zori
song uta
storm monsoon, typhoon
street Ginza
suicide hara-kiri, hari-kari, seppuku
sword catan
untouchable eta
volcano aso(san), fuyi
weight fun, kin, rin, rjoo, momme
wisteria fuji
wooden shoes geta
writing system kana
zither koto
Japanese-American Nisei, Sansei
jape gag, fool, joke, mock, quip
japery buffoonery

Japeth
  father Noah
  son Magog, Tubal, Meshech
japonica bush, shrub, quince, camellia
jar ola, urn, vase, banga, clash, croppa, krater, discord
  coarse earthen crock, terrine
  Egyptian canopic
  fruit mason
  Gr. pelike
  Mex. piñata
  Philippine banga
  rubber lute
  Sp. olla
  two-handled amphora
  very large cadus
  wide-mouthed ewer
jardiniere jug, pot, urn, stand, flowerpot
Jared
  father Mahalaleel
  son Enoch
jargon argot, lingo, slang, zircon, chinook, gibberish, balderdash
jarl earl, headman, chieftain
Jashub's father Bani, Issachar
jasmine bela, papaw, shrub, flower, jessamy, jessamine
Jason
  father Aeson
  love/wife Medea
  men Argonauts
  rival Creusa
  ship Argo
  teacher Chiron, Cheiron
  uncle Pelias
jasper ruby, morlop, quartz, bloodstone
jauk dally, trifle
jaundice bias, envy, yellow, gulsach, icterus, prejudice
jaunt tour, trek, sally, jounce, ramble, excursion
jaunty airy, chic, easy, cocky, perky, finical, stylish
Java, Javanese Djawa
  almond talisay
  berry cubeb

carriage sado(o)
cotton kapok
dancers bedoyo
fig tree gondang
island Bali, Lombok, Madura
measure paal, palen
ox bantens
plum duhal, lomboy
rice field sawah
speech krama, ngoko
squirrel jelerang
temple c(h)andi, tjandi
weight amat, pond, tali
wild dog adjag
javelin dart, lance, spear, assagai, assegai, harpoon
cord amentum
game jerrid
jaw maw, chop, vise, scold, chatter
comb. form gnath(o)
lower mandible
muscle masseter
part chin
pert. to malar, gnathic
upper maxilla
jawab reply, answer, balance, building
jawbone maxilla, mandible
jawless agnathic, agnathous
jayhawker Kansan, fighter, guerrilla, bird of prey
jaylike bird piet, magpie
jazz hot, cool, funky, ragtime, West Coast, progressive, third-stream
Jedidah
  husband Amon
  son Josiah
jeer boo, gibe, hoot, jabe, scoff, sneer, taunt
jeering glaiks, sarcasm
Jeeves creator Wodehouse
Jefferson politician, lawyer, farmer
  home Monticello
Jehiada
  wife Jehosheba
Jehoahaz
  brother Jehoiakim
  father Jehu, Josiah

mother Hamutal
son Joash, Jehoash
Jehoshaphat
  father Asa
  son Jehu
Jehovah God, Jah, Ja(h)ve, Yhva, Yhwa, Yahveh, Yahweh
jehu driver
jejune arid, flat, trite, vapid, insipid, sterile
jellify gel, jelly
jelly jam, colloid, conserve, preserve
  animal gelatin(e)
  base pectin
  grape sapa
  -like gel (material), gelatinous
  meat aspic
jellyfish medusa, acaleph
  group discophora
  part exumbrella
Jena
  glass objective unar
jennet ass, horse, donkey
jeofail mistake, oversight
jequirity licorice
Jerahmeel
  son Oren, Achia
jeremiad tale, lament, tirade, complaint
jerez sherry
Jericho
  publican Zaccheus
  woman Rahab
jerk bob, tic, dolt, flip, hike, shog, tweak
jerked beef charqui, biltong
jerkin coat, jacket, salmon, blackjack
jeroboam bowl, bottle, goblet
jersey gansey, sweater
  tea wintergreen, checkerberry
Jerusalem Zion, Jebus, Salem
  captor Omar
  corn durra, kafir
  mountain Zion, Moriah, Olivet
  oak ambrose
  region Perea
Jerusalem artichoke tuber, girasol(e), topinambou

Jespersen
  language ido
jess strap, thong, ribbon, binding
jessamy fop, dandy
Jesse
  father Obed
  son David
jessur snake, viper, daboia
jester fool, mime, clown, buffoon
  roving student goliard
Jesuit
  bark cinchona
  founder Loyola
  motto A.M.D.G.
  saint Regis
jet ebon, gush, ladle, plane, spurt
  -assisted takeoff JATO
Jethro
  daughter Zipporah
jetty mole, pier, groin, wharf
jeune fille girl, miss
Jew Essene, Hebrew, Semite
  dispersion golah, diaspora
  harp trump, bijuela (Sp.), quimbard
  horn shofar
jewel gem, joy, bijou, stone, darling, treasure
  box casket
  case tye
  connoisseur lapidarist
  setting dop, ouch, pave, bezel
  weight tola, carat, karat
jeweler gemmary
  cup dop(p)
  glass loupe
jewelry gems, beads, trinkets, bijouterie
  adorn with begem
  alloy oroide
  artificial paste, strass
  facet bezel, quoin
  setting pave
Jezebel fury, gorgon, virago
  husband Ahab
  victim Naboth
jib arm, gib, balk, sail, crane
jiffy braid, flisk, hurry, gliffy, instant

jig top, boat, dance, carriage
jigger cup, club, glass, support
jihad, jehad war, strife, contest, crusade
jilt mau, girl, cheat, mitten, reject
jimmy bar, pry, neat, dandy, crowbar
Jimsonweed datura
jingoist chauvinist
jinnee eblis
jinni demon, genie, Alukah, spirit, Yaksha
jinx hex, jonah, voodoo
jitters panic, dither, willies
jivatma ego, soul, atman
Joan of Arc Pucelle
  counselors voices
  victory Orleans
Joan
  spouse Darby
job char, task, berth, stint, position
  soft snap, sinecure
Job
  comforter Boil, Elihu, Bildad
  daughter Kezia, Jemima
  home Uz
  tears coix, adlay, grass, plant
Jocasta
  daughter Ismene, Antigone
  husband Oedipus
  son Oedipus, Eteocles, Polynices
jocose dry, droll, merry
John
  Gaelic Ian
  Irish Sean
  Russ. Ivan
  Sp. Juan
John Brown's Body
  author Benet
johnnycake (corn) pone, hoecake
John of Gaunt Lancaster
John the Baptist
  father Zachary
  mother Elisabeth, Elizabeth
John the Evangelist
  brother James
  father Zebedee
  mother Salome

join add, tie, ally, weld, enroll, mortise
joined conjugal
joiner splicer, carpenter
joint hip, butt, link, seam, junction
  articulated hinge
  grass culm, stem
  lubricator synovia
  pert. to nodal, articular
  plant stem phyton
  put out of dislocate
  right angle ell, tee
  sac bursa
  turn outward valgus
  without acondylose
  wooden tenon
joist beam, sleeper, studding
joke fun, gag, quip, caper, sally
Joktan
  father Eber
  son Ophir
joll lurch
jolly boat yawl
Jolly Roger flag, ensign
  user pirate
Joloano moro, sulu
Jonah crab, jinx
  deliverer whale
Jonathan's father Saul
Jones, John Paul
  ship Bonhomme Richard
  victim Serapis
Jonson, Ben
  author The Fox, Epicene, Volpone, Alchemist
Jordan Petra
  part Moab
  region Basham
  valley Ghor
joree chewink
Joseph
  brother Dan, Gad, Levi, Asher, Judah, Reuben, Benjamin
  buyer Potiphar
  father Jacob
  mother Rachel

son Ephraim
stepson Jesus
josh rib, kid, chaff, banter
Joshua
  associate Caleb
  burial place Gaash
  father Nun
  important place Aijalon
  tree yucca, redbud
Josiah
  father Amon
  mother Jedidah
  son Jehoahaz
Josip Broz Tito
joss idol, crowd, image, master
jostle jar, jog, crowd, elbow
jot ace, iota, whit, tittle, particle
jouk dart, duck, hide, fawn, stulk
joule
  part erg
journey hadj, hike, roam, trek, ramble, travel, passage, expedition
  course itinerary
  division lap, leg
  in circuit eyre
  pert. to viatic, peripatetic
  up anabasis
journeying errant
joust bout, spar, tilt, combat
  field list
  ready to atilt
Jove Jupiter
joy
  muse Tara
joya jewel
Judah see also, Judea; Ain, Aman, Hazor, Shema
  brother Dan, Levi, Joseph, Reuben, Simeon
  daughter-in-law Tamar
  father Jacob
  firstborn Er
  king Ahaz, Urziah
  mother Leah
  queen Athaliah
  son Onan

Judaism see also Hebrew, Israel
  abode of the dead Sheol
  alphabet see Quick Reference List
  ascetic essene
  Bible Tora(h)
  text of miqra
  Book of Psalms Tehillim
  bread matzo(h), hallah
  cabalistic book Zohar
  calendar see Quick Reference List
  convert to ger
  dispersion golah, diaspora
  doctrine Mishna(h), Kodashim
  garment shawl, talis
  harp nebel
  healer Asa
  holidays see Quick Reference List
  horn shofar
  immigrant oleb, halutz
  judge shopet
  law Chok, Tora(h), Talmud, Halacha
  land Zion
  lawgiver Moses
  lyre asor
  marriage broker shadchen
  custom levirate
  miter petalon
  mourning period shivah
  Old Testament division Hagiographa
  patriot family Maccabee
  poems yigdal, Azharoth
  prayer book mahzor, siddur
  prophet Amos, Ezra, Elias, Hosea, Jonah, Micah, Naham, Daniel, Elijah, Elisha, Haggai, Habakkuk, Jeremiah, Zechariah
  prophetess Huldah
  sabbath Saturday
  sacred objects urim
  scroll Sepher Torah
  skullcap kippah, yarmulka
  song hat(t)ikvah
  synagogue schul, temple
  tassel zizith
  teacher rabbi
  temple precentor cantor
  vestment ephod

Judas traitor, betrayer
  suicide place Aceldama
Judea see also Judah
  ancient name Judah
  governor Pilate
  king Asa, Herod
  place Berea
judge try, deem, edile, opine, critic, umpire, arbiter, sentence
  bench banc
  chamber camera
  circuit eyre, iter
  entry after verdict postea
  gavel mace
  group bench
  of dead Osiris
  of Hades Minos
  rigorous rhadamanthus
  robe toga
  subordinate junior, puisne
judgment arret, award, wisdom, censure, verdict
  lack acrisy
  use one's discretion, discretionary
judicial
  assembly court
  journey eyre
judiciary bench
  document writ, decision
Judith
  father Beeri
  home Bethulia
  husband Esau, Manasses
  victim Holofernes
juego game, play
jug gaol, jail, flagon, prison, pitcher
  man-shaped toby
Juggernaut Vishnu
juggle bluff, delude, conjure, shuffle
juice sap, broo, resin, gasoline, electricity
  apple cider
  fruit must, stum, wine, vinegar
jujitsu judo
juju charm, amulet, fetish
jujube ber, elb

Juliana Queen
  house Orange
Juliet
  betrothed Paris
  father Capulet
  lover Romeo
Julius Caesar see Caesar
July 14 Bastille Day
jump
  in Gr. game halma
  stick pogo, pole
jumping
  rodent jerboa
  sickness lata(h), palmus
junco finch, snowbird
junction axil, seam, joint, suture, coupling
June bug dor(r)
June grass poa
Jungfrau peak, mountain
  location Alps
jungle shola
  dweller beast, snake, insect, savage
juniper cade, ezel, cedar, gorse, savin(e), evergreen
junker noble, German, Prussian, conservative
Juno Hera
  consort Jupiter
  messenger Iris
junta group, council, tribunal
junto cabal, coterie, faction
jupe coat, shirt, skirt, stays, tunic, bodice
Jupiter Jove, Zeus, planet
  angel Zadkiel
  consort Hera, Juno
  daughter Bura, Minerva
  epithet Stator
  lover Io
  Roman temple Capitol
  satellite Io, Europa, Callisto
  son Arcas, Castor, Pollux
Jupiter Pluvius rain
jural legal, juristic
Jurassic division Lias
jurema tree, acacia

jurisdiction law, soc, soke, venue, control
  ecclesiastical see, parish, deanery, diocese
  of an emir emirate
juror assizer, talesman, venireman
  group jury, panel
jury panel, peers, dicasts
  attempt to influence embracery
  summons venire
justice due, law, doom, equity, validity
  god Forsete, Forsite
  goddess Maat
  pert. to juridical
  seat banc(us), court, tribunal
justify avow, defend, assert, support
jute tat, desi, gunny, plant, burlap, sacking
Jutlander Dane, German
jutting tor, crag, rock, salient
juvenile kid, actor, green, immature
Juventas Hebe
juxtaposition contact, nearness, proximity

K

K kay, kappa
kaama hartebeest
kaddish hymn, prayer, doxology
kady hat, derby
kae jackdaw
kaffeeklatsch social, gathering
Kaf(f)ir Xosa, Zulu, Bantu
  body of warriors Impi
  corn sorghum
  language Xosa
  servant umfaan
  weapon keri, knobkeroie, knobkerrie
Kafka, Franz
  author Amerika, The Trial, The Castle, Metamorphosis
  character K., Olga, Samsa, Gregor, Joseph K.
kago litter, palanquin
kah plant, carpet, saltwort
kaise ruler, emperor

kaka, kakapo parrot
  genus Nestor
kaki bird, stilt, persimmon
kakkak bittern
kale cole, green, collard, colewort
  sea cole
kalenda calends
kalinite alum
Kalmu(c)k Eleut, Mongol
Kamchatka
  codfish wachna
  salmon mykiss
kamias bilimbi
kanae fish, mullet
Kanaka Hawaiian, Melanesian, Polynesian, Micronesian
kanari almond
Kandh language Kui
kangaroo bilbi, turatt, bettong, marsupial
  female doe, gin, rov
  male boomer
  rat potoroo
  young joey
Kansas see Quick Reference List
Kant
  author Critique of Pure Reason
  category quality, modality, quantity, relation
kapok oil, tree, ceiba, fiber
kaput broken, ruined
karakul fur, lamb, sheep, astrakhan
Karelian lake Seg
karma duty, fate, rite, destiny
Kartvelian Svan(e)
karyotin chromatin
kasha mush, grain, groat, cereal
Kashmir
  alphabet sarada
  capital Srinagar
  deer hangal
  official pundit
  river Jhelum
katchung oil, peanut
Kate shrew
  playwright Shakespeare
kat shrub kafta

kava ava, awa, drink, pepper
  bowl tanoa
kayak canoe, kaiak
kazoo gazoo
kea parrot
Keats
  poem Lamia
Kebbie club, stick, cudgel
ked tick
kedge anchor
keek spy, look, peep
keel vat, ship, ocher, upset, careen, timber, capsize
  part skag, skeg
  right angles to abeam
  shaped carinate
  wedge templet
  without ratite
keelbill ani, ano, bird
keeling codfish
keel over seel, faint, capsize
keen acute, alert, eager, cunning
keenly dearly
keenness edge, acumen, genius, talent, sharpness
keep fend, guard, arrest, husband, maintain, preserve
  back bar, hap, detain, reserve
  going sustain
  in retain
  in view regard
  on continue
  on course cape, head
  out bar, save, except, exclude, withhold
keeper guard, alcade, custos, curator
  door lock nab, risp, stang
  Masonic door tiler
  of golden apples Ithun
  of marches margrave
  of park ranger
keeping care, guard, trust, custody
keepsake token, memento, substance
keest sap, manew, substance
keeve tub, vat, kier, basin
kef tobacco, euphoria, dreaminess
keg tun, cask, firkin
  open unhead

kegler bowler
kelly hat, color, derby, green
kelp ware, varec(h), seaweed
ken view, admit, range, reach, discern
kench bin
Kenilworth
  author Sir Walter Scott
kennel drain, house, sewer, stable, confine
Kent, Kentish
  district Penge
  iceman laet
  sheep romney
  tribal law laes
Kentucky see Quick Reference List
  coffee tree bonduc, chicot
Kenya
  capital Nairobi
  lake Rudolf
  monetary unit shilling
  native/reserve Masai
kerchief curch (Scot.), panuelo, bandan(n)a
kerchoo sneeze
  answer to gesundheit
Keresan Indian Sia
kerf cut, slit, notch, groove
kermis fair, carnival
kernel bunt, core, gist, pith, seed, grain, acinus
  having nucleated
kestrel hawk, falcon, stannel
ketch boat, saic, ship
ketone carone, acetone, camphor
  oily irone, carone
kettle vat, cazo (Sp.), pail, caldron, cauldron
  nose spout
kettledrum naker, tabor, timpani
  cavalry anacra, timbal
  Moorish atabal
kevel bit, peg, bolt, cleat
key quay, reef, pitch, opener, solution
  chain chatelaine
  false glut
  fruit samara
  instr. clavis, manual
  notch ward
  part bit
  pert. to tonal, tonic

skeleton giet, screw
telegraph tapper
keyed up agog, eager, stimulated
keynote theme, tonic, feature
  sign, Gr. music ison
keystone wedge, sagitta, voussoir,
  principle
Keziah
  father Job
khamsin wind
khan inn, title, resthouse, caravansary
Khnemu
  consort Anukit
Khomeini imam
Khyber Pass
  tribe Afridi
Ki
  brother, consort An
  mother Nammu
  son Enlil
Kiang ass, onager
kibble grind, bucket
kibe chap, sore, ulcer, chilblain
kibitzer meddler, converser, spectator
kickshaw toy, food, bauble, gadget
kid hoax, child, banter, leather
  undressed suede
kidney ilk, neer, organ, nature, stripe
  comb. form reni
  Lat. ren
  pert. to renal
  -shaped reniform
  stone jade, calculus, nephrite
Kilauea goddess Pele
kilderkin cask, barrel, measure
Kilimanjaro peak Kibo
kill fake, slay, cancel, deaden, achieve, channel, poniard, slaughter
  by stoning lapidate
  by strangling gar(r)otte
killer whale orc(a), grampus
killing of
  brother/sister fratricide
  father patricide
  king regicide
  mother matricide
  self suicide

small child infanticide
wolf lupicide
Kilmer poem Trees
kiln bake, oven, roast, stove, tiler
kiloliter stere
kilt pleat, skirt, fasten, filibag
  pouch for sporran
kilter order, condition
kimmer girl, witch
kimono sash obi
kin see also kinship; germane
kind ilk, good, sort, genre, benign, species
  comb. form geno
  same homogeneal
kindle beet(e), fire, brood, illume
kindling fag(g)ot, sticks, tinder
kindness favor, bounty, service, goodwill
kindred kin, clan, blood, flesh, related
kine cows, beasts, cattle
kinetic active
king rex (Lat.), rey (Sp.), roi (Fr.), ruler,
  sovereign
  chamber camarilla
  family dynasty
  legendary Lud, Hogni, Sesha, Oberon
  symbol scepter
King Arthur
  abode Avalon
  birthplace Tintagel
  court site Camelot
  death place Camlan
  father Uther
  forest Calydon
  hound Cavall
  knight Galahad, Lancelot, Percivale
  lady Enid
  magician Merlin
  mother Igraine
  queen Guinever(e)
  sword Excalibur
king clover melilot
king crab limulus
kingfish haku, opah, bagara
kingfisher halcyon
King Henry IV
  character Blunt, Henry (Hal), Percy,
    Poins, Scroop

King Lear
  daughter Regan, Goneril, Cordelia
  dog Tray
kinglet bird, wren, lionet
kingly regal, royal, basilic, leonine
King of
  Bath Nash
  Beggars Carew
  Dwarfs Alberich
  Fairies Oberon
  Fomorians Balor
  Golden Touch Midas
  Judea Herod
  Serpents Shesha
  waters Amazon
king's
  bodyguard thane
  evil scrofula
  letter brief
  topper (cards) ace
  yellow orpiment
kink loop, chink, spasm, caprice
  in thread burl
kinkajou potto, mammal
kinship clan, race, blood, family, relation, connection
  father's side agnat(e)
  Mohammedan law nasab
  mother's side enate
kinsman ally, friend
kiosk newsstand, pavillion
kipe basket
Kipling, Rudyard
  hero/novel Kim
  poem L'Envoi
  Shere tiger Khan
kirtle coat, gown, cover, tunic
Kish
  father Ner
  son Saul
kismet fate, moira, destiny
kiss buss, peck, caress, salute, smooch
  -me quick bonnet
  of peace pax
  science philematology
  sculptor (of The Kiss) Rodin
kist box, cist, locker

kit bag, box, kitten, outfit, caboodle
kitchen ben (Scot.), chil (Indian), cuisine, scullery
  garden olitory
  pert. to culinary
  ship galley
  tool corer, ricer, beater, grater, opener, sifter, spatula, colander
kite fly, bird, hawk, soar, raise, rascal
  Europe glede
  genus Elanus
kith friend, neighbors, associates
kittenish coy, frisky, playful
kittiwake bird, gull, waeg, annet
kitty cat, ante, pool, stakes
kiwi roa, bird
  genus Apteryx
kloof glen, gorge, ravine
knable boy, piano
knack art, ease, skill, facility
knap cut, rap, blow, chip, knoll, nibble
knapsack bag, case, wallet
knapweed bluet, bellweed, hardhead
knarred knotty, gnarled
knave jack, cheat, rogue, miscreant
  in clubs pam
  in cribbage nob
knavery fraud, mischief, villainy
knead elt (Scot.), mix, malax, massage
knee bow, joint, supplicate
  armor genouille
  bend kneel, genuflect
  bone cap, rotula, patella
  breeches knickers
kneeling desk prie-dieu
kneepan rotula, patella
knell bell, omen, summon
knickknack toy, bauble, gadget, trifle
knife cut, dirk, stab, blade, bowie, wound
  Burmese dah
  case sheath
  dealer/maker cutler
  Dyak parang
  Hindu kukri
  Irish skean
  large bolo, snee

Malay kris, creese
Maori patu
one-bladed barlow
Philippine bolo, machet(t)e
plaster/paint spatula
sharpener hone, steel, stone, strop
Spanish machet(t)e
surgical fleam, catlin, scalpel
knight eques, lover, gallant, templar
  attendant page, squire
  banner gonfonon
  champion paladin
  cloak tabard
  ensign/flag pennon
  famous Modred, Roland, Caradoc,
    Galahad, Lancelot, Lohengrin
  fight joust
  horse charger, palfrey
  rank above baronet
  rank next armiger
  (of the) road hobo, tramp
  Round Table see King Arthur
  servant varlet
  wife dame, lady
  wreath orle
knighthood chivalry
  confer dub
knightly brave, courteous, chivalrous
knitting craft, union, network
  of a blanket afghan
  machine guide sley
  rod needle
  stitch in purl
  term cast off
knob boss, lump, stud, umbo, bunch,
  handle
  -like nodal
  ornamental boss, knop, stud
  pointed finial
  wood burl, knur
knobby gouty, hilly, knotty
knobkerrie club, kiri, stick, weapon
knobstick cane, club, scab, blackleg
knock hit, rap, blame, decry, strike
  -about actor, sloop, handyman
  down fell, floor, prostrate
  -kneed valgus

  off rob, kill, stop, overcome
  out bash, daze, kayo, beaut, dilly, flatten
knoll hill, knob, lump, mound
knot snag, tuft, joint, nodule, problem,
  sandpiper
  fibrous nep, noil
  free from enode, unravel
  in wood knag
  pert. to nodal
  running slip, noose
  thread burl
  tree knur, gnarl
knotted lace tatting
knotty hard, gouty, craggy, difficult, intricate
know ken, see, wist, discern, realize
  -it-all smarty, wiseacre
  -nothing agnostic, ignoramus
knowing wise, acute, sharp, artful, scient,
  cunning, informed, epistemonic
knowledge ken, lore, ology, wisdom, sapience, erudition
  highest, Plato noesis
  instrument organon
  lack atechnic, nescience
  object scibile, cognitum
  pert. to gnostic
  seeker philonoist
  slight inkling, smatter
  summary encyclop(a)edia
  systematized science
  universal pantology
known couth, famed, famous, renowned
knuckle joint, strike, submit
  bone dib
kobird cuckoo
kobold gnome, nisse, goblin, spirit,
  brownie
koel bird, cuckoo
kohinoor diamond
kohl antimony
  used in mascara, eye makeup
kohlrabi cabbage turnip
koklas fowl, pukras, pheasant
kokoon gnu
kokopu fish, para
Kol
  dialect Ho, Mundari

kola nut, jackal
kopeck coin
  one hundred ruble
kopje hill, mound
Korah
  father Esau, Eliphaz
  mother Oholibamah
Koran Alcoran
  chapter Sura
  compiler's son Ali
  interpreter ulema, alfaquin
  pert. to alcoranic
  register sijil(l)
  scholars, body of Ulema
Korea, Korean Choson
  money won, hwan
  peninsula Ongjin
  river Kum, Hans, Yalu, Naktong
  soldier Rok
  town Fusan, Kanko, Pochon, Moonsan,
    Seishin
  weight won
kosher pure, clean, proper, approved,
  Kashruth
  opposite tref, treif
Koussevitzky, Serg conductor
kowtow fawn, toady, grovel, truckle
kra ape, macaque
kraal hut, pen, crawl, enclosure
Kriemhild
  brother Gunther
  husband Etzel, Attila, Siegfried
  slayer Hildebrand
  victim Hagen
krimmer fur, (lamb)skin
kris dagger
Krishna Vishnu, Juggernaut
  grandson Aniruddha
  mother Devaki
  paradise Goloka
Kornus
  wife Rhea
Krupp work site Essen
krypton
  symbol Kr
kudize hail, praise, acclaim, commend

kudo fame, glory, praise
kudu antelope
kulak farmer, peasant
Kulanapan pomo, Indian
kumiss drink
kumquat fruit
  kin orange
Kuomintang
  council Yuan
Kurd Persian
  ancestors Gordyaean
Kurile island Iturup, Chishima
Kurland Peninsula inhabitant Lett
kurrajong tree, shrub
kurtosis arc, curvature
kusu mouse
kuttar dagger
kvass beer
Kwantung seaport Dairen
kylin unicorn
kylix cup, chalice
kyphosis humpback, hunchback
Kyushu volcano Aso

L

L el, ell
La Rochefoucauld's forte maxims
laager camp
Laban
  daughter Leah, Rachel
labellum lip, petal
labia lips
  minora nympha(e)
labor toil, work, strive, childbirth
  group Artel, union
  omnia vincit
  union negotiation collective bargaining
laboratory
  burner etna, bunsen
  need acids, oleates, test tubes
laborer serf, prole, worker
  Ch. cooly, coolie
  Egyptian fellah

Indian toty
Mex. peon, bracero
migratory okie
Sp. peon, obrero
underground sandhog
unskilled navvy, bohunk
labra lips
Labrador peninsula
labroid fish wrass
laburnum shrub, pea tree, sandalwood
labyrinth maze
builder Daedalus
legendary dweller minotaur
lace whip, weave, string, intertwine
cape mantilla
collar bertha
edging frill
frilled r(o)uche
loop(s) purl
pattern toile
three-cornered fichu
Lacedaemon Sparta
lacert(il)ian gecko, lizard, chameleon
Lachesis fate, weird, goddess
lachrymose teary, mournful
lack need, dearth, without, shortage
desire inappetence
of stress atony
lacking void, short, deficient
brightness dim, lackluster
grace clumsy
reverence impious
Laconia
capital Sparta
lacs, one hundred crore
lactase enzyme
lactescent milky
lacuna gap, space, hiatus
ladder stee, scale
part rung, step, round, spoke, stave,
rundle
ladle dip, scoop, dipper
dip/pour with lave
spout geat
Lady of the Lake Ellen, Nimue, Vivian
ladybird beetle, vedalia

Laertes
sister Ophelia
son Odysseus
lagan jetsam, flotsam
laggard backward, loiterer
lagomorph hare, pika, rabbit
lagoon lake, pond
hare's form
island Ellice
site atoll, coral reef
lair den, cave, haunt, lodge
Laius
son Oedipus
lake loch, pool, lagoon
artificial reservoir
basin playa
bird loon
fish pollan
herring cisco
island in a holm
outlet bayou
study limnology
world's lowest Dead Sea
laky dark red
lalique glass
lamb child, sheep, fatling
breast carre
fur karakul
hide kip
holy agnus
mother ewe
pet cade, cosset
-skin budge
lambent glowing, flickering
lambrequin drapery
Lamech
son Noah, Jabal, Jubal
wife Adah
lamelli
prefix leaf, plate, scale
lamellibranch clam, oyster, mollusk
lamellirostral bird duck, swan, goose
lamentation plaint, wailing, jeremiad
lamia demon(ess), vampire, sorceress
lamiaceous plant mint, bergamot,
rosemary

lamina flake, layer, scale
  brain obex
laminated layered, sheeted
  material plywood
  rock shale
lammergeier vulture, ossifrage
lamp torch, gooseneck, luminaire, flashlight
  decorative lampion
  holder cresset
  miner's Davy
  part wick, burner, chimney, cresset
  waving arati
lamprey eel, cyclostome
  lanate wool(l)y
lance cut, spear, javelin
  barb fluke
  part rest, morne
lancelet amphioxus
Lancelot knight
  liege Arthur
  love Elaine
  mistress Guinevere
  nephew Bors
lancet (surgical) knife, scalpel
  point neb
lancewood yaya
land soil, earth, tract, country
  along river holm
  border rand
  close garth
  cultivated arado, tillage
  grant homestead
  holder thane
  marshy maremma
  mine claymore
  owner of adjacent abutter
  pert. to agrarian, geoponic
  pledged as security wadset
  point of low spit
  reclaimed polder
landau carriage
landloper vagabond
landowner laird, freeholder, proprietor
landscapist topiarist
landtag diet, assembly
language lip, speech, parlance
  artificial ido, esperanto

classical Gr., Lat.
dialect idiom, lingo
difficulty of understanding dysphasia
hybrid jargon
mixed pidgin
Romance French, Catalan, Italian,
  Spanish, Romanian, Portugese,
  Provencal
langur monkey, simpai
laniferous fleecy
lanner(et) falcon
lantana majorana, viburnum
lantern lamp, cresset, lanthorn
  feast bon
  roof louver
  wheel trundle
lanugo down, hair
lanyard cord, rope, thong
Laomedon
  kingdom Troy
  son Priam
Laos kingdom
  language French, Laotian
  monetary unit kip
lapactic laxative, cathartic
lapel flap, rever(s), facing
  stiffener wigan
lapillus rock
lapin fur, rabbit
lapis stone
  lazuli azure blue, sapphirus
Laplander
  sledge pulk(h)a
lappet flap, lobe, label
lapsus slip, lapse
laputan absurd, dreamy, impractical
lapwing peewee, plover
large man-size, outsize
  prefix mega, macro
  scale extensive
  very huge, decuman
largess(e) gifts, bounty
lariat rope, lasso, reata, riata
  eye honda, hondo
lark prank, wagtail, songbird, adventure
  genus Alauda
larrigan moccasin

larva maggot, planula
  beetle grub
  butterfly caterpillar
  case enclosing indusium
  final stage chrysalis
  fly gentle
  frog tadpole
  moth egger, caterpillar
  next form pupa
laryngeal clearing sound ahem
laser inventor Townee
lashings loads, ropes, punishments
lasso rope, reata, riata, lariat
last end, omega, ultimate
  chance Montana
  in succession lattermost
  Mohican Uncas
  person in a race tailender
  supper Cena
  syllable of word ultima
latchkey notch ward
lateen dhow, sail, vessel
lateral sideways, sidewise
  opposed to medial
laterite clay
latex
  plant's milk
  source poppy, milkweed, rubber tree
lathe
  clamp chuck, machine
  operator turner
Latin Roman, Italian, language, Spaniard
  always semper
  and et
  and others et al
  before ante
  being esse
  book liber
  brother frater
  day diem, dies
  discourse sermo
  earth terra
  egg ova, ovum
  fish pisces
  head caput
  highest summa
  holy sanctus

law jus, lex
  man homo
  name nomen
  peace pax
  star stella
  this hoc
  thus sic
  total summa
  water aqua
  we nos
  without sine
  year anno, annus
latite lava
latitude width, scope, extent, breadth
Latona Leto
  progeny Diana, Apollo
latrant barking, snarling, complaining
Latter-Day Saint Mormon
lattice grille, trellis, espalier
Latvia, Latvian Lett(ic)
  coin lat
  monetary unit lat(u)
laugh bray, deride, guffaw, chortle
  able to risible
  pert. to gelastic
  too much cachinnate
lauraceous tree laurel, nutmeg, avocado, camphor
laurel bay, shrub, azalea, cajeput, rhododendron
  bark coto
  family heath, kalmia
  mountain bush, calico
lava rock, magma, latite, taxite
  cinder scoria
  pieces slag, scoria
  stream coulee
lavender mint, aspic, purple
  product oil, perfume
laverock lark
law jus, lex, code, canon, statute, ordinance
  appendix in codicil
  break the infract
  imperial ukase
  kind common, statute, (un)written
  pert. to legal, canonic, forensic
  written statute

lawgiver Draco, Minos, Moses, Solon
lawsuit case, action
  party to suer, litigant, litigator
lawyer barrister, solicitor, mouthpiece
  Bible Blackstone
  cap coif
  patron saint Ives
laxative physic, cathartic, purgative
  drug aloes
  leaf senna
  pulp cassia
lay set, poem, ditty, deposit
  aside table
  down arms surrender, capitulate
  open expose
  siege invest
  waste ravage
layman laic, amateur
lazar leper, beggar
lazy indolent, sluggish
  fellow drone, idler
  Susan tray, turntable
leaching product lye
lead guide, metal, pilot, bullet, minium
  black graphite, plumbago
  oxide litharge
  poisoning plumbism, saturnism
  red minium
  white ceruse
leader head, chief, commander
  in printing dots, dashes
  sheep bellwether
leaf page, petal, tendril
  bud gemma
  central vein midrib
  comb. form phyll(o)
  disease rust, mosaic
  fern frond
  front recto
  -like phylloid
  miner beetle hispa
  part (mid)rib, vein, blade, stalk, stoma, lamina, stipel, petiole, stipules
  point mucro
  pores stoma
  side recto, verso

  tip mucro
  vein rib, nervure
leafless aphyllous
  plant cactus
leafstalk chard, celery, rhubarb
Leah
  father Laban
  husband Jacob
  sister Rachel
  son Levi
leal true, loyal
leam husk
lean cant, spare, incline
  -to roof, shed, shack
leap dive, loup, bound, vault, spring
  ballet entrechat
  year bissextile
Lear
  daughter Regan, Goneril, Cordelia
  dog Tray
  follower Kent
learned wise, erudite, educated, informed
  man sage, pandit(a), pundit, savant, scholar
  people clerisy, literati
learning lore, education
  branch ology, science
  shallow sciolism
lease let, tenure, contract
  grant demise
  party to a lessee, lessor, tenant, landlord
leash curb, rein, lunge, control
  hound limer
  ring terret
leather kid, calf, suede, Morocco
  armor gambeson
  bookbinding skiver
  cutter skiver
  factory tannery
  kind napa, levant, oxhide, chamois
  -like coriaceous
  maker tanner
  saddle mochila
leatherback turtle
leatherfish lija
leatherneck gyrene, marine

leatherwood wicopy
leave depart, vamo(o)se, forsake,
  bequeath
  kind sabbatical
  military furlough
  out omit, elide
  secretly elope, decamp
leaven barm, yeast, sourdough
leaves pages, departs, foliage
  cluster rosette
  having petaled, foliaged, foliaceous
  having two bifoliate
  of foliar
Lebanon, Lebanese
  dance dabkeh
  monetary unit pound
  people Arab
  seaport Tyre, Saida, Tripoli
lebensraum living space
lebistes guppy
lectern ambo, pulpit
Leda
  daughter Helen, Clytemnestra
  husband Tyndareus
  lover, myth. swan, Zeus
  son Castor, Pollux
ledger
  entry debit, credit, interest
lee shelter, protection
  opposed to stoss, windward
leech worm, annelid, parasite
  -like hirudinoid
  sucker acetabulum
leek bulb, allium, scallion
leet court
left gone, departed, larboard
  comb. form l(a)evo
  -handed dubious, southpaw, sinistral
  hand of page levo, verso
  political liberal, radical
  turn haw
leg gam, pin, limb, shank
  bone tibia, fibula
  from knee to ankle crus, shank
  in heraldry gamb
  joint hock, knee, ankle

pert. to sural, crural
  thigh femur
  vein saphena
legal jural, licit, valid, lawful
  arrest caption
  claim lien, demand
  code pandect
  delay mora
  notice monition
  paper deed, writ
  record acta, estreat
  right droit
  tender money
  thing res
  warning caveat
  wrong tort
legally
  competent sui juris
legend myth, saga, fable
legging(s) gaiter, puttee, puttie, gambade
Leghorn hat, chicken, Livorno
legislature congress, parliament
  lame duck rump
legless amphibian caecilian
legume soy, bean, seed, plant, lentil
legumin globulin
lehua tree, myrtle
leister spear, trident
leisure ease, otiose, vacation
leman lover, mistress
lemma bract, membrane
lemming rat, rodent
lemon fruit, citrus
  -juice squeezer reamer
  vitamin C, citrin, ascorbic acid
  peel relish
lemure potto, monkey, sifaka
  arboreal loris
  flying galago, colugo
  kin tarsier
  nocturnal loris
lemuroid potto
length extent
  finger to elbow cubit
  having linear
  of day's march etape

lenis mild, soft, smooth
  opposed to fortis
lenitive laxative, soothing
leno weave, fabric
lens meniscus
  kind convex, concave
  -shaped lentoid, lenticular
lent imprest
Lent
  observance fasting, Penitence
lentigo freckle
L'envoi verse, stanza, inscription
leopard cat, ounce, ocelot, panther
  young whelp
leper lazar, outcast
  hospital spital
  patron saint Giles
lepidolite mica
lepidopteron moth, butterfly
leporid animal hare, rabbit
leprechaun elf, fairy, goblin
leptus mite, larva
lerot dormouse
lesbian erotic, Sappho, homosexual
less minor, smaller
  in music meno
lesson exercise, instruction
  from fable moral
  music etude
let rent, allow, lease, assign, abandon
  down lower, slacken, disappoint
  it be given detur
  it stand sta, stet
  sink vail
lethargic dull, drowsy, comatose
  sleep sopor
Lethe river, oblivion
Leto Latona
  daughter Diana, Artemis
  son Apollo
letter breve, epistle, message
  cross stroke serif
  cut off last apocope
  main stroke stem
  papal bull
  representing a word logogram

short memo, note
  to the exact, literal, precise
lettuce cos, Bibb, salad, Boston, minion,
  iceberg, romaine
leucorrhea whites
Levantine ship, silk
  garment grego, caftan
  state Syria, Lebanon
level flat(ten), rase, raze, plane
  comb. form plani
levulin carbohydrate
lexicographer Roget, wordman,
  compiler
lexicographic work thesaurus,
  dictionary
liang tael, weight
lias rock
libel malign, calumny, slander
libido sex, lust, desire
library bibliotheca
  reading place carrel(l)
  supervisor curator, librarian
libretto book, text, words
Libya, Libyan kingdom
  gulf Sidra
  leader Gaddafi, Gadhafi, Khadafy
lice vermin
  of pedicular
lich corpse
licit legal
lichen alga, moss, fungus
  genus Usnea, Evernia
licorice pea, abrin
lie fib, perjure, mendacity, admissable
  anchored moored
  detector polygraph
lied song, lyric
lierne rib
life breath, animation, existence
  destruction biolysis
  insurance tontine
  pert. to biotic(al)
  prefix bio
  principle jive, atman, prana, spirit
  without dead, amort, azoic
lifting muscle erector, levator

ligament taenia, tendon
  comb. form desmo
ligan jetsam, flotsam
light glim, neon, kleig, illume, illumination, incandescent
  anchor kedge
  around sun aureola
  celestial halo, corona, nimbus
  fuse spit
  giving substance phosphor
  measure lumens
  of reflected catoptric
  pert. to photic
  ring corona
  science optics, photics
  without aphotic
lighthouse phare, beacon
lignaloes aloes
ligneous woody, xyloid
like akin, enjoy, choose, similar
  comb. form ine, oid, home(o)
  ladder scalar
  tail caudal
  wing pteric
likeness image, effigy, similarity
  bad caricature
likewise also, ditto, moreover
lilac shrub, flower, syringa
lily lys, arum, lotus, tulip, squill
  calla arum
  sand soaproot
  -shaped crinoid
limacine mollusk slug, snail
liman bay, marsh, lagoon, estuary
limb arm, edge, branch, margin
  joint knee, elbow
  muscle flexor, levator
limbus border, edging
lime calx, catch, fruit, citron
  bush snare
  comb. form calci
  powder conite
  tree bass(wood), teil, linden, tupelo
limen threshold, stimulation
limestone tufa, chalk, calcite
  crystallized marble

limicoline bird snipe, curlew, plover, killdeer, sandpiper
limn draw, depict, portray
limonene terpene
limpet lamprey, shellfish
limpkin courian
limulus king crab
Lincoln, Abraham
  hat stovepipe
  sobriquet (honest) Abe, railsplitter
  son Robert, Willie
  wife (Mary) Todd
line cord, queue, route, cordon
  cutting secant
  hair ceriph
  intersecting secant, vector
  nautical earing, marline
  threadlike stria
  with bricks revet
linen toile, napery, batiste, lingerie
  cloth, mummy's byssus
  cloth for bookbinding buckram
  fiber flax
  measure cut
  room ewery
lines
  on map hachure
  on optical lens reticle
ling burbot
lingo cant, jargon, patois, dialect
linguist polyglot
linguistics branch syntax, philology, phonology, semantics, morphology
link join, yoke, nexus, copula
linn linden, ravine, cascade
linnet finch, songbird, lintwhite
lintwhite linnet
lion cat, leo, idol, feline
  female lioness
  group pride
  mane crest
  of God Ariel
  young cub, whelp, lionet
lip labial, labium, superficial
  comb. form chil(o)
  sound labial

lipase enzyme
lips labia, kisser
  comb. form labio
  of the labial
liquefy fuse, melt, thaw
  opposed to solidify
liqueur cognac, kummel, cordial, curacao, ratafia, anisette, Benedictine
  glass pony
liquid clear, fluid, transparent
  body tissue lymph
  fatty oil olein
  measuring device jigger, dosimeter
  opposite solid
  waste slops
liquidambar tree, balsam, sweetgum
liquor mead, tiff, drink, juice, bitters
  alcoholic lush, mescal
  bottle magnum
  drink dram, tiff
  glass snifter
  sap nipa
liripipe tippet
list tip, heel, roll, index, careen, calendar
  ancestors pedigree
  saints canon, hagiology
lister plow
listing table, selvage
listlessness ennui, apathy
litany prayer
literal exact, prosaic, accurate, word-for-word
  translation metaphrase
literary learned, lettered
  collection ana, miscellany
  composition novel, parody, vignette
  criticism review, critique
  extracts analecta
  form poem, essay, prose, verse
  pseudonym Elia, Saki
  society Lyceum
lithograph print, chromo
lithoid stonelike
lithomarge clay, kaolin
Lithuania, Lithuanian Balt, Lett
  coin lit(as), ruble
  seaport/territory Memel
litotes meiosis

litter bier, mulch, bedding, clutter, scatter
  bearer cat, dog, pig
  last-born wallydrag
  of pigs farrow
little lil, few, wee, poco, puny, tiny, small, minute, paltry, petite, trivial
  Bear Ursa Minor
  bit fig, morsel
  by little piecemeal
  comb. form micr(o)
littleneck clam, quahog
liturgy mass, rite, ritual
live exist, vivid, endure, inhabit, subsist
  able to viable
  oak encina
lively spry, agile, vivid, vivacious
  music vivo, animato
liver hepar
  disease cirrhosis, hepatitis, porphyria
  function metabolism
  pert. to hepatic, viscera
  secretion bile, gall
  shaped like hepatic
liverwort agrimony, hepatica, bryophyte
  genus Riccia
living being, extant, animate
  on land/in water amphibian
  prefix livi
  thing organism
  within immanent
lizard gila, monitor, reptile, basilisk
  amphibious newt, salamander
  chameleonlike agama
  climbing iguana
  comb. form sauro, saurus
  fish ulae, saury
  genus Uma, Agama
  legless slowworm, blindworm
  wall gecko
llama alpaca, vicuna, ruminant
  habitat Andes
  hair wool
llanero
  weapon bola
llano plain, steppe
lo ecce, look, behold
loa larva

loach carp
loadstar polaris, lodestar
loaf
  of white bread manchet
lobbyist rainmaker
lobe lappet, lobule
  ear earlop
lobo wolf
lobster macruran, crustacean
  claw chela, nipper, pincer
  feeler palp(us), antenna
  part chela, telson, thorax
  trap pot
local branch, nearby, chapter, topical
  relationship ubiety
loch bay, lake, Ness, pond
lock jam, link, tress, confine
  mechanism detent
locofoco cigar, match
locomotive dolly, mogul, iron horse
  coal car tender
  cowcatcher fender
locust tree, cicada, insect
  tree carob, honey, acacia
lode ore, vein, deposit
  cavity vugh
log bole, diary, timber
  measure scalage
  roller decker
  splitter wedge
loganberry bramble
loggerhead dunce, turtle
  bird shrike
loggia arcade, gallery, portico
logia maxims, sayings
  singular logion
logic reasoning
  deductive syllogism
  major premise sumption
logogriph anagram, word puzzle
logrolling birling
lohan monk, Arhat
loin rack, chump, beefcut
  comb. form lumb(o)
  muscle griskin
loins hips
  pert. to lumbar

lomita hill
London
  ancient name Agusta
  bobby's beat point
  district Soho, Chelsea, Lambeth,
    Mayfair, Limehouse
  streetcar tram
lone sole, solo, isolated, solitary
  Star State Texas
long crave, aspire, hanker, prolix, extended
  ago lang syne
  discourse descant
  fish eel, gar
  knife yatagan
  winded wordy, prolix, verbose
longeron spar
longspur bird, finch, sparrow
loo pam, card game
look con, peer, pore, glance, search, observe
  -alike ringer
  askance leer
  obliquely skew, squint
look over case
lookout
  ship conner
  turret bartizan
loom weave, appear
  frame batten
  part pirn, warp, batten, heddle, roller,
    treadle
loop tab, noose, terry
  in electricity circuit
  in lace picot
  in lariat honda
  -like structure ansa
looper (measuring) worm, larva
loose free, lewd, inexact
  end tagrag
  set turn free, release
loquacious voluble, talkative
  bird jay, magpie
  opposite reticent, taciturn
lord earl, peer, liege, master, prince,
  domineer, nobleman
  attendant thane
  of Hosts God, Jehovah
  privileged Palatine

Lorelei siren, Lurlei
  golden possession comb
  victims sailors, mariners
lorgnon monocle, pince-nez, lorgnette
lorikeet lory, parrot
lorry truck, wagon
losel bum, loafer, ne'er-do-well
loss defeat, forfeiture
  of consciousness syncope, syncopation
  of feeling insensate, anesthesia
  of hair alopecia
  of memory amnesia
  of mental power dementia
  of sense of smell anosmia
  of voice aphonia
lot fate, grist, share, parcel
Lot
  city Zoar
  father Haran
  feast Purim
  sister Milcah
  son Moab
  uncle Abraham
lottery game, chance
  kin keno, bingo, lotto, raffle, numbers
lotus herb, shrub, water lily
  tree sadr, jujube
Louisiana see also Quick Reference List
  boat bateau
  land measure arpent
  native Cajun, Caijan, Creole, Acadian
  tobacco perique
louse nit, aphid, cootie, slater, vermin
lovage parsley
love dote, enamor, liking, affection
  apple tomato
  feast agape
  goddess Freya, Venus
  god Amor, Eros, Cupid
  knot amoret
  meeting tryst
  pert. to erotic, amatory
  potion philter, philtre
loving doting, erotic, amorous
  comb. form phile

low deep, menial, vulgar, inferior
  bow curtsy
  brow plebeian
  necked decollete
lowan leipoa, mallee
lower drop, frown, debase, demote, glower, reduce
  world hell, Hades
  world gods Manes
lowest
  animal life am(o)eba
  point nadir
  point of planet's orbit perigee
lox oxygen, salmon
Loyalite Jesuit
LSD lysergic acid diethylamide
  source ergot
luau feast
  dish poi
lubricant oil, dope, castor, grease, vaseline
Lucan
  work Pharsalia
luce fish, pike
luces lights
  singular lux
Lucifer devil, Satan, light bearer
luck lot, chance, fortuity
  of aleatory
lucule sunspot
lugworm annelid
lumbricoid roundworm
luminary sun, moon, star
luminous bright
  energy light
  radiation aura
lunar pale, pallid, crescent
  crater linne
  month moon
  phenomenon eclipse
lung
  membrane pleura
  sound rale
lungfish dipnoan, mudfish
lungi loincloth
lunule lune, half-moon

Lupercus Faunus
Lupin, thief Arsene
Lupus wolf, disease, constellation
lurk prowl, skulk, sneak
Lusitania, now Portugal
lustrum luster, five-year (period)
lute clay, seal, instrument
  Oriental tar
  relative guitar, mandolin
Lutetia Paris
luthern dormer, window
luxate disjoint, dislocate
luxury-lover Lucullus, sybarite
Luzon
  battlesite Bataan, Manila Bay,
    Corregidor
lying false, reclining, mendacious
  downward prone, acumbent
  flat prostrate
  on one's back supine
lymph humor, serum, spring
  -gland swelling bubo
lymphoid tissue of mouth tonsil
lyncean keen-eyed
lynx bobcat, wildcat, constellation
lyre asor, harp, trigon
lyrebird menura
lyric lied, songlike
  muse Erato
  poem hymn, elegy, sonnet, canzone,
    rondeau
  poet odist, lyrist, lyricist
lyrics of opera/oratorio libretto
lytic lysin
lytta worm

M

M em(ma)
Maas Meuse
mabolo plum
macaco lemur, monkey
macadam road, stones
  material tar, stone, asphalt

Macao
  coin avo
  island Taipa, Coloane
macaroni dandy, pasta
  ingredient durum (wheat), semolina
macaroon cooky, cookie, biscuit, ratafia
maccaboy snuff
mace maul, spice, staff
  reed dod
  royal sceptre
  source nutmeg
macedoine salad, medley
machete bolo, knife
Machiavellian crafty, deceitful
machine tool, motor, device, mechanism
  cutting mower, reaper, cropper
  finishing edger
  glazing calendar
  hoisting gin, crab
  part cam, cog, gear, crank, solenoid
  threshing combine
  tool lathe
  weighing trone
machinist's groove t-slot
mackerel fish, tuna, bonita, albacore
  cured bloater
  net spiller
  young spike, tinker
Mackinaw boat, coat, blanket
  trout namaycush
mackle blot, blur, macule
macrocosm world, universe
macrural crustacean prawn, shrimp,
  lobster
mad sore, angry, rabid, upset, insane, frenetic
  monk Rasputin
Madagascar
  native Hova
made crafted, invented, produced, constructed
  of wood xyloid
  up invented, cosmetized, fabricated
Madeira wine, island
  wine tinta
mademoiselle
  abbrev mlle.
madid wet, moist

madras city, cloth, kerchief
  weight pollam
madrigal glee, poem, song
madwort shrub, alyssum
maelstrom whirlpool
maenad nymph, bacchante
maffle muddle, mumble, confuse, squander
mage wizard, magician
magic art, obeah, wizardry
  black voodoo, sorcery
  horse Bayard
  potion philter
  sign sigil
  symbol pentacle
  word sesame
magistrate judge, justice
  civil syndic
  Gr. Ephor
  Roman Pr(a)etor
magnesium silicate talc
magnet loadstone, lodestone
  alloy alnico
  end pole
magnetic electric, mesmeric, attractive
  direction north, south
  force od, odyl(e)
magnificat hymn, poem, song
magnitude size, extent
magnolia shrub, flower, sweet bay
maguey aloe, agave, fiber
magus magician, sorcerer
maharaja
  wife maharani
mahogany tree, caoba, baywood
  of the meliaceous
  pine totara
Maia May, Pleiade
maid girl, lass, virgin, domestic
  of Astolat Elaine
  of Orleans Joan of Arc
maidenhair fern, ginko
mail post, send, armor, dispatch
  boat packet
  pert. to postal
main duct, chief, power, conduit
  body trunk
  point nub, crux, gist

Maine see also Quick Reference List
  native Down-Easter
maize corn, yellow
  ground samp, grits, hominy
majolica pottery
majuscule uncial, capital
make style, create, devise, produce
  airtight seal, lute
  black negrify
  choice opt
  cross sign sain
  indistinct blur
  into law enact
  like imitate
  out the meaning decipher
  position secure entrench
  small(er) minify
  stupid hebetate
  up form, invent
  watertight calk, caulk
  whole heal, mend, repair
  young rejuvenate
mako shark
Malabar monkey wanderoo
Malacca cane, strait
malachite bice, verditer
Malaga wine, grape
malanders eczema, pustules
malar cheekbone
malaria quartan, paludism
  carrier mosquito
malarial paludal
Malaysia
  ape lar, mias
  apple ohia
  bird megapod
  coin ora, tra(h), tampang
  dyeing method bat(t)ik
  language Malay
  measure pau
  title for man tun
  title for woman toh puan
  weight kati, caddy
male he, manly, virile
  animal ram, boar, bull, stag, stallion
  bee drone
  castrated human eunuch

ferret hob
fish milter
hog boar
kangaroo boomer
plant mas
salmon jack
seal seecatch
sheep ram, tup, wether
swan cob
swine boar
malefic evil, harmful
malic acid salt malate
malicious mean, vicious, spiteful
  burning arson
malignant evil, harmful, virulent
  opposite benign
Malines lace, mechlin
malison curse, malediction
malkin hare, dowdy, scarecrow
mallard (wild) duck, drake
  genus Anas
malleate pound
mallee eucalyptus
mallemuck fulmar, albatross
mallet gavel, hammer, pestle
  presiding officer's gavel
  striking part tup
Malmo man Swede
malmsey wine, grape
  grape malvasia, malvoisie
malt barley, liquor
  liquor ale, beer, stout, porter
  liquor's yeast barm
  sugar maltose
Malta
  wind gregale
maltha tar, cement, bitumen
mamba cobra, snake, elapine
mammal primate, suckler
  egg-laying duckbill, platypus
  extinct mammoth, mastodon
  flesh-eating dog, mink, otter, weasel
  lowest order monotreme
  nocturnal bat, lemur
  water seal, otter, whale, sea cow
mammary
  gland udder

mammet doll, idol, puppet
mammilla teat, nipple
mammoth elephant, enormous
  -like animal mastodon
man male, biped, human, person,
  fortify
  bald-headed pilgarlic
  Genesis Adam, Onan
  handy factotum
  Lat. homo
  lecherous wolf, satyr
  -like robot, android, humanoid
  little manikin
  patient Job
  who annoys women masher
manager gerent, director
  opera impressario
manakin bird, dwarf, model
manatee dugong, cowfish, halicore
manavelins orts, leftovers
Manchu Tungus, Mongolian
  dynasty Ta Ch'ing
manciple slave, steward
Mandan Sioux, Indian
mandolin strumming piece plectrum
mandrel lathe, spindle
maned jubate, leonine
manes soul
mange scab
  cause mite
  loss caused by hair
mango fruit, muskmelon
mania craze, obsession
  for dancing tarantism
manifesto edict, declaration
Manila city, hemp, cigar, paper
  hemp source abaca
maniples, three cohort
manna food, lerp
manner air, mien, method, fashion
  of dress guise
  of speaking diction
  of walking gait, waddle
manners mores, behavior
  study of ethology
manorial court leet
mansard roof, attic, garret

manse parsonage
manta cape, shawl, devilfish
manteau cloak, mantle
mantel ledge, shelf
  ornamental band frieze
mantis crab/shrimp squilla
manual handbook, textbook
  training sloid
manufacturing leftovers shorts
manuscript ms., handwritten
  copier scribe
  leaf folio
  to be set in type copy
manx cat, celt, gael
many myriad, manifold, numerous
  comb. form poly, myria
Maori
  canoe waka
  parrot tui
  weapon patu
map plat, chart, orrery
  line(s) isobar, hachure, osocheim
  maker mercator, cartographer
  maker's abbr. rd., isl., rte.
maple tree, wood, sirup, syrup
  -leaf land Canada
  seed samara
  tree box elder, sycamore
maquis guerrilla
marabou stork, argala
marabout tomb, hermit
maraca rattle
Maracanda Samarkand
marasca cherry
  product liqueur
marble mib, cold, aggie, carrara, shooter, sculpture
  flooring terazzo
  imitation scagliola
  worker's tool burin
March file, month, border, advance
  date Ides
  day's etape
  for dead dirge
marchen tale, story
Mardi Gras carnival, festival
  day Tuesday

home New Orleans
king Rex
mare dam, yaud, horse, dobbin, equine
  tail cloud
  young colt, filly
margarite pearl
margay cat, ocelot
marginal note apostil(le), scholium
marguerite daisy, chrysanthemum
marijuana pot, hemp, ganza, narcotic
  cigarette holder roach clip
marine fleet, naval, soldier
  plant seaweed
  plant group benthos
mariner
  victim (fictional) albatross
mariposa flower lily, tulip
mark scar, stain, symbol, vestige
  adverse demerit
  black stigma
  critical obelus
  for identification dog tag
  missile's target
  of bondage yoke, brand, collar
  of disgrace brand, stigma
  of omission caret, ellipsis
  over syllable breve
  proofreader's dele, stet, caret
  Twain Clemens
  with line striate
  with spots mottle, speckle
marker peg, liner, scorer, milestone
  channel buoy
  grave barrow
  stone cairn
market sell, store, bazaar
  place agora, plaza, emporium
marking instrument scribe
marlin spearfish
marmalade jam, confection
  material peel, rind, fruit
  tree chico, mamey, sapodilla
marmoset mico, monkey, tamarin
marmot rodent, woodchuck, prairie dog
Marquand, John
  sleuth Mr. Moto
marriage Hymen, wedding, nuptials

broker schatchen
dowry dot
hater misogamist
obstacle annulling diriment
pert. to marital
second digamy
vow troth
marrow pith, medulla
bones knees
Mars Ares, planet
comb. form areo
moon Deimos, Phobos
sister Bellona
son Remus
marsh bog, fen, quag, morass, wetland
bird coot, rail, sora
fever helodes
grass reed, sedge
hen coot, rail
plant tule, cattail, bullrush
marshy boggy, fenny
inlet/outlet bayou
marsupial tait, koala, wombat, kangaroo
marsupium formation pouch
marten sable, mammal
fur baum
martin martlet, swallow
martinet tyrant, disciplinarian
Martinique
music beguine
volcano pelee
Maryland see also Quick Reference List
founder Calvert
mask visor, vizard, conceal, disguise
half loup, domino
masker mummer
mason stonecutter
bench banker
chisel broach, tooler
mortarboard hawk
mass wad, clot, lump, liturgy, majority, magnitude
for the dead requiem
meeting rally
of bacteria clump
solidified concretion

Massachusetts see Quick Reference List
massacre carnage
organized pogrom
mast pole, spar, acorns
platform lookout, maintop
support bibb
master dom, boss, chief, sahib, control
pert. to herile
stroke coup
masterpiece magnum opus, chef-d'-oeuvre
mastic resin, cement, liquor
tree acoma
masticating animal cow, deer, goat, bison, camel, llama, giraffe, antelope
mastication product cud
mat snarl, carpet, matrix
leaf yapa
sleeping petate
matador torero, toreador, bullfighter
queue coleta
red cloth used by muleta, muletilla
sword estoque
match fit, team, equal, contest, vesuvian
boxing bout, set-to
stick linstock
wax/wooden vesta
matchmaker schatchen
indefatigable Eros, Cupid
mateless single, azygous
maternal
relationship enation
matgrass nard, marram
mathematical exact, precise, accurate
arc radian
figure graph, diagram
line vector
ratio sine
term (co)sine, constant
matrass flask, bolthead
matrimonial marital, nuptial, conjugal
matted cespitose
matter copy, pith, affair, content
classification animal, mineral, organic, vegetable
in law res
Matterhorn mountain, Mont Cervin
mattock hack, pick(ax)

mattress
  stuffing material ceiba, flock, kapok
maturation meiosis, reduction
Mau Mau land Kenya
maud rug, wrap, plaid, shawl
  clothing for shepherd
mauler
  Manassas (Jack) Dempsey, soubriquet
maumet idol, puppet
Mauser rifle, pistol
mavis bird, thrush
max.
  opposite min.
maxilla jawbone
maxim saw, adage, axiom, gnome, motto,
  precept
  collection sutra
May prime, heyday, maiden, springtime
  apple plant, mandrake
  Day folk dance Morris
  fifteen ides
  tree hawthorn
maybe perhaps, possibly, perchance
maze stupefy, labyrinth
  exit aid clew
mazzard cherry
McCoy, the real genuine
mdse. merchandise
meadow lea, grassland
  barley rie
  grass poa, fescue
  lark troupial
  mouse vole
  poet. mead
meal chow, mess, agape, flour, farina, repast
  coarse samp, hominy, cornmeal
  family potluck
meals board
mean low, base, poor, nasty, snide,
  common, humble, vicious, wretched
  person caitiff
meaning sense, purport
  ambiguous cryptic
means agency, method, riches, resources
  for communicating knowledge
    organon
  of defense muniment

of escape loophole
of expression medium, outlet
measles roseola, rubeola
measure
  cloth ell
  comb. form metro
  depth fathom
  dry peck, rotl, quart, bushel
  equality isometry
  nautical knot, fathom
  of mensural
  of earth geodesy
  of energy entropy
  of wood cord
  paper ream, quire
  sound volume decibel
  wine butt
  wire mil
  yarn lea, spindle
measurement meterage, mensuration
  contents/weight metage
  standard/unit module
meat beef, food, pork, veal, flesh, steak,
  tripe, mutton, tissue, poultry, venison
  and vegetable dish olla, stew, ragout
  carving board trencher
  eater carnivore
  in gravy au jus
  jelly aspic
  leg/ribs cutlet
  paste pem(m)ican
  slice collop
  spiced salami, bologna, sausage,
    pastrami
  strips biltong
meatless maigre, marinari, vegetarian
Mecca
  pilgramage Hadj
  shrine Caaba, Kaaba
medal badge, medallion
  back verso
  face obverse
  space exergue
medals disk, badge, plaque
  of numismatic
Medea sorceress
  father Aeetes

husband Jason
rival Creusa
Medes
  language Avestan
medical iatric, curative
  comb. form iatro
  professional symbol Caduceus
  student medic(o), intern(e)
  suffix oma, itis
medicinal iatric
  bark pereira, cinchona, viburnum
  gum kino
  herb aloe, senna, arnica
  plant rue, tansy, urena, ipecac, simple, spurge, boneset
  root artar, jalap, ginseng, zedoary
  shrub alem
medicine cure, drug, remedy
  cure-all elixir, panacea
  dropper pipette
  measure dose
  mock placebo
  science of iatrology
medieval
  coat gambeson
  flag pennon
  lyric alba
  servant sewer
  shield ecu, pavis
  sport tilt, joust
  tunic gipon, jupon
  vassal vavasor
  weapon mace, lance, oncin, sword
Mediterranean sea, inland, landlocked
  bush caper
  evergreen laurustine
  fish omber
  grass diss
  pine pinaster
  principality Monaco
  resin mastic
  shrub laurustine
  trading ship padrone
  tree carob
  wind solano, mistral, ptesian, sirocco, levanter
medium mean(s), agency, average

response oracle
session seance
spiritualistic psychic
medley melange, mixture, fantasia, pastiche
medrick gull, tern
medulla pith, marrow
Medusa gorgon, jellyfish
  hair snake(s)
  sister Stheno, Euryale
  slayer Perseus
medusan jellyfish
meerschaum pipe, mineral, seafoam
meet equal, seemly, convene
  face-to-face confront
meeting bee, date, rally, caucus, huddle, powwow, session, assembly, conclave, gathering, symposium, conference
  clandestine tryst
  full attendance plenary
  lovers' tryst, rendezvous
  place of "Big Three" Yalta, Potsdam, Casablanca
  room camarilla
  to elect pope conclave
Megiddo Armageddon
Mein Kampf
  author Adolf Hitler
mel honey
melancholic spell hump
Melanesian
  islands Fiji, Solomon
  language Santo Admiralty
melanin pigment
melanous, opposite xanthous
Melba, soprano Nellie
Meleager argonaut
  mother Althea
melicocca genip
melilot clover
melli
  comb. form honey
melodic ariose, lyrical
  phrase ostinato
melody air, aria, strain, cavatina
  counterpoint descant
meloid beetle

melt fuse, soften, liquefy, dissolve
  fat render
  ore smelt
melting pot crucible
Melville, Herman
  character Ahab, whale, Moby Dick, Billy Budd
membrane pia, web, velum, frenum, velamen, covering
  animal eye tapetum
  bird's beak cere
  comb. form hymen(o)
  enclosing caul
  eyeball sclera
  uniting toes/fingers web(bing)
memorabilia ana
memorable notable, worthwhile
  period era, epoch
memory remembrance, recollection, reminiscence
  loss amnesia
  pert. to mnesic
  science to improve mnemonics
Memphis
  god Ptah
  ruler Pharoah
menad nymph, bacchante
Mendel, botanist Gregor
  forte genetics, heredity
Menelaus
  brother Agamemnon
  daughter Hermione
  father Atreus
  wife Helen
meniscus lens, crescent
Mennonite Amish
mentally
  alert acute
  sound sane, lucid
mentum chin
Mephisto(pheles), debtor of Faust(us)
Mercator mapmaker
Merchant of Venice
  character Tubal, Portia, Antonio, Shylock
merchants' guild Hanse
mercuric
  chloride calomel

Mercury Azoth, Hermes, planet, messenger, quicksilver
  shoes talaria
  staff caduceus
mercy killing euthanasia
mere
  nonsense falderal
  nothing fiddlestick
merganser smee, smew, harle, sheldrake
meridian apex, noon, prime, zenith
merino wool, yarn, sheep
meros thigh, surface
Merrimac river, frigate, ironclad
mescal agave, cactus, liquor
mesmeric hypnotic, magnetic
  force od
Mesopotamia Iraq, Babylonia
  wind shamal
messenger envoy, herald, nuncio
  of the gods Hermes, Mercury
Messrs. misters, messieurs
metal tin, iron, lead, copper, aluminum
  assaying vessel test, cupel
  coating rust, zinc, patina
  cutting tool hacksaw
  dross slag
  fastener t-nut
  for coins flan, planchet
  lightest lithium
  marker die, stamp
  mixture alloy
  plate, cut trepan
  purify smelt
  refine smelt
  shaped for coins flan
  suit mail, armor, hauberk
metalloid arsenic, silicon
metalware, enameled tole
Metamorphoses
  author Ovid
  character Thisbe, Pyramus
metaphorlike figure of speech trope, simile
  mixed catachresis
meteor leonid, rainbow, fireball
  train tail
meteorologic prefix strato

metheglin mead, liquor
  material honey
Methodism
  founder Wesley
Methuselah
  famous for age
  father Enoch
  grandson Noah
metis mulatto
metrical
  accent/stress ictus
  time unit mora
metro subway
mewl whine, whimper
Mexico, Mexican
  Aztec emperor Montezuma
  bandit bandido, ladrone
  beverage mescal, tequila
  bird verdin, tinamou
  bread tortilla
  cactus chaute, mescal, peyote
  coin peso, centavo
  dance raspa
  Indian Zuni, Aztec, Lipan, Mayan,
    Otomi, Toltec
  laborer peon, bracero
  mixed-blood mestizo
  pine ocote
  poppy chicalote
  temple reocalli
  weight arroba
Miami county Dade
Michaelmas daisy aster
Michigan see also Quick Reference List
  river Cass
microspores pollen
Midas touch gold
middle hub, mid, center, median
  comb. form medi(o)
  ear drum, tympanum
middy plebe, blouse
mien air, look, manner, bearing, demeanor,
  appearance
migale mouse, shrew
miggle taw, migs
mignon dainty, pretty
migratory nomadic, wandering

bird tern, wi(d)geon
butterfly monarch
creature locust, lemming
horde swarm, Mongols
mildew mold, blight, fungus
mile
  nautical knot
  one-eighth furlong
  one-third li
military army, corps, militia, soldiers
  cap kepi, busby, shako
  force army, corps, legion, militia
  formation phalanx
  group army, division
  jail brig
  messenger estafet
  movement march, deployment
  roll muster
  station camp, fort, garrison
  storehouse depot, etape, arsenal
  truck amtrac, camion
milk lac, suck, extract, emulsion
  comb. form lact(o)
  curd casein
  curdled clabber
  giving milch
  pert. to lactic, lacteal
  sugar lactose
  with au lait
  without yeld
milkfish awa, sabalo, tarpon
milkwort senega
miller moth, machine
millet grain, grass, panic, pearl
  sorghumlike milo
million
  comb. form mega
mim shy, quiet, demure
mimosa herb, acacia
  descriptive word for shrinking
mind nous, psyche, reason, purpose
  bear in remember
  call to recollect
  of the mental, phrenic
mine dig, pit, source, tunnel, explosive
  car/truck hutch
  entrance adit

kind coal, gold, silver, diamond
passage stulm, winze
safety lamp davy
vein lode
worker miner, pitman, collier
mineral ore, talc, barite, spinel, fluorite
black coal, graphite
blue iolite, lazulite
glassy silica
hardest diamond
magnetite lodestar
mixture magma
radioactive carnotite
silicate mica
softest talc
truck corf
vein lode
miniature
tree bonsai
minify reduce
opposite magnify
minister serve, curate, vizier
assistant deacon
home manse, rectory, parsonage
Minnehaha
love Hiawatha
Minnesota see Quick Reference List
minnow gudgeon, moonfish
minor petty, youth, nonage, underage
details minutiae
offense misdemeanor
planet Amor, Eros, Ceres, Hermes,
planetoids
Minorite Friar, Franciscan
Minos
kingdom Crete
monster minotaur
mint herb, candy, stamp, fabricate
genus Mentha
product coin(s)
Minuit's bargain New York
minute wee, tiny, petty, instant, miniscule
comb. form micro
groove stria
minutiae details
Mira star
constellation Cetus

miracle feat, sign, anomy, wonder
scene Cana, Lourdes
Miriam
brother Aaron, Moses
Miranda
father Prospero
misanthrope (man) hater
kind cynic
miscellanea ana
misdeed sin, crime, fault
miser niggard, skinflint
of fiction Marner, Scrooge
misle mist, drizzle
misogynist woman hater
missal prayer book
missel thrush
missile arrow, rocket, projectile
detecting device radar
part warhead
returning boomerang
whaler's harpoon
Mississippi see also Quick Reference List
native tadpole
Missouri see Quick Reference List
misstep trip, error, faux pas
mistral wind
misunderstanding imbroglio
misuse abuse, mistreat
of words malapropism
mixed impure, motley, mongrel
blood, person of metis, mulatto
language jargon, pidgin
metaphor catachresis
mizzen sail
mnemonic subject memory
Mnemosyne
daughters Muses
moa bird, ratite
Moab kingdom
father Lot
Moby Dick
author Herman Melville
mochila knapsack
mochy damp, misty, muggy
mock defy, false, mimic, scoff, deride, imitate
attack feint
up model, dummy

modal auxiliary verb can, may, must, could, might, would, should
model design, pattern, exemplar, standard, prototype
  for imitation lodestar
  of perfection ideal, paragon
modified leaf bract
modus way, means
  operandi procedure
  vivendi compromise
mogo hatchet
moha millet
mohair fiber, fabric, garment
  source angora
Mohammed Mahomet, Mahound
  birthplace Mecca
  burial place Medina
  flight Hegira
  follower Islam, Muslim
  successor Calif
  wife Aisha
Mohammedan
  angel Azrael
  bible Koran, Alcoran
  canonical law Sharia
  crusade Jehad, Jihad
  festival Bairam
  god Allah
  infidel Kafir
  law Sunna(h)
  noble Amir, Emir
  priest Imam
  saint Pir
  scholars Ulema
  sect member Shiite, Sunnite
  slave mameluke
  woman's clothing izar
moire silk, tabby, fabric
moisture
  comb. form hygr(o)
  condensed dew, mist, rain, distillate
molasses treacle
  source cane, sorgo
mold die, fen, calm, cast, model
  pert. to humic
moldable fictile
molding ogee, fillet, cornice, shaping

cornice cyma
curved nebule
edge arris
material ormolu
mole spy, pier, quay, mammal, platypus
molecule particle
  component atom
molluscoid
  by-product pearl
mollusk clam, helix, snail, chiton, oyster, abalone, scallop, periwinkle
  arm tentacle
  beaked octopus
  fake slug, queer
  genus Murex, Oliva
  shell conch, cowry
  teeth redula
moly garlic
moment sec, flash, point, instant
  of truth crisis
Monday see also Quick Reference List
  Black cold
  blue depressing (colloq.)
  Easter day after Easter
money coin, fund, lucre, tender
  box arca, kist, till
  bronze aes
  changer shroff, cambist
  market bourse
  sl. moola, boodle, lettuce, scratch
  substitute scrip, coupon
Mongol, Mongolian Tungus, Kalmuck
  dynasty Yuan
  coin tugrik
  priest Lama, Shaman
  tribesman Buryat
  weight ian
monk Lama, Friar, Votary, Carmelite, Dominican, Franciscan
  ever silent Trappist
  head Abbot
  settlement Scete
  title Fra
monkey fool, simian, primate
  Asiatic langur
  bread baobab
  green guenon

marmoset tamarin
red patas
sacred rhesus
spider quata, ateles
monocotyledon plant lily, palm, orchid
monolith column, pillar, obelisk
monostich poem, verse, epigram
monotreme echidna, anteater, duckbill
monster ogre, huge, freak, enormous
  comb. form terat(o)
  female gorgon, Medusa
  fire-breathing dragon, chimera
  hundred-eyed Argus
  many-headed Hydra
  myth. Sphinx, Centaur, Griffin, Hippogriff
  snake-haired Medusa
  winged Geryon
Montana see Quick Reference List
Monte Cristo
  author Alexandre Dumas
  hero Dantes
month see also Quick Reference List
  by the permensem
  first day calend(i)s, kalends
  last ult(imo)
monument tribute, memorial
  honoring the dead cenotaph
  of stone(s) cairn, dolmen
moon Diana, month, satellite
  between half and full gibbous
  dark area mare
  hole crater
  on the wane decrescent
  pert. to lunar, selenic
  poetic lamp
  point farthest from earth apogee
  point nearest earth perigee
  shadow umbra
Moorish Moresque, Moriscan
  coin maravedi
  fabric tiraz
  garment jupon
moor rope painter
moose elk, deer, alces
  female cow
  male bull
  pouch bel

moral chaste, decent, ethical, honorable
  allegorical story with fable, apologue
  law decalog(ue)
morals
  pert. to ethics
moray eel, elgin, conger
more plus, again, further, additional
  cry for encore
  in music piu
morello cherry
moreover and, also, else, besides, further, likewise
mores habits, customs, manners
morganite beryl
Mormon Danite
  church founder Smith
  priest elder
  sacred instrument urim
morning eos, dawn, matin, aurora, daybreak
  glory plant, ipomean,
  star Venus, Saturn
  sunrise matutinal
Morocco, Moroccan Berber, leather, Marrakech
  coin rial
  dynasty founder Ali
  hat fez
  international zone Tangier
  monetary unit dirham
Morpheus, god of dreams
morphine
  addicts' analgesic drug methadone
mortal fatal, human, deadly
  opposite venial
mortar bowl, cannon, cement
  mixer rab
  sound-proofing pugging
mortise join, fasten
mosaic inlay, collage
  material tile, tessera
  work intarsia
Moscow Moskva
  citadel Kremlin
  square/writer Pushkin
Moses leader, lawgiver
  brother Aaron
  people led by Israelites

place of death Nebo
sister Miriam
wife Zipporah
Moslem Islam(ic), Berber, Saracen,
  Mohammedan; see also Muslim
  coin dinar
  converts ansar
  devil Eblis
  holy city Mecca, Medina
  holy man Imam
  idol Maumet
  lady begum
  language Urdu, Arabic
  measure ardeb
  messiah Mahdi
  monk Santon
  mystic Suni
  nomad kurd
  pilgrimage hadj
  prayer salat
  religious festival Bairam
  temple mosque
  tomb tabut
  weight rotl
mosquito culex, insect, onopheles
  genus Aedes, Culex, Anopheles
  larva w(r)iggler
mot word, repartee, witticism
moth io, luna, egger, gypsy, insect, miller,
  browntail
  group tortricid
  larva looper
  night-flying noctuid
motion gesture, movement
  pert. to motive, kinetic
  producing motor, motile
motorcyclist biker, Hailwood
mott(e) grove
mottle spot, blotch, dapple, streak
motto adage, gnome, maxim, device, slogan
  in a book epigraph
moulding see molding
mound dune, heap, pile, tell, knoll, hillock
  domelike stupa
mountain heap, pile, mound, range
  antelope klipspringer
  Apollo's Parnassus

Asia Minor Ida
biblical Nebo, Horeb, Sinai, Ararat
chain Sierra, range
climber's aid piton, crampon
comb. form/prefix oro
crest spur, arete
formation spur, arete, ridge
gap col, pass
goat ibex, tahr
highest Everest
legendary Meru
movable Ossa
pass col, gap, ghat, defile
ridge arete, sawback
sheep bighorn, mouflon
sickness puna, veta
trail marker karn
mourning
  band crape, crepe
  cloak butterfly
  clothes weeds
  song dirge
mouth lips, stoma, opening, orifice
  comb. form ori, stome
  gaping rictus
  opening rictus
  part lip, uvula, velum, tongue
  pert. to buccal, stomatic
  river delta, frith, estuary
  to pharynx passage fauces
  open agape
mouths ora
move act, stir, budge, shift, touch, affect,
  advance, animate
  able to mobile, motile
  along mosey, sashay
  confusedly mill
  in circles eddy, purl, swirl
  movie camera/TV pan
  on casters truckle, trundle
  sidewise edge, sidle
  sinuously snake, writhe
  slowly inch, worm, crawl
  to and fro wag, swing, shuttle, vibrate
  toward something approach, gravitate
movement action, motion
  in music tempo, rhythm

of charged particles cataphoresis
of organism taxis
of the sea tide, current
movie kino, cinema
  camera platform dolly
  comb. form cine
  film, one thousand feet reel
  low budget quickie
  script scenario
  shot clinch, close-up
  sound adjustment sync
moving motile, current, stirring
  about ambulant
  area around body periphery
  comb. form kineto
  in circular path gyral
mowing implement reaper, scythe, sickle
moxa plant, cautery
Mozambique
  native Yao, Bantu
Mozart
  city Salzburg
  rival Salieri
much lot, lots, many, plenty
  in music molto
mucilage glue, paste, arabin,
adhesive mucous slime, slimy, viscous, blennoid
  comb. form myx(o)
mudfish bowfin, dipnoan
mudguard wing (Brit.), fender
mudworm ipo
mufti ulema, "civies"
muggins fool, game, domino
mugwump Republican, independent
mulatto metis, creole, quadroon
mulberry tree, sycamine
  bark tapa
  tree genus Morus, Cecropia
mule hinny, shavetail
  driver skinner
  female mare
  young foal
mulla(h) teacher, interpreter
multiplied creature centipede
mumbo jumbo idol, fetish, gibberish

mummy corpse
  cloth byssus
mundungo tobacco
Mundy work Om
muntjac deer, ratwa
murder kill, slay, bump off, homicide
  by drowning noyade
  by suffocation burke
murderous frenzy amok, berserk
murex whelk
murid rat, disciple
murmuring sound sussurus
murre auk, guillemot
murrelet (sea)bird
musaceous plant banana
muscid insect housefly
muscle brawn, sinew, tissue, sphincter
  attachment tendon
  comb. form my(o)
  contraction tic, spasm, cramps
  disease myopathy
  jaw masseter
  loin psoas
  protuberance venter
  tension tonus
muscles brawn, psoas, thews
  science myology
  wasting dystrophy
muscovado sugar
muscular burly, brawny, strong
  elasticity tonus
  fatigue myasthenia
  impotence ataxia
muse mull, dream, ponder, meditate
Muse goddess
  astronomy Urania
  chief Calliope
  comedy Thalia
  dance Terpsichore
  epic poetry Calliope
  history Clio
  love Erato
  music Euterpe
  poetry Erato
  tragedy Melpomene
Muses
  domain Aonia, Parnassus

fountain Hippocrene
home Helicon
mountain Helicon, Parnassus
names Clio, Erato, Thalia, Urania,
  Euterpe, Calliope, Polymnia,
  Melpomene, Terpsichore
of the Pierian
place where worshipped Pieria
spring Castalia
museum gallery
  custodian curator
  part court
mushroom morel, agaric, fungus,
  champignon
  alkaloid muscarin(e)
  cap pileus
  covering volva
  poisonous agaric, amanita, toadstool
  underground truffle
music air, tune, harmony
  adapter arranger
  canto passus
  clef base, treble, baritone
  concluding passage coda
  for nine nonet
  for practice etude
  for two duet
  high part treble
  major scale gamut
  measured beat moto, pulse, tempo
  moderately, slow andante
  rate of speed lento, tempo, allegro,
    andante
  sacred motet, choral(e)
  short song ode
  sign presa, segno
musical lyric(al), melic, canorous, melodious
  ballad derry
  character key, clef, flat, rest, sharp
  combination chord
  drama opera
  ending coda
  excerpt morceau
  exercise etude
  instrument lute, lyre, reed, viol(in),
    brass, flute, piano, sitar, cornet, guitar,
    percussion

brass wind cornet, trumpet, trombone
keyboard organ, piano, spinet, clavier,
  accordion
string chord, catgut
stringed asor, lute, lyre, rote, vina,
  viol, banjo, rebec, viola, cither(n),
  citole, guitar, violin, zither, bandore,
  samisen, ukelele, dulcimer, mandolin,
  samebuke, clavichord
trumpetlike tuba, clarion
wind reed, tuba, flute, organ, clarinet,
  saxophone
instruments, collectively brass, traps,
  winds, strings, percussion
interlude, short verset
introduction overture
movement scherzo
note of old fe, ut, are, ela, elk
passage in fast tempo presto
pitch tone
sounds, science of harmonics
trill tremolo
vibrato trill
work opus
musician
  patron saint Cecilia
musk
  cat civet, scent
muskellunge pike
musket dragon, jingal, firearm, culverin
  flintlock fusil
muskmelon atimon, casaba, cantaloupe
Muslim see also Moslem
  cap kopia
  court Agama
  fasting month Ramadan
muslin adati, mosal, shela, batiste
  bag tillot
  striped doria
mussel clam, unio, mollusk
  product pearl
must alba, mold, sapa, essential
mustached sea animal walrus
mustang pony, horse, bronco
mustard weed, woad, turnip, condiment
  dye woad
  gas vesicant

plaster sinapism
pod silique
wild charlock
mustee mestizo, octoroon
musteline animal mink, otter, weasel,
   polecat, wolverine
muster gather, summon
   in enlist
   out disband
mutant sport
mutation change, evolution
   in linguistics umlaut
mutton meat, flesh, sheep
   bird oii
   chop kabobs, kebobs
   fish sama
   stew haricot
mutually destructive intercine
myna(h) bird
myrmicid ant
Myrmidon adherent, follower
myrrh cicely
myrtle guava, shrub, cajeput, periwinkle
   berry allspice
mystic essene, occult, sufist, enigmatic
   art cabala, voodoo, alchemy
   union with God theocrasy
   word abraxas, abracadabra
   writing rune
mythical fabulous, imaginary, legendary
   animal griffin
   antelope yale
   being centaur
   flyer Icarus, Daedelus
   giant Ymer, Ymir, Jotun, Fafnir, Cyclops
   horse Pegasus, unicorn
   hunter Orion
   island/continent Atlantis
   land Lemuria
   monster dragon, sphinx, chimera,
      minotaur
   river Styx
   sisters Gorgons
   wolf Fenrir

N

N en, nu
Na sodium
Nabal
   home Maon
   wife Abigail
nabob dives, Midas, viceroy
   deputy Nawab
Nabokov novel Ada, Pnin, Lolita,
   Pale Fire
nacelle car, basket, chassis, cockpit
nacket boy, cake
nacre (mother-of-pearl), shellfish
nacrite kaolin(e)
nadir
   opposite zenith
naga snake
nahoor sha, sheep, bharal
Nahor
   son Terah
   wife Milcah
naiad nymph, mussel, hydriad
nail brad, stud, tack, trap, plate, talon, clench
   drive at slant toe
   Fr. clou
   headless sprig
   ingrowing acronyx
   marking on lunule
   shoemaker's brad, sparable
   size penny
   wooden fid, peg
nais nymph
namaycush fish, togue, trout
name alias, agnomen, declare, epithet,
   moniker, christen, identity
   assumed pen, alias, pseudonym
   bad caconym
   consisting of onomastic
   derived from father patronym
   derived from mother matronym
   family agnomen, cognomen
   female
      beautiful Bell(a), Belle
      beauty Ada(h)

beloved Amy, Vida
bird Ava, Avis
bitter Mara, Mari(e), Mary, Moll(y), Moya, Poll(y)
chaste Karen, Catherine
clinging Ivy
compassionate Ruth
destiny Carma
eagle Arva
felicity Naomi
good Bonnie
grace Ann(a), Nina, Nancy
happy Ida
high or holy Elga, Olga, Holly
honey Millie, Melissa
jewel Opal, Ruby, Pearl
life Eve, Zoe, Vita
lovable Mila
maiden Cora
mistress Martha
one Mona
peace Freda, Irene, Olive
poem Edda
power Dyna
rainbow Iris
royal Rani
snow Neva
sound Echo
true Vera
feminine of
  David Vida
  John Jane, Jean, Joan, Janet
  Joseph Josepha, Josephine
  Solomon Salome
first forename, praenomen
maiden nee
male
  amiable Elmo
  beloved David
  bitter Omar
  blind Homer
  cautious Cato
  cheerful Tate
  courageous Neil
  dove Jonah, Jonas
  fighter Boris
  free Frank, Francis

  God's grace Jess(e)
  healer or physician Asa, Jason
  judge Dan
  laughter Isaac
  Lord is God Joel
  love Lief
  man Enos
  of the forest Silas, Sylvester
  peace Fritz
  red-haired Rufus
  safe Titus
  wanderer Errol
  watchful Ira
of a thing noun
of two terms dionym
written backward ananym
namesake homonym
Nandu rhea
Naomi Mara
  daughter-in-law Ruth
  land settled in Moab
naos cella, shrine, temple
nap ras, down, fuzz, snooze
  long shag
  raising machine gig
  to raise tease(l)
nape scruff, niddick
  of sheep's neck scrag
napery linen
Naphtali
  mother Bilhah
  son Guni, Jezer
Naples Napoli
  coin carlin(e)
  secret society Camorra
Napoleon (Bonaparte)
  battle Waterloo
  birthplace Corsica
  exiled to Elba, St. Helena
  laws Napoleonic Code
  wife Josephine, Marie-Louise
napu deerlet
Naraka hell
narcissus plant, egoist, flower
  loved by Echo
narcotic
  dose locus

package deck, bindle
plant hemp, poppy, cannabis, mandrake
seller dealer, pusher
nardoo nardu, plant, clover
nares nose, nostrils
narghile pipe, hooka(h)
nark spy, tease, informer
narrative fable, story, history, recital
poem epic, epos
narrow close, rigid, small, lineal, confined
comb. form sten(o)
inlet ria
-mindedness bias, bigotry
narthex hall, foyer, porch, portico
nashgab gossip
nasi patriarch, president
nasicorn rhinoceros
nasutiform noselike
nat demon, spirit
Nata
wife Nana
natatorium pool, tank
native ite, son, natal, denizen
natterjack toad
natural raw, easy, wild, innate, primitive,
unspoiled
condition norm
group race, ethnicism
location situs
principle guna
naturalist Muir, animist, biologist
nature ilk, bent, bios, tenor, climate,
essence, quality
god Pan
goddess Artemis
pert. to cosmo
spirit Nat
worship physiolatry
nauntle fuss, raise, strut
nautical naval, marine, maritime
before afore
below alow
cease avast
chain tye
fasten batten
hook becket
stop avast

tighten frap
tilting alist
water's surface ryme
Nautilus mollusk, submarine
Navaho hut hogan
nave hub, apse, center
navel umbilicus
navigation cabotage
call ahoy
signal bell, flag
nawab ruler
neal temper
neap pole, tide
near next, aside, close, short, almost, stingy,
adjacent, approach
comb. form par(a)
-sighted myopic, purblind
Near East Levant
native Arab, Kurd, Turk
Nebraska see Quick Reference List
nebris fawnskin
nebula vapor, galaxy
nebulous hazy, vague, cloudy
envelope coma, chevelure
necessity use, need, want
of life air, food, bread, water, aliment
neck woo, swire, cervix, channel
-and-neck tie, even, close
armor gorget
artery carotid
back nape, nucha, scruff
frill jabot, ruche
hair mane
horse withers
part gula, throat
pert. to nuchal, wattled
thin scrag
necromancy goety, magic, sorcery
necropsy autopsy
nectar drink, honey
bird sunbird
of gods ambrosia
neddy donkey
needle vex, bodkin, obelisk, pointer
bug genus Ranatra
comb. form acu
finisher eyer

medical hypodermic
pointed acerate, acerose
shaped aciform, acicular, spicular
needlefish gar, earl, pipefish
neep turnip
nef clock
negative not, anti, film, x-ray, negate
ion anion
pole cathode
prefix im, un, dis, non
Negro Luri, Zula, Hubshi, Bushman,
Ethiopian, Hottentot
Afr. Vai, Vei, Dahoman
dance juba
dialect Gullah
Egypt Nubian
ghost Juba
Niger Ibo, Nupe
secret society Egbo, Mau-Mau
Sudan Egba, Hausa
white and Mustee
negus beverage
neither right nor wrong adiaphorous
Neleus
son Nestor
nelumbo lily, lotus
nemoral sylvan
nema eelworm
neoplasm tumor, growth
neoteric new, late, novel
nep catnip
Nepal, Nepalese
coin anna, mohar
Mongoloid Rais
native Kha
peak Api
nephelite lenad, mineral
nephew nepote (Scot.)
Neptune sea god
Celtic Ler
emblem trident
consort Salacia
son Triton
Ner
son Abner
Nereides
steed seahorse

Nereus
wife Doris
nerfling id, ide, fish
Nero tyrant, emperor, fiddler
successor Galba
victim Seneca
wife Octavia
Nero Wolfe
creator Rex Stout
nerve grit, cheek, vigor, energy, sciatic
cell neuron
center brain, cortex, plexus
comb. form neur(o)
cranial optic, vagus, auditory
motor efferent
network rete, retia, plexus
sensory afferent
nerve cell framework stroma
nervous edgy, jittery, timorous
malady tic, aphasia, neuritis
ness cape, suffix
nest bed, den, lair, abode, aerie, colony
build nidify
builder ant, bee, bird, wasp, mouse, hornet
-building fish acara, stickleback
of boxes inro
squirrel's dray, drey
Nestor sage, counselor
net gin, gain, trap, snare, fabric, profit
bag reticule
-like retiary
Netherlands see Holland
netop crony, friend
nettle vex, plant, offend
genus Urtica
rash hives, urticaria
network web, mesh, system, complex
arterial vas
nerve rete, plexus
neume sequence
neurite axone
neuroglia glia
neutral even, bland, unbiased, impartial,
indefinite, noncombatant
equilibrium astatic, balanced
Nevada see Quick Reference List
neve ice, firn, snow

nevus mole, freckle
new novel, young, another, original
  comb. form neo
New Caledonia
  bird kagu
Newfoundland
  log house tilt
New Guinea Papua
  people/tribesman Karon
New Hampshire see Quick Reference
  List
New Jersey see Quick Reference List
New Mexico see also Quick Reference
  List
  art colony Taos
  turpentine tree tarata(h)
New Testament
  gospel John, Luke, Mark, Matthew
  letter epistle
New York see also Quick Reference List
  City Olean, Gotham
New Zealand(er) Kiwi, Maori, Antipodes
  bell bird mako
  fish ihi, hiku
  shrub karo, tutu, kowhai
  wages utu
  war club mere
newel post
news word, report, tidings, dispatch
  -boy camelot
  -monger gossip
  paragraph item, squib
  -stand kiosk
newspaper
  article item, squib
  file morgue
  hoax canard
  stand kiosk, stall
newt eft, triton, salamander
next neist, beside, closest, in order
  (comb. form) eka
nexus tie, bond, link
ngaio kio, tree
Nicaragua
  coin peso, centavo
  measure vara, milla, suerte, manzana
  weight bag, caja

nickel jit, coin
  alloy invar, konel, monel
  symbol Ni
nickname
  form prosonomasia
  Chamberlain, Wilt The Stilt
  Churchill, Winston Winnie
  Clemenceau, George Tiger
  Edison, Thomas Wizard of Menlo Park
  Elizabeth I Virgin Queen
  Hemingway, Ernest Papa
  Jackson, Andrew Old Hickory
  Lincoln, Abraham Honest Abe
  Napolean I Little Corporal
  Richard I Lion-Hearted
  Ruth, Babe Bambino
nide nest, brood, litter
nidus nest
Nigeria, Nigerian
  native Aro, Ibo, Ijo, Beni, Eboe
  region Benin
  tree afara
  walled city Kano
night
  bird nightingale
  comb. form nyct(i)(o)
  goddess Nyx, Hecate
  pert. to nocturnal
nightcap drink, biggin
nighthawk pisk
Nightingale bulbul, Florence, philomel
nightjar potoo, nighthawk
nightshade herb, henbane, belladonna
nihil nil, nothing
Nile river; see also Egypt
  bird ibis
  boat baris, cangia
  dam Aswan
  houseboat dahabeah
  native Nilot
  Negro Jur, Luo, Suk
nilgai antelope
nim tree margosa
nimb halo
nimbus aura, vapor, gloria
nimshi fool
nine IX, ennead

comb. form ennea
day's devotion Novena
-eyes lamprey
-headed monster Hydra
inches span
-killer shrike
-pins skittles
ninth nonus (Lat.), enneatic
  day before ides Nones
  recurring every nonan
ninut magpie
Niobe
  brother Pelops
  father Tantalus
  husband Amphion
nipa a(t)tap, palm, drink
nis nix, nisse, kubold, brownie
nisi unless
nisse goblin, sprite
Nisus
  daughter Scylla
nit egg, speck, insect
niter potash, saltpeter
  comb. form nitro
nithing coward
nitron radon
nitrogen gas
  comb. form azo
  compound azin(e)
niveau level
Njorth
  son Frey(r)
  wife Skathi
no Baal, none, drama (Jp.), denial
  one nix, nemo, none, nobody
Noah
  dove Columba
  father Lamech
  grandson Aram
  great grandson Uz
  pert. to Noetic, Noachian
  son Ham, S(h)em, Japheth
nob jack
nobleman
  pert. to ducal
nobleness of birth eugeny
noctuid moth, worm

noctule bat
nocturnal night
  carnivore ratel
  mammal bat, lemur, raccoon
noddy auk, fool, noodle
node knot, point, tumor
  of a poem plot
  of a stem joint
nodule mass, granule
  stone geode
Noel carol, Christmas (Fr.)
noir black (Fr.)
noisette hazel
noisily larum, loudly
nom de plume pen name, pseudonym
noma ulcer
nomad Arab, Moor, Gypsy, river, Bedouin,
  Saracen
nonage infancy, minority, pupilage
nonce present, purpose, occasion
nonconductor resin, bakelite
none nane (Scot.)
nonessential unneeded, incidental
  in religion adiaphorus
nongypsy gajo
nonpasserine bird tody, hoopoe,
  motmot
nonsense bosh, trash, babble, rubbish,
  twaddle, folderol, balderdash
  creature goop, snark
nook cant, cove, herne, cranny
nope bullfinch
Norn fate, Wyrd, Skuld
Norse Dane, Ogier, Norwegian, Scandinavian
  Adam Ask(r), Buri
  alphabet runic
  collection of songs/epic edda
  deity Ran, Odin, Woden
  giant Ymer, Fafnir
  giantess Groa, Natt
  king (myth.) Atli
  poem rune
  queen of underworld Hel(a)
  saint Olaf
  serpent (myth.) Midgard
  viking Rollo
  watchdog (myth.) Garm(r)

North polar, arctic, boreal
  Africa see Africa
  Pole discoverer Peary
  star Polaris, Cynosure, Lodestar, Polestar
  wind boreas
North Carolina see Quick Reference List
North Dakota see Quick Reference List
Norway, Norwegian
  bird rype, ptarmigan
  coin ore, krone
  early ruler Haakon
  measure fot, pot
  weight lod, pund
  writer Ibsen
nose beak, conk, scent, snoop, proboscis
  bee's lore
  cartilage septum
  having flat simous
  having large nasute
  openings nares
  partition vomer, septum
  pert. to narial, rhinal
nosebleed epistaxis
noselite lenad
Nostradamus seer, prophet, astrologer
nostril naris, blowhole
  pert. to narial, narine
not nay, nor, negative
  in style passé, stale
  prefix il, im, in, ir, un, non
  wanted superfluous
note IOU, espy, fame, billet
  endorsement or guarantee aval
  explanatory scholium
  half minim
  marginal scholium, adversaria, annotation
  tail filum
nothing zero, blank, trifle, bagatelle
  more than mere
notice
  book blurb
  death obit
  good rave
  honorable citation
  official edict, bulletin

not kosher tref, trefah
notum back
notus southwind
noumenal real, ontal
noun name, thing
  common gender form epicene
  form case, gender
  suffix et, ana, ery, fer, ier, ion, ise, ist
  two cases dipote
  verbal gerund
nous we/us (Fr.), mind, reason
nouveau riche parvenu, upstart
novelette conte, novella
Nox Nyx
  brother Erebus
  father Chaos
nubia wrap, cloud, scarf
nucha nape, neck
nuclear
  element proton
  machine betatron
nudibranch conch, snail, mollusk
nugae jests, trifles
nuisance bane, evil, pest, plague, vexation, annoyance
  remover abator
nullah gorge, gully, ravine
nullo game, task
number sum, digit, amount, reckon, see also Quick Reference List
  describable by scalar
  extra encore
  irrational surd
  pure scalar
  suffix st, th, eth
  whole integer
numbered
  biblical mene
numeral style Roman, Arabic, Hebrew
numerical prefix bi, tri, uni, quad
Numidia city Hippo
numinous awe
nun sister, recluse, votaress, cloistress
  bird monase, titmouse
  dress habit, wimple
  hood faille
  moth tussock

Nun
  son Joshua
nuncupative oral, spoken, designative
nunni blesbok, antelope
nupson fool
nuque nape, neck
nur gnarl
nursery
  day or public creche
nurse shark gata
nut(s) core, fool, pith, problem, fastener
  bearing nuciferous
  pert. to nucal
  tanning bomah
Nut
  children Ra, Isis, Osiris
nuthatch
  genus Bird, Sitta
nutmeg tree, spice, calabash
  husk mace
nymph Echo, pupa, houri, larva, sylph,
  damsel, kelpie
  beloved by Pan Syrinx
  changed into laurel Daphne
  fountain Naiad, Egeria
  in love with Narcissus Echo
  laurel/tree Daphne
  mountain Oread
  queen Mab
  sea siren, Nereid, Scylla, oceanid
  water Nais, Undine
  wood Dryad
nyssa
  genus Tree, Tupelo
nystagmus tic, wink
Nyx, Nox night
  daughter Day, Eris, light
  father Chaos
  husband Erebus
  son Charon

O

O oh, omicron
O. Henry William Porter

oak tree, brave
  bark crut
  beauty moth
  fruit mast, acorn, camata, bellote
  genus Quercus
  holm ilex
  immature fruit camata
  types bur, pin, red, holm, live, post,
    black, holly, scrub, swamp, water,
    white, barren, willow, chestnut
  white roble
oaky hard
oam steam
oar scull, paddle
  blade peel, wash
  part loom, palm
  -shaped remiform
oasis ojo, spa, wadi
oat(s)
  genus Avena
  head panicle
obeah charm, fetish, voodoo
Obed
  father Boaz
  mother Ruth
  son Jess(e)
obedient plant dragonhead
obelisk pylon, column, guglia, needle
Oberon king, poem, fairy, opera
  wife Titania
obi sash, charm, fetish, girdle
object aim, goal, cavil, design
  lesson example
  sacred urim
  to mind
objet d'art vase, curio, bibelot, figurine
oblate monk, dedicate
  opposite prolate
obnok tax
oboe reed, shawm, hautboy, musette
obsequies wake, rites, funeral
obsidian lava, iztle, iztli, lapis
obstacle, insurmountable impasse
obtain by threat extort
obtund dull, blunt, quell, deaden
obvious clear, liable, visible
  not arcane, hidden, subtle

obvolution fold, twist
oca plant, oxalis, sorrel
Occident west, Hesperia
occultism magic, cabala, mystery
occurring
  at eight-day intervals octan
  at nightfall acronical
  at regular intervals horal
  at twilight crepuscular
  every fourth year penteteric
  every seven days hebdomadal
ocean main, brine, drink, expanse
  floating matter flotsam
  motion tide
  on the asea
Oceanid nymph
Oceanus
  daughter Doris, Eurynome
  father Uranus
  mother Gaea
  wife Tethys
ocellus eye(let), stemma
ocher ore, pigment
  black wadd
  Indian or Sp. almagra
  red tiver
  yellow sil
ocrea sheath
octave eight
  of a feast utas
Octavia
  brother Augustus
  husband Antony
octopus hee, squid, cuttle
  arm tentacle
  secretion ink
  ten arms decapod
octoroon metis, mestee, mustee, mestizo
ocuby rum
odds edge, chance, discord, variance
  and ends orts, brott, refuse, scraps,
    seconds, fragments
ode hymn, lyric, psalm
  kind pindaric
odic lyric
  electric forces od, elod
Odin Woden, Wotan

brother Ve, Vili
daughter-in-law Nanna
father Bor
son Tyr, Vali, Balder
wife Rind(r), Frigg
odor fume, aroma, scent, smell
  of cooking fumet, nidor
Odyssey
  author Homer
  sorceress Circe
Oedipus
  daughter Antigone
  father Laius
  mother Jocasta
  sister Creon
  son Eteocles
  victim sphinx
  wife Jocasta
Oeneus
  kingdom Calydon
  wife Althaea
oestrid bot, fly, larva
oeuvre opus, work
of de (Fr.), off, from
  each ana, per
offense onset, pique, affront, umbrage
  against law crime, delict, felony, infraction
  civil tort
  offer present
offering bid, donation, sacrifice
  as a vow corban
  resistant to force renitent, recalcitrant
office post, wike(n), station
  divine akoluthia
  paid without work sinecure
  purchase/sale barratry
officer agent, sheriff, functionary
  assistant to aide, deputy
  Brit. Royal Guard Exon
  noncommissioned chief, corporal,
    sergeant
  of king's stables avener
official VIP, Bashaw, approved, functionary,
  authoritative
  approval visa, vise, license
  decree writ, ukase
  weights sealer

oflete wafer, offering
Ogier Dane, hero, prince, Norseman
ogtiern son, lord, master
Ohio see Quick Reference List
oii muttonbird
oil lube, bribe, smear, grease,
    smooth, lubricant
  beetle meloe
  bottle cruet
  cask rier
  comb. form oleo
  dry well duster
  fish escolar
  flaxseed linseed
  lamp lantern, lucigen
  made from butter ghee
  orange blossom neroli
  pert. to oleic
  skin sebum
  tree eboe, poon, tung, mahwa
oilseed til, flax, sesame
ointment balm, nard, ceroma, unguent
  biblical spikenard
  wax cerate
Oise tributary Aisne
Oklahoma see Quick Reference List
  people Sooners
old aged, stale, archaic, ogygian,
    obsolete, senescent
  age, pert. to gerontal, gerontic
  age, study of geriatrics, nostology
Old
  Bailey Gaol, jail
  Faithful geyser
  Gooseberry Satan
  Hickory Andrew Jackson
  Noll Oliver Cromwell
  Sod Erin
Old Testament
  land of riches Ophir
  object urim
  people Phud, Phut
  writer Elohist
olea olive
oleander
  genus Shrub, Nerium
olena turmeric

oleoresin tolu, anime, elemi, balsam
olinda bug weevil
olive tree, drupe, fruit
  fly genus Dacus
  genus Olea
  inferior moron
  stuffed pimola
  wild oleaster
olive oil
  comb. form elaio
oliver hammer
olla jar, jug
olla-podrida medley, potpourri,
    hodgepodge
oloroso sherry
olp(h) bullfinch
Olsin
  father Finn
Olympian (Diana) Artemis, (Juno) Hera,
    (Mars) Ares, (Mercury) Hermes,
    (Minerva) Athena, (Neptune) Poseidon,
    (Pluto) Dis, (Venus) Aphrodite,
    (Vesta) Hestia, (Vulcan) Hephaestus,
    (Zeus) Jove, Jupiter
Olympic
  cupbearer Ganymede
Olympic Games see Quick Reference
    List
Olympus
  pert. to godlike, Olympian, celestial
  region by Pieria
Oman
  coin gaj
Omar Khayyam
  country Iran (Persia)
omber card basto
omega last
omicron tiny, short, little
  ceti Mira, star
omission default, neglect,
    oversight
  mark caret
  of vowel elision
  pretended paralepsis
omit delete, ignore, overlook
  in pronunciation elide
omni all, everywhere, omniscient

Omri
  successor Ahab
on
  account of for
  and on forever, tedious
  the contrary rather
  the other hand but
  time prompt, punctual
Ona Fuegian
onager ass
Onam
  son Jada
once anis (Scot.), erst, quondam
  more anew, echo, again, encore
oncorhynchus
  genus Salmon
ondoyant undy, wavy
one
  after the other seriatum
  behind the other tandem
  comb. form mon(o), uni, heno
  -footed uniped
  hundred and forty-four gross
  hundred thousand lac
  million million trillion
  -sided askew, unilateral
  thousand mil
  trillion (comb. form) treg(a)
one and one-half
  comb. form sesqui
O'Neill, Eugene
  heroine Anna
oneself
  belief in solipsism
onion boil, bulb, cepa, cibol, plant
  bulb set
  genus Allium
  small shallot, eschalot, scallion
onomatopoeic echoic, imitative
oopak tea
oorial sha, sheep, urial
opah fish, cravo
opal gem, resin, hyalite
  fire girasol
open ajar, agape, liable, public, artless,
    evident, unclasp, unlocked
  air alfresco

bursting dehiscence
country wold, weald
plain vega, prairie
opening cave, rima, slit, canal, stoma,
    eyelet, passage, vacancy, aperture,
    introduction
  in chess gambit
  slitlike rima
  small pore
opera
  aria solo
  Bellini Norma
  Bizet Carmen
  comic actor Buffo
  Flotow Martha
  Gounod Faust
  hat gibus, topper, stovepipe
  Massenet Manon, Thais, Sappho
  Puccini Tosca, Boheme
  Strauss Bat, Salome, Fledermaus
  Verdi Aida, Ernani, Othello
  Wagner Rienzi, Parsifal
opinion idea, view, belief, estimate,
    conclusion
  expressed credo
opium drug, opiate
  seed maw
  source poppy
oppidan civic, urban, townsman
Ops
  consort Saturn
  daughter Ceres
  festival opalia
  son Zeus, Poseidon
optical
  apparatus lens, glass, telescope,
    microscope
  illusion mirage
  instr. alidade
oquassa fish, trout
or
  heraldry gold, yellow
oracle seer, augur, mentor, prophet
  Apollo's Delphic
  pert. to pythonic
orange
  bird tanager

Bowl site Miami
Chinese mandarin
Genus Citrus
heraldry tenne
kind blood, navel, osage, seville
seed pip
seedless navel
-shaped oblate
orangewood tree osage
oratorio Messiah, Seasons
  coda stretto
Oratory, Fathers of
  founder Neri
orbital point apsis, nadir, apogee
orchid
  Afr. genus Disa
  appendage caudicle
  edible root salep
  genus Disa, Listera
  male purple, cullion
  part anther
  plant drug salep
  tea faham
  tuber salep
Orcus Hades
order bid, form, genus, group, ordain
  connected seriatim
  cosmic tao, rita
  grammar taxis
  law writ
  writ precipe
orderliness system, neatness
ordinary lala, soso, plain
  court probate
ore tin, coin, iron, rock, metal,
  mineral
  box flosh
  deposit lode, mine
  excavation stope
  horizontal layer stope
  iron pigment ocher
  loading platform plat
  receptacle mortar
  vein lode, scrin
  worthless slag, matte
Oregon see Quick Reference List
  coin beaver

crab apple powitch
fabled monster Bigfoot
wind chinook
Oreortyx quail
Orestes
  father Agamemnon
  mother Clytemnestra
  sister Electra
  wife Hermione
orf(e) ide, fish
organ
  bristlelike seta
  elongated tentacle
  footlike pes
  of insect antenna, stinger
  of motion muscle
  respiratory lung
  secreting gland
  tactile feeler
organic inherent, nonmineral, structural,
  fundamental
  body zooid
  compound amine, ketol
  remains, without azoic
organism monas, plant, amoeba, person
  of certain plants spore
  potential idorgan
  swimming on sea nekton
organized body corps army, navy,
  posse, commando
Oriana
  lover Amadis
oribi antelope
Orient, Oriental Asian, bright, ortive,
  Eastern, precious, Levantine
  carpet Kali, Sarouk
  coin see specific country
  destiny Kismet
  dwelling dar
  kettledrum anacara
  laborer coolie
  market sook, souk
  measure dra, para(h); see also
    specific country
  mendicant priest fakir
  people, ancient Seres
  salute salaam

ship dhow
taxi ricksha(w)
weight see specific country
origin on earth epigene
oriole bird, pirol, loriot
  genus Oriolus
Orion Rigel, constellation
  slayer Artemis
orison prayer, speech
orlop deck
ormer abalone
ormolu gilt, gold, alloy
ornament seme, gutta, bedizen, spangle, decorate
  circular rosette
  raised boss, stud
Orozco
  specialty mural
orp fret, weep
Orpheus
  birthplace Pieria
  parent Apollo, Calliope
orthorhombic
  mineral iolite
ortolan bird, sora, bunting
oscine bird crow, vireo, tanager
osier rod, twig, wand, wicker, willow
  band wicke(r)
Osiris
  brother Set(h)
  parent Geb, Nut
  son Horus, Anubis
  wife Isis
Osmanli Turk
ossuary tomb, grave
ostiole os, stoma, aperture
ostracoderm
  order anaspida
ostrich nandu
  feather boa, plume
  genus Rhea, Struthio
  -like bird emu, rhea, ratite, cassowary
otary seal
Othello Moor
  character in play Iago, Bianca, Cassio, Emilia
  wife Desdemona

other else, left, more, rest, former, additional
  comb. form allo, heter(o)
others rest, residue
  and et al
otherwise or, else, alias, differently
  in music ossia
otidium ear, otocyst
otter
  genus Lutra
  sea kalan
Ottoman Turk
  court porte
  governor pasha
ouakari monkey
ouch bezel, brooch, exclamation
ouphe elf, goblin
out ex, end, off, away, scram, begone
  of dehors
  of date passé
  of sorts cross, grouchy
  prefix ec, ecto
outas clamor
outbreak riot, ruckus, tumult
  sudden spurt
outcast Cain, exile, leper, pariah, Ishmael, castaway
  Jp. eta, Ronin
outer utter, foreign, external
  opposed to ental, inner
outhouse shed, privy, toilet
outlaw ban, tabu, taboo
  Oriental ronin, dacoit
outlying
  district suburb, environ, purlieu
outmoded dated, passé, obsolete
outre bizarre, strange, extravagant
outrigger boat, proa, float
outside alien, outer, exterior
  comb. form ecto
outward ectad, outer, formal, visible
  turn evert
ouzel piet, thrush
oval ovoid, oblong, elliptic(al)
ovate
  inversely obovate
oven kiln, oast, stove

annealing glass leer, lehr
goddess Fornax
mop scovel
over dead, more, beyond, excess, athwart, finished
   and above atop, best, atour
   prefix sur, hyper, super, supra
overcoat benny, capote, ulster
   close-fitting surtout
   loose raglan, paletot
   sleeveless inverness
overreach cozen, strain, defraud
override veto, nullify, abrogate
overscrupulous strict, prudish
overshoe boot, arctic, galosh, rubber
overspread fog, pall, scatter
overtop dwarf, excel, eclipse
Ovid
   birthplace Sulmo
   burial place Tomi(s)
   work Fasti, Medea, Amores, Tristia
ovule egg, nit, germ, seed, embryo
   outer integument primine
ovum egg, seed, spore
   comb. form ova
owal(l) due, bobo, owing, unpaid, obliged, payable, indebted, ascribable
owl hawk, lulu, gnome, ullet, snowy, barred
   and Pussycat author Edward Lear
   genus Strix, Ninox, Syrnium
   hoot ululu
   pert. to strigine
   S.A. utum
   short-eared momo
own retain, concede, possess, divulge
   comb. form idio
ox(en) bull, kine, beeve, bison, steer, bullock
   cart ar(a)ba
   comb. form bovi
   extinct wild urus
   India guar, zebu, gayal
   kind neat, nowt
   pair span, yoke
   stomach tripe
   working av

oxalic acid salt lemon
oxalis oca, sorrel
oxeye bird, fish, daisy, flower, plover, chamomile
oxide calx, rust, salt
   calcium lime
   sodium soda
oxygen
   allotropic ozone
   binary compound oxide
   metal compound oxid(e)
   radical oxyl
oyster bivalve, mollusk
   bed bank, stew, layer, claire
   catcher bird, tirma
   common family edulis
   fish toad, tautog
   genus Ostrea
   grass kelp
   ova spawn
   shell husk, test, shuck
   spawn ova, spat, clutch
oysterfish toad, tautog
Oz books
   author L. Frank Baum

P

P pi, pee
pa, pah fort, papa, village
pac boot
paca cavy, labba, agouti, rodent
Pacific
   island(s) Aru, Yap, Bali, Fiji, Guam, Lifu, Rapa, Truk, Uvea, Wake, Atoll, Ducie, Munga, Samoa, Upolu, Ellice, Komodo, Saipan, Tahiti, Okinawa
   pine hala, matsu
   tree kou, ipil, taro
Pacific Ocean
   discoverer Vasco Balboa
   shark mako
   stepping stones Aleutians
pacifist bolo, peacenik, peacemaker
   colloq. dove

pack
  animal ass, mule, burrow
  horse sumpter
packing paper, straw, waste
  box crate
  clay lute
  plant cannery
  water-tight gasket
packsaddle aparejo
Pacolet dwarf, horse
Pactolian golden
pad mat, walk, stuff
  of hay wase
  sl. bed, apartment
  with powder sachet
paddlefish spadefish
paddy rice(field), Irishman
paddywack rage, beating
Paderewski, Ignace pianist
  opera Manru
padnag horse
Padus Po River
paean ode, hymn, song, praise
pagan paynim, heathen, ungodly
  god Baal, idol
Paganini, Nicolo violinist
page call, child, record, servant
  left-hand verso
  number folio
  right-hand recto
  sl. buttons
  title rubric
Pagliacci
  character Canio, Nedda, Tonio
  composer Leoncavallo
pagoda ta(a), coin, tower, temple
pagurian crab
Pahlavi
  realm Iran
pain ache, care, wound, grieve
  comb. form algia
  dull ache
  pert. to asonal
  relayer nerve
paint coat, daub, adorn, color, stain
  comb. form picto
  first coat base, primer

glossy enamel
in dots stipple
paintings oil, canvas, portrait, stilllife
  collection gallery
  cult Dadaism
  method grisaille
  on dry plaster secco
  style genre, impasto
  wall mural
  watercolor aquarelle
Pakistan, Pakistani Sikh, Pathan,
  Bengali
  language Hindi, Bengali, Punjabi
  pass Bolan
pal ally, chum, buddy, cully
palace officer paladin
Palamedes
  enemy Ulysses
  war Trojan
palate taste, relish
  pert. to uranic
  soft velum
pale
  face ashen, white man/woman, caucasian
  yellow flaxen
Palestine Canaan, Israel
  ancient Palestinian Hivite, Amorite
  animal daman
  coin mil
  conqueror Turk
  part Canaan
  plain Sharon
  weight zuza
  village Bethel
palet quoit
paletot jacket, overcoat
palfrey horse
paling fencing
palladium
  symbol Pd
Palladium of Rome Ancile
Pallas Athena
pallion bit, piece, nodule
Pall Mall site West End
palm hand, tree, foist, prize, steal, laurel
  Afr. doum, raffia, palmyra
  Arizona date

Asia nipa, areca, betel
book tara, taliera
cabbage saw, palmetto
Ceylon talipot
dwarf fan genus Sabal
edible fruit date, nipa, coconut
feather gomuti
Florida royal, palmetto
genus Nipa, Areca, Cocos, Sabal, Bacaba, Raphia
leaf ol(l)a, frond
lily ti, toi
mat yapa, petate
New Zealand nikau
pith sago
reedlike stem rattan
sap toddy
spiny grugru
stem cane, rattan
wine sura, toddy
palmetto saw
genus Serenoa
palmyra tree brab, tala, talipot
pampas plains
cat pajero
Pan Faunus
Panama, Panamanians hat, darien
coin balboa
gulf Darien
locks Gatun
measure celemin
tree copa, yaya
Panama Canal
engineer de Lesseps
lake Gatun
panax herb
panda wah, bearcat
Pandora
brother Prometheus
daughter Pyrrha
husband Epimetheus
panfish (king) crab, horseshoe
Pangim native Goan
pangolin manis, anteater
panpipe syrinx
Pantagruel giant
companion Panurge

father Gargantua
mother Badebec
pantalan wharf
Panthea
husband Abradatus
pantheon tomb, temple
panther cat, pard, puma, cougar, leopard
-like animal ocelot
pants jeans, slacks, trousers
leather chaps, chaparajos
papa pa, dad, potato, priest
papal apostolic, pontifical
book of edicts decretal
cape or collar fanon
letter/seal bull
scarf or veil orale
papaya fruit, pa(w)paw
genus Carica
paper essay, theme, writing, document
clothlike tapa, papyrus
cutter slitter
damaged retree
folded once folio
medicinal powders charta
pulp ulla
thin pelure
untrimmed edge deckle
paprika
vitamin citrin
par value face, nominal
parable fable, allegory, similitude
objective moral, proverb
parabole simile
paradigm model, example, pattern
paradise Eden, utopia, elysium
Buddhist Jodo, Gokuraku
Muslim Jenna
river Gihon
Paradise Lost
angel Ariel, Uriel
paragram pun
Paraguay
coin peso
Indian Guarani
tea mate, yerba
weight quintal

parallel equal, analogous, correspond
  render collimate
parallelogram rhomb(us)
paralysis palsy, stroke
  comb. form plegy
paramo plain
parang knife
parapet wall, rampart
  part crete
  V-shaped redan
parasite smut, leech, louse, fungus,
  sycophant
  animal flea, mite, tick, cuckoo
  fungus lichen
  marine remora, sponge
  plant aphid, thrips, entophyte
  worm tape, round, trichina
paravane otter
Parcae Fates
parcel out mete, allot, ration
parchment skin, forel, paper,
  vellum
  manuscript palimpsest
  roll pell
pardon remit, spare, forgive
  general amnesty
parent sire, mater, pater, source
  undivided holethnos
parenthetical aside er
pareu skirt
parfleche rawhide
parget plaster
Paris (city)
  airport Orly
  patron saint Genevieve
  river Seine
  Roman name Lutetia
  subway metro
Paris
  father Priam
  mother Hecuba
  rival Romeo
  victim Achilles
  wife Orenone
parliament member lord

Parnassian poet, butterfly
parrot echo, kaka, poll, mimic,
  corella, cockatoo
  Afr. joke
  Brazil ara(ra), tiriba
  genus Psittacus
  gray jako
  green cagit
  long-tailed macaw
  Malay lory
  Philippine cagit
  sheep-killing kea
  small lorilet, parakeet
Parse, Parsee Zoroastrian
  holy book Avesta
  priest Mobed
  Towers of Silent Dakmas
parsley plant, lovage, sanicle
  derivative apiol(e)
parsnip root, plant
  water genus Sium
parson bird poe, tui, rook
part, parts dole, some, quota, behalf,
  components
  basic core
  choice elite
  comb. form demi, hemi, meri, semi
  highest apex
  main body
  minor bit
  narrow neck
  rootlike radicle
  small bit
  totality unity
  two binary
  with lose, sell
partan crab
Parthenon temple
  designer Ictinus
  sculptor Phidias
  site Athens, Acropolis
Parthenope siren
Parthenos virgin
particle gen, atom, iota, shred, speck,
  morsel, granule, scintilla

atom proton, neutron, electron
cosmic meson
electrified ion
parti-colored pied, variegated
partisan pike, biased, devotee
  comb. form crat
  unwavering zealot
partlet hen, band, collar, woman
partner mate, buddy, consort
  comedian's stooge
  paid escort, gigolo
partridge yutu, titar, chukar
  call juck, juke
  flock covey
  kind quail, grouse, tinamou
  sand seesee
  young cheeper
partylike gala
Pascal work Pensées
Pasch(a) Easter, Passover
pasear walk, promenade
pasha dey, emir
Pasiphae
  daughter Phaedra
  husband Minus
  son Minotaur
pasquinade squib, satire, lampoon
pass col, gap, bygo, omit, pinch, expire, strait, neglect, overtake
  Alpine col
  Indian mountain ghat
  in sports bye
  matador's faena
  off foist
  over omit
  through reeve
  up reject
  words about bandy
passage duct, route, channel, sanction
  between two walls slype, arcade
  mine stope
  one end closed sac, impasse
passer of bad checks kiter
passeriform bird irena
Passover feast, Pasch(a)

bread matzos, matzohs
commencement evening Nisan
first night Seder
pert. to paschal
passus canto
past ago, eld, beyond, bygone, ancient
  master expert
  tense preterit(e)
paste gem, hit, pap, glue, stick
  rice ame
  jewelry strass
  mineral matter magma
Pasternak, Boris author
  novel (Dr.) Zhivago
Pasteur, Louis
  treatment rabies
pasticcio cento, medley, pastiche
pastoral poem, song, rustic, bucolic, country
  crook pedum, crosier
  pert. to rural, bucolic, agrestic, geoponic
  poem idyl, eclogue
  staff peda
pasture lea, agist, graze, herbage
  grass rye, grama, clover
patagium parachute
patand base
paten disc, plate
path lane, orbit, access, footway
  math locus
Pathan Afghan, Moslem
pathos suffering
  false bathos
  opposite ethos
patois cant, argot, lingo, patter, speech
patron saint, sponsor, protector
  animals Pan, Faunus, St. Francis
  art Mascenas
  beggars Giles
  Broadway angel
  children Nicholas
  cripples Giles
  England George
  husbandry Grange

Ireland Patrick
lawyers Ives
literature Maecenas
musicians Cecilia
Russia Nicholas
sailors Elmo
Scotland Andrew
shoemakers Crispin
wine growers Vincent
patroon tract, patron
land manor
patsy stooge, fall guy
Paul
associate Titus
birthplace Tarsus
original name Saul
place of conversion Damascus
Paul Bunyan lumberjack
ox Babe
paulownia tree kiri
pavane dance
pavis cover, protect
Pavlova, Anna ballerina, ballet dancer
pavo peacock, constellation
pawnbroker money lender
shop spout
sl. uncle
pawpaw papaya
pay ante, wage, salary, stipend
attention heed, listen
back refund, reimburse
dirt ore, gold
one's share ante
penalty aby
up pony
paynim pagan, heathen
payola bribe
Pb lead
pea gram, seed, legume
chick gram, cicer, garbanzo
India, split dal
soup fog
seeds palse
-shaped pisiform
tree agati
vine earthpea
peabird oriole

peace pax, calm, amity, quiet, tranquility
goddess Irene
pipe calumet
symbol dove, toga, olive branch
peaceable placid, serene, henotic
peach Crosby, Elberta, Crawford,
freestone, clingstone
blue paon
clingstone pavy
constellation pavo
genus Pavo
heraldic pawn
origin almond
stone pit, putamen
peacoat jacket
peacock mao, bird, pavo
butterfly io
female hen, peahen
fish wrasse
flower poinciana
like a vain
pert. to pavonine
tail spot eye
peag(e) tax, toll, beads, wampum
peak Alp, apex, crest, point, climax, zenith
Eng. Scafell
ice serac
rocky Alp, crag
Rocky Mountain Logan, Pikes
snow-capped calotte
pear pome, fruit, melon, prickly
cider perry
late autumn Bosc
prickly Tuna, Nopal
genus Opuntia
-shaped bulbous, pyriform
stone pyrene
pearl gem, onion, margarite
eye cataract
Harbor Oahu
imitation seed, olivet
of Antilles Cuba
of Orient Manila
opal cacholong
pearlwort
genus Sagina

pearmain apple
Peary, Robert
  discovery North Pole
peasant boor, carl, hind, peon, rustic, swain, coolie, tiller
  Egypt fellah
  East India ryot
  Eng. churl
  Ireland kern(e)
  Scot. cotter
pease crow tern
peat fuel, turf
  bog moss
  cutter piner (Scot.)
  spade slane
pebble scree
  fig-shaped sycite
pech pant, sign, breath
pecht fairy, gnome, pygmy
peck dot, carp, hole, kiss, measure
  at nag, tease
pectinoid bivalve scallop
ped basket, hamper
pedal digit toe
pedestal leg, foot, gaine, support, foundation
  part die, base, dado, plinth
  projecting socle
pedometer odograph
peduncle knot, stem, stalk
  plant scape
peeper tom, frog, snoop, voyeur
Peeping Tom voyeur
  lady he looked at Godiva
peep show raree
Peer Gynt
  author Henrik Ibsen
  mother Ase
  suite author Edvard Grieg
peetweet sandpiper
peg bind, plug, dowel, tooth, reason, strike
  golfer's tee
  mountain climber's piton
  wood pin, skeg, spile
Pegasus winged horse

  rider Bellerophon
  source Medusa
pekan weasel
pelagic marine
  phenomenon tide
Pele Peel, Edson, soccer star
Peleus
  brother Telamon
  father Aeacus
  son Pelides, Achilles
  wife Thetis
pelf booty
pelham bit
Pelias
  nephew Jason
pelicanlike bird solan
pelmet valance
Peloponnesus
  city Sparta
  river god Alpheus
Pelops
  father Tantalus
  son Atreus
pelota ball, jai alai
  basket/racket cesta
  court fronton
pelvic bone ilium
  pert. to iliac
pen crib, hutch, quill, stylus, confine, enclosure
  fish crawl
  point neb, nib
  sl. jail
  text ronde
pen name see pseudonym
pendulum weight bob
Penelope weaver
  father Icarius
  father-in-law Laertes
  husband Odysseus (Ulysses)
  suitor Agelaus
penetralia secret, privacy
penguin auk, bird, Johnny
  genus Eudyptula
  home pole, rookery
  small Adélie
Penn, William Quaker

penna feather
pennant jack, prize, banner
  pirates' Roger
  yacht burgee
Pennsylvania see also Quick Reference List
  sect Amish, Mennonite
Pentateuch law, Bible, Tora(h)
  first book Genesis
Pentheus
  grandfather Cadmus
  mother Agave
pentyl amyl
penumbra shadow
people(s) kin, clan, mankind, populace,
  proletariat
  ancient Asian Seres
  group ethos
  lowest order mob, rabble,
    canaille
  pert. to ethnic, demotic
peplos scarf, shawl
pepo gourd, melon, squash
pepper pelt, spice, attack, capsicum,
  condiment
  betel ikmo, itmo
  intoxicant kava
  Java cubeb
  picker Peter Piper
  shrub kava
  species betel, cayenne
Pepys, Samuel diarist
pequod whaler
  captain Ahab
per by, each
  annum yearly, annually
  diem daily
  se itself, directly
perch sit, fish, roost
  fish mado, okow, pope, barse
  genus Perca
  -like darter
Percheron horse
Pere Goriot
  author Honore Balzac
peregrine hawk, alien, falcon
perfect holy, exact, ideal, model, utter,
  correct

comb. form telev
realm nirvana
perforated pierced, riddled
  marker stencil
  sphere bead
perfume odor, attar, scent, bouquet,
  redolence
  base musk
  Oriental myth
  pad sachet
  with burning spice incense
peri elf, fairy, houri
  cousin nisse
periapt amulet
Pericles
  consort Aspasia
period end, term, epoch, limit, point,
  stage, estrus
  brief spell
  inactive lull
  of extension grace
  of race's apex hemera
  seclusion retreat
  unbroken stretch
periwinkle snail, mussel, myrtle
permanent stable, abiding, constant,
  persistent
  condition hexis, status
permit to travel passport
pern buzzard
pernio chilblain
perpendicular erect, plumb, sheer,
  upright, vertical
  geometry apothem
perplexed asea, anxious, intricate,
  embarrassed
perquod whereby
Perry Mason
  creator E. S. Gardner
  secretary Della Street
  T.V. actor Raymond Burr
perse blue
Perse
  daughter Circe, Pasiphae
  father Oceanus
  husband Helios
  son Aeetes, Perses

Persephone
  parent Zeus, Demeter
Perseus
  father Zeus
  mother Danae
  star Atik
  wife Andromeda
Persia, Persian see Iran
persiennes blinds
persimmon fruit, chapote
  family ebony
person one, chap, self
  beatified beatus
  canonized saint
  charitable Samaritan
  detested anathema
  disgruntled sorehead
  enterprising go-getter
  of bad luck jinx, Jonah
  of distinction VIP, star, notable
  of good luck mascot
  left-handed southpaw, portsider
  loud-voiced stentor
  timid milquetoast
  white ofay, honky (sl.)
personal own
  comb. form idio
personification embodiment
  of rumor Fama
  of truth Una
Peru, Peruvian
  ancient Inca
  bark cinchona
  coin sol, libra, dinero, peseta
  dance cueca
  goddess Mama
  llama paco, alpaca
  partridge yutu
  volcano El Misti
  wind puna, sures
peruke wig, hair
peshkash tax, present, offering
peso coin
  silver duro
pess hassock
pestle grind, pound, masher, pulverize
  vessel mortar

petal ala(e), corolla
  without apetalous
petard devise, firecracker
petasus cap, hat
Peter Rock, Tsar, Simon
  father Jonas
Peter Pan
  author James Barrie
  dog Nana
  pirate Smee
Petrarch
  beloved Laura
petrel bird, titi
Petrograd Leningrad, St. Petersburg
petroleum oil
  derivative butane, grease, naphtha,
    gasoline
petty base, mean, minor, trivial
  fault peccadillo
pewee flycatcher
pewit gull, lapwing
peyote plant, cactus, mescal
Phaedo
  school Elian
Phaedra
  father Minos
  husband Theseus
phalera boss, disk, cameo
phantasm ghost, specter, spectre,
  illusion
Phaon
  consort Sappho
Pharaoh king, ruler, Rameses
  ancestor Ra
  chicken vulture
  fig sycamore
  mouse ichneumon
pheasant fowl, cheer, monaul
  Afr./Asia tragopan
  Austral. leipoa
  brood nid(e)
  finch waxbill
  India monal
phenol orcine, thymol
  derivative salol, cresol
Phidias
  statue Athena

philabeg kilt
Philippine, Filipino Atta, Tagal
  ant, white anai, anay
  canoe banca, vinta
  child bata
  coconut meat copra
  coin peso, conant
  discoverer Ferdinand Magellan
  farmer tao
  food staple saba, taro
  hemp abaca
  house bahay
  idol Anito
  knife bolo, itac
  liquor beno, pangasi
  lizard ibid
  measure chupa, apatan
  native Ata, Ita, Aeta, Moro, Igorot
  nut pili
  parrot cagit
  plant alem
  plum duhat, lanseh
  rice paga
  sash tapis
  skirt saya
  volcano Apo
  water buffalo carabao
  white man cachil
Philippine-Malayan Italone
Philistine barbarian, hypocrite
  city Gath
  foe Samson
  giant Goliath
  god Baal, Dagon
Philomela nightingale
  father Pandion
  sister Procne
philosopher of Syracuse Dion
philosophical cool, sedate, erudite,
  sapient, rational
  element rect
  unit monad
philosophy
  ancient cynic, stoic
  natural physics
  school Eleatic
phloem bark, bast, tissue

phoca seal
Phoebad seeress, prophetess
Phoebe moon, Diana, peewee, Selene,
  Artemis
Phoebus sol, sun, Apollo
Phoenicia, Phoenician
  ancient city/state Tyre, Sidon
  dialect Punic
  god Baal
  goddess Tanit(h), Astarte
  king Agenor
phonetic oral, vocal
  sound palatal
  system romic
photo film, picture, likeness
  copy stat, photostat
  finish by a nose
photography
  inventor Niepce, Talbot, Daguerre
phratry clan
Phrixos
  father Athamus
  mother Nephele
  sister Helle
Phrygian
  god Men, Atys, Attis
  king Midas
physician medic, curer, healer, doctor
  comb. form iatro
  pert. to iatric
  symbol Caduceus
pi jumble, mixture
pibroch bagpipe, instrument
picador wit, jester, bullfighter
Picasso, Pablo artist, painter
  painting Guernica
Piccadilly London street
  Circus London section
pick best, call, pike, elite, glean, gather
  at nag
  on abuse, tease
  out choose, select
pickax(e) gurlet
pickling
  herb dill, garlic
  solution brine, souse, marinade
picot loop

picotee carnation
Pickwick Papers
  author Charles Dickens
Picnic
  author William Inge
pictograph glyph
picture image, photo, scene, reflect
  border mat
  composite montage
  long panel
  painted on wall mural, fresco
  puzzle rebus
  stand easel
Picture of Dorian Gray
  author Oscar Wilde
piebald pied, dappled, mongrel, pintado, variegated
piece bit, gun, coin, tune, unit, scrap, shred, detail, repair
  armor tace, tane, corselet
  of eight peso, real
  out eke
  together patch
  worker jobber
pieplant rhubarb
pier key, anta, berth, jetty, stilt, wharf
  architectural anta
  base socle
  space slip
piet ouzel, magpie
pig(s) bar, hog, mold, pork, slob, bacon, ingot, swine, farrow, porker, glutton
  female sow, gilt
  -like animal peccary, aardvark
  litter farrow
  male boar, barrow
  pickled feet souse
  young elt, grice, shoat
pigeon nun, dove, piper, cushat, isabel, turbit, carrier, fantail, jacobin, trumpeter
  Austral. wonga
  call coo
  carrier homer, homing
  clay skeet, target
  extinct dodo
  genus Goura, Columba
  hawk merlin

  house cote, rook(ery)
  pert. to peristeronic
  variety nun, ruff, homer, pouter, tumbler
  young piper
pigment dye, tint, color, paint, stain
  black tar, soot
  blue bice, smalt, iolite, azurite
  board palette
  brown bister, bistre, umber
  lack achrom(i)a
  orange-red realgar
  pale yellow etiolin
  without albino, achromic
pignus pawn, pledge
pigpen sty, mess, reeve, piggery
pigtail pla(i)t, braid, queue
pikelet crumpet, pancake
Pilate, Pontius procurator, Roman governor
  wife Claudia
pilchard fumado
  young sardine
pile cock, money, mound, stack, gather, pillar, accumulate
  driver gin, ram, beetle, fistuca
  of hay cock, rick, stack
  of stones cairn, scree
  sl. fortune
pileus (skull)cap
pilgrim crusader, wayfarer
  garb at Mecca ihram
  to Holy Land palmer
pilgrimage to Mecca hadj, hajj
Pilgrim's Progress
  author John Bunyan
  character Demas
pillar beam, pier, shaft, column, support
  of ore jam
  pert. to stele, stelar
  tapering obelisk
  with figures osiride
Pillars of Hercules Abila, Calpe, Gibralter
pillbox hat, container, fortification
pill bug louse (sl.)
pillow
  covering tick, pillowcase
  stuffing ceiba, eider, kapok

pilm dust
pilot ace, lead, flyer, conduct
  bird plover
  boat helmsman
  cow pintano
  fish remora, whitefish
  seat cockpit
  snake bull, copperhead
  test solo
  whale blackfish
Pima cotton, Indian (tribe)
pimola olive
pimple scar pock(mark)
pin bolt, nail, fasten, secure
  machine cotter
  plant tacca
  rifle tige
  small peg, lill
  wooden fid, peg, coag, coak, dowel
Pinafore
  authors Gilbert and Sullivan
pincer(s) tong(s), plier(s)
  claw chela
Pindaric form ode
pine ache, hone, tree, yearn
  fruit cone
  leaf needle
  nut piñon, pinyon
  product tar, resin, turpentine
pineapple nana, pina, ananas
  genus Puya
  segment pip
  sl. bomb, grenade
  weed marigold
pinion arm, wing, quill, feather
pink stab, color, flower, scallop
  flower genus Silene
  pill cure-all
pinnacle top, apex, peak, crest
  glacial ice serac
  rocky tor
Pinocchio
  author Lorenzini Collodi
pinochle term dix, meld, kitty
pinpoint aim, dot, fix, trifle
pintail duck, smee
pinxter flower azalea, honeysuckle

pip ace, seed, spot, chirp
pipe oboe, reed, briar, sound, conduit
  dream hope, illusion
  flanged end taft
  joint ell, tee, union
  -like tubate
  Oriental hooka(h), nargileh
  pastoral reed
  peace calumet
  shepherd's oat, larigot
  short dudeen
pipefish gar, earl, snacot
pipit titlark, wekeen
pippin seed, apple
pirate Kidd, Drake, robber, Rogers, corsair,
  buccaneer
  flag Roger
  gallows yardarm
  literary plagiarist
  state Tunisia
pirol oriole
piscine pond, pool (Fr.), basin
  propeller fin
Pisgah
  climber Moses
  summit Nebo
pishu lynx
pismire ant, emmet
pismo clam
piste path, spoor
pit dent, seed, abyss, cavity, crater, fovea,
  lacuna
  baking imu
  bottomless abaddon
  of theater parquet
  viper habu
pita fiber, agave, bread
pitchblende derivative radium,
  uranium
pitcher ewer, crock, tosser, creamer
  false move balk
  left-handed southpaw
  motion windup
  place mound
  -shaped urceolate
  -shaped vessel alguiere
pitchhole cahut

pith nub, gist, center, kernel, tissue, medulla, quintessence
  helmet topi, topee
  tree of Nile ambash, ambatch
pitman miner, overseer (gambling)
pivot slew, turn, hinge, wheel
  City Geelong
  pin pintle, kingbolt
pixy elf, goblin, sprite
Pizzaro, Francisco explorer, conquistador
  country Peru, Spain
place put, set, lieu, bestow, locate, region, deposit, station
  apart enisle, separate
  beneath infrapose
  camping etape
  comb. form gea, topo
  intermediate limbo
  of
    nether darkness erebus
    rapid growth hotbed
    safety haven, refuge
    torment gehenna
    secret den, hideout, safe house
    side by side collocate
    snugly ensconce
    storage depot
    trial venue
plague harry, tease, harass, disease, epidemic
  carrier rat
  of locusts
  pert. to loimic
plaice flounder
plain frank, homely, simple, lowland, distinct
  Arctic tundra
  Argentine pampa
  Asia chol
  elevated mesa
  Eur. steppe
  salt-covered salada
  treeless llano, pampa, veldt, tundra, prairie, savanna(h)
plaited braided, browden
  rope sennit
  trimming ruche
plane flat, tool, grade, level, surface, aircraft
  chart mercator

  inclined ramp, chute
  on the same coplanar
planet Mars, moon, star, Earth, Pluto, Venus, world, Saturn, Uranus, Jupiter, Mercury, Neptune
  brightest Venus
  nearest sun Mercury
  red Mars
planetarium orrery
plant(s)
  adapted to dryness cactus, xerophyte
  algae genus Nostoc
  Alpine edelweiss
  ambrosia genus Ragweed
  ammoniac oshac
  anise anet, dill, cumin
  apoplexy esca
  araceous arum, lily, taro, cabbage
  aromatic mint, nard, anise, tansy, thyme, lavender, tarragon
  arrowroot pia, musa, canna, tacca, ararao
  Asiatic fiber ramie
  Assam tea, tche
  auricula primrose
  Austral. correa, alstonia
  bean family licorice
  bitter rue
    leaves tansy
    vetch ers
  bramble briar, furze, gorse, thorn
  bud cion
  bulb camas(s), quamash
  burning bush wahoo
  cactus cereus, mescal, saguaro
  calyx leaf sepal
  castor kiki
  catnip family nep(eta)
  cherry, laurel cerasus
  Chinese ramie
  chlorophyll-lacking albino
  climbing ivy, bine, vine, liana, philodendron
  clover medic, alsike, lucern(e), alfalfa, melilot, trefoil
  comb. form. phyto
  corn lily ixia
  cutting slip

dill anet
disease rot, gall, rust, scale, fungus, blister, erinose
dogwood osier, sumac, cornel, cornus
dwarf cum(m)in
everlasting orpine
flag, sweet calamus
flowerless fern, moss, lichen, acrogen
fragrant root orris
garlic, wild moly
hawthorne azarole, mayflower
healing sanicle
heather ling, besom, erica
honesty moonwort
indigo anil
iris family lis, flag, irid, orris
juice gum, sap, milk, resin
life flora
male mas
medicinal jalap, senna, tansy, arnica, lobelia
Mex. chia, datil, salvia
mock orange syringa
mosslike hepatica
mustard family cress, alyssum
onionlike leek, chive, shallot
order ericales
part axil, stipel
perennial carex, sedum
pos boll
poisonous genus Datura
rat poison squill, oleander
root radix
roselike avens
seedless fern
pert. to agamic
shoot rod, sprig, stolon
soap amole
S. Afr. aloe
starch-yielding pia, taro
stem bine, shaft, caulis
joint node
tissue pith
strawberry frasier
sweet flag calamus
tapioca cassava
taro root eddo(es)

tissue, relating to tapetal
trifoliate clover, shamrock
vinegar-flavoring tarragon
wild-growing agrestal
Plantagenets Angevin
plantain weed, banana, fleawort
  eater touraco
  spike chat
plantation farm, estate, hacienda
  cacti nopalry
  coffee finca
  Gone with the Wind Tara
  sugar trapiche
  willow holt
plaster daub, compo, cover, mortar
  artist's gesso
  coarse grout, parget, stucco
  of Paris yeso, gesso, gypsum
  support lath
  tool trowel, spatula
  wax cerate
plastered drunk (sl.)
plasterer mason
  glue size
platanist susu
platano banana
plate coat, dish, tile, print, sheet, silver, plaque, illustration
  Eucharist paten
  horny scute
  shaped like ship nef
  thin lamella
  throwing disc, discus
platen roller
platform map, deck, bench, floor
  floating raft
  for execution scaffold
  portable skid, pallet
  raised dais, solea, stand, podium, tribune
  revolving turntable
platinum
  comb. form metal, platin(o)
  symbol Pt
  wire oese
Plato
  idea eidos
  knowledge, highest noesis

school academe
work Grito, Meno, Phaedo, Republic
Platonic philosophy follower academist
platyfish moonfish
platypus duckbill
Plautus
  forte comedy
  language Lat.
play act, fun, drama, enact, frolic
  around gad(about)
  at love flirt
  backer angel
  between acts interval, intermission
  down minimize
  first performance debut, premiere
  silent pantomime
  that folds turkey
  the wrong card renege
playa lake, basin, beach
playing cards
  deck tarots, fifty-two
  extra jokers
  hand deal
  shuffle riffle
  spot pip
  suits clubs, hearts, spades, diamonds
playtime recess
plea nolo, alibi, request
  to end abater
pleasure fun, joy, mirth, gaiety, relish
  god Bes
  insensitivity to anhedonia
  pert. to hedonic
  seeker sport, hedonist, playboy/girl
  trip junket
  voyage cruise
Pleiades Atlantides
  constellation Taurus
  half sisters Maia, Electra, Merope, Alcyone, Celaeno, Sterope, Taygete
  father Atlas
  mother Pleione
plenty ample, enough, opulence
  goddess Ops
  horn of cornucopia
plenum space, assembly, plethora
  opposite vacuum

plexus rete, tangle, network
plinth base, block, socle
  flat orlo
plot map, cabal, design, connive, conspire
  garden bed
  ground lot, grave
  play node
plouk knob, pimple
plow dig, till, furrow
  blade or cutter share, colter, coulter
  handle stilt
  land arable
plug boost, caulk, tampon, stopper, tobacco
  clay bod
  colloq. line, pitch
  fire hydrant
  in TV/radio commercial
plum drupe, fruit, prize, prune, damson, lomboy
  -colored puce
  date sapote
  dried prune
  green gage
  wild sloe
plumber's tool snake, torch, wrench
plume crest, egret, preen, quill
  heron's aigret(te)
Plutarch
  work Lives, Biography
Pluto Dis, dog, Orcas, planet
  kingdom Hades
  wife Persephone, Proserpina
Plutus
  father Jasion
  mother Demeter
pneuma soul, neume, spirit
pneumogastric nerve vagus
Po
  river Padus
  tribesman Lombard
  tributary Adda
Pocahontas
  father Powhatan
  husband Rolfe
pochard duck, fowl, smee
pochette violin, handbag, envelope

pod sac, carob, pouch, shell, container
  tree locust
podagra gout
Poe, Edgar Allan poet
  bird raven
  character Pym
  house Usher
  poem Raven, Lenore, Ulalume
poem ode, rhyme, verse
  bucolic eclogue
  collection sylra, anthology
  division canto, verse
  eight-line triolet
  fourteen-line sonnet
  heroic epic, epos
  love sonnet
  mournful elegy
  nonsensical doggerel, limerick
  satirical iambic
  six stanzas sestina
poetess Jong, Plath, Lowell, Millay, Parker, Sappho
poetry poesy, verse
  god Bragi
  line stich
  muse Erato, Thalia, Calliope
poets, collectively Parnassians
Pogo
  friend Owl
poi food, paste
  source taro
point aim, dot, barb, shape, detail, needle, object, period, prickle, sharpen
  curve node
  highest acme, apex, zenith, apogee
  lowest nadir, perigee
  pert. to focal, apical
  strong fort, forte
  utmost extreme
pointed brief, aimed, marked, concise, conical, leveled
  as a leaf apiculate
  end barb, cusp
  missile bolt, dart, arrow
  shaft goad, pike, arrow, spear
  tip apiculus

pointer dog, rod, hint, stick
  teacher's cue, fescue
poison bane, taint, toxin, virus, corrupt
  arrow inee, wagogo
  comb. form toxic(o)
  hemlock coni(i)ne
  ivy genus Rhus
  tree upas
poisonous fatal, toxic, lethal, noxious, malignant
  fish fugu (Jp.)
  gas arsine, phosgene
  herb henbane
  lizard gila
  plant mandrake
  weed loco
pokeweed poke, pocan, scoke
Poland, Polish Pole, Slav, Sarmatia
  cake baba
  coin abia, zlot(y), ducat, grosz
  composer Frederic Chopin
  dance polka
  dynasty Piast
  measure cal, mila, morg, pret
  scientist Marie and Pierre Curie
  weight lut
pole rod, axis, sprit, region
  negative cathode
  positive anode
  to pole axial
polecat skunk, zoril, ferret
polish wax, buff
  material sand, emery, rabat, rouge, pumice
political
  division town, ward, shire, state, county, province, township, community
  faction bloc, clan, junta, party
  gathering rally, convention
  hack heeler
  list slate
pollard deer, goat
pollen dust, meal, flour, spore
  bearing antheral, staminate
  part anther
Pollux and Castor Gemini, twins
  father Zeus
  mother Leda

polo
- **division of play** chuck(k)er
- **mount** pony, horse
- **stick** mallet
- **team** four

Polonius
- **daughter** Ophelia
- **servant** Reynaldo
- **son** Laertes

Polo, Marco Venetian traveler

Polynesia, Polynesian Maori, Kanaka, Malayo
- **apple** kevi
- **banana** fei
- **burial place** ahu
- **butterfly** io
- **dance** hula, siva
- **demon** atua
- **fish** aua
- **garment** malo, pareu, sarong
- **god** Oro, Atua, Maui
- **goddess** Pelé
- **oven or pit** umu
- **sky** langi
- **wages** utu
- **yam** ube

Polyphemus moth, Cyclops
- **captive** Ulysses, Odysseus

Polyxena
- **father** Priam
- **lover** Achilles
- **mother** Hecuba

polyzoan hydra, polyp, sea anemone
- **skeleton** coral

pomaceous fruit pear, apple, quince

Pomp and Circumstance
- **composer** Edward Elgar

pompano alewife, poppyfish

Pompeii
- **heroine** Ione
- **scene of defeat** Thapsus

Ponce de Leon
- **discovery** Florida
- **searched for** Fountain of Youth

Ponchielli opera (La) Gioconda

pony glass, horse, measure
- **student's** crib

pooka goblin, specter

pool game, pond, flash, kitty, cartel, puddle
- **artificial** tank
- **mine** sump
- **tree** dilo, keena
- **triangle** rack
- **waterfall** linn

poon tree dilo

poor base, cheap, needy, barren, feeble
- **Clare** nun, sister
- **-house** almshouse
- **joe** heron
- **John** cod, food
- **player** dub
- **sl.** lousy, low grade
- **sport** sorehead

pop soda, burst, shoot, father
- **-art hero** Andy Warhol
- **the question** propose

Pope pontiff
- **cathedral** Lateran
- **collar** fanon, orale
- **crown** tiara
- **given name** Leo, Paul, Pius, Urban, Adrian
- **name of twelve** Pius

Pope, Alexander poet
- **love** Gonne

popes, collectively papacy

Popeye sailor, comic strip
- **rival** Bluto
- **sweetheart** Olive Oyl

popinjay fop, dandy, parrot, coxcomb, macaroni, woodpecker

poplar alamo, aspen, tulip, lombardy
- **balsam** liar
- **species** bahan
- **white** abele

Poppaea Sabina
- **husband** Nero

poppy opium, flower
- **genus** Papaver
- **sap** latex
- **seed** maw

population count census

porbeagle shark

porcelain ceramics, china(ware)
  ingredient clay, kaolin
  types Ming, Derby, Spode, Sevres,
    Limoges
porcupine urson, rodent
  fish diodon
  spine quill
Portia
  alias Balthazar
  lover Bassanio
  maid Nerissa
Portugal, Portuguese
  boat moleta
  coin conto, crown, dobra, escudo
  commune Braga
  folk song fado
  lady doña
  monetary unit escudo
  title dom
  saint sao
  weight grao, onca, libra, marco
Poseidon Neptune
  father Cronus
  mother Rhea
  scepter Trident
  wife Amphritrite
positive photo, certain, constant, dogmatic,
  explicit
  not minus, negative
  pole anode
  saying dictum
  sign plus
positivism Comtism, certainty,
  assurance
  founder Auguste Comte
possession wealth, property
  assume again revest
  legal title, estate
posset drink, pamper
post mail, stake, inform
  airplane (race) pylon
  boat capstan
  doorway/window jamb(e)
  staircase newel
postea entry, record
posterior rear, dorsal, hinder
  opposite anterior

postscript codicil, addition
pot bet, olla, crock, kitty, skillet
  handle bool
  stand trivet
  wheel noria
potato imo, spud, tuber
  bud eye
  disease pox, curl, scab, wilt
  starch farina
  sweet oca, yam
potherb kale, wort, chard, spinach
  pert. to olitory
potman waiter
potpourri jumble, medley, mishmash,
  pasticcio
pottery ceramics, porcelain
  dish ramekin
  Hindu uda
  pert. to ceramic
  wheel disk, lathe, throw
poultry fowl, chickens
  breed Ancona, Dorking, Leghorn,
    Langshan
  dealer eggler
  farm hennery
  yard barton
pour flow, gush, rain, stream
  off decant
  to the gods libate
pout mope, moue, sulk, pique
powder dust, talc, pounce, cosmetic
  case bandolier
  ground brag
  perfumed sachet
powdered floury
  heraldry seme
power vis, sway, vigor, ability, control
  comb. form dyna
  intellectual wit, genius
  lack atony
  natural odyl(e)
  third cube
  unit volt, watt
prad horse
prairie plain, steppe
  dog marmot
  hen grouse

soil gumbo
squirrel gopher
vehicle schooner
wolf coyote
praise laud, bless, exalt, kudos, plaudit
  hunger for esurience
prandium meal, dinner, repast
pray ask, beg, invoke, request
  Yiddish daven
prayer ave, bene, matin, orison, vesper
  beads rosary
  form litany
  nine-day novena
  short grace, benediction
  tower minaret
precept act, code, canon, maxim, behest,
  command, instruction
precious dear, arrant, costly, beloved,
  beautiful
  sl. very
  stone gem, ruby, topaz, diamond, emerald
  -stone cutter lapidary
precocious child prodigy
predatory
  bird owl, hawk, eagle, vulture
  insect mantis
predicate base
prefab nissen (hut), quonset (hut)
prefatory note foreword
prefix put before
  about peri
  across trans
  against anti
  backward retro
  bad mal
  before pre, ante
  between meta
  blood hemo
  both ambi
  distant tel(e)
  eight oct(o)
  equal iso
  false pseud(o)
  far tel(e)
  fire pyr(o)
  half demi, hemi, semi
  many mult(i)

mountain oro
outer ect(o), exo
over supra
single mono
thought ideo
under sub
with syn
within endo
wrong mis
prehistoric
  comb. form pale(o)
  human caveman
  upright stone menhir
preliminary preceding, prefatory
  meeting caucus
  race heat
  statement foreword, preamble
premises, series of sorites
preoccupation
  with sex erot(ic)ism
prepare prime, ready, train
  copy edit
  for action gird, unlimber
preposition for, out, from, into, onto,
  unto, after
prepossession bias
prerogative right, privilege
  king's regalia
preserve can, smoke, pickle, protect
  by drying dehydrate, dessicate
  game sanctuary
  with salt corn
presidential
  disapproval veto
  reception levee
Preston
  milieu Yukon
pretended courage bluff, bravado
pretense air, ruse, sham, claim
  of virtue hypocrisy
pretentious pompous
  art kitsch
pretext
  for war belli, casus
prevent avert, block, deter, hamper,
  impede, thwart, obriate
  legally estop

preventative
  court order injunction
Priam
  children Paris, Creusa, Hector, Troilus, Cassandra
  domain Troy
  father Laomedon
  wife Hecuba
price fee, cost, rate, value, worth, charge
  go down in stock market bear
  go up in stock market bull
  list catalog(ue)
prickly burry, spiny, thorny, echinate
  bush rose, brier
  heat lichen, miliaria
  shrub bramble
  weed nettle
pride vanity, conceit
  disdainful hauteur
  lion's mane, group, litter
  ruffled pique
priest cleric, minister, clergyman
  assistant acolyte
  gift of mortuary
  newly ordained neophyte
  shaven head tonsure
  skullcap zucchetto
priests
  group of twenty fetial
primitive basic, crude, ancient
  comb. form pale(o)
  fish coelancanth
prince ras, king, rajah, monarch, principe
princeling satrap
princess Infanta
  carried by bull Europa
principle rule, maxim, tenet, theorem
  first rudiments
  main keystone
print
  blurred/double mackle
  in red letters rubricate
printer's
  apprentice devil
  ink pad dabber
  proof galley
  roller bray

printing edition
  process offset
  system for the blind Braille
  trial impression proof
Priscilla
  husband John Alden
  suitor Miles Standish
prison cage, jail, penitentiary
  guard screw (sl.)
  oubliette cell hole
  sl. jug, pen, stir, clink
  underground dungeon
private secret, intimate, personal
  entrance postern
  eye detective
  information tip
  remarks ad libs, asides
  wrong tort
privileges, equality of isonomy
pro for, professional
  bono publico
  tempore temporary
proceed issue, advance
  without power coast
process action, course, outgrowth
  of decline decadence
  server sheriff
Procne
  husband Tereus
  parent Pandion
  transformation swallow
prodrome symptom
produced on earth's surface epigene
producing
  abundantly feracious
professional pro
  non lay, amateur
profit gain, avail, benefit
  clear net, velvet
  easy gravy
  sudden, great killing
prog forage, plunder
prohibit ban, stop, veto, taboo, enjoin, forbid
prohibitive price dear, costly
projectile ball, bullet, rocket, missile

part warhead, war nose
path trajectory
prolonged dry weather drought
Prometheus
  boon to man fire
prominence
  between eyebrows glabella
Promised Land Sion, Zion, Canaan
promissory note IOU, debt
  sl. marker
pronged thing fork, rake, antler,
  trident
pronounce utter, declare
  indistinctly slur, mumble
pronunciamento manifesto
proofreader's mark dele, stet, caret
propeller rotor, screw, driver
  driving force thrust
  part hub, blade
proper meet, prim, suitable
  order eutaxy
  sl. kosher
property chattel, holdings, ownership
  claim lien
  reverted escheat
  willed to someone legacy
prophesy forecast, prediction
  by lots sortilege
prophets, book of the Nebiim
proposed international language
  Ido, Esperanto
Proserpina Cora, Persephone
  husband Pluto
  mother Ceres
prosit toast
Prospero
  slave Caliban
  sprite Ariel
prosy dull, jejune
protein fibrin, albumin, globulin
  egg yolk vitellin
Protestant
  Anglo-Saxon WASP
protrusion of organ hernia
Proust, Marcel novelist
proverb adage, axiom, saying,
  parable

proving directly d(e)ictic
provisions larder, groceries
  search for forage
prow bow, nose
prowl lurk, rove, skulk
proximal next, nearest
  opposite distal
prude prig
Prussian German, Junker
psalm hymn, laud, venite, introit
  word selah
pseudonym alias, pen name, nom de
  plume
  Arouet Voltaire
  Austen Dapsang
  Bronte Currer Bell
  Clemens Mark Twain
  Dickens Boz
  Dudevant George Sand
  Lamb Elia
  Millay Nancy Boyd
  Porter O Henry
  Stein Alice Toklas
  Thibault Anatole France
Psiloriti, Mount Ida
  location Crete
psoas loin, muscle
Psyche mind, soul
  love Cupid
psyche, part id, ego, superego
Pt, in chemistry platinum
pteropod clione, mollusk
pterygold winglike
public open, overt, common, community
  auction vendue
  disclosure exposé
  land ager
  opinion consensus
Puccini, Giacomo composer
  heroine Mimi, Tosca
  opera Tosca, Boheme, Turandot, Manon
    Lescaut
pucka, pukka good, real, genuine
puddling tool rabble
pudendum vulva
puff gust, whiff, breath, pastry, praise
  adder snake

bird barbet, monasa
of wind flatus
up bloat, swell
puffin bird
puggree scarf
pugh bah, pish
pugnacious bellicose, combative, quarrelsome
man bruiser (sl.)
pulex flea
pull tug, haul, move, pluck
apart pan, rip
down raze, reduce
off effect, accomplish
sl. influence
up stakes leave, depart
pulp pap, pith, chyme
apple/fruit pomace
product paper
sl. magazine
pulse beat, throb
beat absence acrotism
of the sphygmic
pulverizing device mill, spider
Punch and Judy
character puppet
dog Toby
punchinello clown, buffoon
punctuation mark dash, (semi)colon, comma, hyphen, period, brackets
Punic
citizen Carthaginian
War battlesite Zama
punishment rap, penalty
of penal, punitive
voluntary penance
Punjab
native Jat, Sikh
punka(h) fan
punster wag, wit
pupil
contraction myosis
organ eye
purchase
or sale of office barratry
purification catharsis, disinfection
by holy water baptism

purslane herb, weed
purulence pus
push impel, shove, hustle, propel
along plod
on proceed
over setup (sl.)
pusher (sl.)
commodity of LSD, pot, heroin, marijuana
put set, impel, place, state
aside discard
down crush, quash, humble, record
forth effort work, exert
forward present, propose
off delay, evade, divert
on don, josh (sl.), clothe
on the block auction
out oust, evict, dismiss
side by side juxtapose
to work harness
up with bear
Putnam, Israel Revolutionary general
putsch uprising, rebellion
puttee putty, gaiter
putting area green
puttyroot orchid
Putumayo river Ica
puzzle rebus, stump, enigma, nonplus, perplex
word logograph
pygarg addax
Pygmalion
author George Bernard Shaw
statue Galatea
pygmy
antelope oribi
pyralidid moth
pyramid
builders Egyptians
site El Giza
Pyrenese
goat ibex
highest point Aneto
pyrexia fever
pyrite fool's gold
Pyrrhonism skepticism

Pythagoras
  birthplace Samos
  forte mathematics
Pythias
  friend Damon
pythoness soothsayer
pyx box, ciborium
pyxis box, case, vase

Q

Q cue, queue
  Gr. Kappa
Qara Qum's/Qatar
  capital Doha
q.e.d. quod erat demonstrandum
qua as, bird, heron
quabird heron
quack cry, faker, fraud, crocus
  crier duck
  doctor's aide toady
  mediane herb, nostrum
quad jail, block, campus, sibling
quadra fillet, plinth
quadragenarian fortyish
quadragesimal forty, Lenten
quadrangle square, tetragon
quadrant arc, fourth, instrument
  graduated edge limb
quadrate suit, ideal, square, balanced
quadriga cart, chariot
quadrille cards, dance
  card matador
  sight vane
quadrillion peta (comb. form)
quadrivium
  part music, geometry, astronomy
quadroon hybrid, mulatto
quadrumane ape, primate, chimpanzee
quadruped mammal, four-legged
  example ass, camel, hippo, rhino, tapir,
    zebra, donkey, giraffe
quaere inquiry, question
quaestor judge, official, paymaster
quaff sip, gulp, drink

quag quake, quiver, quagmire
quaggalike animal zebra, donkey
quaggy miry, soft, boggy, flabby, yielding
quagmire bog, hag, mire, marsh, dilemma
quahaug, quahog clam
  young littleneck
quail bird, wilt, colin, recoil, wince
  flock bevy, covey
  young cheeper, squealer
quail snipe dowitcher
quaint odd, crafty, fanciful, singular
  humor droll(ery)
quake rese, shake, waver, shiver, vibrate
Quaker Friend, broadbrim
  city Philadelphia
  colonist Penn
  founder George Fox
  gray acier
  midweek Wednesday
quaker ladies bluet, flower
quaking shaky, trepid
  tree aspen, poplar
qualification ability, condition, requisite,
  modification
qualified able, eligible, competent
qualify fit, pass, entitle, describe
qualifying word adverb, adjective
quality cost, sort, nature, caliber, characteristic
  distinguishing trait
  of tone timbre, resonance
  poor/bad bum, punk
  special deluxe
qualm pall, nausea, twinge, misgiving,
  compunction
qualmish queer, queasy
quamash lily, ca(m)mas(s), prairie
quandary fix, pickle, puzzle, dilemma,
  nonplus
quannet file
quant pole, punt, propel
quantity dose, grist, hoard, amount,
  portion, allowance
  fixed constant
  full complement
  indefinite any, some
  irrational surd
  large raft, slew, bushel

not prescribed scalar
per unit rate
prescribed dose
small lick, scantling
Quantrill
  men raiders
quantum unit, amount, portion
  of radiation energy photon
quarantine ban, exclude, isolate
  building/ship lazaretto
  signal yellow jack
quaranty court
quarentene rood, furlong
quark caw, croak
quarl(e) tile, brick
quarrel pane, spat, argue, bicker, chisel, altercation
quarrelsome hostile, petulant, bellicose, litigious
quarrying tool trapan, trepan
quarry game, prey, chase, excavate, excavation
quarryman stonecutter
quart see also Quick Reference List, Metric
  eighth gill
  four gallon
  fourth cup, measure
  two flagon
quartan fever, malaria
quarter coin, span, allot, mercy, billet, fourth, division, neighborhood
  circle quadrant
  note crotchet
  phase diphase
  round orolo
quartern gill, quarter
quarters camp, room, abode, shelter
  nautical cabin, steerage, wardroom
  winter hibernacle
  women's harem
  sl. digs
quartz onyx, sand, flint, prase, silex, topaz, crystal, amethyst
quartzite itabarite
quash drop, void, annul, crush, cancel, suppress
  legally abate

quasi as if, seemingly
quat boil, pimple, tetrad, satiate
quaternion tetrad
  turning factor versor
quatrain poem, stanza
quaver trill, shake, tremble, vibrate
quawk caw, heron, screech
quay dock, pier, levee, wharf, landing
queach bog, fen, swamp, thicket
quean jade, slut, hussy, shrew, wench, prostitute
Quebec
  acre arpent
  cape Gaspe
  county Laval
  patron saint Anne
  peninsula Gaspe
  town Sorel
  vehicle caleche
quebrada brook, gorge, ravine
Quechua Inca(n), Andean, Indian, Peruvian
queechy puny, weak, feeble, sickly
queen regina, monarch, sovereign
  Anne's lace carrot
  beheaded Marie Antoinette
  fairy Mab, Una, Titania
  legendary Dido
  widowed dowager
Queen City Cincinnati
queenly noble, regal, royal, reginal
queen of
  Adriatic Venice
  Antilles Cuba
  Calydon Althea
  East Zenobia
  gods Hera, Juno, Sati
  hearts Elizabeth
  heaven Mary, Astarte
  Iceland Brunhilde
  Ithaca Penelope
  Isles Albion
  jungle Sheena
  Lydia Omphale
  Moslems begum
  Nile Cleopatra
  nymphs Mab

Olympia Hera
Palmyra Zenobia
Roman gods Juno
Sheba Balkis
spades Basta
Thebes Dirce, Jocasta
Queen of Spades
  author Aleksandr Pushkin
  composer Pyotr Ilich Tchaikovsky
queen's
  arm musket
  delight oil, herb, perennial
  flower myrtle, bloodwood
Queensland
  capital/river/seaport Brisbane
  explorer James Cook
queer odd, weird, cranky, bizarre, singular,
  homosexual
  bird/person nut, crank, oddball
  notion kink
  sl. spoil, counterfeit
queest ringdove
queet coot
quell calm, cool, crush, quash, assuage
quelque chose trifle
queme snug, tidy, handy, quiet
Quemoy
  neighbor Amoy
quench delay, slake, appease, diminish
quenelle meatball
quercetin dye, flavin(e)
quercitron dye, oak
quercus genus Oaks
querent inquirer, plaintiff
querida (Sp.) lover, darling, sweetheart
querken choke, stifle
querl coil, twist
quern mill, grinder
querulous fretful, peevish, quizzical,
  complaining
query ask, doubt, concern, inquiry
quest ask, hunt, search, pursuit
question ask, quiz, doubt, issue, inquiry,
  problem
  -and-answer teaching catechesis
  baffling poser
  denoting interrogational

mark erotema, eroteme
  rhetorical eperotesis
questionable moot, dubious, suspect,
  equivocal
questionnaire form, poll, survey
quetzal bird, trogon
queue line, braid, pigtail
  torero's coleta
quey heifer
quiaquia scad, cigarfish
quibble cog, pun, carp, bicker, wrangle
quica opossum, sarigue
quick fast, agile, fleet, rapid, swift, snappy,
  pregnant
  assets cash
  bread muffin, biscuit
  in learning apt
  look glance, eyebeam
  -tempered irascible
  witticism sally
quicker than ere, before
quicklime rusma
quickly fast, presto, rapidly, vigorous
quicksand flew, syrt(is), morass
quickset slip, hedge, thicket
quicksilver azoth, mercury
quid cud, chew, trade, return
  pro quo substitute
quiddany jelly, sirup, syrup
quiddit subtlety
quidnunc frump, snoop, gossip,
  busybody
quiescent quiet, still, latent, placid
quiet mum, calm, allay, silent
  interval lull
  secretly clandestine
quietus death, repose, mittimus
quiff curl, girl, puff
quill pen, remex, spine, barrel, feather
  feathers calami, remiges
  porcupine spine
quillai soapbark
quillet tube
quilt pad, duvet, eider, caddow,
  bedcover
quilting party bee
quince bel, pome

quinine kina
  source cinchona
  water tonic
quink brant
quinoa seeds, pigweed, goosefoot
quinoline derivative analgen
quint stop, organ
quintuplets Dionne, Fischer
quip mot, pun, jest, saying
quire fold, choir, paper
quirk kink, clock, twist, caprice
quirquincho pichi, armadillo
quirt whip, romal
quis woodcock
quisling rat, traitor, collaborator
  fifth columnist Vidkun
quit free, stop, forgo, desist, abdicate
quitch weed, grass
quitclaim acquit, release, transfer
quite all, stark, wholly, entirely
  so exactly, precisely
quits even
quittance repay, reprisal, discharge
quitter slag, piker, coward, shirker
quiver shake, tremor, nimble, tremble,
  vibrate
  content arrows
quivering aspen, ashake, blubbery
quivering tree aspen, palpitant
  leaf aspen
quiverleaf aspen
Quixote
  giant windmill
  horse Rosinante
  love Dulcinea
  squire/friend Sancho Panza
  title don
quixotic absurd, utopian, romantic,
  impractical
quiz ask, exam(ination), joke, probe
  kid prodigy
quizzical odd, amusing, curious, searching
quizzing glass monocle, eyeglass
quod jug, jail, prison
quodlibet debate, medley, subtlety
quoin coin, lock, corner, keystone
quoit disc, ring(er), throw

pin hob
  target peg, tee
quomodo means, manner
quondam once, former, whilom, erstwhile
Quonset hut prefab
  British type Nissen
quop throb
quorum group, council, company,
  majority
quota share, divide, allotment
quotation cital, excerpt, citation
  ending speech/story/song tag
  mark guillemet (Fr.)
  opening chapter epigraph
  reader speculator, stockholder
quoth said, spoke
quotha indeed, forsooth
quotidian daily, ordinary
quotient result
quotity group, collection
Quo Vadis
  author Henryk Sienkiewicz
  character Nero, Lygia, Peter, Vinicius,
    Petronius

R

R ar
  Greek rho
  in chemistry radical
  in mathematics ratio, radius
  pronunciation like l lallation
Ra sun god
  crown aten
  in chemistry radium
  symbol sun disk
  wife Mut
raad catfish
rabato ruff, collar
rabbi Amora, teacher
  teachings Mishna(h)
rabbit hare, rodent, cottontail
  breeding place warren
  ears antenna
  family leporid

female doe
fur con(e)y, lapin
-fur hat castor
-hunting dog harrier
male buck
pen hutch
rock hyrax
tail scut
variety lop, Dutch
young bunny
rabble mob, canaille
rouser agitator
the masses
Rabelais, Francois Fr. satirist
Rabelaisian earthy
RCA trademark Nipper
race stirps, lineage, pedigree
channel flume
division Negroid, Caucasian,
   Mongoloid
engine rev
of dwarfs nibelungen
pert. to ethnic
prelims heats
short dash, sprint
start breakaway
water arroyo
white Caucasian
yellow Mongoloid
racecourse oval, turf, track
circuit lap
comb. form drome
marker lane, pylon
official starter
racehorse
disability spavin, glanders, stringhalt
enclosure/exercise area paddock
kind pacer, mudder, plater, trotter
winless maiden
racer (black) snake, hot rod, sprinter
course lane
racetrack oval
character tout, tipster, dopester
cover tanbark
fence rail
Rachel
father Laban

husband Jacob
son Joseph, Benjamin
rachis stem, spine, backbone
Rachmaninoff, Sergei composer/pianist
Racine, Jean Fr. poet
masterpiece Phedre, Phaedra (Eng.)
racing
colors silks
program card, form
scull shell, wherry
rack gin, score, stand, strain, grating,
   torture
display easel
hat tree
horse's gait, pace
racket
sl. line, noise, business, profession
string catgut
raconteur
forte stories, anecdotes
Radames
love Aida
radar
device, for short TFR
image blip
-like device sonar
screen flash blip
sound beep, racon
system shoran
radian arc
radiant aglow, bright, beaming
comb. form heli(o)
radicel root(let)
radio wireless
active shower fallout
aerial antenna
dash in dah
frequency band channel
interference static
operator, amateur ham
signal for aviators beam
sign-off roger
tube grid, detector, rectifier
radioactive
matter niton, radon, nobelium, carnotite
particles geigers
radioactivity measure curie

radium
   discoverer Marie, Pierre Curie
   source uranite, pitchblende
radix base, root, etymon, radical
radon gas, niton
raft lot, balsa, platform, collection
   log catamaran
ragamuffin tatterdemalion
Raggedy doll Andy, Anne
raggee ragi, grass
raglan general, topcoat, overcoat
ragweed ambrosia, cocklebur
ragwort jacoby, groundsel
raid foray, invade, sortie, assault
   sl. pinch
rail bird, coot, sora, weka, fence, heron,
   scoff
   kin notornis
   -like bird courlan
railing
   fence parapet, balustrade
railroad herd, line, rush
   baggage car van
   bridge trestle
   center yard
   crossing gate
   engine serviceman hostler
   freight car gondola
   handcar velocipede
   line end terminus
   side track spur
   siding turnout
   single track monorail
   stop for locomotives tank town
   supply car tender
   switch device frog, shunt
   tie timber, sleeper
rain shower, precipitation
   briefly spit
   fine mist mizzle, serein
   forest selva
   formed by pluvial
   frozen hail, sleet
   gauge udometer
   mist scud
   sudden brash, spate
   tree saman, zamia

rainbow arc(h), bow, meteor
   bridge bifrost
   color like pavonine
   goddess Iris
   pert. to iridal
   trout steelhead
rainmaker lobbyist
raise jack, lift, erect, hoist, collect,
   nurture
   in relief emboss
   nap tease(l)
   to third power cube
raisin grape, sultana
   in pudding plum
raison d'etat, d'etre
rajah
   wife rani, ranee
ralline bird rail
ram tup, pound, sheep, district
   constellation Aries
   -headed god Ammon
   horn shofar, shophar
   ship's beak
Ramadan, Ramazan fasting
Rambouillet (merino) sheep, district
ramekin/ramequin dish
Rameses monarch, pharaoh
   domain Egypt
ramie hemp, fiber
ramjet engine, athodyd
Ramona
   author Helen Jackson
rampaging person amok, berserk,
   berserker, juramentado
Ramses
   goddess Anta
ramson root, garlic
ramus branch
rana frog
range row, area, rank, gamut, stove, train,
   extent, limits, Sierra
   finder stadia, telemeter
   of emotion gamut
   of vision scan, scope, eyesight
   Rocky Mountains Teton, Uinta
rani/ranee queen
   husband raja(h)

Ranier prince
  domain Monaco
rank tier, grade, eminence, position
  and file soldiers, followers
  having genetic
  of lower puisne
ransom
  person held hostage, redeem
ranunculaceous plant peony, anemone, larkspur
ranunculus crowfoot, buttercup
rapacious greedy, predatory, voracious, avaricious
  bird shrike
  fish piranha
rape cole, pulp, seize, fodder, ravish, cabbage, plunder
  soil/seed colza
rapid swift, abrupt, ripple
  comb. form tachy
  fire staccato, fusillade
rapids chute, dells, dalles
rappee snuff
rapping tattoo, tapping
rapscallion rogue, rascal
raptorial bird owl, hawk, eagle, falcon, vulture
rara avis bird, oner, rarity
rarebit rabbit
rareripe fruit peach
rasher ham, bacon, slice, portion
Rasmussen, Knud Arctic explorer
rasorial gallinaceous
  bird hen, chicken, pheasant
Raspe
  character Munchausen
Rasputin, Grigori Russian monk
rasse civet
rat vole, rodent, vermin
  genus Mus
  hair pad
  kind mole
  poison ratsbane
  rodent resembling mouse, hamster
  sl. deserter, informer, stool pigeon
ratafia cookie, liqueur, macaroon
rataplan drumbeat

rate class, ratio, scold, esteem
  exchange agio
  of mass to volume density
ratel badgerlike animal
ratfish chimaera
Ratibor river Oder
ratio pi, cos, sine, quotient, proportion
rational principle logos
rations food, allotment
  bag haversack
ratite emu, moa, ostrich
  genus Apteryx
ratoon shoot, sprout
rats, of murine
rattlepate ass, fool
rattlesnake viper, cascabel, sidewinder
  bite rue
  plantain orchid
rattletrap mouth, jalopy, rickety
raun roe, spawn
raven crow, prey, corby, devour
  author Edgar Allan Poe
  cry caw
  genus Corvus
  like a corvine
  of Odin Hugin
  quote nevermore
raw sore, bleak, uncooked
  cotton lint
  material ore, stock, stuff, staple
  sl. unfair
rawhide whip, leather, parfleche
  kind shagreen
ray beam, petal, skate, trace, sawfish
  eagle obispo
  fish dorn
  kind X, beta, gamma, laser, ultraviolet
  -like part radius
rayon jersey, ratine, acetate, textile, viscose
  corded/ribbed repp
  sheer voile
  twilled serge
razor shave(r)
  -billed bird auk, alca
  clam solen
  sharpen hone, strop

Rb (in chemistry) rubidium
re about, anent, regarding
  echoing reboant
reaction reflex, tropism, response
read con, pore, study, peruse
  inability to alexia
  metrically scan
  superficially skim
reads alike forward and backward
   palindrome
  example Madam I'm Adam
real coin, true, pucka, actual
  plural reis
  thing McCoy
real estate
  claim tax, lien
  pert. to predial
realism opposite idealism
realistic practical
  opposite visionary
ream enlarge, quantity
reamer tool, borer, drift, broach
Reaper mower, harvester
  Grim death
rear aft, back, build, ramp, rise, breed,
   nurse, raise
  horse's stend, pesade
  young bird fledge
rearrange switch, permute
reason argue, logos, motive, sanity, justify
  against oppugn
  deprive of dement
  for being end, raison d'etre
  pert. to noetic
  with rightly, logically
reasoning logic
  basis premise
  correct logical
  false idolism, sophism
  faulty syllogism, paralogism
  subtle, difficult metaphysics
reata lasso, noose
Rebecca, Rebekah
  brother Laban
  diminutive Reba, Becky
  father Bethuel
  husband Isaac

  mother Milcah
  son Esau, Jacob
rebel
  angel Belial
rebus puzzle, riddle
recede ebb, draw back
receiver radio, recipient, treasurer
  stolen goods fence
  trust property bailee, trustee
recent lately, current
  comb. form neo
receptacle bin, box, basin, vessel
  flower torus
  holy water font, stoup
Recife Pernambuco
reciprocal repay, mutual, return
  comb. form allelo
recite relate, narrate
  loudly declaim
  mechanically patter
  monotonously chant, drone
reck heed
reckless rash, wild, madcap, wanton,
   heedless
reclaimed land polder
reconnaissance survey, examination
record tab, dope, file, register
  copy estreat
  formal minutes, document
  historical annals
  personal diary, dossier
  police blotter
  ship log
records
  place for public archives
recovery in law trover, replevin
recrement dross, waste
rectifier adjuster
  tube diode
recto right
  opposite left, verso
recurring period cycle
red color, radical
  -and-blue color purple
  ape orangutan
  arsenic realgar
  breast robin, sandpiper

cedar savin(e), juniper
corpuscle deficiency anemia
corundum ruby
deep ruby, garnet
deer spay, staggart
desert Nefud
-eyed fish carp, rudd
fir pine, spruce, Douglas
gum eucalyptus, strophulus
in heraldry gules
inscribed in rubric
lead minium
letter memorable
pigment chica, roset
planet Mars
squirrel chickaree
star Mars, Antares
viper copperhead
Red Cross
  concern calamity, disaster
  founder Clara Barton
redd tidy up
redeemer Goel, Savior, Jesus Christ
Redemptorist founder Liguori
redfin carp, fish
redhead duck, carrottop, woodpecker
  kin pochard, widgeon
redmouth fish, grunt
redness
  excessive erythrism
  of skin rubefaction
redowalike dance polka, waltz
Red Sea Erythrean
  Kingdom Yemen
Red Square landmark Kremlin
redundancy excess, nimiety, pleonasm,
  tautology
reduplicate
  in botany valvate
redwood sequoia
reed oat, grass, plant, stalk
  bird bobolink
  instrument oboe, organ, bassoon,
    clarinet, saxaphone
  loom sley
  poet. arrow
  weaver's sley

reef
  coral cay, key
  mining lode, vein
reel
  for thread spool, bobbin, filature
  of cocoon silk filature
refer point, allude, assign
  to vide
referendum plebiscite
refine distill, polish, purify, improve
  by distillation rectify
  by melting smelt
  vessel used cupel
reflet luster
reformer moralist, Jacob Riis
  religious Martin Luther
refuse nill, ejecta, reject, naysay, rubbish
  consent to veto
  metal scum, dross
  table ort, scrap
  wine lees
Regan
  father Lear
  sister Goneril, Cordelia
regent interrex
  of the sun Uriel
regicide
  victim king
regiment unit, cadre, order
  flag pennon
  member soldier, grenadier
Regin
  son Sigurd, Siegfried
region area, zone, realm, locale
  comb. form nesia
  pert. to areal
  upper ether
  warm tropics
  woodless plain, tundra, steppe
register
  cash damper
  legal docket
regma maple, schizocarp
regulating box rheostat
rehearsal practice, training
  kind dress, dry run
rehoboam hat, bowl

Rehoboam king
  father Solomon
  son Abijah
reign rule, govern, prevail
  of a family dynasty
  pert. to regnal
reindeer caribou
  genus Rangifer
  man Lapp
rejoinder reply, answer
related akin, allied, germane
  by blood kin(dred), sib
  on father's side agnate
  on mother's side enate
relationship
  sympathetic rapport
relative amount ratio
relatives kith, kindred, kinfolk
  favoritism to nepotism
release free, undo, untie, exempt, liberate,
    statement
  claim remise, waiver
  a mass of ice calve
reliance on experience empirical
relic curio, souvenir
  cabinet etager(e)
  sacred halidom
religious nun, monk, friar, pious, devout,
    conscientious
  beggar fakir
  belief creed
  devotion novena
  expedition crusade
  image icon
  journey pilgrimage
  offering oblation, sacrifice
  order Jesuit, Marist, Templar, Dominican,
    Franciscan
  reformer Huss, Luther
  saying logia
  vigil watch
relish curry, enjoy, gusto, sapor, radish,
    chutney, mustard, condiment
  fish egg caviar
  jelled aspic
remain bide, last, stay, tarry, endure
  balanced librate

firm stand (pat)
  undecided fire, hang, pend, procrastinate
remark barb, note, word, aside
  correct mouthful (sl.)
  embarrassing boner, faux pas
  indirect innuendo
  witty quip, sally, bon mot
Rembrandt Dut. painter
  work Titus
remedy cure, heal, antidote, treatment
  cure-all elixir, panacea
  quack nostrum, placebo
  soothing balm
remex quill, feather, oarsman
remo(u)lade sauce, dressing
remora clog, fish, pega, delay
remote alien, aloof, vague, distant
  goal thule
  most ultima
remove oust, eject, expel
  from grave disinter
  from office oust, depose
  impurities distill, refine
  in law eloin
  water dehydrate
Remus
  brother/slayer Romulus
  father Mars
  foster mother wolf
  mother Rhea
Renard fox
Renoir, Pierre Auguste Fr. painter
rensselaerite talc
rep cloth, fabric
repair fix, mend, remedy, restore
  hole/tear darn
repartee mot, retort, rejoinder
  engage in fence
  skilled at witty
repast meal, treat, refection
  pert. to prandial
repeat
  mus. bis
  performance encore
  sign segno (mus.)
repeating rifle inventor Peter Wilhelm
    Mauser

repertoire/repertory list, stock
repetition copy, recitation, recurrence
  in music reprise
  mechanical rote
  of performance encore, replay
  of sound echo
repine fret, grouse, complain
replica copy, carbon, facsimile
repondez s'il vous plait RSVP
report rumor, gossip, account, hansard,
  denounce, broadcast, reputation
  false canard, slander
reporter
  concern data, scoop
  routine legwork
repository safe, confidant, sepulcher
representation image, mimesis, allegory
  of heavenly bodies orrery
  ridiculous travesty
reprisal revenge, quittance, vengeance,
  retaliation
reproduce asexually clone
reproductive
  cell ovum, sperm, gamete
  gland gonad
  organ ovary, testis
reptile lizard, turtle, saurian, alligator,
  lacert(il)ian
  age Mesozoic
  carnivorous tuatara
  extinct dinosaur, pterosaur
  footless apod, snake
  fossil stegosaurus
  mythical salamander
  Nile crocodile
  pert. to saurian
  scale scutum, platelet
  study herpetology
republic democracy
  author Plato
  of letters literati
  imaginary Oceania
  Republican Whig
  mascot elephant
  party GOP
  recalcitrant mugwump
repute odor, esteem, reputation

request
  formal rogation
requiem hymn, mass, dirge
requiescat in pace RIP
reredos screen, partition
reremouse bat
res point, thing
research study
  center lab(oratory)
reseau network
reseda mignonette
resemblance ringer (sl.), likeness, similarity
reservation
  in law salvo, saying, exception
reserves National Guard
  armed forces militia
reservoir store, supply, cistern, reserve,
  receptacle
  overflow spilth
residence home, abode, biding, domicile
  rural bower, cottage
  stately mansion
residential street terrace
resin, rosin alkyd, amber, pitch, shellac(k)
  aromatic copaiba
  cathartic scammony
  fossil amber
  gum copal, myrrh, mastic, resinoid
  incense myrrh, sandarac
  perfume-making benzoin
  purified shellac
  solvent ether
  synthetic bakelite, silicone
  thermoplastic saran
  varnish anime
resinous tree fir, pine, balsam
resort spa, recourse
  place frequented haunt
  Riviera Cannes
Respighi, Ottorino composer
respiration breathing
  comb. form spiro
  difficult dyspn(o)ea
  organ lung
  normal eupnoea
rest seat, relax, sleep, repose, recline,
  vacation

sl. break, breather
midday siesta
reading caesura
restaurant diner, bistro, eatery, cabaret
bench banquette
compartment booth
restive balky, unruly, fretful, impatient
restorative anodyne, salutary
restore
printer's mark stet
to health recuperate
result in cause
resurrection rebirth, revival
experienced by Jesus, Lazarus
resuscitation revival, anabiosis
ret damp, soak, macerate
retable shelf, gradin
retainers, body of retinue
retaining wall revetment
retch gag, keck, puke, vomit
rete/reticulum plexus, network
retem juniper
retepore mollusk
retiarius gladiator
retort quip, reply, sally, riposte, repartee,
apparatus
retraction palinode
retreat lair, nest, asylum, pullout,
sanctum
kind convent, hermitage,
monastery
shaded bower
signal chamade
underground abri, cave
retribution goddess Ate
retributive justice nemesis
return in kind reciprocate
Return of the Native
author Thomas Hardy
Reuben
brother Joseph
father Jacob
mother Leah
Reuel
father Esau, Essau
reunion get-together
with Brahma Nirvana

reus defendant
reveille call, dian(a), rouse, signal,
awaken
revelations Apocalypse
revelry festivity, saturnalia
cry evoe
revenue income
bishop's annat
reverence awe, worship, adoration
gesture kneeling, genuflection
lacking impious
revers lapel
reversion return
of property escheat
to type atavism
review report, inspect, critique
adverse pan
enthusiastic rave
one who does critic
revivalist evangelist
revolting horrid, loathsome, offensive
revolution gyre, rotation, rebellion
general, Am. Revolution Gates,
Arnold, Greene, Washington
revolutionary fighter minuteman
revolutionist reb(el), anarch
revolutions per minute RPM, revs
revolving part rotor, rotator
Reynard fox
rezai coverlet
Rh factor rhesus
Rhea Ops, Ratite
child Hera, Zeus, Hades, Hestia
father Uranus
husband Cronus
rhesus monkey, macaque
rhetorical florid, bombastic
rheumatism
of back/loins lumbago
remedy salol
weed pipsissewa
Rhine Rijn, river
city on the Mannheim
magic hoard Rheingold
nymph Lurlei, Lorelei
pert. to Rhenish
wine Hock, Moselle

rhino(ceros) cash, abada, money
- **beetle** uany
- **bird** bee eater
- **black** borele
- **cousin** tapir
- **one-horned** badak
- **two-horned** keitloa

rhizoid rootlike

rhizopod testacean

rhoda rose

Rhode Island see also Quick Reference List
- **founder** Roger Williams

Rhodes Rodi, Cecil
- **ancient wonder** Colossus

Rhodesia
- **language** Bantu, Shona
- **tribe** llas

rhomb, rhomboid lozenge, parallelogram

Rhone tributary Isere, Saone

rhubarb hassle, pieplant
- **genus** Rheum

rhus tree sumac(h)

rhythmic metrical
- **accent** ictus
- **rise and fall** heave

riata rope, lasso, lariat

rib kid, vein, wife, tease
- **in architecture** lierne
- **leaf** nervure
- **pert. to** costal

ribaldry japery

ribbon bow, braid, strip, decoration
- **badge** cordon
- **binding** lisere
- **decorative** riband
- **document/seal** label
- **fish** cutlass
- **knot** cockade
- **-like part** t(a)enia
- **paper** ticker tape, register tape
- **trimming** galloon

ribs
- **having** costate
- **without** decostate

rice grain, grass, cereal
- **dish, spicy/meat** pilau
- **field** paddy
- **husk** bran
- **paste** ame
- **wine** sake

rice rail sora

Richard I
- **of England** Lionheart, Coeur de Lion

Richelieu cardinal
- **successor** Mazarin

riches
- **demon** Mammon
- **region** Eldorado
- **worship** plutomania

rich man Midas, nabob, Cropsus, plutocrat, millionaire

ricin protein

rick heap, scold, stack, jingle

Rickenbacker, Eddie Amer. flying ace

ricksha(w) samlor, jinrikisha

rictus gape, mask

riddle sieve, puzzle, enigma, conundrum
- **picture** rebus

ridge aas, ruga, seam, wale, crest, cuesta
- **cloth** wale
- **glacial** osar, esker, drumlin
- **pert. to** cardinal
- **sand** dene, dune
- **skin** welt

ridicule gibe, jeer, mock, irony, roast, satire, sarcasm
- **deity** Momus
- **object** laughingstock

riding
- **outfit** rig, habit
- **pants** breeches, jodhpurs
- **school** manege
- **shoe** solleret, jodhpur boot
- **whip** crop, quirt

rifle gun, rob, carbine, pillage, repeater
- **ball** minie
- **chamber** magazine
- **person/man** jager
- **pin** tige

Riga city, balsam
- **Gulf island** Oesel
- **native** Latvian

right fit, title, correct, license
- **comb. form** rect(i)

hand dextra
legal droit, title
of way easement
sl. roger
to mail free frank
turn gee
word mot juste
rights
  equality isonomy
  relating to jural
Rigoletto
  composer GuiseppeVerdi
  heroine Gilda
rigor fury, harshness, austerity
  companion mortis
Riis, Jacob social reformer
Rijn Rhine
Rilke, Rainer Ger. poet
rim lip, orle, brink, border, margin
  cap's projecting visor
  pipe flange
  roof's eave
  wheel felly, felloe
Rinaldo's steed Bayard
ring rim, arena, knell, sound
  comb. form gyro
  of chain link
  of guards cordon
  of light halo
  of rope grommet
  of rubber gasket, O-ring
  pert. to annular
ringing clam, bright, chiming, resonant
  sound in ear tinnitus
rings
  interlocking gimmal
  series coil
Rio Bravo, Grande
  de Oro, Janiero
Rip van Winkle
  author Washington Irving
ris de veau sweetbread
rise flow, rebel, stand, aspire, expand
  again resurrect
  and fall heave
  and float in the air levitate
rissole meatball

Ritter knight
Ritz, Cesar Swiss hotelman
river
  arm estuary
  bank ripa, levee
  barge gondola
  beautiful Ohio
  bend oxbow
  blue, poet. Danube
  bottom bed
  comb. form potamo
  crossed by Caeser Rubicon
  current eddy, rapids
  dam weir
  edge bank, levee
  island holm
  log run sluiceway
  myth. Styx
  nymph naiad
  of oblivion Lethe
  of sorrows Acheron
  outlet bayou, mouth
  rapid sault
  winding of ess
Rivera, Diego Mex. painter
Riviera
  beach plage (Fr.)
  resort Cannes
rizzom ear, stalk, straw
Rn, in chemistry radon
road route, freeway, highway, expressway
  bend hairpin
  charge toll
  edge berm, curb, shoulder
  map abbrev. rte
  military agger
  runner bird, cock, cuckoo
  surface tar, concrete, macadam
roadster car, auto, horse, bicycle, runabout
  seat rumble
roan bay, horse
roaring brisk, noisy
  game curling
  Meg cannon
roast pan, broil, brown, criticize
  meat kabobs

prepare truss
stick skewer
rob flay, reave, plunder
  a boat/truck/airplane hijack
  Roy canoe, drink
  sl. cop, pinch
robber thief, outlaw, bandido, brigand
  cattle rustler
  den hideout
  sea pirate, corsair
robe gown, toga, vestment
  bishop's chimar, chimer
  long-sleeved caftan, kaftan
  loose simar
  monk's frock
Robin Hood outlaw
  chaplain Friar Tuck
  companion Will Scarlet, Little John
  sweetheart Maid Marian
  weapon longbow, quarterstaff
Robinson Crusoe
  author Daniel Defoe
  man Friday
roc bird, simurg
  passenger Sin(d)bad
rock candy, shake, stone
  black basalt
  boring tool trepon
  carving petroglyph
  comb. form lith(o), petr(o), saxi
  crushed ballast
  ejected by volcano lapillus
  growths lichen
  molten magma
  myth. Scylla
  pert. to petric
  suffix ite, yte
  volcanic lava, latite, perlite
rocket asroc, speed, projectile
  firing platform launching pad
  load warhead
Rockne, Knute football coach
  school Notre Dame
rocks
  of the oldest archean
  sl. gem, money, diamond
  study geology, lithology, petrology

rocky dizzy, shaky, craggy
  cliff scar
  hill tor
Rocky Mountain
  animal goat
  peak Logan, Pikes
  range Teton, Wasatch
  sheep bighorn
  wind chinook
rod pole, stem, wand, perch, pistol, toggle
  billiards cue
  divination dowsing
  sl. gat, piece
  square perch
rodent rat, mole, paca, vole, mouse, gerbil
  genus Mus
  jumping jerboa
  pert. to rosorial
  water beaver, muskrat
Rodin, Auguste Fr. sculptor
  famous work Thinker
roe ova, eggs, milt, coral, spawn, (fish) caviar
Roentgen see X-ray
rogan bowl
roger OK, over
Roi (Fr.) king
  heir Dauphin
  realm France
  wife Reine
Roland
  emperor Charlemagne
  enemy Gano
  friend Oliver
  horse Veillantif
  love Aude
  sword Durendal
roll cake, list, peal, wrap, lurch, elapse, enfold, brioche, catalog(ue), drumbeat, register
  along trundle
  back reduce
  hard bagel, kaiser
  in wallow
  of cloth bolt
  of coins rouleau
  of hair bun, chignon

of paper web, bolt
parchment scroll
sl. rob, wad, money
Rollo Viking
rom buzz, gypsy
Rome, Roman Eternal City
  abode of gods Olympus
  adviser to king Egeria
  amphitheater colosseum
  agreement pacta
  assembly forum, senate, comitia
  bathhouses thermae
  Caesar's title imperator
  cap pileus
  chariot essed
  circus arena hippodrome
  circus fighter gladiator
  citadel arx
  coin aes, semis, denarius
  commoner plebeian
  concert hall odeum
  court atrium
  date ides, nones
  emperor Otho, Otto, Carus, Galba, Nerva, Titus, Probus, Trajan, Hadrian, Caligula
  empire founder Augustus
  farewell addio
  fiddler Nero
  first emperor Augustus
  founder Romulus
  games ludi
  general Sulla, Titus, Drusus, Marius, Scipio, Agrippa, Cassius, Agricola, Lucullus
  god
    fire Vulcan
    gates Janus
    herds Pan
    household Lar, Lares, Penates
    night Somnus
    pastoral Faunus
    sea Neptune
    sleep Morpheus
    sun Sol
    underworld Dis, Orcus
    wine Bacchus
    woods Sylvanus

  goddess dea
    beauty Venus
    dawn Aurora
    earth Terra
    fertility Fauna
    fire Vesta
    flowers Flora
    fruits Pomona
    hope Spes
    hunting Diana
    love Venus
    marriage Juno
    moon Luna
    night Nox
    sea Mare
    underworld Proserpina
    war/wisdom Minerva
  headband vitta
  helmet galea
  highway via, iter
  hill Palatine, Capitoline
  jar amphora
  language Latin, Italian
  law lex
  meal cena, gena
  monster (myth.) Lamia, Typhon
  name nomen
  noble patrician
  orator Cato, Caesar, Cicero
  people Sabines, Etruscans
  philosopher Seneca
  poet Ovid, Lucan, Virgil, Juvenal, Lucretius
  pound libra
  river Tiber, Lethe
  soothsayer Haruspex
  tablet tessera
  theatrical arch proscenium
  urn capanna
  vase pyxis
  writing tablet diptych
Romeo lover
  and Juliet character Friar, Paris, Tybalt, Capulet, Mercutio, Montague
  father Montague
  rival Paris

Romulus Quirinus
  brother Remus
  father Mars
  mother Rhea
rondure circle, sphere
ronin (Jp.) outlaw, outcast
roof top, gambrel, shelter
  arched vault
  border eave
  comb. form stego
  covering tar, slate, terne, gravel, thatch, shingle
  drain gutter
  opening scuttle, skylight
  point (final) epi
  rounded dome, cupola
  slate rag
  sloped shed, lean-to
  two-sloped Mansard
  window dormer
  without homeless, hypethral
rookery building, tenement
  inhabitant auk, penguin
room cell, space, closet, chamber, quarter
  band, ornamental frieze
  conversation exedra, locutory
  harem ada, oda
  hot bath caldarium
  inner ben
  private boudoir
  storage shed, attic
rooming house kip
roorback lie, hoax, libel
roose extol, praise
Roosevelt, Franklin D. see also Quick Reference List
  dog Fala
  mother Sara
rooster cock, bantam, chanticleer
  castrated capon
  comb. form caruncle
  young broiler, cockerel
root core, plug, cheer, origin, rhizome
  aromatic orrice, ginseng, horseradish
  comb. form rhiz(o)
  dried rhatany
  edible yam, taro, potato, radish, cassava

  growth tubercle
  outer layer exoderm
  pert. to radicle
  shoot sucker, tiller
  starch arum
  substance zedoary
  word etymon
rope tie, cord, cable, lasso
  -and-pulley block tackle
  cattle catcher's bola, lasso
  dancer/walker funambulist
  fiber hemp, jute, nylon, sisal
  guiding dragline
  holder becket
  in lure, entice
  knotted at end colt
  ship's tye, line, vang, hawser, shroud
  wire cable
rorqual whale, finback, razorback
rosaceous rosy, blushing
  plant agrimony, strawberry
rosary beads, chaplet
rose color, damask, flower, perfume
  city Portland
  extract attar
  of Sharon Althea
  petal oil attar
  under the sub rosa
  wild brier, eglantine
Rose Bowl arena
  site Pasadena, California
rosebush fruit hip
rosette cockade
Rosinante jade, horse, steed
  master Quixote
ross bark, peel, waste
Rossini, Gioacchino
  opera Othello, William Tell, Barber of Seville
rot ret, decay, spoil, putrefy, decompose
  grass flukewort
  sl. bosh, bushwah, rubbish, nonsense
rotch(e) dovekey, guillemot
rote custom, system, routine
  by memory

rotten evil, foul, fetid, nasty, carrion, corrupt
  comb. form sapr(o)
rottenstone Tripoli
rough crude, coarse, jagged, rustic, agrestic
  -and-tumble fight brawl, melee, set-to
  cloth shag, terry
  comb. form trachy
  -edged erose
  skin shagreen
rouky foggy, misty
roulette game, epicycloid
  man croupier
  term bas, noir (black), passe, rouge (red), manque
round course, plump, circular
  clam quahog
  make circinate
  protuberance knob, umbo
  robin letter, contest
  Table knight Kay, Bors, Balan, Galahad, Geraint, Tristan, Lancelot, Parsifal, Percival
  trip excursion
roundabout indirect
  expression ambage
  way detour
roundhead Swede, Puritan
roundworm ascarid, parasite
Rousseau, Henri
  hero Emile
route gest, trail, direction
  circuitous detour
  straight beeline
routine rota, regular, humdrum
  task chore
rove gad, card, roam
  for adventure errant
  for plunder forage, maraud
row oar, file, fuss, tier
  of cut grass swath
  of planted seeds drill
rowan tree ash, sorb
rowen hay, field, grass, aftermath
royal noble, august, kingly
  agaric mushroom
  color purple

crown tiara, coronet
house Tudor, Stuart, Windsor, Romanov, Hapsburg
initials HRH
rock snake python
standard emblem
royalty
  symbol ermine
Roy Rogers
  horse Trigger
  wife Dale
rub gall, wipe, chafe, polish, stroke, obstacle
  down comb, curry, massage
  elbows fraternize
  out kill, erase
Rubaiyat
  author Omar Khayyàm
rubber eraser, ebonite, masseur
  boot wader, Wellington
  city Akron
  product basis latex
  roller squeegee
  tree ule, seringa
rube yokel, rustic, bumpkin, hay shaker
rubella rash, measles
Rubicon river
  crossed by Caesar
ruche frill, trimming
rudd carp, fish, vireo
rudder helm
  guide steer
  handle wheel, tiller
  part yoke
ruff bird, fish, trump, ruffle, disorder
  female ree, reeve
ruffle at the neck jabot, ruche
ruga fold, crease, wrinkle
rugby football
  formation scrum
  score try
rule norm, canon, order, theorem
  Brittannia composer Thomas Arne
  out bar, forbid
  over manage, supervise
ruler czar, tsar, tzar, emir, monarch, potentate

absolute shah, despot, tyrant
family dynasty
one of three triumvir
one of two duarch
wife rani, queen, empress, czarina, tsarina, tzarina
rules of
  conduct code
  infraction foul
  Order author Robert
Rumania, Rumanian
  coin ban, leu, ley
  composer Enesco
  folk dance Hora
rumble brawl, growl, uproar, thunder
  seat dickey
rumen cud, paunch
ruminant chewing, meditative
  female cow, doe, ewe, nanny
  genus Bos, Capra
  male ram, buck, billy
  type ox, yak, goat, bison, camel, steer, alpaca, buffalo, giraffe
rummer cup, glass
rummy gin, odd, sot, game, strange
  sl. sot, drunk
Rumpelstiltskin dwarf
run leak, incur, manage, sprint, publish, smuggle
  across meet
  aground founder
  away flee, abscond
  cricket bye
  down poor, outline, summary
  -of-the-mill so-so, ordinary
  off print, decamp
  out evade, expel, spill
  over exceed
  through stab, examine, practice
  up enlarge, increase
runcible spoon fork
rundlet tun, cask
rune magic, script, secret
runic alphabet futhark
running going, linear, contest, successive
  birch snowberry
  board footboard

knot noose
toad natterjack
Russia, Russian Rossiya, Muscovy
  alcoholic drink kvass, vodka
  assembly duma, rada
  calendar Julian
  carriage dros(h)ky, troika, tarantass
  chalet dacha
  citadel/gov't Kremlin
  coin ruble, kope(c)k
  commune kolhoz
  community mir
  Cossack Slav
  dance ziganka, kazatsky
  dramatist Gogol
  empress czarina, tsarina, tzarina
  exile's place Siberia
  farmer Ivan, kulak
  fish beluga
  founder Ivan
  guitar balalaika
  horse team troika
  house dacha
  ibex tek
  measure lof, verst, archine
  mother of cities Kiev
  museum Hermitage
  no nyet
  news agency Tass, Novosti
  novelist Gorky, Tolstoy
  peasant kulak, muzjik
  peninsula Crimea
  poet Pushkin
  revolutionary leader Lenin, Trotsky
  ruling family Romanov
  saint Olga
  satellite Sputnik
  scarf babushka
  soup borsch
  spa Ems
  teapot/urn samovar
  weight pud, dola, pood
  windstorm buran
  wolfhound alan, Borzoi
  yes da
rust film, oxide, fungus, corrode, deteriorate

on bronze patina
plant ferrugo
rustler thief
object cattle
Rustum
father Zal
son Sohrab
rutabaga Swede, turnip
Ruth
husband Boaz
mother-in law Naomi
sister Eileen
son Obed
Ruthenia, Ruthenian Ukranian, Little Russia
rye grass, gypsy, cereal, whiskey
disease ergot, blackrust
grass darnel
ryke (Scot.) reach
ryot tenant, peasant
Ryukyu island Okinawa

S

S ess
-curve ogee
mark pothook
-shaped ess, sigmate, sigmoid
Sa, in chemistry samarium
Saarinen, Eero architect
Sabaist
object of worship stars
sabalo milkfish
Sabine goddess Vacuna
sable fur, dark, sobol, lemming
genus Mustela
imitation kolinsky
pert. to zibel(l)ine
sac bursa, pouch, Indian
SAC Strategic Air Command
Sacar
son Ahiam
sacerdotal hieratic, priestly
sachem chief, Sagamore
sackcloth

symbol mourning, penitence
sack fire, container
fiber jute, gunny, burlap
sacred holy, pious, divine
bean lotus
beetle scarab
bird ibis
bull apis, hapi
city Mecca, Jerusalem
comb. form hagi(o), hiero
cow untouchable
fig tree pipal
fountain Hippocrene
literature Veda
most sacrosant
opposite profane, secular
plant ragtree
scriptures Bible, Koran
song motet, psalm
wine vessel ama
word om, logos
sacrifice oblation, offering
burning place pile, altar
by killing immolate
human suttee
sacrificial
animal lamb, bullock
fire igni
rite libation
sacristy
pert. to vestral
sad blue, trist, tragic, lugubrious
comb. form tragi
saddle load, seat, encumber
bag alforja
blanket tilpah
cloth manta, panel
footrest stirrup
front part pommel
girth cinch
pack aparejo
part pad, horn, cantle, latigo
rock oyster
sl. pigskin
stirrup iron, gambado
Sadducee
opposite Pharisee

safe siker, vault, coffer, secure, untouched
  cracker yegg(man), peteman
  place port, haven
safety security
  device armor, valve, Mae West
  lamp davy
  pin fibula
  zone island
saga edda, epic, Iliad
Sagamore chief, sachem
sage herb, seer, wise, prudent
  cheese cheddar
  cock grouse
  Chelsea Thomas Carlyle
  Concord Ralph Waldo Emerson
  Ferney Voltaire
  Monticello Thomas Jefferson
Sagitta arrow, keystone, constellation
saguaro cactus
Sahara arid, desert, wasteland
  fertile area Fezzan
  people Arabs, Nomads, Berbers
  wind leste
saic ketch
sail lug, float, glide, cruise, depart, jigger
  boat yawl, ketch, sloop, yacht, frigate,
    galleon, schooner
  close to wind luff
  haul up trice
  hoist clew-up, clue-up
  kind jib, main, royal, lateen
  pert. to velic
  poet. sheet
  rope tye, halyard
sailor's
  bad luck Jonah, Jonas
  call ahoy, avast
  carving scrimshaw
  dish scouse
  drink grog
  hat sou(th)wester
  patroness Eulalia
  patron saint Elmo
  rebellion mutiny
  underwear skivy
  yes aye
saint holy, sacred, canonize

  Andrew's cross saltier
  Anthony's fire erysipelas
  Barbabas' prayer Ave Maria
  declare person a canonize
  Francis' birthplace Assisi
  homage to a dulia
  tomb shrine
  Vitus' dance chorea
saker falcon
Sakti Maya
salaam bow, greeting, obeisance
Saladin
  foes Crusaders
Salammbo
  author Gustave Flaubert
Salem
  witchcraft trial judge Sewall
salep tuber
  source orchid
salicaceous tree poplar, willow
salient point detail, feature
Salix willow genus
salmacis nymph
salmon coho, jack, mort, holia, sprod,
    chinuck, quinnat
  eggs roe
  female raun, baggit
  male cock, kipper
  one-year-old bluecap
  red sockeye
  salted/smoked lox
  silver coho
  trap slap
  young parr, smolt, grilse, samlet
Salome
  father Herod(ias)
  grandfather Herod
  known for Dance of Seven Veils
salt sal, humor, sailor, season
  acid oleate
  bed vat
  deposit lick, mine
  marsh salina
  pert. to saline
  pork sowbelly
  rock halite
  water brine

salted corned
saltpeter niter, nitre
saltwort kali, barilla
Salus Hygeia
  concern health
salute bow, hail, greet, honor
  flag dip
  gun salvo
salvation rescue, preservation
  Army founder William Booth
  pert. to soterical
samaj church
samara chat, key fruit
  tree bearing ash, elm, maple
Samaritan god Tartak
same alike, ditto, equal, identical
  comb. form iso, homo
Samhain Eve Halloween
Samoa, Samoan Polynesian
  bird iao
  cloth tapa
  council fono
  loincloth lava-lava
  maiden taupo
  mollusk asi
  owl lulu
  warrior toa
sampan boat
  derivative sam three
  pan wood
Samson
  betrayed by Delilah
  place of death Gaza
  vulnerability hair
Samuel
  mentor Eli
  mother Hannah
  son Abiah
  victim Agag
San saint
  Antonio shrine Alamo
  Simeon Hearst castle
Sancho Panza
  master Don Quixote
  mule Dapple
sanctuary bema, grit, asylum, refuge
sand beach, abrade, polish, smooth

bank cay, shoal
bar reef, spit, shelf
dollar sea urchin
dune towan
flea chigger
hill dene, dune
lily soaproot
sl. grit, courage
snake eryx
sandal
  winged talaria
  wooden patten
  woven huarache
sandalwood algum, incense
  island Sumba
Sandburg, Carl poet
sandpiper bird, ruff, stilt, teeter
  female reeve
  relative plover
sandstone paar, berea, arkose, medina
  block sarsen
  pert. to arenilitic
Sandwich Islands (formerly) Hawaii
sanforize preshrink
sangfroid cool, poise, composure
Sangraal (Holy) Grail
sans (Fr.) without
  pareil peerless
  souci gay, castle
  Souci site Potsdam
Sanskrit Indic, Vedic
  dialect pali
  god Vayu, Indra
  epic character Sita
  soul atman
Santa Claus St. Nicholas
  reindeer Comet, Cupid, Vixen, Dancer,
    Dasher, Donner, Blitzen, Prancer,
    Rudolph
santon monk, hermit
sap dig, fool, fluid, trench, weaken,
  undermine
  dried gum
  tree milk, latex, maple, balata
sapajou grison, monkey, capuchin
sapodilla acana, bustic, sapota, plum tree,
  marmalade

Sapphira
  weakness lying
Sappho
  consort Phaon
  home Lesbos
  work poetry
sapsago cheese
sapsucker woodpecker
Saracen Arab, Moor, Moslem
  foe Crusader
  leader Saladin
Sarah
  husband Abraham
  slave Hagar
  son Isaac
sardine lour, herring, pilchard
Sardinia, Sardinian
  coin carline
  language Catalan
  ruling house Savoy
sark shirt, island, chemise
sarmentose plant strawberry
sarong comboy, pareus
  made famous by Dorothy Lamour
Sarpedon
  parent Zeus, Europa
sasin buck, antelope
sassaby antelope
Sassenach Saxon, lowlander
Satan devil, Lucifer, Abaddon, Mephisto
  cohort Azazel
  son imp
Satchmo Louis Armstrong, trumpet
  player
satellite moon, Pioneer, Sputnik, Explorer,
  follower
  path orbit
  shadow umbra
  weather Tiros
satin pod honesty
satirize attack, expose, denounce,
  ridicule
  in verse berime
satisfactory o.k., pat, enough
  sl. cool, jake
Saturday Sabbath
  pert. to sabbatine

Saturn Cronus, planet
  in alchemy lead
  wife Ops
saturniid moth
satyr faun, deity, lecher, Silenus
  god attended by Bacchus
  staff thyrsus
sauce chili, curry, flavor, mornay,
  dressing
  thickener roux
  type Bernaise, Bordelaise, Hollandaise
Saudi Arabia
  desert Red, Nefud
  inhabitant Arab, bedouin
  monetary unit riyal
Saul
  concubine Rizpah
  daughter Michal
  father Kish
  kingdom Israel
  son Jonathan
  successor David
saunter lag, gait, idle, stroll, ramble
  across street jaywalk
saurian lizard, reptile, dinosaur
sausage
  casing bung
  -shaped allantoid
Savage Island Niue
savin(e) juniper
savoir-faire tact, diplomacy
saw cut, rede, maxim, motto, observed
  blade web
  comb. form serri
  cut kerf
  -toothed serrate
sawbuck ten(spot) (sl.), stand
sawdust coom, scobs
sawing frame horse
Saxon English
  king Harold
  lady Godiva
sayings
  attributed to Jesus logia
  collection ana
  distinguishing shibboleths
Sb, in chemistry stibium, antimony

scads lots, many, much, oodles
scale climb, falke, gamut, clamber, measure
  animal squama
  charges tariff
  comb. form lepid(o) scutum
  measuring vernier
  notes do, fa, la, me, re, ti, sol
scallop quin, crena, badge, mollusk
scalp skin, cheat
  disease scall, favus
  tumor wen
scaly base, mean, mangy, scabby, scurfy
  comb. form lepid(o)
scampi prawn
scandent plant vine
Scandinavia, Scandinavian Dane, Finn,
  Lapp, Nordic, Swede, squarehead
  coin ore
  country Norway, Sweden, Denmark,
    Iceland
  explorer Eric the Red
  folklore creature troll
  giantess Urth, Wyrd
  god Loki, Thor, Alfadir
  heaven myth. Asgard, Asgarth
  inlet fiord, fjord
  measure alen
  plateau fjeld
  weight lod
scar mar, wound, blemish
  pert. to uloid
  tissue keloid, adhesions
Scaramouche scamp, rascal, braggart
  author Rafael Sabatini
scarecrow malkin, bugaboo, straw man
scarf sash, ascot, foulard, kerchief
  clerical stole, tippet
  head babushka (Russ.)
  sun helmet puggry
scarlet red, lewd
  bird tanager
Scarlett O'Hara
  home Tara
  husband Rhett Butler
scatter strew, dispel, litter, disperse, sprinkle
  by blowing winnow
  for lost scent cast

scent clue, odor, smell, track, perfume
  kitchen aroma, nidor
  left by animal drag
  of wine bouquet
schelm rogue, rascal
schemer artist, plotter
Schicklgruber
  son Adolph Hitler
schistosome fluke
schizocarp fruit
schmaltz fat, corn, sentimentality
schnapps gin, spirits
scholar pupil, pundit, savant, classicist
  day extern
  inferior pedant
  literary harmonist
  Moslem Ulem
scholarly
  paper thesis
  people literati
school pod, cult, ecole (Fr.), lycée, teach,
  train, lyceum, cultivate, academe,
  academy
  banner pennant
  boy, new scum
  grounds campus
  of birds pod
  of fish shoal
  of whales gam, pod
  pert. to academic, scholarly
  riding manege
schoolmaster's rod feruke, ferule
Schubert, Franz composer, Little
  (symphony), Tragic (symphony),
  Sad Waltz, Rosamunde, Mourning
  Waltz
  composer Franz
  classic Ave Maria
sciatic area hip
science art, skill
  comb. form techno
science
  boxing fisticuffs
  causes etiology
  human behavior psychology
  law making nomology
  motion kinetics, dynamics

origins etiology
plants botany
words semantics
principles logic
scilicet to wit, namely
Scipio
  victim Carthage, Hannibal
sciurine animal marmot, squirrel
scombroid fish tuna, bonito, mackerel
scop bard, poet
Scorpio
  brightest star Antares
Scotland, Scottish Gael, Pict, kiltie, Caledonian
  ago syne
  bagpipe music pibroch, coronach
  bank brae
  beggar randy
  biscuit scone
  boy loon
  breeches trews
  brook sike
  burn stream
  cap Glengarry, Tam o' Shanter
  cat malkin
  charm cantrip
  chest kist
  chief thane
  child wean, bairn
  clan chief thane
  coin demy, lion, baubee
  cup tass, tassie
  devil deil, mohound
  dish haggis
  dog sealyham, deerhound
  fellow carl(e)
  girl lassie, quean, cummer
  go gae, gang
  good gude
  hawk allan
  Highlander Celt, Gael
  hill dod(d), inch
  hill(side) brae
  kilt filibeg
  kiss pree
  lake lin, loch, katrine
  little sma

  Lowlander Sassenach
  Lowlands Lallan
  measure cran
  men's undergarment trews
  money siller
  more mair
  mus. instr. bagpipe
  national emblem thistle
  negative, no dinna, nae
  New Year's Eve Hogmanay
  one ane, yin
  peasant cotter, crofter
  pig grice
  pipe cutty
  plaid maud, tartan
  poet Burns, Hogg, Edina, Dunbar
  prefix to names Mac
  pronunciation burr
  rock skerry
  servant gilly, gillie
  shirt sark
  since syne
  sister titty
  skirt kilt
  spirit banshee
  sweetheart Jo(e)
  tartan pattern sett, plaid
  tobacco pouch spleuchan
  topper/hat tam
  town bur(g)h
  true leal
  uncle eam, (y)eme
  village rew
  wear under kilts trews
  weight trone
  woman randy, cummer, carline
  woman, unmarried quean
Scourge of God Attila
scrambled pied, disorderly
scrap ort, junk, shred, morsel, tatter
  glass cullet
scrape hoe, claw, grit, difficulty
  bottom scour, dredge
  ground in golf sclaff
scraps
  literary ana
scratching ground for food rasorial

screen sift, pavis, shield, shroud, seclude, partition
  altar reredos
  bulletproof mant(e)let
  chimney bonnet
  material mesh, vetiver
  mesh sieve
screw turn, miser, twist
  thread helix
  -like spiral
scriptural biblical
  analysis exegesis
  interpreter exegete
  Moslem Alcoran
  occult cabala
  part lesson
scrivello tusk
scrod codfish, haddock
scroll list, roll
  Hebrew Torah, mezuza(h)
  -shaped turbinate
  tabletlike cartouch(e)
  writing makimono
Scrooge miser
scullery contents pans, pots
scrupulous to excess finicky, prudish
sculpin bullhead, hardhead, sea raven
sculptor carver
  framework armature
  tool chisel, graver, caliper
  work (pert. to) glyphic
scye armhole
Scylla rock
  father Nisus
  lover Minos
  whirlpool opposite charybdis
scyphozoan jellyfish
scythe bea, sickle
  bearer death
  cut, one stroke swath
  handle nib, snath, snead
sea mer (Fr.), deep, wave, ocean, swell
  anemone polyp, actinia
  bat devilfish
  bird gull, skua, gannet, albatross
  borne afloat

  -born goddess Aphrodite
  calf seal
  cow walrus, manatee
  creature, legendary merman, mermaid
  devil octopus, angelfish
  dog tar, sailor
  foam spume, meerschaum
  god Ler, Aegir, Triton, Nereus, Neptune, Proteus, Poseidon
  grave locker
  marker dan, buoy
  mile knot, naut
  nettle medusa, jellyfish, acaleph
  of the naval, marine, pelagic
  pen polyp
  poet. foam, brine, briny
  prefix mari
  serpent Elops
  surface movement lipper
  swell surf
  urchin echinus, echinoid
  wall jetty, breakwater
  with many islands archipelago
  worthy staunch
seal close, stamp, mammal, signet, initial
  bottle/tube capsule
  letter cachet
  off trap
  papal bull
  wax lac
sealed completely hermetic
seals carnivores
  breeding place rookery
  flock pod
  limb flipper
  pelt sculp
  pert. to phocine
  young pup, calf, harp
seamen's chapel Bethel
seance meeting, sitting
  leader medium, spiritualist
  writing device Ouija
search seek, probe, quest, forage
  for food forage
  for Holy Grail quest
  for talent scout

party posse
a person frisk
thoroughly comb
seasickness mal de mer
seaside strip boardwalk
seasons Horae
  goddess Dike, Horae, Eirene
seat
  bishop's metropolis
  church pew, sedilia
  coach dicky
  of judgment tribunal
  on elephant houdah, howdah
  on horse/camel saddle
  tier gradin
seaweed kelp, varec, tangle, sargasso
  extract agar
  genus Alaria
  purple sion
  red dulse
  study algology
seaworm sao, lurg
second aid, abet, moment, attendant
  childhood dotage, senility
  growth crop rowen
  lieutenant shavetail (sl.)
  self alter ego
  -story man burglar
  team scrub
secret arcane, covert, hidden, cryptic
  agent spy, saboteur
  meeting conclave
  place hideout, sanctum
  remedy elixir
  society Poro, Mafia, Ku Klux, camorra
  writing code
secundine afterbirth
security pledge, safety, surety
  for payment bond, lien, collateral
Seder
  event Exodus
seed sow, bean, germ, plant
  -bearing organ pistil
  bud plumule
  case bur(r), pod, cypsela
  comb. form sperm, spermat(o)

immature ovule
organ pistil
oyster spat
pod cypsela
without agamous
seeds
  comb. form carpo
  row of planted drill
  study carpology
seeled bird hawk, falcon
segment
  body somatone
  -shaped toric
sego lily, plant
seidel mug
seize for debt attach, distrain
Sekhet
  husband Ptah
Selassie, Haile emperor
self ego
  comb. form auto
  confidence aplomb, panache
  cremation suttee
  defense art judo, karate, jujutsu
  destruction suicide, immolation
  esteem pride, vanity
  evident obvious, axiomatic
  important pompous
  love narc(iss)ism
  pert. to personal
  reproach remorse
  respect pride
  righteous pharisaical
  worship autolatry
sell over official price scalp
Semele
  husband Zeus
  father Cadmus
  son Bacchus, Dionysus
  sister Ino
Seminole chief Osceola
Semite Jew, Arab, Assyrian, Babylonian,
  Phoenician
  god Baal, Hadad, Shamash
send mail, forward, dispatch
  back remit, return

flying rout
for summon
forth emit
out exile, expel, deport
packing dismiss
up jail (sl.)
Senegal
  gazelle korin
seneschal kay, major domo
sense sight, meaning, perceive
  and Sensibility author Jane Austen
  sight optic
  smell olfaction
  taste gustation
sensitive plant mimosa
sensitivity erethism
sentence
  one word monepic
  construction syntax
  part verb, adverb, object, subject, predicate
  types simple, complex, compound
sentinel guard, picket
  mounted lookout
sepal leaf
separate part, split, secede, alienate
  forcibly rend, wrench
  into parts dismember
  prefix dis
Sephardim Jews
  original country Spain, Portugal
  dialect Ladino
sepoy policeman
seppuku hara-kiri, suicide
September 13, Roman calendar Ides
seraglio harem, zenana
Serb, Serbia Slav
  coin dinar
  comb. form Serbo
  measure ralo
sere dry, wax, dried, threadbare
serein mist, rain
serf helot, slave
  female neif
  liberated manumit
series set, chain, sequence
  of columns colonnade
  of six hexad

sermon lecture, discourse
  subject text
serow jagia, antelope
serpent snake, reptile, entwine
  comb. form ophi(o)
  nine-headed Hydra
  pert. to anguine
  worship ophism
serranoid fish redhind, cabrilla
servant hind, salve, menial, ancillary
  boy page, gossoon
  garment livery
  feudal sergeant
  pert. to famulary
  retired emeritus
serving portion
  boy knave
  man potman
  stand dumbwaiter
serviette napkin
sesame seed gingili
set fix, seat, rigid, batch
  afloat launch
  aside reject, reserve
  down (as a fact) posit
  firmly infix
  in motion activate
  of nine ennead
  of rules code
  on fire kindle
  sail cast off
  up erect, exalt
  upon attack, browden
Set god, Seth, deity
  brother Osiris
  father Geb
  mother Nut
  victim Osiris
seta bristle
Seth
  brother Abel, Cain
  parents Eve, Adam
  son Enos
settle
  on land illegally squat (sl.)
  strike mediate

seven sept, zeta, heptad
  comb. form hept(a)
  days week, hebdomad
  deadly sins envy, lust, anger, pride, sloth, gluttony, covetousness
  Hills of Rome Caelian, Viminal, Aventine, Palatine, Quirinal, Esquiline, Capitoline
  wonders of the world sphinx, pharos, Ephesus, Phidias, colossus, pyramids, mausoleum
seventeen-year locust cicada
Seward's folly Alaska
sewer opening manhole
sewing-machine
  inventor Elias Howe
sex gender
  comb. form geno
  hormone steroid
sexes, common to both epicene
shade blind, color, trace, trees, umbra
  blue Alice
  light pastel
  lines hatch
  of difference or meaning nuance
shades, the Hades
shadow dog, omen, shade, vestige
  astronomer's umbra
  man without Ascian
  of death Sheol
  outline silhouette
  without Ascian
Shadrach
  fellow captives Meshach, Abednego
  persecutor Nebuchadnezzar
shagbark hickory
Shaker founder Ann Lee
Shakespeare, William
  actors Booth, Olivier, Geilgud, Barrymore
  home Avon, Stratford
  plays Lear, Caesar, Hamlet, Macbeth, Othello, Tempest, Twelfth Night
shako
  decoration pom-pom
  cap headdress
shakti Devi, force, power

shallop boat, dinghy
shallot bulb, onion
  kin leek
shamal wind
Shamash sun god
  consort Ai, Aya
  worship center Larsa, Sippar
Shamo Gobi
shandrydan cart, chaise
Shangri-la utopia, paradise
shank leg, shaft
  in botany footstalk
  pert. to crural
sharecropper metayer
shark man-eater, swindler
  blue pointer mako
  loan usurer
  nurse gata
  small tope, lamia, sharklet
  young puppy
sharp keen, tart, clear, acute, clever, vitriolic
  sl. adept, expert
  comb. form oxy, acet(o)
  cry yelp
  -edged/witted keen
  -eyed one lynx, eagle
  reply retort
  taste tang, tart
Shasta daisy, mount, volcano
shavetail mule, (2nd) lieutenant
Shavian forte wit
shaw wood, grove
Shawnee chief Tecumseh
shearing machine clipper, cropper
sheatfish wels, catfish
Sheba Saba
  queen of Balkis
shedding of skin ecdysis
Sheean, Vincent writer
sheep sha, urial, merino, bleater, karakul
  castrated wether
  coat fleece
  dog collie
  female ewe
  flock fold, dryband
  genus Ovis

kept together fold
male ram, tup, wether
mark brand
pen fold, kraal
pert. to ovine
-skin dealer fellmonger
wool fleece
young hog, teg, (y)eanling, lamb
shekel coin, money
shell cover, shuck, mollusk, cartridge
abalone ormer
boat hull
casing gaine
defective dud
enclosed in a obtected
hole crater
large conch
money peag(e), se(a)wan, cowrie, wampum
Shelley, Percy Bysshe poet
poem Adonais
shelter haven, protect, retreat
dove's cote
hillside abri
overhanging canopy
soldier's (pup) tent
Shem
father Noah
son Lud, Aram, Asshur
Sheol hell, grave, Hades
shepherd lead, tend
concern flock, sheep
clock salsify
god Pan, Faunus
pert. to bucolic, pastoral
staff kent, peda, crook
shepherdess bergere, Amaryllis
Sheridan play Rivals
Sherlock Holmes
creator Arthur Conan Doyle
friend Watson
Sherwood Forest hero Robin Hood
Shetland Island
inlet voe
measure ure
tax scat
shibboleth slogan, password, test word

shield ecu (Fr.), armor, cover, defend
arm buckler
Athena's/Zeus' (A)egis
bearer escudero
center point fess
large pavis
Roman testudo
-shaped scutate, clypeate
strap enarme
shillelagh club, cudgel
shin kick, shank, tibia
pert. to cnemial
Shinto Sintu
deity Kami
temple sha
temple gate torii
ship send, vessel, embark
ancient bireme, galleon, trireme
bow flag jack
breadth beam
capacity tonnage
carpenter chips
chains tyes
crew member hand, mate, sailor, stoker, seaman, yeoman
forward part bow, prow, stem
group fleet
hospital sick bay
jail brig, hulk
left-side port, larboard
load bulk, cargo
myth. Argo
not seagoing hulk
path lane
poet. bark, keel
rear aft
record log
sink a scuttle
tender pinnace, cockboat
torpedoed May 1915 Lusitania
water in the hold bilge
windless becalmed
window porthole
shipwrecked
goods jetsam, flotsam
person castaway

shirt
  type polo, skivvy, chemise
  -collar stiffener stay
  -front ornament stud
  -sleeve button cuff link
shock
  absorber snubber
  mental trauma
  to reality sober
shoe brogan, blucher, footwear
  baby bootee
  canvas sneaker
  flap tongue
  form/model last, tree
  maker cordwainer
  mender cobbler
  mule's planch
  part heel, rand, (in)sole
  winged talaria
  wooden sabot
shoelace lachet
  tip aiglet
shoemaker cobbler, farrier
  apprentice snob
  patron saint Crispin
  tool butt, els(h)in, hammer
shoot chit, dart, fire, stem, twig, throw
  firearm fire
  from cover snipe, ambush
  objective target
shore beach, brace, coast, rivage
  pert. to littoral
  poet. strand
short brief, scant, abrupt, concise
  comb. form brevi, brachy
  -lived ephemeral
  of lacking, wanting
  ride spin
  -sighted myopic
  sl. shy
  story conte
  tail scut
shortchange cheat
shorthand Gregg, Pitman, stenotype
  character pot, hook
  sign phonogram
Shostakovich, Dmitri composer

shou deer
shoulder push, carry, epaul
  comb. form omo
  muscle deltoid
  of the scapular
  pack knapsack
  pert. to alar, humeral
  to shoulder serried
show guide, evince, expose, display, exhibition
  anger fume
  aquatic aquacade
  in usher
  off flaunt, parade
shower party, spray, bestow
  fall in a cascade
  meteor Leonid
showman, famous Cody, Rose, Barnum, Carroll, Ringling, Ziegfeld
shrew scold, vixen
  long-tailed sorex
  name of Shakespeare's Kate
  pert. to soricine
  sister of Shakespeare's Kate Bianca
shrimp kid, shaver, crustacean
  covering mail
Shrove Tuesday Mardi Gras
shrub bush, plant
  bean family ulex
  berry currant, blueberry
  bushy tod, cade
  climbing liana, clematis
  dwarfed bonsai
  fence hedge (row)
  genus Olea, Erica, Spirea
  holly family ilex
  rubber source guayule
  tea family camellia
shut bar, close
  -eye (sl.) sleep
  in confine, invalid
  out ban, exclude
  up closet, immure, silence
Shylock usurer, moneylender
  daughter Jessica
  friend Tubal
siamang gibbon

Siamese
  see Thailand
Sibelius, Jean composer
  work Finlandia
Siberia, Siberian Vogul, Samoyed(e)
  antelope saiga
  fish nelma
  forest Taiga, Urman
  fur sable
  ibex tek
  leopard ounce
  wasteland/plain steppe
  wildcat manul
  windstorm buran
sic thus, attack, so much
Sicily, Sicilian
  inhabitant, legendary Cyclops
  landmark Etna
  measure salma, caffiso
  secret society Mafia
  Trinacrian god Adranus
  volcano Etna
  wine Marsala
Siddhartha Buddha
side team, facet, aspect
  by side abreast
  interest hobby
  -kick pal, buddy, alter ego
  pain stitch
  pert. to lateral
  -step avoid, dodge
  view profile
sideboard buffet, credenza
sidero
  comb. form iron, star
sideways askance, lateral, indirect
  move sidle
  walker crab
Siegfried
  mother Sieglinde
  slayer Hagen
  sword Balmung
  vulnerable place shoulder
sierelike cribrate
Sigmund
  father Volsung
  son Sigurd

sword Gram
wife Hiordis
sign(s) mark, token, symptom, indication
  affirmative nod
  away convey
  in magic sigil
  omission caret
  pert. to semic
  Zodiac Leo, Aries, Libra, Virgo, Cancer,
    Gemini, Pisces, Taurus, Scorpio,
    Aquarius, Capricorn, Sagittarius
signal warn, alarm, token
  actor's cue
  distress SOS, mayday
  eye wink
  Indian smoke
  seance tap
  system code
Sigurd
  father Sigmund
  foster father Regin
  horse Grani
  slayer Hogni
  wife Gudrun
Silas Marner
  author George Eliot
silence, goddess Angerona
Silenus deity, satyr
  foster son Bacchus
silk pekin, tulle, foulard
  cocoon bave
  for mourning almas
  hat topper
  -like sericeous
  raw grege
  rough rajah
  source eria, cocoon
  unspun sleave
  weight pari
  yarn tram
  yarn size denier
silkworm eri(a), tusser, bombyx
  covering cocoon
  food mulberry
silver coin, siller, sycee, flatware
  comb. form argyro
  containing lunar

fluoride tachiol
in alchemy luna
lace filigree
symbol Ag
-tongued eloquent
unminted sycee, bullion
silverware decoration gadroon
Simenon
  author Georges
  detective/novel Maigret
Simeon
  father Jacob
  mother Leah
similar akin, like, such
  comb. form homeo
simnel biscuit, fruitcake
simoleon dollar (sl.)
sin, canonical heresy, idolatry
Sinai mountain Horeb
Sinbad sailor
  bird roc
since ago, hence, before now,
    inasmuch as
Singapore
  founder Raffles
  old name Temasek
single sole, unwed, individual
  comb. form uni, mono, haplo
  file tandem
  -handed unaided
  thing unit
singular
  opposite plural
sinister
  opposite dexter
sipping tube straw
siren of the Nile Cleopatra
Sisera
  enemy Barak
  slayer Jael
sister
  pert. to soral
  Superior abbess
  younger cadette (Fr.)
Sistine Chapel
  features frescoes
  Madonna painter Raphael

Sitting Bull
  antagonist George Custer
  tribe Sioux
Sitwell
  poet Edith, Osbert
six hexad, sestet
  comb. form hexa
  pert. to senary
size area, mass, cover, stiffen
  book page duodecimo
  indefinite nth
  yarn lea, forty, dernier
skate fish, glide
  blade runner
  order raja
  place rink
skein hank, mesh
  of yarn hasp
skerry reef
ski
  race slalom
  run schuss
skill talent, ability, finesse, prowess
  comb. form techno
skin coat, shell, strip, epidermis
  comb. form derm(o), derma, dermat(o)
  dark melanic
  deeper layer cutis
  design on tattoo
  diver's aid scuba
  flaw wrinkle
  Lat. cutis
  oil sebum
  opening pore
  person with abnormal white
    albino
  pert. to dermal, cutaneous
  shed molt
  sl. cheat, defraud, swindle
  without apellous
skirt border, garment, periphery, petticoat
  armor tasse
  ballet dancer's tutu
  divided culotte
  sl. girl, woman
  steel lamboys
  triangular part gore

skull head, sconce
  part bregma, cranium, calvaria
  pert. to cranial
  soft spot fontanel
skullcap beanie
  Arabian chechia
  cardinal's berrettino
  clergy's callot(te)
  felt pileus
  Hebrew kippah, yarmulke
slang cant, argot, lingo, patois
  suffix eroo
slant tilt, angle, slope, incline
  comb. form clino
  line solidus
slapdash sloppy, offhand
slave serf, helot, vassal, servant
  biblical Hagar
  block catasta
  dealin mango
  driver taskmaster
  educated hetaera
  liberate manumit
  traveling group coffle
sleep repose, slumber
  comb. form hypno
  deep stupor
  god Somnus, Hypnus, Morpheus
  inability to insomnia
  lightly doze
  pert. to somnial
  short (cat)nap, siesta, snooze
Sleepy Hollow
  author Washington Irving
sleeve hole scye
slice
  bacon rasher
  meat collop
slightest least
  amount grain
  sound peep
slingshot catapult
  killer with David
slip boner, lapse, slide, garment, mistake
  away elapse
  back relapse

by pass
knot noose
up error
slogan motto, phrase, catchword
slope grade, slant, splay
  comb. form clino
slot track, groove, aperture
  -machine coin slug
  -machine windfall jackpot
sloth sin, inertia, laziness
  three-toed ai
  two-toed unau
slow
  comb. form brady
  in music largo, lento, tardo, andante
  leak drip
  train local
  -witted dull, dense
slug snail, strike, loiter
  genus Limax, Elysia
  pert. to limacine
  sea trepang
sly cagy, foxy, shrewd
  look leer, ogle
  remark catty (sl.)
small low, tiny, bantam, little, trivial,
  minuscule
  allowance pittance
  amount drop
  animal runt, bantam
  bite nip
  car compact
  coin mite
  comb. form micr(o), lepto, steno
  fry tots
  hollow areola
  piece snip(pet)
  portion modicum
  prefix micro
  quantity bit, iota, spot
  talk chitchat
smartly dressed natty, dapper
smell scent, flavor
  comb. form osmo
  loss anosmia
  offensive fetor, stink, stench

pert. to olfactory
pleasant aroma
stale musty
smelling salts inhalant, hartshorn
smew duck, merganser
smile beam, grin, simper
  Mona Lisa's cryptic, enigmatic
smoke
  fragrance incense
  -jack funnel
  out flush
  screen camouflage
smolt clear, salmon, smooth
smooth oily, soft, slick, serene
  comb. form lio
  feathers preen
  over gloss
  -tongued glib, oily
  with rock pumice
smuggled
  goods contraband
  whiskey moonshine
snail mollusk, escargot
  genus Nerita, Oleacina
  shell caracole, periwinkle
snake reptile, serpent
  comb. form ophi(o)
  charmer's flute pungi
  crusher boa, python
  deity zombi
  -haired woman Gorgon, Medusa
  -horned cerastes
  marine chital
  sea kerril
  -skin shedding ecdysis
  study ophiology
snapdragon figwort
snark boojum
snee dirk
snickersnee knife
snit tizzy
snook robalo
snow firn, sleet, mislead (sl.), precipitation
  living in neval
  of nival
  on a glacier neve

sl. opium, heroin, cocaine
slide, mass avalanche
White's friends dwarfs
snowdrop anemone
snub check, ignore, retort
  nose(d) pug
so sic, ergo, very
  be it amen, altercate
  far thus
  -so average
soak wet, steep, saturate
  in brine/vinegar marinate
  sl. hit, pawn, charge
  up sorb
soap cleanser, detergent
  foam suds
  ingredient lye
  material tallow
  opera melodrama
  pharmaceutical sapo
  plant amole
  sl. money
So Big
  author Edna Ferber
  heroine Selina
soccer football
  player, famed Pele
social party, convivial
  affair ball, soiree
  asset tact, grace
  climber upstart
  Contract author Jean Rousseau
  error faux pas
  finesse tact
  insect ant, bee
  men only stag, smoker
  outcast leper, pariah
  register blue book
  system regime
society company, association
  comb. form socio
  entrance into debut
  for animals SPCA
  Island Tahiti
Society of Friends Quakers
  founder George Fox

sockeye salmon
Socrates
  biographer Plato
  dialogue Meno, Phaedo, Apologia
  disciple Plato
  wife Xanthippe
sodium Na, natrium
  carbonate trona
  chlorate NaClo
  comb. form natro
  nitrate caliche, saltpeter
Sodom's neighbor Gomorrah
soft mild, gentle, velvety, yielding
  and limp flabby
  and sweet dulcet
  feathers down, eider
  job snap, sinecure
  mass pulp
  pedal play down
  soap flatter, blarney (sl.)
soil sod, dirty, earth, defile
  comb. form geo, agro
  goddess Demeter
  organic humus
  poet. glebe
  unfruitful barren, desert, sterile
sola alone
solan goose gannet
solar room, story, tropic, heliacal
  deity Shu
  disk aten, aton
  streak facula
  system model orrery
  system part planet
soldier fighter, warrior
  fellow buddy
  killed/wounded casualty
  of fortune adventurer
  old vet(eran)
  sl. G.I., sadsack, doughboy
  vacation pass, leave, furlough
Soldiers Three
  author Rudyard Kipling
sole fish, foot, only, solitary
  foot's vola, pelma, plantar
  part shank
  pert. to plantar

solid firm, cubic, sphere
  comb. form stereo
  ground terra firma
  six-sided cube
solidum sum, dado
solitary monk, alone, hermit, eremite, recluse
  comb. form eremo
Solomon king, sage, wise man
  ally Hiram
  father David
  gold from Ophir
  mother Bathsheba
  sayings maxims, proverbs
  temple shamir
solus alone
some any, part, about
  time later, one day
something
  easy pie, snap
  imagined figment
  notable/outstanding daisy
somewhat rather, aliquid
  suffix ish
son heir, progeny
  favorite Benjamin
  of God Savior
  of, prefix Fitz, Mac
  pert. to filial
  roi's Dauphin
  Scot. Mac
song
  baby's lullaby
  comb. form malaco
  evening vespers
  folk ballad
  identification theme
  improvisation vamp
  last words tag
  love serenade
  morning matin
  of Solomon/of Songs canticles
  operatic aria
  pert. to melic
  poet. rune
  prefix melo
  sacred hymn, motet, psalm
  words lyrics

songs, anthology of garland
sonnet poem, song, verse
  last six lines sestet
soogan rope, blanket
soosoo dolphin
soothsaying augury
Sophocles
  play Oedipus
Sorb Slav, apple
  descendants Wends
sorceress Circe, witch, Gorgon
sore angry, lesion, tender, touchy,
   pustule
  dressing gauze, patch
  mustard application poultice
soricine animal shrew
sorrel horse, plant
  wood oca
sort ilk, part, sift, genus
  of somewhat
sotol, plantlike yucca
sotto below, under
soucar banker, straight
soul spirit, embodiment
  dead person's manes
  personified psyche
  without brute
sound safe, audio, noise, valid, stable
  comb. form phon(o)
  dull thud
  gleeful chortle
  gutteral grate, grunt
  harsh jar, rasp
  lung rale
  mournful knell
  of contentment purr
  of laughter peal
  of yearning sigh
  off speak
  pert. to tonal
  science acoustic(s)
  thin, sharp squeak
  unit of measurement mach,
   decibel
  voiceless cedilla
  whispering susurrus
  without mute, tacit, silent

Sousa, John Phillip
  employment marine, bandmaster
  soubriquet march king
South African Boer, Afrikaner
  assembly raad
  aunt tanta
  beverage mate
  bushman Qung
  Dut. Boer, Taal
  foreigner uitlander
  monetary unit rand
  monkey vervet
  mulatto griqua
  plain veldt
  policy, former apartheid
  spirit tikolosh
  stream aar
  tribal council Indaba
  warrior impi
  whip sjambok
South American Latin
  animal llama, alpaca, vicuña
  bird jacu, guan, rhea, agami, topaz, condor
  coin condor
  dance samba, tango, beguine
  duck pato
  hat jipijapa
  herdsman gaucho, llanero
  Indian hut toldo
  liquor chicha
  lizard teju, coati
  measure vara
  mountains Andes
  ostrich ehea
  palm ita, grugru
  parrot macaw
  rabbit tapeti
  serpent aboma
  strait Magellan
  tree mora, balsa, carob
  vulture condor
  weapon bola
  wind pampero
South Carolina see also Quick
   Reference List
  native weasel
South Dakota see Quick Reference List

southern austral
  cross crux
  France midi
  States Dixie
South Pole explorer Roald Amundsen
South Sea
  canoe prau, proa
  garment pareo, pareu, comboy, sarong
  island drink/shrub kava(kava)
  loincloth lava-lava
  native Kanaka, Samoan, Balinese, Tahitian, Polynesian
south wind notus, auster
sow pig, plant, sluice, scatter, broadcast
  young gilt, piglet
sowens porridge
Soviet see Russian
soy bean soja, soya
space gap, rank, void, extent, duration
  agency NASA (abbr.)
  beacon pulsar, quasar
  between eyes lore
  -craft capsule Specs
  -craft part module
  -craft to moon Apollo
  -craft to Venus Mariner
  dog Laika, Streika
  filler shim
  in biology lacuna
  monkey Enos
  pert. to spatial
  -ship blister module
  small areda
  void chasm
  wall niche
spade dig, graft, shovel
  kind scavel
  plasterer's server
  sharp spud
Spain, Spanish España, Iberia, Hesperia
  afternoon tarde
  article el, la, un, las, los, una
  as como
  aunt tia
  baby niña, neña
  bayonet yucca

bear oso
berry, dried pasa
blanket manta, poncho, serape
boy niño
cape Trafalgar
chaperon duen(n)a
cheer olé, bravo
club(house) casino
coin peso, dobla, peseta, centavo, doubloon
composer Manuel de Falla
council junta
cup taza
cupid Amorino, Amoretto
dance jota, tango, bolero, carioca, flamenco
dear caro
dish olla, paella, bacalao
farm ranco, granja, hacienda
forest monte
friend amigo
game pelota, jai alai
girl niña, chica
god of love Amadis
grape malaga
gypsy dance flamenco
half-breed ladino, mestizo
hall sala
hat sombrero
hill alto, alcor
holiday/feast fiesta
hour hora
house casa
jail calabozo
landmark escorial, alhambra
little poco
Madrid boulevard Prado
man hombre
measure vara, linea, cantara
mother madre
none/nothing nada
painter Dali, Goya, Miro, Picasso
park alameda
police rurale
prefix hispano
rabbi Maimonides

ruling house Bourbon
sherry Jerez
street calle
sweet dulce
thank you gracias
tomorrow mañana
uncle tio
weapon arma, bola
weight peso, carga, marco, tonelada
woman mujer, señora
spark woo, court, light, kindle, particle
  gives off ignescent
  stream arc
sparoid fish porgy
sparrowgrass asparagus
sparse thin, scanty, meager
  opposite dense, crowded
Sparta, Spartan hardy, warlike,
  Lacedaemon
  festival Carneia
  king Leonidas, Tyndareus
  magistrate ephor
  queen Leda
  serf/slave helot
spasm fit, kink, throe
  muscle cramp, crick
  of pain throe
  series clonos
  twitch tic
Spassky, Boris chess champ
spatterdash legging
spatterdock lily
spavined lame
spayed hen foulard
speak carp, utter, declaim, declare
  against oppose
  angrily snarl
  at length expatiate
  comb. form lalo
  imperfectly lisp, mumble, stutter
  inability to alalia
  irreverently blaspheme
  of refer, mention
  offhand extemporize
  pert. to oratorical
  slowly drawl

  unable to dumb, mute
  under the breath mumble, mutter
speaker
  annoys a heckler
  loud stentor
  of many languages polyglot
spear dart, pierce, harpoon
  African assegai
  body shaft
  Neptune's trident
  point pike
  -shaped hastate
  three-pronged leister, trident
spearfish marlin
specialist
  city planning urbanist
  money matters planner, economist
specie coin, money
  factory mint
speculation vision, surmise
  reckless flier, flyer
speech lip, sermon, tongue, oration,
  utterance
  abusive tirade
  art oratory, rhetoric
  blunder solecism
  comb. form log(o)
  defect lisp, stammer, dysphonia,
    impediment
  expert phonetist
  farewell valedictory
  figure of simile, metaphor
  formal address, oration
  goddess Vac
  incoherent jargon, gibberish
  peculiar idiom
  sl. spiel
  surplusage padding
  without mute, silent, aphasic
  world language Esperanto
speed rev, rate, rush, velocity
  full amain
  measuring device tachometer,
    speedometer
  of sound mach
  writing shorthand

spelean cavelike
spell, in another alphabet transliterate
spelunk den, lair, cavern
spence larder, pantry
spend the summer (a)estivate
sperm seed, semen
  whale cachalot
spheroid example football
sphinx moth, monster
  head ram, hawk
  land Egypt
  mother Echidna
  query riddle
spider mite, trivet, skillet, arachnid
  comb. form arachn(o)
  girl turned into Arachne
  monkey quata, ateles
  nest nidus
  trap web
  venomous hermit, tarantula, black
    widow
  web-spinning organ spinneret
spike nail, prong, antler, secure,
  frustrate
  -like spinate
  mountain climber's piton
Spillane, Mickey
  hero Hammer
spinal balas, rachidian
  column spine
  column, having vertebrate
  cord myelon
  layer dura
spiral helix, helical
  comb. form helico
  like a spiroid
  motion gyre
spirit
  air Ariel
  evil Ate, Ker, Lilith
  female banshee
  fire Agni
  good genie
  of censure Momus
  of people ethos
spirits mood, liquor, brandy
  night-walking lemures

  of the dead manes
  of wine alcohol
spiritual
  apathy acedia
  opposite corporeal
spiritus frumenti whiskey
spiteful snide, malicious, offensive,
  vindictive
  woman cat
split rift, cleave, divide, schism
  capable of being fissile
  open break, dehisce
  pea dal
  sl. leave
spoiled eggs addle
spoilsport wet blanket
spokes radii
spoon
  fed pampered
  large ladle
  -shaped spatulate
spoor scent, track, trail
Sporades island Samos
sportsman's vest tattersall
spot fleck, place, blemish
  playing card pip
  sl. jam, trouble
spotted fever typhus
spout gush, nozzle, stream
  sl. pawn(shop)
  steam jet
  whale's blowhole
spread oleo, feast, extend, unfold, scatter,
  stretch
  as plaster teer
  false rumors asperse
  grass ted, tedder
  here and there strew, scatter
  rapidly mushroom
  sl. meal, feast
  thick slather
  thin bray
spring leap, bound, season, source
  abruptly bolt
  Apollo's Castalia
  back rebound
  biblical Ain

deposit trona
festival May Day
holiday Easter
mineral spa
of fontal
pert. to vernal
poet. font
poet's Castalia
sl. free, release
up arise, sprout
sprinkling aspersion
with holy water asperges, irrigating
sprit boom, dart, pole, spar
sprout bud, son, growth
comb. form blast(o)
spruce trig, trim, groom, conifer
sl. natty, spiffy
spud potato
toollike spade, chisel
up titivate
spurt jet, gush, stream
of energy lick
Spyri, Johanna author
heroine Heidi
square fair, plaza, tally, settle, quadrate
column pilaster
dance reel, lanc(i)ers, hoedown, quadrille
-dance need caller
public plaza
root of nine three
shooter fair dealer
sl. hick, hayseed
squeeze hug, neck, crowd, wring, compress
the chin chuck
squid mollusk, cuttlefish
arm tentacle
pen quill
secretion ink
shell pen
squirrel xerus, rodent, pentail
burrowing gopher
flying assapan
genus Sciurus
nest dray, drey
skin vair, calabar
sri holy, lakshmi, fortunate

St. see Saint
stabile stationary
opposite labile, mobile
stables, royal mews
staccato
opposite legato
stacte spice
staff rod, cane, wand, retinue, truncheon
bearer verger
bishop's crosier
in music stave
mountain climber's alpenstock
of life bread
shepherd's crook
symbol clef
winged Caduceus
stag hart, pollard, informer
horn rial, bezantler
horn's tine prong, brocket
stage dais, dock, show, present, produce
curtain backdrop
front apron, orchestra
hand grip, callboy
overact on ham, emote
pert. to scenic
prop drop, curtain, footlights
side scene coulisse
sl. legit
whisper aside
staggered arrangement zigzag
Stagirite Aristotle
staining art marbling
stair step, stile
face riser
post newel
series flights
staircase gri(e)ce, perron
bend ramp
guard handrail
post newel, baluster
ship's companionway
spiral caracole
stalk cane, culm, stem, filament
having a petiolate
without sessile
stamp(s) beat, mark, tool, impress, postage
collecting philately

fencing appel
substitute indicia
stamping
  ground haunt, locale, hangout
  plate die
stand face, halt, view, stall, resist, attitude, position
  against oppose
  artist's easel
  by maintain
  conductor's podium
  cup's zarf
  high tower
  in substitute
  orator's soapbox
  small taboret
  three-legged tripod, trivet
  two-legged bipod
standard bearer gonfalonier
stang pain
stanza envoi, verse, strophe
  eight-line triolet
  four-line quatrain, tetrastich
  seven-line heptastich
  six-line sextain, hexastich
star sun, excel, planet, leading
  brightest Cor, Lucida, Sirius
  cluster galaxy, asterism, Milky Way
  comb. form astro, sider(o)
  exploding nova
  fallen alga
  five-pointed pentacle
  pert. to a sidereal
  poet. lamp
  shooting meteor
  spangled, in heraldry seme
  worshiper sabaist
starch amylum, amidine, carbohydrate
  comb. form amyl
  source arum, corn, taro, potato, cassava
starling bird, mino, trout, pastor, enclosure
starnose mole
Star-Spangled Banner
  author Francis Scott Key
state etat, mood, declare, condition
  ideal utopia
  of affairs case

of balance equipoise
of excitement ferment
of mind mood, morale
of suspended animation anabiosis
pert. to federal
under foreign control protectorate
United see Quick Reference List
statement bill, remark, report, manifesto
  assumed correct premise
  authoritative dictum
  defamatory libel
  mathematical theorem
  self-contradictory paradox
statue effigy, marble, carving, figurine
  base pedestal
  gigantic colossus
  that came to life Galatea
  weeping Niobe
Statue of Liberty
  poetess Emma Lazarus
  sculptor Frederic-Auguste Bartholdi
staying power stamina, endurance
staylace a(i)glet
steady calm, firm, stable, staid, constant
  opposite jerky, shaky, astatic, unstable
stealer of cattle rustler
steel inure, metal, toughen
  poet. sword, dagger
  process Henry Bessemer
  with inlaid gold damask
steeper teapot, cistern
stegomyia mosquito
steinkirk cravat
stem arise, stalk, pedicel, petiole, peduncle
  comb. form caul(o)
  covering ocrea
  of arrow stele
  pert. to cauline
  rootlike rhizome
  underground corm, tuber
steno (comb. form) thin, small, narrow
step gait, pace, dance, stair, tread
  dance pas
  down resign, abdicate
  heavily plod, trample
  in intervene

lightly trip
softly pad, tiptoe
stepmother, of/like a novercal
steps, outdoor stile, perron
sternum breastbone
  attachment rib
Stevenson
  author Robert Louis
  statesman Adlai
stick rod, wand, cling, adhere, ferule, pierce
  bamboo lathi
  celery stalk
  insect emesa
  match linstock
  pointer fescue
  up for defend
stiff bum, hard, proper, exacting
  -necked stubborn
  sl. corpse
Stilton cheese
stimulant tonic, bracer, beverage
  in coffee caffeine
  in tea thein
sting bite, smart, nettle
  sl. dupe, cheat, shaft
stinging nippy, caustic, irritating
  ant kelep
  sensation urtication
  taste pungent
stirk cow, heifer, bullock
stirrup gambado, support, footrest
  bone stapes
  cup drink, toast
  straps chapelet
stitch sew, ache, tack, baste
  bird ihi
stocking hose
  bishop's caliga, bushkin
  foot only ped
  footless hushion
  soleless traheen
stoic spartan, impassive
  philosopher Seneca
Stoic school founder Zeno
Stokowski, Leopold conductor
stomach gut, bear, desire, abdomen, appetite

ache colic
animal's paunch
bird's craw, crop
comb. form gastro
opening pylorus
pert. to gastric
washing out of lavage
stone pelt, rock, pebble, dentrite
  abrasive emery
  -age human caveman
  -age period eolithic, neolithic
  broke penniless
  carved cameo
  carver graver
  change into petrify
  comb. form lite, lith(o), lyte, petr(o)
  cutter mason
  -cutter's chisel drove
  druid sarsen
  engraving intaglio
  measure perch
  particles grit
  pert. to lithoid(al)
  philosopher's carmut, elixir
  pile talus
  prefix litho
  sharpening hone, whet
  tablet stele
  uncut naif
  woman turned to Niobe
Stonewall Jackson general
stooge foil
stop end, block, check, close, arrest
  hole plug
  legally estop
  nautical avast
  short balk
  temporarily pause
  watch timer
store fund, save, amass, garner
  cargo steve
  hidden cache
  military PX, canteen
  sl. stash
stork's bill geranium
storm gust, rage, wind, assault, expunge
  god Zu, Rudra

sand tebbad
snow buran
story lie, myth, tier, legend
  animal fable
  continued serial
  exaggerated yarn
  exclusive beat, scoop
  false fable, canard
  heroic saga
  part passus
  short conte, parable
  sl. fib
  teller raconteur
  with moral lesson parable,
    allegory
stoss
  opposite alee
stot ox, bull, steer, bounce, stagger
Stowe, Harriet Beecher author
  character Eva, Topsy, Legree
  work Uncle Tom's Cabin
Stradivarius Strad, violin
straight pure, erect, unmixed
  comb. form rect(i), euthy
  edge liner, ruler
  -faced deadpan
  man foil, stooge
  out direct
  route beeline
strain air, tax, force, melody
  blood breed, stock, lineage
  comb. form tono
  great stress
strait narrow, channel, isthmus, Malacca,
  Magellan, Gibralter
  -laced stuffy, priggish
strange odd, alien, quaint, uncommon
  comb. form xen(o)
strap tie, belt, whip, girth, secure
  falcon's jess
  for leading animal lead, halter
  -shaped lorate, ligulate
straphanger standee
Stravinsky, Igor composer
  work Firebird, Petrouchka, Rites of Spring
straw culm, stem, stalk, fodder, trifle
  bale truss

bed pallet
bunch wisp, whisk
color flaxen
cover plant mulch
in the wind omen, sign
stack mow, rick
vote poll
weaving rafia
strawberry fraise, runner
  bush wahoo
stream flow, pour, creek, spout, arroyo
  dry bed arroyo
  of lava coulee
  swift, violent torrent
  underground aar
street via, easy, lane, main, road, calle,
  avenue, one-way, dead end
strength brawn, might, power
  deprive of sap, weaken, unnerve
  diminish water, dilute
  liquor proof
  poet. puissance
  regain rally
streptomycin
  discoverer Selman Waksman
stretched
  out prolate
  tight taut
  to dry tentered
stretching muscle tensor
strife war, feud, combat, quarrel
  civil stasis
strigil fluting
strike hit, smite, attack, buffet
  and rebound carom
  breaker fink, scab
  demonstrator picket
  dumb amaze, astound
  kind sit-in, hunger
  out fan, erase, cancel
  series pelt
string cord, josh, lace, line, twine
  of beads rosary
  of (racing) horses stable
  -quartet instruments viol, cello,
    viola, violin
  up hang, lynch

stringed instrument harp, koto, lyre, banjo, piano, violin, zither, ukelele
strip bare, divest, undress
  of land neck
  of leaves defoliate
  of tree trunk flitch
  -tease dancer ecdysiast
striped bandy, striate, zonate
  lengthwise vittate
stroke blow, shot, caress
  brilliant ace, coup
  cutting chop, slice
  endlike coup de grace
  lucky coup, fluke
  oblique bricole
  of luck windfall
Stromboli island, volcano
strong firm, robust, virile, intense
  -arm man (sl.) bouncer, goon
  current riptide, undertow
  man Atlas, Samson
  muscled brawny
  point forte
  scented olid
strudel pastry
strummer guitarist
struthious bird emu, rhea, theal, ostrich
student pupil, disciple
  Annapolis midshipman
  fellow classmate
  former alum, alumnus, dropout, graduate
  girl coed
  in charge monitor
  initiation haze
  military school cadet
  West Point cadet
studies
  academic arts, sciences, humanities
  self-chosen electives
  series course
study
  closely pore, examine
  course seminar
  hard bone (up)

study of
  animals zoography
  bees apiology
  fingerprints dactylography
  flowers anthoecology
  horses hippology
  insects entomology
  mountains orology
  population larithmics
  wine enology
  words etymology
stumbling block obstacle, hindrance
stumps legs, baffles
stunted
  person runt
  tree scrag, bonsai
stupa mound, tower
stupid, to be rendered hebetate
stupor coma, trance, lethargy
  comb. form narco
  pert. to carotic
sturgeon
  gray/white beluga
  roe caviar
  small sterlet
Stygian gloomy, infernal
style mode, brand, manner, needle, technique
  art genre
  out of dated, passé
  painting Dada, genre, Cubism
  show off ostentatious
  with gusto, panache
stylized flower (fleur) de lis
Styx river, Lethe
  ferryman Charon
  location Hades, underworld
su- juris, generis
subject text, theme, liable, servant
  change to another metastasis
  main motif
  point moot
  to change mutable
  to dislike aversion
  to mistakes erratic
  to third degree sweat
submerged continent Atlantis

subscription
  to newspaper abonnement (Fr.)
subsequently later, presently, afterward
substance core, mass, spirit, essence, material
  animal gelatin
  dissolving resolvent
  expansive gas
  rubberish gutta
  simple element
  transparent glass, celluloid
  white alba
substitute, temporary ersatz, stopgap
subway tube, metro, tunnel
  entrance kiosk, turnstile
succory chicory
succubus demoness
such sic (Lat.), kind, similar
suckfish remora, lamprey
Sudan, Sudanese Fulah, Mossi, Haussa
  antelope oterop
  language Toshi, Mandingo
  sultanate Wadai
  weapon trumbash
Suez Canal
  builder Ferdinand-Marie de Lesseps
suffering loss, agony, distress
  comb. form path(o)
  person involved in martyr, victim
suffix postfix
  adjective ent, ial, ish, ist, ous
  comparative ier, ior
  diminutive ule, ette
  lacking less
  superlative est
sugar
  alcohol sorbitol
  burnt caramel
  cane sucrose
  comb. form sacchar(o)
  crude gur
  lump cube
  milk lactose
  sl. money
  source beet, cane, maple
suit kind, cards, dress, match
  of armor panoply

  of mail armor
  playing card clubs, hearts, spades, diamonds
  tarot card cups, wands, swords, pentacles
  to a tee
Sullivan's collaborator Gilbert
Sumatra
  animal balu, orang
  deer napu
  language Nias
  measure paal
summer ete (Fr.)
  beverage ade
  pert. to (a)estival
  theater stock
summon call, rouse, subpoena
  by calling name page
  by magic conjure
  roll call muster
  to a meeting convoke
  to court cite, sist
sumpter mule, packhorse
sun sol, bask, star, bleach
  comb. form heli(o)
  dog parhelion
  god see god, goddess
  greatest distance from apsis
  halo corona
  obscuring of the eclipse
  pert. to solar, heliacal
  poet. lamp, Phoebus
  point farthest from aphelion
  shadow umbra
  worship heliolatry
Sunday
  following Easter Low, Quasimodo
  mid-Lent Laetare
  pert. to dominical
  special Palm, Easter
sundial horologe
  pointer gnomon
sundog parhelion
sunfish bream, roach, cichlid, bluegill
  genus Mola
sunflower maid Clytie
sunset, occurring at acronical

superabundance plethora
superficial cursory, shallow
  polish veneer
superhumeral amice
superlative acme, tops, ultra
  absolute elative
  suffix est
supersonic noise boom
supine
  opposite prone
supplement add
  in law codicil
support abet, second, uphold, buttress
  chief mainstay
  idea/cause espouse
  main pillar
suppository pessary
suppress news story kill
supreme being Allah, monad
Supreme Court high court
  nickname (historical) nine old men
surcoat cloak, jupon, topcoat
sure secure, stable, confident
  thing (sl.) cinch, in the bag
surface area, facet, exterior
  antique patina
  flat plane
  front obverse
  pert. to facial
  slanting cant
  toward ectad
  wing on plane airfoil
surfbird plover
surgical
  compress stupe
  instr. trepan, scalpel
  operation (comb. form) tomy
  sewing suture
  thread seton, catgut
Suribachi
  location Iwo Jima
Surinam
  hut benab
  toad pipa(l)
  tree balata
surmounting atop, prevailing
surplice cotta, ephod

surrealist Salvador Dali
surrender cede, yield, resign
  conditionally capitulate
  sign white flag
surtout (over)coat
surveying
  instr. level, stadia, caliper, transit
  nail spad
susceptible to error fallible
suslik sisel, gopher, squirrel
suspension delay, stoppage
  of court sentence probation
  of hostilities truce
  of proceedings recess, adjournment
Susskind, David TV producer/host
susu dolphin
swag pit, list, spoil, swing
  sl. loot, plunder
swallowwort celandine
swamp fen, flood, morass, slough
  fever malaria
  pert. to paludal
  trees mangrove
  vapor miasm(a)
swan sweat, declare, surprise
  constellation Cygnus
  female pen
  genus Olor
  male cob
  river Avon
  young cygnet
Swann's Way
  author Marcel Proust
swaraj home rule
swarmer ant, bee, insect, locust
swat hit, clout
  sultan of Babe Ruth
swear vow, curse, pledge
  falsely perjure
  off renounce
  to secrecy tile
  word profanity
sweat ooze, exude, egesta
  causing hidrotic
Sweden, Swedish Sverige
  coin ore, crown, krona
  dance polska

measure stang
nightingale Jenny Lind
noble title graf
parliament Riksdag
prize Nobel
tribe Geatas
writer August Strindberg
sweet candy, honey, pleasant
  and soft dolce
  clover melilot
  drink nectar
  flag calamus
  smelling olent
  sounding dulcet, melodic
sweetbread ris de veau
sweetfish ayu
sweetheart beau, Jill, beloved, valentine
  Scot. jo
  sl. steady
sweetsop ates
swellfish puffer
swelling puff, bulge, edema
  armpit/groin bubo
  comb. form c(o)ele
  foot chilblain
  pert. to nodal, edematose
sweven dream, vision
swift bird, fleet, rapid, lizard
  comb. form tachy
Swift, Jonathan
  flying island Laputa
  hero Gulliver
  lady friend Stella (fictional)
  pen name Drapier
swile seal
swimmer of English Channel
    Gertrude Ederle
swimming natant, flooded, vertigo
  pool tank, natatorium
  stroke/style crawl, breast, butterfly
  suit tank, bikini, trunks, maillot
swine hog, pig, sow, boar
  female sow, gilt
  flesh pork
  genus Sus
  litter farrow
  male boar

pert. to porcine
  young shoat, piglet, porker
switchman shunter
Swiss, Switzerland Suisse, Helvetia
  ax piolet
  card game jass
  cottage chalet
  designer Corbusier
  Family Robinson author Wyss
  food bernerplatte
  herdsman senn
  hero William Tell
  lake Zug, Geneva, Lucerne, Neuchatel
  measure elle, im(m)i
  money batz
  mountain Jungfrau
  painter Paul Klee
  pert. to Alpen
  plant edelweiss
  psychologist Carl Jung
  song yodel
  wind bise
swivet, in a agog
sword epée, cutlas(s), rapier, falchion
  belt baldric
  handle haft, hilt
  Highlander's claymore
  knob pommel
  legendary Balmung, Excalibur
  poet. steel
  -shaped ensate, xiphoid, ensiform
  short dirk
  Siegfried's Balmung
  St. George's Ascalon
  two-edged pata
swordfish aus, dorado, espada
  saw serra
syagush caracal
sycamine mulberry
syce groom
syconium fig
sycosis victim beard
Syleus
  slayer Hercules
syllable
  added prefix, suffix
  deletion apocope

last ultima
next to last penult
short breve
stressed arsis
sylvan rustic, woody
  deity Pan, Faun(us), satyr
symbol token, emblem
  bad luck opal
  bondage yoke
  Brit. lion, John Bull
  death crossbones
  grief rue
  immortality ph(o)enix
  peace dove
  phallic linga(m)
  purity lily
  saintliness halo
  strength Atlas, sinew
  sun aten
  universe mandalga
  wisdom owl
sympathetic humane, piteous
  response echo
symphony
  form sonata
  division movement
  of Beethoven for Napoleon
    Eroica
symptoms
  continuing syndrome
  pert. to semiotic, semiology
synagogue shul, temple
  officer parnas
  platform bima, almemar
  singer cantor
synthetic sham, artificial
  silk nylon, rayon
Syracuse
  founder Archias
Syria, Syrian Hittite, Saracen,
    Levantine
  bishop abba
  buried city Dura
  goat angora
  goddess Ashtoreth
  peasant fellah
  religious follower Druse

script serta
seaport Tripoli
weight cola
wind simoon
syringa lilac, shrub
syrinx nymph, panpipe
syrphus fly gnat
system order, circle, theory, method
  betting parimutuel
  of rules code
  of weights troy, avoirdupois
  of worship cult, ritual
  orderly cosmos
systematic orderly
  arrangement schema
systematics taxonomy
syzygy dipody
szopelka oboe

T

T tee
  -shaped tau
ta (Ch.) tantalum
taa pagoda
Taal Afrikaans
tab pan, flap, check, tongue
  shoe aiglet, latchet
  sl. record
tabanid horsefly
tabard cape, gown, mantle
tabby cloth moire, moreen
tabby moth genus Aglossa
table food, list, rota, canon, put off,
    postpone
  calculating abacus
  centerpiece epergne
  communion altar
  linen napery
  philosopher deipnosophist
  three-legged tripod, trivet
  workman's siege
tableland mesa, plain, plateau
  Central Asia pamirs
  S. Afr. karoo

tablespoon
  abbrev. tbsp.
tablet pad, pill, panel, sheet, plaque, troche, lozenge, writing pad
  stone slab, stele
  symbolic pax
tableware dishes, plates, utensils, chinaware, silverware
taboo, tabu ban, no-no, outlawed, forbidden, prohibited, unacceptable, unmentionable
tabulate list, rank, rate, chart, grade, index, arrange, catalog, compute, organize, catagorize
tabor camp, drum, timbrel
tace
  music silent
tachina fly
tacit implied, inferred, unspoken, undeclared, understood
taciturn aloof, quiet, silent, reserved, tight-lipped, uncommunicative
tack add, peg, pin, clap, jibe, join, nail, affix, annex, spike, attach, laveer
  glazier's brad, point
tackle throw, tools, attach, take on, attempt, derrick, embrace, endeavor, undertake, implements, accoutrements
tacky dowdy, gluey, gummy, seedy, shabby, sticky, unkempt, slovenly, disordered
tact finesse, diplomacy, discretion, considerate, savoir-faire (Fr.)
tactic way, line, plan, method, policy, scheme, strategy
tactics maneuvers, military operations
tactless curt, rude, brash, boorish, imprudent, insensitive, thoughtless, undiplomatic, inconsiderate
tael, 1/10th mace
taffeta florid, gaudy, samite
taffy candy, blarney, flattery, Welshman
tag add, card, flap, mark, name, slip, stub, affix, label, append, frazzle, earmark, designation
  metal dog, a(i)glet
Tagalog see also Malayan, Philippines
  mother ina

peasant tao
wine alac
Tahiti, Tahitian Polynesian
  artist Gauguin
  author Stevenson
  apple hevi
  canoe pahi
  capital Papeete
  centipede veri
  god Taaroa
  robe maro
  ocean Pacific
Tai, Thai Siamese
  race Lao
taiga forests
tail dog, scut, follow, shadow
  boar's wreath
  coin's verso
  comb. form uro
  furry scut
  having a caudate
  pert. to caudal
  short bun, scut
  without acaudal
tail end back, rear, rump, caudal, backside, buttocks
tailleurs anura, frogs, amphibian
  amphibial family frog, tenrec, ranidae
tailor fit, sew, make, redo, adapt, alter, devise, modify, sartor, fashion, clothier, costumer, couturier, dressmaker, seamstress
  iron goose
  lapboard panel
  work sartorial
taint mar, rot, blot, flaw, ruin, soil, spot, turn, dirty, fauly, smear, spoil, stain, damage, debase
Taiwan Formosa, terraced bay
  capital Taipei
  channel Bashi
  deer sika
  feast pai-pai
  museum National Palace
  people Yami, Hakka, Hoklo, Chinese, Malayan, Fukienese, Taiwanese, Indonesian, Polynesian

religion Taoism, animism, Buddhism, Christianity, Confucianism
storm monsoon, typhoon
tea oolong
Taj Mahal
  builder Jahan-gir
  site Agra
tajo trench
take bag, nab, grasp, usurp, capture, swallow, embezzle
  advantage of abuse, misuse, exploit, profit from
  away adeem, heave, seize, wrest, curtail, detract
  back recall, recant, renege, return, disavow, retract, withdraw
  captive snag, catch, capture, ensnare, apprehend
  off ape, fly, doff, lift, leave, detach, remove, burlesque
  on bear, hire, accept, engage, shoulder, undertake
  one's breath away daze, stun, shock, stupefy, astonish
  possession seize, escheat, confiscate, appropriate
  sl. cheat, trick
  shape form
  shelter nestle
  some partake
  stock check, assess, survey, examine, inspect, inventory
  to court sue
  turns share, rotate, alternate
  umbrage resent
  up weapons arm
  without authority usurp
takin gazelle
talapoin monk(ey), guenon
Talaria
  location ankles
  of Hermes wings, sandals
talc powder, agalite, steatite, soapstone
tale epic, myth, saga, yarn, fable, novel, story, fiction, recital, hearsay, anecdote, narrative
  adventure gest(e)

bearer gossip, blabber, quidnunc, storyteller
medieval lai
Norse saga
of sorrow jeremiad
traditional saga, fairy
Tale of Two Cities
  author Charles Dickens
  hero Sydney Carton
  heroine Lucie Manette
  setting French Revolution
Talese, Gay
  author Honor Thy Father, Thy Neighbor's Wife
taliera palm, tara
talipot palm
talisman charm, amulet, fetish, phylactery, lucky piece
  beetle scarab
  stone agate
  talismanic magical
talk gab, jaw, rap, say, cant, chat, argot, lingo, prate, speak, spiel, state, utter, babble, confer, gossip, jargon, parley, preach, address, chatter, dialect, discuss, express, lecture, prattle, chit chat, converse, dialogue, language, discourse, conversation
  back sass
  big brag, boast
  freely descant
  glib patter
  light banter
  sales spiel
  sl. lip
  wildly rave
talkative windy, prolix, verbose, effusive, loquacious
tall big, high, lanky, elevated, towering, embellished
  chest highboy
  tale yarn, fish story, fabrication, cock-and-bull story
tallow suet, sevum, grease
  pert. to stearic
  product soap, candle
  sediment greaves
  tree cera, roka

tally add, sum, jibe, list, mark, score, total, reckon, square, tabulate
Talmud
  commentary Gemara
  parts in Gemara, Mishnah
  title Abba
talon claw, nail
Talos
  guarded Crete
  made by Hephaestus
  slayer Daedalus
  uncle Daedalus
Tamar
  brother Amnon, Absalom, Chileab, Solomon
  daughter Maachiah
  father David, Absalom
  father-in-law Judah
  husband Er, Onan, Juday, Uriah
  mother Maacah
  son Zarah, Pharez
tamarack tree, larch
tamarau buffalo, carabao
tame curb, damp, flat, meek, mild, rein, break, train, bridle, docile, gentle, subdue, control, repress, domestic, regulate, restrain, suppress, submissive
Tamil Dravidian
  caste member Vellala
Taming of the Shrew, The
  author William Shakespeare
  character Bianca, Gremio, Tranio, Baptista, Lucentio, Hortensio, Katharina (Kate), Petruchio, Vincentio
Tammuz
  god of shepherds
  Hebrew month fourth
  love Ishtar
  origin Sumerian
tamper mix, meddle, tinker, interfere, intervene, mess around
tan beige, brown, khaki, sorrel
tanager bird, yeni, habia, lindo
  genus Piranga
tang reek, punch, savor, flavor, acridity, piquancy, tartness, spiciness

Tanganyika Zanzibar
  mountain Kilimanjaro
tangible real, solid, obvious, physical, corporeal
Tangier
  measure kula, mudd
tangle fix, net, web, knot, ravel, twist, jumble, labyrinth
Tanis Zoan
tank vat, boiler, vehicle, aquarium, reservoir
  rainwater cistern
  weapon bazooka
tankard facer, hanap, vessel
tanner's gum kino
  shrub sumac(h)
  solution bate, amaltas
  substance splate
Tanoan Indian, Isleta
  See also Indian(s), Pueblo
Tantalus
  daughter Niobe
  father Zeus
  king of Pisa, Phrygia
  punishment thirst, hunger
  son Pelops
  wife Clytemnestra
tantamount like, equal, analogous
tantivy haste(n), rapid
tantrum storm, rampage, outburst
Taoism
  right conduct te
tap pat, rap, drum, peck, valve, spigot, uncork, unplug, draw upon
tape affix
  braided inkle
  needle bodkin
taper dip, wax, light, candle, narrow, decrease, come to a point
tapered terete
tapering spired, conical, fusiform
  piece shim
tapestry arras, tapis, fabric
  comb. reed
  kind Brugges, Gobelin
  warp thread lisse
tapeworm cestode, entozoan
  genus Taenia

tapiocalike food salep
　source cassava
tapir anta, seladang
　pride of snout
tappet cam
taproom bar, pub, saloon, tavern
tar salt, pitch, sailor
　mineral brea, pitch, maltha
　product creosol
taradiddle fib, lie
Taranaki volcano Egmont
tarboosh fez, turban
tardy late, slow, slack, belated, remiss, crawling, creeping, slowpoke, procrastinating
tare weed, plant, vetch
targe shield
target aim, butt, goal, mark
　center eye, blank
　easy sitting duck
　of blame scapegoat
Tar Heel North Carolinian
Tarkington, Booth
　author of Penrod, Seventeen, Alice Adams, Kate Fennigate, The Man from Home, Monsieur Beaucaire, The World Does Not Move, The Magnificent Ambersons
tarnish dim, blot, dull, foul, soil, spot, dirty, errode, stain, taint, darken, defame, defile, vilify, blemish, corrode, degrade, oxidize, discolor, dishonor, discredit, stigmatize
taro gabi, koko, plant
　dish (paste) poi
　root(s) eddo(es)
　West Indies tania
tarot
　cards/deck seventy-eight
　division major arcana, minor arcana, lesser arcana, greater arcana
　face card king, page, knave, queen, valet, knight
　Fr. tarau, tarot
　Ger. tarok
　It. naibes, attutti, tarocchi
　major arcana Fool, Moon, Death, Justice, Judgment, Hanged Man, Wheel of Fortune
　suit cup, coin, wand, baton, money, sword, cudgel, pentacle
tarpaulin tarp, dropcloth
tarpon fish, elops, sabalo
　genus Elops
　related to chiro
tarragon Artemisia dracunculus
　flavor licorice
　Fr. estragon
　origin Siberia
　use fish, salad, sauce, mayonnaise
tarry lag, dally, dawdle, linger, procrastinate
tarsus hock, ankle, shank
tart pie, sour, tangy
tartar argol, calculus
Tartar Hu, Turk, Tatar
　dynasty Kin, Wei
　horseman Slav
　king khan
　nobleman murza
Tartarus Hades
Tartuffe comedy, hypocrite
　author Moliere
Tarzan Lord of Greystoke, Lord of the Jungle
　author Edgar Rice Burroughs
　mate Jane
　monkey Cheeta
task job, duty, stint, metier, assignment
　punishing pensum
　routine chore
　take to scold, lecture
Tasmania
　bay Storm, Oyster
　cape Grim
　capital Hobart
　city Launceston
　country Australia
　devil Dasgure
　strait Bass
tass cup, goblet
tassel tag, thrum, cordelle
taste sup, sapor, liking, palate, relish, sample

absence of ageus(t)ia
delighting the friand
Fr. soupçon
strong tang
tasteful elegant, esthetic, attractive
tasteless rude, weak, bland, gaudy, garish, insipid, flavorless
tasty spicy, tangy, yummy, savory, delicious, palatable, scrumptious
Tatius Titus
ruled with Romulus
tatterdemalion ragamuffin
tatters shreds, threads
tattersall checkered
tattler blab, gossip, informer, quidnunc, talebearer, rumormonger, troublemaker
tau ankh, crux, tace
taunt rag, jeer, sneer, tease, deride, harass, provoke, make fun of
taurine bull, bovine, Taurus
taurotragus eland, oreas
tautog chub, blackfish
tavern bar, pub, saloon, brasserie, watering hole, cocktail lounge
taverna shop, tent, booth, tavern
taw tan, harden, marble
tawdry cheap, tacky, vulgar, flamboyant, ostentacious
tax duty, levy, toll, stent, assess, burden, custom, excise,
assess on default doomage
church tithe
feudal tallage
kind city, sales, state, county, excise, income, luxury, inheritance
on hides hidage
salt gabelle
taxicab hack
taxite lava
taxonomy
study of structure contrast
taxus genus Yew
Taygeta star, pleiad
Taylor, Elizabeth
born London
movies Giant, Cleopatra, A Place in the Sun, National Velvet, Cat on a Hot Tin

Roof, Father of the Bride, Suddenly Last Summer, Who's Afraid of Virginia Woolf
tazza cup, bowl, vase
Tchaikovsky, Peter composer
born Russia
works Manfred, Mazeppa, Ionlanthe, Pathetic (symphony no. 6), Swan Lake, Joan of Arc, Nutcracker, Eugene Onegin, Winter Dreams, Caprice, Romeo and Juliet, The Enchantress, Sleeping Beauty, Eighteen-Twelve Overture
tea
Asia cha, congo(u), hyson, oolong
black pekoe
bowl chawan
box caddy
Brazil holly mate, yerba
cake scone
China congo(u), hyson, oopak, oolong
drug in thein(e), caffeine
English Earl Grey, breakfast
extract adenine
genus Thea
plant kat, thea
table teapoy
urn samovar
weak blash
teacher coach, tutor, docent, mentor, pundit, scribe, pedagog(us)
Jewish rab(bi), melamid, melammed
Moslem alim, mulla(h)
pointer fescue
Russ. starets
unattached docent
teaching tutelage, training, schooling, instruction
of a fable moral
pert. to pedagogic
teakettle suke, suky
teal duck, fowl
team ally, band, gang, side, unit, group, unite, clique, faction, coalition, consolidate
spirit solidarity, esprit de corps
teammate partner, colleague

tear rip, run, bead, bolt, dart, dash, drop, part, rive, slit, binge
  heraldry larme
  pert. to lacrimal
  sl. spree
  up by roots pluck, arache, assart
tear down level, raise
teardrop design larme
tearful moist, maudlin
  mother Niobe
teasel comb, herb, plant, boneset
teaspoon
  abbrev. tsp
technical trade, mechanical
technique way, method, system, formula, know-how
teck cravat
ted toad, spread, scatter
tedious slow, tiring, irksome, intensive
teem gush, overflow
teeth
  cavity tissue pulp
  decay caries
  deposit tartar
  double molars, grinders
  grinding bruxism
  hard tissue dentin
  having all alike isodont
  long-pointed fangs, tusks
  sockets alveoli
  without edentated, edentulous
teeter reel, totter
teetotaler abstainer
teetotum top, toy
teg doe, woman, fleece
Tegeates
  father Lycaon
tegua sandal
Tegucigalpa
  capital of Honduras
tegula tile, alula
tegument coat, skin, cortex
Tehran, Teheran
  capital Iran
  ruler Pahlavi
tela web, tissue, membrane
telamon atlas, column, pilaster

Telamon
  brother Peleus
  companion Hercules
  father Aeacus
  half-brother Phocus
  king of Salamis
  member of Argonauts
  mother Endeis
  son Ajax
  wife Glauce, Eriboea
telecost fish eel, apoda
Telegonus
  father Proeus, Odysseus
  killed Odysseus
  killed by Hercules
  mother Circe
  wife Io, Penelope
telegraph
  instrument part key, anvil, tapper
  inventor Samuel Morse
  signal dah, dit, dot, dash
Telemachus
  father Ulysses, Odysseus
  mother Penelope
  son Latinus
Telemus
  father Eurymus
  occupation seer
  warned Polyphemus
telepathy ESP, clairvoyance, extrasensory perception
telephone
  inventor Alexander Graham Bell
  receiver cymaphen
telephotographic lens adon
Telephus
  father Hercules
  king of Mysia
  mother Auge
telescope
  inventor Kepler, Galileo, Lippershey
telescope site Palomar
television TV, tube, telly, video
  award Emmy
  cable coaxial
  camera platform dolly
  interference snow

inventor Baird, Zworykin, Farnsworth
lens zoom
tell ask, say, count, speak, state, utter, write, advise, direct, inform, recite, relate, report, reveal, apprise, divulge, recount, describe, disclose, calculate, chronicle, communicate
Tell
home Uri
telluride altaite, hessite
telson somite, segment
of king crab pleon
Temenus
brother Aristodemus, Cresphontes
father Pelasgus, Aristomachus
temerity gall, cheek, nerve, audacity, boldness, chutzpah
tempera painting secco
Tempest, The
author William Shakespeare
character Ariel, Alonso, Antonio, Caliban, Gonzalo, Miranda, Prospero, Ferdinand, Sebastian
tempestuous fiery, frantic, furious, turbulent, passionate
Templar knight, crusader
temple kirk, huaca, church, chapel, shrine, basilica, cathedral, synagogue, tabernacle, meeting house, teocalli sidepiece
basin laver
builder, early Jewish Micah
chief chamber naos, cella
Chinese taa, pagoda
gateway torii
inner cella
pert. to hieron
portico narthex
Shinto sha
vestibule pronaos
tempo beat, clip, gait, pace, rate, time, meter, pulse
pert. to agogic
rapid presto
slow lento
very slow grave
tempus time
fugit time flies

ten decad(e)
acres decare
-century note grand
decibels bel
-gallon hat sombrero
prefix dec(a), deka
square chains acre
thousand grand, myriad
Ten Commandments Decalogue
location Mount Sinai
first Thou shalt have no other Gods before me
second Thou shalt not bow down before graven images
third Thou shalt not take the name of the Lord thy God in vain
fourth Remember the Sabbath Day and keep it holy
fifth Honor thy father and thy mother
sixth Thou shalt not kill
seventh Thou shalt not commit adultery
eight Thou shalt not steal
ninth Thou shalt not bear false witness against thy neighbor
tenth Thou shalt not covet
tenacious firm, dogged, adamant, resolute, stubborn, pigheaded, steadfast, relentless
animal bulldog, pit bull
tenant lessee, renter
farm croft
feudal leud(e), vassal, socager
neglect to pay rent cesser
tribute cens (Fr.)
tend lean, be apt, foster, nurture, predispose
tendency aim, habit, trend, course, leaning, direction, propensity, inclination
tender give, soft, sore, frail, benign, feeble, gentle
tenderfoot novice, rookie, apprentice
Tender Is the Night
author F. Scott Fitzgerald
character Abe North, Dick Diver, Nicole Diver, Tommy Barban, Rosemary Hoyt
tending toward an end telic
tendon thew, sinew

broad, flat aponeurosis
comb. form teno
tendril shoot, cirrus, sprout, stipule
Tennessee see also Quick Reference List
nickname Old Franklin
Tennyson, Alfred author
works Ulysses, In Memoriam, Morte d'Arthur, The Idylls of the King, The Charge of the Light Brigade
heroine Enid, Maud, Elaine
heroine's home Astolat
In Memoriam subject Hallam
tenon coo, tusk, tooth, dovetail
tenor gist, sense, intent, nature, meaning, connotation
tense rigid, stiff, tight, on edge, uneasy, fidgety, uptight, agitated
opposite loose, slack
past preterite
verb past, future, perfect, present
tensile ductile, plastic
tent pup, lodge, probe, canopy, teepee, wigwam, shelter, pavilion
circular yurt
covering fly, tilt
dweller Arab, Kedar, nomad, Scenite
India pawl
large field marquee
maker Omar
surgical plug
tentacle arm, palp, feeler, tendril
without acerous
tenth
comb. form deci
muse Sappho
part tithe
tenure rule, term, time, reign, occupancy, incumbency, administration
of land socage
teocalli temple
tequila
drink margarita, Chapala, El Diablo
tera church, monastery
Terah
father Nahor
son Abraham
teraph idol, image

terbium symbol Tb
terebinth teil, tree, turpentine
teredo (ship)worm, borer
terefah, trefah not kosher
Tereus
father Ares
prince of Thrace
raped Philomela
son Itylus
wife Procne
tergal back, aboral, dorsal
tergum back
term era, tag, name, time, rhema, state, period, boundary
in office tenure
math sine, cosine
of life age, sands
termagant scold, shrew, vixen, virago
terminal end, pole, anode, depot, final, cathode
negative cathode
of a leaf apiculus
positive anode
terminate end, cease, close, bring to an end
termite ant, anal, anay
variety desert, dry wood, damp wood, powderpost, rotten wood, soldierless, subterranean
tern bird, fowl, pirr, noddy, starn
genus Anous, Sterna
Hawaii noio
terpene nerol
derivative camphor
Terpsichore muse
concern dancing
terra
firma earth
cotta clay
terrace dais, roof, patio, street, plateau, balcony
in series parterre
wall podium
terra-cotta clay, reddish-brown
terrain area, tract, setting, topography
terrapin emyd, turtle, tortoise
family Emydidae

order chelonia
red-billed slider
terrestrial land, global
terret ring
terrible bad, awful, great, harsh, brutal, fierce, horrid, severe, hideous, alarming, dreadful, appalling, monstrous
terrify alarm, daunt, scare, frighten
terrine stew
territory area, domain, region
  division amt
terry loop
terse brief, crisp, short, abrupt
tertiary period neocene, pliocene
tesselate tile, mosaic
test quiz, check, probe, prove, examination
  flight trial run
  operation shakedown
  ore assay
  paper litmus
  series gauntlet
testa coat, shell
testament legacy
Testament Bible, scriptures
testify swear, declare, bear witness
testy moody, crabby, sullen, irascible
teston coin
tete-a-tete chat, talk, conversation
tether tie, leash, secure
Tethys Titan
  brother Cronus
  daughters three thousand
  father Uranus
  husband Oceanus
  mother Gaea
tetrachord
  music nete, meson
tetrad four, quadrivalent
tetter fret, eczema, herpes, lichen, psoriasis
Teutonic Dutch, German, Gothic, Nordic, British, English, Germanic, Scandinavian
  ancient tribe Ubi(i)
  barbarian Goth
  demon alp

letter rune
people Gepidae
Texas see also Quick Reference List
  fort Alamo
  tree pecan
textile cloth, fiber, fabric
  dealer mercer
  worker reeder
Thackeray, William Makepeace
  author of Vanity Fair, The Virginians
  character Becky (Sharp), Amelia, Esmond
  tale country Paflagonia
Thai, Thailand Lao, Shaw, Siam
  capital Bangkok
  coin att, bia, bhat, catty, fuang, tical
  demon nat
  fruit camut, durian, pomelo
  garment panung, sarong, saffron robes
  lake Nong Lahan
  leader king, Phraruang
  measure sok, cohi, niou, sesti, tanan
  sea Andaman
  temple wat
  tree teak
  twins Eng, Chang
  weight bat, catty, fuang
Thais opera, courtesan
  character Athanael
  composer Jules-Emile-Frederic Massenet
thalassic marine, neritic, aquatic, oceanic, pelagic
Thales mathematician
  predicted sun's eclipse
Thalia muse, grace
  concern comedy, poetry
  lover Zeus
  sisters Clio, Graces, Charities
  slayer Erato
Thallo
  goddess of spring flowers
Thames
  landmark Eton, bridge
Thanatos
  mother Nyx
  personified Death

thank be grateful
thankful obliged, indebted, appreciative
thankless person vain, ingrate, heedless, ungrateful, inconsiderate
thanks benediction, appreciation
thanks be to God Deo gratias (Lat.)
Thanksgiving
  originated by Pilgrims
  typical food corn, turkey, pumpkin pie, cranberry sauce
  symbol cornucopia
thank you
  Fr. merci
  Ger. danke
  It. grazie
  Jp. domo
  Sp. gracias
thank you very much
  Fr. merci bien, merci beaucoup
  Ger. danke schon
  Jp. domo arigato
  Sp. mucho gracias
that as, so, who, what, which, because
  is ie, id est
  is to say viz (Lat.), namely, videlicit (Lat.)
  not lest
thatch
  grass neti
  palm nipa
  peg scob
  support wattle
that's life c'est la vie (Fr.)
thaumaturgy magic
  work miracle
thaw melt, soften, dissolve
the
  Fr. la, le, les
  Ger. das, der, die
  It. il, la, le, egli, ella
  Sp. el, la, las, los
  same idem, ditto
theater, theatre drama, legit, opera, stage, cinema
  award Tony
  box loge
  classic lyceum

floor pit
full SRO
Gr. odeon
-in-the-round arena
part scena, stage
theatrical hammy, showy, flashy, dramatic, thespian, extravagant
theatrical trick coup de theatre (Fr.)
Theban, Thebes
  blind soothsayer Tiresias
  deity Mut, Amon
  founder Cadmus
  king Creon, Laius, Lycus, Oedipus
  one of the seven against Tydeus
  poet Pindar
  wicked queen Dirce
theca sac, cell, capsule
theft robbery, pilfering, swindle
theme focus, motif, topic, thesis, treatise, leitmotif, dissertation
  literary motif
  mus. tema
  title lemma
Themis goddess, Titan
  concern law, harmony, justice
  father Uranus
  holds scale
  husband Iapetus
  mother Gaea
  mother of Fates, Horae, Moerae, Seasons
  sister Phoebe
  son Prometheus
Themiste
  father Laomedon
  mother Eurydice
  son Anchises
thence whence, therefore, in due course
Theoclymenus seer
  father Proteus
  king of Egypt
  mother Psamathe
theological holy, sacred, dogmatic, canonical, ecclesiastical
theorbo lute
theoretical academic
  opposite applied, empirical, practical

theorize posit, surmise, speculate, hypothesize

theory idea, believe, notion, concept, doctrine, postulate, hypothesis, supposition
  Darwin evolution
  Einstein relativity
  Newton gravity

therapeutic healing, remedial

there at, yon(der), that, thence, thither
  it is voila (Fr.)

thereafter later, afterward(s), from then on, subsequently

therefore so, ergo, then, hence, accordingly, consequently

thereupon then, thereon, directly, suddenly

Therimachus
  father Hercules
  mother Megary
  killed by Hercules

thermometer
  invented by Galileo

theropod dinosaur

thersitical abusive, scurrilous

the same as like, equal to, tantamount to

thesaurus lexicon, cyclopedia, dictionary, synonymicon
  compiler Peter Roget

Thescelosaurus dinosaur
  period Cretaceous

Theseus
  father Aegeus
  king of Athens
  lover Ariadne
  mother Aethra
  son Acamas, Demonphon, Hippolytus, Melanippus
  victim Minotaur
  wife Phaedra

thesis essay, article, proposition, dissertation
  opposite arsis, antithesis

thesis essay, paper, critique, composition

thespian actor, player, actress, performer, tragedian

thespis forte tragedy

Thestius
  father Ares
  king of Aetolia
  mother Demonice

Thestor
  daughter Theonoe, Leucippe
  son Calchas

Thetis
  husband Peleus
  sister Eurynome
  son Achilles

thick fat, dull, broad, crass, husky, obtuse, compact
  as thieves close
  -headed dense
  skinned hard, callous, impervious, pachydermatous
  -skulled dull, stupid
  slice slab
  soup puree, pottage

thief crook, gonif, gonof, bandit, stealer, larcener, swindler
  cattle rustler
  compulsive kleptomaniac
  literary lifter, plagiarist
  sells loot to fence

thigh ham, leg, coxa, hock, meros
  bone femur
  comb. form mer(o)
  of the femoral
  part flank
  pert. to crural

thill plank, shaft, thwart

thimble cap, ring, sput, bushing
  machine sleeve
  rigger cheat, swindler

thimblerig shell game

thin lean, slim, lanky, flimsy, meager, sparse, subtle
  -blooded pale, weak, anemic, sickly
  coat/layer film, veneer
  comb. form steno
  disk wafer
  glue size
  out peter, water, weaken, adulterate
  paper tissue
  plate leaf, wedge
  scale flake, lamina
  -skinned touchy, sensitive

thing idea, item, being, cause, affair, object, article, happening
  accomplished act, deed, fait accompli
  added appendix, insertion, addendum
  aforesaid ditto
  already done fait accompli (Fr.)
  -amagig gizmo, gadget, contraption
  an easy snap, cinch
  complete unto itself unity
  cursed anathema
  extra bonus
  following sequel
  found trove
  indefinite so and so, nondescript
  ineffectual dud
  in law res
  invariable constant
  of remembrance token, memento
  out of place estray
  precious curio, relic
  reasoned noumena
  sensed phenomena, phenomenon
  to be done job, task, chore, agenda
  unusual freak, oddity
  valueless nihil (Lat.), trifle, picayune
things goods, effects, belongings
  done res gestae
  edible esculents
  forbidden vetanda
  for sale wares, services
  hidden penetralia
  holy hagia
  linked by nature cognates
  movables chattels
  worth remembering memorabilia
think plan, weigh, judge, meditate, deliberate
  alike agree
  logically reason
  out plan, scheme
  over brood, cogitate
  through ponder, analyze, evaluate
  up create, invent, concoct, contrive
  well of admire, look up to
thinker sage, egghead, scholar, mastermind, metaphysician
Thinker
  sculptor Auguste Rodin

thinness rarity, tenuity
third
  day tertian
  estate tiers etat (Fr.)
  in music tierce
  power cube
  row cee
thirst lust, pant, desire, yearning, hankering
this hoc, here
  minute now, pronto
  one haec
Thisbe Babylonian
  death by suicide
  loved Pyramus
thistle burr, arnica, cosmos
  genus Layia
  -like plants carlina, artichoke
thistledown tufts, pappus
tho also, still
thole peg, bear, allow, fulcrum, oarlock
Thomas, Ambroise
  opera Mignon
thong lash, knout, romal, strap, sandal, fastening
  -shaped lorate
Thor Sisech
  concern rain, thunder
  father Odin
  stepson Ull
  weapon hammer
  wife Sif
thorax chest
  insect's trunk
Thoreau, Henry David
  author of Walden (Life in the Woods), Civil Disobedience
thorn briar, spine, prickle, trouble, irritant
  apple meter, datura
  back ray, fish, skate
  comb. form spini
  -like spina(te)
thorny hard, ought, spiked, critical, formidable, troublesome
thorough full, pure, total, absolute, definitive, unmitigated, all-inclusive

thoroughbred purebred, blueblood, pedigreed, racehorse, aristocrat
thoroughfare street, roadway, thruway, expressway, interstate
thoroughwort plant, boneset
thought idea, belief, opinion
  continuous meditation
  force phrenism
  to transfer telepathy
thoughtful caring pensive, considerate
thoughtless rash, unkind, impolite, neglectful, inattentive
thousand mil(le)
  comb. form kilo, milli
  dollars grand (sl.)
  -headed snake S(h)esha
  years chiliad, millennium
thou too tu quoque (Lat.)
thrall slave, servant, servitude
thrash beat, cane, flog, maul, whip, spank, pommel
Thrasydemus
  squire for Sarpedon
  killed by Patroclus
Thrasymedes
  brother Antilochus
  father Nestor
thread cord, lisle, filament
  bare worn
  ball clew, clue
  comb. form mit(o), nema
  cross woof, reticle
  guiding clew
  lengthwise warp
  -like filar, linear, nemaline
  linen inkle
  shoe latchet lace, lingel, lingle
  silk tram
  worm filaria, nematode
threat risk, danger, menace, endanger, terrorize
three trio, see also Quick Reference List
  dimensional solid
  -fold ternal, ternate
  group of tern, trio, triad
  in one oil, triune
  of a kind leash

prefix ter, tri(o)
-toed bird stilt, woodpecker
-toed sloth ai
three
  B's (mus.) Bach, Brahms, Beethoven
  Graces Aglaia, Thalia, Euphrosyne
  Holy (mus.) Weber, Webern, Schoenberg
  Kingdoms Wu, Shu, Wei
  Musketeers Athos, Aramis, Porthos
  R's reading, (w)riting, (a)rithmetic
  Wise Men Gaspar, Melchior, Balthasar
Thriae nymph
  nurse to Apollo
  teacher of Hermes
thrice prefix ter, tri
thrift prudence, frugality, moderation, parsimoniousness
  -less lavish, wasteful, extravagant
thrill stir, excite
thrive boom, burgeon, prosper
throat maw, neck, gorge, gullet, passage, pharynx
  comb. form lemo
  covering barb
  nautical jaw(s), nock
  part fauces, larynx, tonsil, glottis, trachea
  pert. to gular, jugular, esophageal
  swelling goiter
  upper gula
throb pulsate, oscillate, palpitate
throes pangs, tumult, anguish, turmoil, confusion, disruption
throttle gag, block, choke, silence, strangle
through, thru by, via, among, finished
  and through utterly, completely
  comb. form di(a)
  my fault mea culpa (Lat.)
Through the Looking Glass
  author Lewis Carroll
  character Gnat, Lion, Alice, Dinah, Red King, Unicorn, Red Queen, Red Knight, White King, Tweedledee, Tweedledum, White Queen, Black Kitten, White Kitten, White Knight, Humpty Dumpty
throughout about, during, perfect
  comb. form per

throw dash, hurl, toss, flury
  away scrap, discard
  back revert, reversion
  down fling
  off emit, exude
  out oust, eject, remove
  over jilt
  overboard jettison
  stones at stone, lapidate
  up puke, spew, vomit
  water on douse
thrum drum, waste, recite, tassel
thrush bird, ouzel, robin, missel
  disease soor, aphtha, fungus
  genus Turdus
  ground pitta
  Hawaii omao
  India shama
thrust ram, push, drive, force, lunge, propel, impetus, momentum
  aside dump, cast aside
  at assail, attack
  out eject, protrude
thud bang, thump
thug hood, mugger, mobster, ruffian, gangster
thuja pine, cedar
Thule
  part Iceland, Norway
thulium, symbol Tm
thumb digit, hitch, finger, handle, phalanx, hitchhike, flip through, leaf through
  nail brief, short, concise
  pert. to thenar
Thumbelina
  author Hans Christian Andersen
thunder peal, rage, bronte, fulminate
  bolt lightning
  comb. form bront(o)
  god Thor, Zeus, Donar, Taranis
  storm of Cuba bayamo
  storm of West Indies houvari
  struck aghast, amazed, dumbfounded
  witch baba
thunderfish raad, loach
Thurber, James
  author The New Yorker, Is Sex Necessary, The Catbird Seat, The Owl in the Attic, My Life and Hard Times, The Thurber Carnival, The Secret Life of Walter Mitty
thurible censer
Thursday see also Quick Reference List
  god Thor
  Holy Skire
  observance Holy Thursday, Thanksgiving, Corpus Christi, Ascension Thursday
thus so, sic, yet, ergo, hence, consequently
  always to tyrants sic semper tyrannis
  Lat. ita, sic
thwart bar, stop, oppose, inhibit
Thyestes
  brother Atreus
  daughter Pelopia
  father Pelops
  half-brother Chrysippus
  mother Hippodamia
  sister-in-law Aerope
  son Aegisthus
thylacine tiger, yabbi
Thymoetes
  king of Athens
  elder of Trojans
thyroid
  growth/enlargement goiter
tiara crown, coronet, headdress
Tibet, Tibetan Tangut, Sitsang
  animal panda
  antelope goa, sus
  banner tanka
  capital Lhasa
  coin tanga
  dance cham, achelhamo
  deer shou
  dog lhasa apso
  drink chang
  garment chuba
  kingdom Nepal
  leader Dalai Lama
  legend yeti, abominable snowman
  leopard ounce
  monastery lamasery
  monk/priest lama

ox yak
palace Potalaf
religion Bonko, Lamaism
tibia bone, shin, cnemis
  pert. to cnemial
tick tap, mite, check, click, insect
  fowl argas
  genus Argas, Cimex, Ixodes, Ixodidae
  sheep ked
ticket pass, coupon,
  sl. tag, ducat, label
  stub rain check
tickle amuse, cheer, tingle, delight, titillate
tidal
  basin inlet, sound, lagoon
  flow ebb, bore, estuary
  wave eagre
tidbit treat, morsel
tide flow, befall, current
  low, lowest of high, pert. to neap
tidings news, declaration, announcement
tidy neat, prim, spruce, orderly
  make redo
  up clean, neaten, straighten
tie rod, band, belt, join, knot, rope, equal,
  cement, engage, fasten, connect, kinship,
  allegiance, connection, affiliation
  down restrain
  fast belay
  tightly bind
  up moor, delay
tier row, rank, level
tiff huff, rage, tizzy, quarrel, disagreement
tiffin tea, lunch, repast
tiger cat, shir, feline
  family felidae
  young cub, whelp
Tigger
  character in Winnie-the-Pooh
  author Milne
tight full, hard, snug, blind, exact, scarce,
  compact
  -fisted stingy, penurious, parsimonious
  -fitting snug, constricting
  -laced prim, inhibited, puritanical
  -lipped mum, laconic, reserved,
    secretive

place fix, jam, spot
  sl. drunk, tipsy, smashed
  -wad miser, piker
tighten fasten, secure, constrict
  one's belt scrimp, economize, pinch
    pennies
til plant, sesame
tile hat, drain
  curved pantile
  large slab
  pattern mosaic
  pert. to tegular
  roofing pantile
till sow, farm, plow, prepare, cultivate
tillage land, culture
  fit for arable
tilt tip, lean, joust, altercation
Timandra
  brother Castor, Pollux
  cursed by Aphrodite
  father Tyndareus
  husband Echemus, Phyleus
  mother Leda
  sister Helen Clytemnestra
  son Meges
timber log, bitt, fuel, wood
  crack anemosis
  defect conk
  grooved coulisse
  lands wood, forest
  peg pin, cork
  rot doat
  tree fir, yew, pine
  wolf lobo
timbre pitch
time beat, days, year, cycle, epoch, hours,
  tempo, moment, period, duration,
  generation
  before eve
  being nonce
  comb. form chron(o)
  division eon, hour, week, year, month
  error in order of anachronism
  fast DST, Lent
  flies tempus fugit (Lat.)
  past ago, once, yore
  pert. to eral

piece clock, sundial, hourglass, horologue
saving efficient
to come future
without end forever, eternity
worn old, aged, obsolete antiquated
timid shy, afraid, cowardly, spineless, apprehensive, fainthearted
Timor
capitol Dili
country Portugal, Indonesia
Timor coin avo
timorous meek, bashful, submissive
tin can, coat, metal, preserve
box trummel
fish torpedo
foil for mirrors tain
pert. to stannic
symbol Sn, see also Quick Reference List
tinamou bird, yutu
tinean moth
tined, three tridentate
tinge cast, color, shade, trace, nuance
Tinker Bell
character in Peter Pan
author Barrie
tin lizzie car, jalopy, automobile
tinsel glitter, pretense, decoration, ostentation
tint hue, tone, pigment
tintinnabulum bell, rhyme
tip cap, top, barb, clue, hint, lean, tilt, crest, point, topple, vertex, sharpen, pinnacle
off hint, warn
over upset, capsize
pen's neb, nib
tippet fur, cape, amice, scarf, muffler
tipple drink, guzzle, beverage
tipsy high, blind, drunk, juiced, loaded, intoxicated
tirade lecture, diatribe, denunciation, vilification
Tirane capital of Albania
tire bore, weary, disgust, exhaust, fatigue, lose interest
tire wheel
inventor Dunlop, Thomson

tired beat, weary, pooped, sleepy, tuckered
Tiresias seer, prophet, soothsayer
blinded by Athena
character in Odysseus, Oedipus Rex
father Everes
grandfather Udaeus
home Thebes
mother Chariclo
Tisamenus seer
father Orestes
killed by Heraclidae
leader of Boeotians
mother Hermione
tissue fat, bast, meat, flesh, fabric
comb. form hist(o)
connecting tendon, stroma
decay caries, atrophy
hardening sclerosis
pert. to telar
weblike tela, plexus
titan giant, mogul
Titan Coeus, Creus, Crius, Cronus, Iapetus, Oceanus, Hyperion
female (Titaness) Rhea, Theia, Phoebe, Tethys, Themis, Mnemosyne
father Uranus
mother Ge, Gaea, Gaia
Titania fairy, queen
husband Oberon
titanic huge, mammoth, herculean, monumental
Titanium see also Quick Reference List
principal ore ilmenite
symbol Ti
tithe tax, tenth
pert. to decimal
titi monkey
Titian Tiziano Vecellio, artist, painter
born Italy
works Pieta, The Rape of Europa, The Pesaro Madonna, The Venus of Urbino, Bacchus and Ariadne, The Young Englishman, Venus and the Lute Player, The Assumption of the Virgin
titillate charm, allure, excite, tickle, provoke
titivate tidy, spruce

titlark bird, pipit
title deed, assign, notice, record, placard, appelation
  ecclesiastic dom, fra, abba
  feminine dame, hanum, milady
  masculine sir, master, mister
  personage peer, noble
  pert. to titular
titmouse nun, bird, yaup, tomtit
tittup caper, prance
Titus Andronicus
  author William Shakespeare
  daughter Lavinia
  queen Tamora
Tivoli
  ancient Roman name Tibur
tizzy tailspin
Tlepolemus
  father Hercules
  killed by Sarpedon
  mother Astyochia
tmesis diacope
TNT trotyl, dynamite, explosive
to ad, for, into, with, closed, toward, against, together
  be esse (Lat.), etre (Fr.)
  comb. form ac, ad
  come behind, pending
  each his own suum cique
  that time until
  the end af
  the point ad rem
  this hereto
  wit viz, namely, scilicet
toa warrior
toad bufo, frog, pipa, bufonid
  fish sa(r)po
  flax flaxweed, fluellen, gallwort
  genus Bufo, Hyla
  group of knot
  largest agua
  order anuria
  stone bufonite
  stool canker, fungus
  tongueless genus aglossa
  tree hyla
toady fawn, zany, earwig, flunky, lackey,

mucker, placebo, bootlick, parasite, backscratcher
toast toss, brown, grill, rouse, cheers, pledge, salute, cheerio, preface, wassail
  and ale swig
  oneself leep
tobacco capa, plant, burley, vuelta, caporal, knaster, latakia, uppowoc
  ash dottel, dottle
  dried tobacum
  coarse caporal
  in ropes bogie
  Indian gagroot, pukeweed, eyebright
  juice ambeer
  kiln oast
  left in pipe dottel
  low grade shag
  mild return
  paste goracco
  Persian shiraz, tumbek
  Peruvian sana
  plant, heart of leaf ratoon
  pouch doss
  pulverized snuff
  shreds shag
  -smoke hater misocapnist
  worker looper, leafboy, leafgirl
Tobacco Road
  author Erskine Caldwell
  character Ada, Love, Dude, Ellie, Pearl, Jeeter
tobbogan coast, sleigh, cariole
Tobias
  father Tobit
  grandfather Tobiel
  wife Sara
Tocqueville, Alexis de author
  work Democracy in America
tocsin bell, alarm, alarum, warning
today now, this day, this time, on this day, the present, modern times, in this day and age
  pert. to diurnal
toddle waddle, wobble
toddler tot, tyke, child, youngster
tode boat, haul, sled

to-do ado, fuss, stir, work, bustle, flurry, hoopla

toe obey, digit, phalanx
  comb. form dactyl
  great hallux
  pert. to digital
  plate shod
  small minimus

to err is human errare humanum est (Lat.)

toff nob, dandy, swell

toga garb, gown, robe, garment

together mass, union, united, (con)jointly, married, mutually, accompanying
  prefix com, con, syn

toil grub, hack, muck, plod, work, labor, drudge, strive, industry, elbow grease, apply oneself

toiler peon, swot, prole, slave, worker, servant, workhorse, wage earner

toilet can, loo, john, commode, crapper, lavatory, outhouse, rest room, water closet
  case etui, etwee
  water cologne, perfume

toilsome hard, sweaty, arduous

token gift, proof, signal, auspice, memento, evidence, keepsake, signacle
  affection amoret, keepsake
  luck charm, hansel
  respect salute
  victory palm, laurel

Tokyo Eastern capital
  former name Edo, Yedo

Tola Hebrew judge
  father Issachar

tolerable okay, so-so, livable, patible, bearable, passable

tolerance fairness, patience, compassion, forbearance

tolerant easy, patient, lenient, liberal, placable, permissive

to life le(c)hayim (Heb.)

Tolkein, J.R.R. author
  works The Hobbit, Silmarillon, The Lord of the Rings

toll fee, tax, duty, jowl, loss, pike, knell, peage, caphar, excise, keelage, passage, pierage, destruction, annihilation

tolliker dummy

Tolstoy, Leo author
  works War and Peace, Anna Karenina, Resurrection, The Kreutzer Sonata, The Death of Ivan Ilyitch

Toltec
  anc. capital Tula
  tribe Itza

toluene diluent

tolypeutine apar, armadillo

Tom
  of Lincoln bell
  Thumb dwarf
  Tulliver's river Floss

tomahawk hatchet, neolith

tomato berry, cherry
  sauce ketchup, marinara
  soup gazpacho

tomb crypt, mastaba, catacomb, mausoleum, sepulcher, resting place
  cave speos
  church sacellum
  for bones of dead ossuary
  Moslem tabut
  prehistoric kurgan
  saints shrine

tomboy girl, romp, gamine, hoyden, madcap, tomrig, strumpet

tomcat gib, tommy, podger, womanizer

tomfoolery play, antics, nonsense, high jinks, skylarking, foolishness, lollygagging

Tom Jones
  author Henry Fielding
  character Tom, Betty, Jenny, George, Sophia, Square, Thwackum, Allworthy, Fitzpatrick

tommyrot bull, crap, hooey, baloney, hogwash, rubbish, balderdash

tomorrow manana (Sp.), morrow, the future

Tom Sawyer
  aunt Polly
  author Mark Twain, Samuel Clemens
  brother Sid

girl Becky Thatcher
pal Injun Joe, Huckleberry Finn
ton
  abbrev. t
tone(s) key, cast, feel, color, shade, sound,
    energy, attitude
  artificial unit nil
  broken crack
  comb. form phon(o)
  deep bass
  dominant animus
  down mute, tame, soften, subdue
  high-pitched pip
  key keynote
  lack mute, atony, silence
  loud forte
  low semisoun
  monotonous drone
  nasal twang
  rhythmical cadence
  series octav
  significant accent
  up brace
tongs server, forceps, grampus
tongue gab, chib, flap, organ, prate,
    dialect, language, lorriker
  bell clapper
  bone hyoid
  comb. form glosso
  disease agrom
  fish sole
  Jew's-harp tang
  -lash scold
  -less aglossal
  -like process ligula
  mollusc radula
  part of bud, uvula, fauces, lingua, septum
  pert. to lingual
  piveted pawl
  shoe flap, kilty, kiltie
  -tied mute, silent, flustered
  tip corona
  wagon neap, pole
tonic do, aloe, keep, prime, bracer, sambul,
    pick-me-up
tonsil gland
  inflammation quinsy

tonsure cut, trim, spot
too also, in addition to
  bad alas
  Fr. trop
  late tardy
  much excess, nimiety
  soon premature
tool(s) dupe, pawn, means, device, gadget,
    puppet, stooge, cat's paw, machine,
    utensil, vehicle, apparatus, implement
  ability to use chrestic
  bookbinder gouge
  carpenter adz, awl, peg, saw, adze, nail,
    rasp, vise, auger, edger, gouge, lathe,
    plane, ruler, screw, bodkin, chisel,
    hammer, router, sander, screwdriver
  cleaving frow, hatchet
  cutting adz(e), die, burr, file, razor,
    hatchet, scissors
  drilling bit, drill, countersink
  edge bit
  engraver burin
  farmer ax, axe, hoe, plow, rake, spade,
    cradle, harrow, plough, scythe, seeder,
    shovel, sickle, tiller, trowel, hayfork,
    cultivator
  flat spatula
  kit etui, chest
  marble worker fraise
  mechanic zax, file, vise, bevel, lathe,
    pliers, crowbar, calipers
  mining gad, pick
  theft ratten
too little dearth, scarcity, shortage,
    deficient, insufficient
too many de trop (Fr.)
too much excess, profuse, overflow,
    plethora, inundation
toot honk, blast, trumpet, wingding
tooth cog, cusp, fang, tusk, molar,
    grinder, incisor, cuspid, serration
  canine cuspid
  cavity caries
  comb. form odonto
  grinding surface mensa
  having but one monodont
  less edentate, edentulous

molar wang
part cusp, pulp, root, dentin, trigon
projecting buck, snag
pulp nerve
sockets alveoli
toothed serrated
top cap, tip, toy, apex, culm, head, cover, crest, excel, trump, surmount
altar mensa
  box coupon, proof of purchase
  coat overcoat
  hat gibus, stovepipe
  hill knoll
  ornament epi, finial
  roof deck
  spin with fingers teetotum
  thundercloud incus
  wave comb
topaz pycnite, pycnium
  sign fidelity
tope rig, boat, wren, dheri, drink, shark, stupa
topi cap, helmet
topic item, text, hobby, thema, gambit, matter, subject
  of discourse theme
topical timely, current localized, particular, contemporary
topographic terrain
topple tip, tile, wobble
tops aces, A-one, best
  opposite pits (sl.)
topsy-turvy messy, chaotic, inverted, disorderly
tor crag, peak, pinnacle
tora law, tetel, Torah, antelope, law of Moses
torch lamp, lunt, pine, blaze, brand, flare
  -bearer keryx, linkman, daduchus
torii gateway
torment rag, try, bait, bale, fret, pine, rack, curse, tease, harass, anguish, bedevil, perplex, cruciate, lacerate
  extreme agony
tormenter bully, tyrant, browbeater
tormina colic, pains
tornado storm, cyclone, twister, typhoon
  belt Midwest

torpedo ray, fish, shell, missile, tin fish, projectile
  sl. gunman, criminal
torpid dull, lazy, numb, inert, sodden, languid, comatose
torpor coma, sleep, lethargy
torrent flow, rush, stream
torrid sultry, austral, boiling
tort libel, wrong
torte dobos
tortilla (Mex.) taco, shell, burrito, tostada
tortoise emyd, bekko, turtle, terrapin
  genus Emys
  marsh gopher
  pert. to chelonian
  shell carapace
torture pain, abuse, agony, trial, harrow, ordeal, distress, suffering, punishment
  device rack, wheel
tory bandit, outlaw, loyalist, conservative
toss lob, cast, hike, pass, shag, tout, chuck, fling, heave, pitch, throw, dandle
  about thrash
  aside bandy
  coin sky
tosspot sot, drunkard
tota grivet, monkey
total sum, tab, tale, count, gross, summa, whole, entire, perfect, absolute, complete, surmount
totalitarian fascist, tyrannous, dictatorial, unrepresentative
totally good, wholly
totem post xat
to the letter exact, precise
To the Lighthouse
  author Virginia Woolf
  character Prue, James, Camilla, Lily Briscoe, Mr. Charmichael
to the point direct, explicit, pertinent
to this extent quoad hoc (Lat.)
toto baby
Toto Wizard of Oz
  author Frank L. Baum
totter reel, sway, wobble, vacillate
toucan bird, toco, aracari

touch pet, abut, join, meet, stir, sway, vein, flair, pinch, rouse, shave, style, taste, caress, fondle, stroke, contact, texture, converge, deal with
  comb. form tac
  examine by palpate
  -hole vent
  organ palp, feeler, finger, antenna
  pert. to haptic, tactile
  -stone test, basanite, criterion
  -wood punk, tinder, amadou
  pert. to agaric
tough hard, mean, wily, cruel, rigid, rough, solid, knotty, rugged, savage, trying, callous, complex, hoodlum, onerous, ruffian, vicious, exacting, toilsome, difficult, obstinate, formidable, perplexing, bewildering, troublesome
Toulouse-Lautrec, Henri painter
  born Albi, France
works Friends, The Inspection, At the Moulin Rouge, Au Salon de la Rue des Moulins, Jane Avril at the Jardin de Paris, Cirque Fernando the Equestrienne, In the Parlor at the Rue des Moulins, The English Girl at Le Star Le Havre, La Goulue Entering the Moulin Rouge
toupee wig, carpet, peruke, hairpiece
  sl. rug
tour trip, swing, visit, junket, safari, voyage, journey, excursion
  de force feat, stunt
  of duty station
tourist tripper, voyager, traveler, sightseer, globetrotter
tournament game, match, jousts, tourney, competition
tourneur dealer
tourniquet stanch, twister
tousle mess, rumple, disarray
tow lug, drag, haul, pull, stupe
towai tree, birch, kamahi
toward into, gainward
  center centrad
  comb. form ac, ad, af, ag al, ap, at, il, im, in, intro, pros
  one side aslant

  the end sf
  the head anterior
  the rear aback, backward
  the right dextrad
  the side laterad
  the stern after
tower rise, soar, babel, spire, mount, pylon, spire, belfry, castle, exceed, minaret
  bell carillon
  Buddhist tope
  coke scrubber
  fort spur
  glacial ice serac
  Indian/Moslem minar(et)
  medieval donjon
  pyramidal sik(h)ara, sikhra
  sentinel guerite
  signal bantayan
  small turret
  small round rondel
  Spain atalaya
  spherical cupola, steeple
  wind badgir
towering eminent, ambitious
towhee bird, finch, chewink
town ham, camp, city, stad, toon, bayan, brugh, burgh, place, stand, stead, ville, ciudad (Sp.), pueblo, borough
  desolated gubat, ghost town
  fortified burg
  main street main drag
  map plat
  pert. to civic, urban, oppidan
  small village, whistle-stop
  unimportant podunk
  walled chester
town hall cabildo, rathaus (Ger.), stadhouse
townsman towny, burgher, citizen, inhabitant
Toxeus
  father Oeneus
  killed by Oeneus
  mother Althaea
toxin venom, poison
  alkaloid venom, brucin
  protein abrin
toxophilite Eros, Cupid, archer

toy play, tiny, flirt, bauble, trinket, plaything
  bear teddy
  stiltlike pogo stick
  stringed yoyo
trabea toga
trace run, cast, echo, hint, lick, mark, show, sign, ghost, print, shade, touch, derive, sketch, surmise, vestige, simulacrum
tracer outliner, searcher
trachea artery, windpipe
trachyte domite
track rut, way, clue, draw, hunt, lane, page, path, race, rail, road, trail, course, runway
  animal pug (mark), spoor
  deer slot, spoor
  railroad lead, spur, stub, trunk, siding, approach, backbone, mainline
  running flat, cinders
  ship wake
trackman spiker
tract area, flat, zone, clime, coast, drive, field, patch, barony, extent, region, enclave, terrain, district, province
  boggy morass
  dry searing
  forestless stepp
  sandy den, dene, lande
  shrubby monte
  waterless thirst
traction draft, friction
tractor cat, mule, crawler, bulldozer, caterpillar
  trailer rig, semi
trade job, coup, deal, sell, swap, craft, barter, metier (Fr.), calling, faculty, business, exchange
  agreement/association cartel
  -man huckster (sl.)
  -mark brand
  unlawful graft, contraband
tradition story, cabala, custom, legend, sunnah, halakah, folklore, convention
traditional old, usual, typical, classic, ancestral, established
traduce slur, defame, malign, scandal, slander

traffic deal, doings, bootleg, commuters, enterprise, transactions
tragacanth gum, tree, shrub
tragedy grief, misery, sorrow, calamity, disaster
  muse Melpomene
tragic sad, fatal, deadly, woeful, dramatic, grievous, lamentable, heartbreaking
tragopan fowl, pheasant
trail pad, drag, foil, hunt, path, slot, blaze, crawl, route, shadow
  blazer leader, pioneer, forerunner, pathfinder, trendsetter
  fish loom
  marker cairn
  wagon rudloff
train aim, line, focus, teach, direct, school, series, cortege, practice, rehearse, discipline
  fast limited
  overhead el(evated)
  slow local
  underground tube, metro, subway
trainee boot, cadet, rookie, apprentice
traipse wald, tramp, sashay
trait mark, vein, charm, knack, element
traitor judas, apostate, squealer
trample crush, stomp, flatter, run over
tranquil quiet, serene, pacific, restful, peaceful
tranquilize calm, still, pacify, soothe, appease
transact do, conduct
transcend exceed, surpass
transcribe copy, exscribe
transept plage, porch
transfer cede, deed, give, pass, carry, cross, grant, shift, change, switch, cession, traduce, virement
  design decal
  dye exhaust
  energy flow
  heat convect
  legal deed, lease
  pigment flush
transfix dart, stake, thrill

transform shift, change, convert, catalyze, heterize
transformer dimmer, variac, booster
transgress err, sin, overgo, violate, infringe, trespass
transient passing, fugitive
transition shift, passage
transitive active
translate make, wend, render, convert, interpret
translucent lucid, lucent
transmission message, passage, broadcast, conveyance, transmittal, communication
transmit emit, send, convey, impart, forward, describe
transparent clear, lucid, obvious, diaphanous
  comb. form hyal(o)
  mineral mica, quartz
  opp. opaque
transparency slide
transport bear, bus, pass, send, ship, ferry, carriage
  logs bob
  ore slush
transpose reverse
transverse cross, oblique
transvestism eonism
trap coy, get, pit, set, fall, hook, lace, nail, wait, catch, leash, plant, snatch
  bird scrape
  feet caltrops
  poker sandbag
  rat clam
  salmon putt
  sand bunker
Trappist monk, Merton
trapshooting skeet
  target (clay) pigeon
trash rot, junk, raff, trag, dreck, waste, kitsch, paltry, refuse, garbage
trashy cheap, paltry, shoddy, riffraff
travel mush, trip, wend, cruise, voyage, journey, travail, traverse
  across snow mush
  aimlessly wander
  along ground taxi

  at random drift
  back and forth commute
  by foot hike, perambulate
  fast streak
  pert. to viatic
  through woods bushwack
traveler farer, ganger, kilroy, sailor, viator, drummer, pilgrim, trekker, waygoer, argonaut, explorer, voyageur
  group caravan
traverse deny, move, pass, cross, range, refute
  rear parados
travesty parody, satire, burlesque
trawl net, fish, troll
tray board, float, scale, susan, server, coaster
  crumb voider
  type galley
treacherous dirty, false, punic, fickle, yellow, imposing
treacle syrup, remedy, molasses
tread pad, foot, step, track, defoul, footing, footstep
  heavily trample
  on foil
  warily pussyfoot
treason revolt, sedition
treasure covet, hoard, prize, store, value, wealth
Treasure Island
  author Robert Louis Stevenson
  character Ben Gunn, Smollett, Dr. Livesey, Jim Hawkins, Long John Silver
treasurer banker, bursar, purser, financier, accountant, minister of finance, secretary of the treasurer
treat joy, gift, give, apply, cover, favor, grant, imbue, attend, doctor, thrill, delight, gratification
  badly abuse, scorn
  carelessly bandy
  clouds seed
  flour agenize
  illness pomster
  lightly palter

steel harvey
tenderly pet, TLC
treatise book, thesis, discourse, exposition
  elementary donet, primer, grammar
  on fruit trees pomona
  preface isagoge
treatment cure, behavior, demeanor, entreaty
  bad misusage
  cold freeze
  contemptuous spurn
  dire dole
  severe rough
  medical iatria
treaty deal, pact, compact, entente, formal agreement
tree forest, timber, boscage
  Abyssinia, dried flower cusso
  acacia babul, cooba(h), siris
    Austral. myall
  alder arn
    genus Alnus
  algarroba carob, calden
  allspice pimento
  apple shea, sorb
    genus Malus
  aromatic clusia, labiate
  babul garad
  bark tan, crut
  bay laurel
  bee linden
  beech buck, fagus, myrtle
    Chile roble
  birch betula
  black gum nyssa, tupelo
    haw sloe
  Borneo bilian
  branches ranage
  Buddhist sacred pipal
  cabbage angelim
  candlenut ama, kukul, bankul
  Ceylon tala
  citrus shaddock
  coffee chicot
  comb. form dendri(o)
  coral dapdap
  cottonwood alamo

cursed warytree
custard atta, sweetsom
dead runt, snag, rampick, rampike
decayed dotterel
devil dita
dogwood genus Cornus
drupe bearing bito
dwarf bush, scrub, arbuscle
elm genus Ulmus, Celtis
eucalyptus gum, yate
evergreen fir, yew, holm, pine, holly, olive
  New Zealand tarata
fabaceous agati
family stemma, descent, pedigree
fir balsam
  genus Abies
forgetfulness lotus
fruit cordon
geneological arbor jesse
gingerbread dum, doom
glasswort jume, kali
grove tope
Guinea akee
hickory species carya, pecan
honeyberry genip
in stream sawyer
left in cutting holdover
-less wold
light wood balsa
lime bass, teil
live oak encina
locust kowhai, courbaril
  pod carob
loquat biwa
maple genus Acer
moss lichen, usnea
moth egger
oil ebo(e), poon, tung, mahwa
olive genus Olea
on wall rider
papaya carica, pawpaw
pea agati
pear bosc, pyrus, seckel, bartlett
  prickly nopal
pert. to arboreal
pine ocate

plum genus Prunus
  wild Sloe
poisonous bunk, upas, sassy, hemlock
poplar abele, alamo, aspen
rain zaman, genisaro
rowan ash, sorb
rows stich
rubber ule, para, caucho
sandalwood algum
sassafras ague
science silvics
shea karite
stately palm
swamp alder, maple
taxus genus Yew
toad genus Hyla
trained espalier
trunk bole, caber
willow osier
  genus Itea
trees
  clear of assart, deforest
  clump of toll, stell
  growth of sylvage
  in forest stand
trefoil arch, medic, plant, clover
trelliswork pergola
tremble quake, shake, wiver, didder, dither,
  falter, thrill, totter, tremor, stagger, shudder
trench moat, sike, bayou, ditch, drain,
  coffer, furrow, gullet
  below forest fire gutter
  irrigation float, sugsloot
  embankment drain, parados
  knife bayonet
trenchant keen, sharp, incisive
trend bias, flow, tone, sense, current,
  fashion, movement, tendency
trendy in, chic, modish, stylish,
  fashionable
tres very (Fr.)
tress hair, lock, man, strand, ringlet
trial bout, doom, test, cross
  inconclusive mistrial
  pert. to empiric
  severe ordeal
  site venue

triangle trigon(e), trinity, instrument
  draw circle in escribe
  heraldry giron
  insert gore
  -shaped deltoid, scalene, isoceles,
    equilateral
  side leg
tribe clan, sept, group
  emblem (Indian) totem
  head chief
  New Zealand ati
  Roman Latin, Sabine, Etruscan
trichord lyre
tricks
  device gimmick
  win all capot
Trieste
  measure orna, orne
trifle bit, dally, flirt, palter, dessert
  insignificant fico, bagatelle
trifoliate three-leaved
  plant clover, shamrock
triglyphs, space between metope
trigo wheat
trigonometric figure co(sine)
Trilby
  author Daphne duMaurier
  character Svengali
trillion (comb. form) trega
Trinidad
  capital Port-of Spain
  fish guppy
  music calypso
  tree mora
trio
  fictional Musketeers
  myth fates, furies, graces
  one of a
    hope, faith, charity
    Tom, Dick, Harry
    Athos, Aramis, Porthos
triplet(s) tercet, siblings
  one trine
Tripoli
  coin piastre
  measure dra(a)
  ruler dey

trippet cam
triptych panel, (writing) tablet
  wing volet
trismus lockjaw, tetanus
Tristram, Tristan
  beloved Isolt, Iseult, Isolde
  uncle Mark
  villain Melot
trite expression cliché, bromide
triton eft, newt, satellite (of Neptune)
trivet knife, stand, stool, tripod
trochilus scotia, warbler, hummingbird
trochlea pully
Troilus and Cressida
  character Ajax, Helen, Paris, Hector,
    Nestor
  father Priam
  mother Hecuba
Trojan Ilian, Darden
  country Troy
  epic Iliad
  hero Hector, Aeneas
  horse builder Epeus
  king Priam
  war cause Helen
  warrior Agenor
trombone sackbut
  mouthpiece bocal
  part bell, slide
trona urao
troops army, battery, soldiers
  group band, squad, brigade
  quarters etape, barracks
  reserve echelon
tropical hot, torrid
  disease yaws, malaria, beriberi
  fish opah
  herb loofa
  tree palm, balsa, guara
tropo (comb. form) turn
Tros
  son Ilus
trotyl TNT
trough hod, basin, feeder, channel, conduit
  inclined chute
  mining sluice
Troy Ilion, Ilium, Troas

defender Aeneas
founder Ilus
Gr. general Agamemnon
king Paris, Priam
myth. Tros
pert. to Iliac
truck van, dolly, lorry, wagon, pickup
  trailer rig, semi
truffle fungus, earthnut, mushroom
trumpet horn, bugle, clarion
  bell codon
  belt baldric
  blare tantara
  call sennet
  caller Gabriel
  mouth codon
  muffler mute
  shell triton
trumpet-creeper plant, tecoma
trumpeter bird, fish, agami, musician
  perch mado
trunk bole, stem, caber, torso, coffer
  animal's soma, snout
  tree burl
trusty convict
truth
  drug pentothal
  goddess Maat
  personification Una
  self-evident axiom
tsamba flour, barley
tsetse fly mau, kivu, muscid
  disease caused by nagana, encephalitis
  genus Glossina
tsine ox, banteng
tub vat, bath, skeel, firkin
  -handled cowl
  wooden soe
tuba mouthpiece bocal
Tubal
  father Japheth
  grandfather Noah
tuber eddo, jalap, potato, truffle
  orchid salep
Tuesday
  god Tiu, Tyr
  Shrove Mardi Gras

tuft wisp, crest, tussock
- **bird's head** cop
- **botany** coma
- **feathers** alula
- **pert. to** comal

Tuileries palace, gardens

tule bulrush
- **genus** Scirpus
- **root** wapatoo

tumbleweed bugseed, pigweed, amaranth

tumor yaw, moro, growth, keloid, swelling
- **comb. form** coele
- **fleshy** sarcoma
- **glandular** adenoma
- **small** wen, papilla
- **suffix** oma

tun vat, cask, drink
- **half** pipe
- **shell/fossil** dolite

tung oil product varnish

tungsten wolfram
- **chemical symbol** W
- **ore** cal

Tunis, Tunisia
- **cape** Bon
- **capital** Tunis
- **measure** zah, cafiz
- **money** dinar
- **ruler** dey, pasha
- **weight** rotl, artel, kantar

tup ram, sheep, mallet

tupelo gum, tree, nyssa

tur pea, goat

turban cap, pata, mandil
- **cloth** lungi
- **flower** tulip

turbot flatfish

turdine bird thrush
- **pert. to** turdidae

turkey
- **buzzard** vulture
- **female** hen
- **male** tom
- **sl.** failure
- **trot** dance
- **wild** bustard
- **young** po(u)lt

Turkey, Turkish, Turk Porte, Tartar, Osmanli, Ottoman
- **boat** mahone
- **cap** fez, calpac
- **cape** Baba
- **capital** Ankara
- **carpet** Smyrna
- **coin** lira, para, asper, iklik, beshlik
- **fermented drink** boza, airan
- **garment** colman
- **harem** serai
  - **ladies** kadein
- **measure** kilo, almud, parmack
- **name** Ali, Kemal
- **non-Moslem** raia
- **palace** serai
- **peasant** raya
- **pipe** chibouk
- **prayer rug** melas
- **rug** konia
- **sword** yataghan
- **weight** mane, roti, maund, cantar, chequi

turn
- **aside** divert, swerve
- **frontward** obvert
- **inside out** evert, invert
- **left** haw, port
- **out of course** veer, deviate
- **over** keel, spill
- **right** gee, starboard
- **to side** splay

turnip swede, rutabaga, vegetable
- **-shaped** napiform
- **wild** rape, navew

turnstone bird, plover, redleg

turpentine oleoresin
- **resin** alk, pitch, galipot
- **tree** pine, tarata

turtle cooter, jurara, terrapin
- **back** carapace
- **freshwater** emyd
- **genus** Emys, Chelone
- **giant** arrau
- **marine** caretta
- **snapping** torup

Tuscany
- **city** Pisa

island Elba
river Arno
tut hush, king, rebuke
tutta all, whole
tuyere tew, pipe, nozzle, opening
twelfth part uncia
twenty corge, kappa, score
  comb. form icosa
  pert. to icosian
  years vicennial
twice bi(s), doubly
  prefix di, dis
twilight dusk, evening, obscure, nightfall
  pert. to crepuscular
twin dual, pair, counterpart
  one gemel
  Siamese Eng, Chang
  stars Castor, Gemini, Pollux
twist warp, wind, dance, gnarl, whirl, contort
  inward intort
  to and fro wrench, wriggle
twisted cam, (a)wry, complex, tortile
  cord torsade
  spirally torse
two
  and a half inches nail
  -bit (sl.) cheap, quarter
  -celled bolocular
  colors dichromic
  consisting of dyad, bivalent
  -edged ancipital
  -faced false
    god Janus
  -fingered bidigitate
  -fold dual, double
  -footed biped
  -forked bifurcated
  -handed bimanual, ambidextrous
    animals bimana
  -headed ancipital
  of a kind pair, brace
  -pronged bident
  -sided bilateral, hypocritical
  -spot deuce
  -time cheat
Tyche fortuna, goddess
tylopod camel

type kind, sort, genre, model, pattern
  face kern, runic
  kind pica, agate, elite, ionic, pearl, ronde, minion
  metal piece quad
  part face, foot, nick
  script ronde
  set font
  slanted italic
  style ionic, runic, caslon, script
  tray galley
typewriter
  roller platen
  type pica, elite
typographical error typo, erratum
Tyr Tiu, Zeus, Jupiter
  parent Odin
tyre milk, wine, curds
Tyre
  king Belus, Hiram
  prince Pericles
  princess Dido
tzigane gypsy

U

U eu
  -shaped bone hyoid
  -turn hairpin
uang beetle
Ubangi tributary Uele
ubermensch overman, superman
uberous fruitful, abundant
uca crab
Ucayali tributary Apurimac
udder
  part teat, nipple, quarter
  product milk
Uganda
  capital Entebbe, Kampala
  cattle ankoli
  kingdom Buganda
ughten dawn, dusk, twilight
ugly
  duckling swan

sight eyesore
symbol toad
Ugrian Avar
uhlan German, lancer, soldier
uintaite asphalt
uitlander foreigner
ukase decree
Ukraine, Ukrainian
  assembly rada
  capital Kiev
  coin grivna, schagiv
  dance gopak, kazatzky
  holy city Kiev
  native Cossack
  seaport Odessa
Ulalume
  author Edgar Allan Poe
Ulan Bator Urga, Khoto
ulcer noma, sore, canker
  kind peptic
ule caucho
  fluid latex
ulema mufti
ulmus elm
ulna bone, cubitus
  end ancon
Ulster (over)coat, county
  lake Erne
ult ultimo, ultimate
Ultima Thule Ireland
ultra beyond, extreme, radical
  modern avant-garde
  nationalist chauvinist
ultramarine blue, pigment
ulu knife
Ulysses Odysseus
  author James Joyce
  character Bloom, Molly
  country Ithaca
  dog Argos
  enchantress Circe
  enemy Poseidon
  father Laertes
  friend Mentor
  mother Anticlea
  plant moly

  name given to Cyclops Noman
  son Telemachus
  voyage odyssey
  wife Penelope
umbelliferous plant carrot, parsley
umber shade, pigment
  bird umbrette
umbo beak, boss, knob
umbra fish, ghost, shade, shadow
umbrella gamp, cover, chatta, screen, parasol, bumbershoot (Br.)
  cloth gloria
  -like flower umbel
  -like fungus mushroom
  -like thing canopy
  of leaves talipot
  part rib
  tree magnolia
Umbria
  town Assisi
  river Tevere
umiak boat, canoe, kayak
umlaut dieresis
  in linguistics mutation
UN FAO, IDA, WHO, GATT, ICAO, UNRRA, agency, UNESCO
una catboat
unaccented lene, atonic, stressless
  vowel sound schwa
unaging eternal, youthful
Unalaskan Aleut
unalloyed pure, genuine
unanimously una voce
unau sloth
unbleached blae, ecru
  fabric beige
unbeliever pagan, atheist, heretic, infidel, agnostic
unborn
  in uterus fetus
unbosom tell, reveal
unbranched antler dag
unbranded cow maverick
unburnt brick adobe
unbury exhume
uncanonical apocryphal

unchaste bawdy, wanton, lasicivious
uncia coin, inch, ounce, twelfth
unciform hook-shaped
uncle eam, oom, unk, nunks, pawnbroker (sl.)
  cry yield, surrender
  pert. to avuncular
Uncle Remus
  author Harris
  character Brer Fox, Brer Rabbit
Uncle Tom's Cabin
  author Harriet Beecher Stowe
  characters Eva, Eliza, Topsy, Legree
unco news, very, great, weird, notable,
   remarkable
uncoined metal bullion
unconfirmed news tip, rumor, gossip,
   hearsay
unconscious torpid, mindless, inanimate
  render stun
  sl. out, blotto
  state coma(tose), swoon, apsychia,
   narcosis
unconventional one rebel, Bohemian
unction oil, unguent, ointment
  give extreme anele
und so weiter (Ger.) etc., et cetera
unde, in heraldry wavy
under
  obligation bound, indebted
  par ill, sick, (golf) term
  prefix hyp, sub
underage minor, immature
underbrush covert, abature, thicket
undercroft crypt
underground hidden, secret
  being dwarf, gnome, troll
  burial place crypt, catacomb
  drain sewer
  fighter maquis, sapper, partisan
  fungus truffle, earthnut, tuckahoe
  passage tunnel
  railway tube, metro, subway
  worker sandhog
underlying principle elixir
underpinning, sl. legs, supports

undersea
  boat U-boat, submarine
  eye periscope
undershirt jersey, skivvy, singlet
understanding nous, entre, sense, accord
  between nations entente
understatement litotes
undertaking venture, guarantee
  written cautio(nes)
undertow eddy, riptide, vortex
underwater submarine
  apparatus scuba, caisson, snorkel
  captain Nemo
  explorer Piccard, Cousteau
  ledge reef
  missile torpedo
  plant benthos
  prefix hyp(o)
  sound detector sofar, sonar
  swimmer frogman
underworld
  boatman Charon
  deity Bran, Pluto, Osiris, Dispater
  goddess Belili, Hecate, Trivia
  king Yama
  pert. to chthonic
  queen Hel
  river Styx, Lethe, Acheron
  watchdog Cerberus
undeveloped latent
  quality potential
undine nymph, sylph, seamaid
undressed skin kip, pelt
Undset, Sigrid Norweigan novelist
undulant fever brucellosis
undulating object wave, worm, snake,
   ripple
uneasy stiff, fidgety, restive
  feeling malaise
unequal impar, uneven, irregular
  angled scalene
  comb. form aniso
  condition odds
uneven erose, rough, spotty, varying
  condition asperity
  contest lopsided

unexamined a priori
unexpressed tacit, unsaid
unfading flower amaranth, everlasting
unfermented grapejuice stum
unfledged callow
  bird eyas, nestling
ungodly sinful, dreadful, impious
ungual growth claw, hoof, nail, talon
unicellular
  animal amoeba, protozoan
  plant spore, bacterium
unicorn lin, reem, monocero
  fish unie, filefish
  whale narwhal
uniform even, level, outfit, steady
  cord fourragére, aiguillette
  in color flat, flot
  servant's livery
  shoulder ornament epaulet(te)
uninflected aptotic
unio mussel
union fusion, merger, alliance, marriage, coalition
  business cartel, syndicate, partnership
  "jack" flag (Brit.)
  member cardholder
  merchants hanse
  trade guild
unison concord, harmony
  sing/utter in chorus
unit one, item, piece
  caloric therm
  electrical ohm, volt, watt, ampere
  of energy erg, joule
  of light lux, lumen
  of pressure barad, pound
  of resistance to ohm
  of value point
  wire mil
United States see America
  presidents and Indians see Quick Reference List
univalve snail, mollusk
universe
  of the cosmic

university
  grounds campus
  official dean, bursar, regent, president
  professorship chair, tenure
unknown unco, obscure
  person John/Jane Doe
unlawful illegal, illicit
  goods contraband
  importing smuggle
  to distill bootleg (liquor)
  to hunt poach(ing)
  to intrude trespass
unleavened azymous
unmarried
  law sole
unpopularity odium
unreasoning devotion fetish
unredeemed territory irredenta
unrelated fremd (Yiddish)
unscrupulous person cheat, crook, swindler
untamed state wild, ferity
untanned hide kip, pelt
untidy person pig, slob, sloven
  place pigsty, mare's nest
until till, unto, up to, before, pending
unto till, until
untouchable leper, distant, sudra
untreated raw, virgin
unvarying sound drone, monotone
unvoiced surd, muted
unwonted rare, unusual
unwritten blank
  but understood tacit
  law custom, tradition
up over, above, aloft
  and coming promising
  and moving astir, awake
  in the air asea, unsettled
  in arms angry, irate, miffed
  prefix ana
  -to-the-minute red-hot
Updike, John
  novel Centaur, Couples, Rabbit Redux

upholstery stuffing flock
upon atop, over, up and over
  prefix ep(i)
upper bunk, ramp, berth, superior
  air ether, ozone
  case capital
  crust elite
  limit ceiling
  lips flews
upright good, just, piano, honest
  comb. form ortho
  support jamb, stud
upscuddle quarrel
Uracus asp, cobra
urane rat, curare
Urania muse, Aphrodite
  pert. to celestial
  son Hymen
  sphere astronomy
Uranus
  children Rhea, Titan, Cronus, Furies,
    Saturn, Cyclops
  discoverer John Herschel
  moon Ariel, Oberon, Titania, Umbriel
  mother/wife Ge, Gaea, Gaia
  satellite Ariel
urban civic, oppidan, citified
  division ward
urease enzyme
uredo hives, urticaria
Urfa Edessa
Uriah
  wife Bathsheba
urial, ooriah sha, sheep
Uriel angel, archangel
Urim
  partner Thummim
Uris, Leon
  novels QBVII, Exodus
urisk brownie
urn jar, bury, Kist, container
  figurative grave
  for bones ossuary
  for tea samovar
  -shaped urceolate

Urne-Buriall
  author Browne
urodela newts, salamander
Ursa Bear
  pert. to ursine
Urth Norn
urticaria hives, uredo
urubu vulture
Uruguay
  capital Montevideo
  coin peso, centesimo
  cowboy gaucho
  discoverer Bartholomeu Diaz
  language Spanish
  measure vara, suete, cuadra
  weight quintal
urus ox, tur, aurochs
us we, uns (Ger.), nous (Fr.)
use try, value, employ, exploit, function
  as example cite
  divining rod dowse
  efforts exert, strive
  over again salvage, secondhand
  to be of avail
  up eat, tire, expend, corrode, deplete
  wastefully fritter, squander
Uspallata Pass
  site Andes
usquebaugh whiskey
U.S.S.R. see Russia
usury gombeen
Utah see also Quick Reference List
  natives Mormons
Uther
  son Arthur
Utopia, Utopian ideal, edenic
  author Thomas More
  Harrington's Oceana
  imaginary Shangri-La
Uttar Pradesh
  capital Lucknow
  part Oudh
utterance aside, ditty, expression
  soft murmur, whisper
  voiceless surd, spirate

utu reward
uva fruit, grape
uxorial wifely
Uzbek
  capital Tashkent
  city Khiva

V

V vee
  -shaped piece pie, vee, slice, wedge
  symbol victory
vaca cow (Sp.)
vacancy gap, chasm, inanity, vacuity,
  interstice
vacant idle, open, silly, void, empty,
  wanting
vacation
  place spa, beach, resort, shore, country
  person camper, tourist
vaccination
  inventor Edward Jenner
vaccine serum
  polio, discover Jonas Salk
vacillate reel, sway, waver, seesaw, totter,
  stagger
vacuous dull, empty, unfilled
vacuum void
  opposite plenum
  pump pulsometer
  tube diode, tetrode
vade mecum manual, handbook
vadium bail, pawn, pledge
vagabond vag, rove, scamp, rascal,
  drifter
vagary whim, fancy, breach, caprice,
  conceit, crotchet
vagrant hobo, caird, rover, tramp, nomadic
  lives in Bowery, jungle, skid row
vague dim, lax, hazy, loose, unfixed,
  indefinite
vail tip, use, doff, lower, yield, submit, decline
vain idle, flory, silly, trivial, useless, conceited, ineffectual, unsuccessful
  bird peacock

boasting fanfaronade
manners airs
person fop, dandy, coxcomb
to do in futile, wild goose chase
vainglorious proud, boastful
vair fur, squirrel fur
Vaishnavas
  deity Vishnu
  priest gusain
vakass amice
valance pelmet, curtain, drapery
valediction adieu, address, farewell
Valence
  river Rhone
valency power, value, importance
valentine card, lover, sweetheart
  derivation (myth.) Pan, Faunus
  feast Lupercalia
valerian drug, herb, plant, hemlock
valetudinarian sickly, invalid
valgus knock-kneed
Valhalla
  maiden Valkyrie
  palace of Odin (Wotan)
Vali
  mother Rind(r)
valid just, true, legal, sound, cogent, robust,
  binding, effective
  opposite null, void, invalid
valise bag, case, grip, suitcase
Valjean
  discoverer Javert
  friend Marius
  portegé Cosette
Valkyrie Brunnhilde
  love Sigard
vallancy wig
vallation wall, rampart, entrenchment
vallecula furrow, channel, depression
Valletta
  capital of Malta
  native Maltese
  without rivers, lakes
valley brae, cove, dale, glen, basin, hollow,
  depression
  between volcanic cones atrio
  deep canyon

entrance jaws
moon rill(e)
vallum wall, rampart
valor Arete, bounty, spirit, virtue, bravery, courage, boldness
valse waltz, triste
valuable discovery find
value rate, prize, worth, admire, reasonable
  equal parity
  highly cherish
  mean average
  more prefer
  net reserve
  of little trifle, bagatelle
  reduction depreciation
valve tap, poppet, spigot
  engine choke, poppet, throttle
  heart mitral
  sliding piston
vamoose lam, scat, scram, depart, decamp
vampire bat, lamia, siren, corpse
  famous Dracula
van from (Dut.), lorry, wagon, shovel, fourgon, forefront
  man mover, hauler
Vance, Philo sleuth
vandal Hun, plunderer
  act mar, deface
Vandyke beard, artist, collar, goatee
vane arm, blade, feather, weathercock
  feather web, vexillum
Van Gogh, Vincent painter
  town Arles
vanguard front, avant-garde
vanilla orchid, flavoring
  substance coumarin
vanity pride, conceit, egotism, falsity, worthlessness; see also vain
  case etui
  symbol peacock
Vanity Fair
  character Amelia, Becky
vanquish get, rout, subdue, expunge, overcome
vantage fee, gain, profit, advantage
  point coign, position
vapid dry, dull, insipid, tedious, lifeless

vapor fog, bray, reek, cloud, fancy, steam, exhalation
  aircraft's contrail
  comb. form atm(o)
  frozen hail, frost, sleet
  in air fog, mist
  mass wrack
  measuring device tonometer
vaporizer etna, steamer
vaquero cowboy, herdsman
Varangian Scandinavian
varec kelp, seaweed
variation change, mutation, deviation
  slight shade, nuance
varicella chicken pox
varicolored motley, varied, mottled, rainbow, variegated
varicose varix, dilated, swollen
  pert. to veins
varied daedal, diverse, various
variegated pied, menald, dappled, flecked, speckled, varicolored
variety show vaudeville
variola smallpox
  scar variole, pockmark
variolate cowpox, horsepox
variole foveola
various many, sundry, diverse, manifold, varicolored
varlet page, gippo, menial, rascal
varmint sharp, cunning, predator, despicable, obnoxious
varnish spar, japan, embellish
  ingredient lac, copal, elemi, resin, dammar
varsity team (first string)
  eight-member stroke
  of junior, senior
varus bowlegged
vas duct, pledge, vessel
vase urn, echew, tazza, crater, amphora, potiche
  handle ansa
  support pedestal
vassal esne, serf, slave, subject
  pert. to feudal
  tax paid tribute

vassalage homage, service, servitude, territory, dependence, subjection
vat bac, tub, coomb, barrel
  for bleaching keir
vatic inspired, oracular, prophetic
Vatican
  art gallery Belvedere
  chapel Sistine
  chapel ceiling artist Michelangelo
  guard's nationality Swiss
  official datary
  statuary group Laocoon
Vaud Canton
  capital Lausanne
vaudeville acts, revue, entertainment
  act skit, song, dance
vault cope, dome, leap, bound, curvet, spring
  burial tomb, crypt
  underground cellar, dungeon
Ve
  brother Odin
veal calf, meat, veau/gigot (Fr.)
  cutlet schnitzel
  stew goulash
vector host, carrier
  opposite scalar
vedette boat, vigil, watch, sentry, sentinel
Vedic Pali, Sanskrit
  artisans of gods Ribhus
  cosmic order Rita
  fire god Agni
  god Aditya
  goddess Ushas
  sky serpent ahi
  sun god Savitar
  text Sakha
vee fin, fiver
veer yaw, slue, turn, deviate
veery thrush
vega tract, meadow
Vega Lyra, star
vegetable plant, legume
  basket scuttle
  carbonized lignite
  caterpillar aweto
  dealer huckster, greengrocer

  decayed duff, humus
  ferment yeast
  green sabzi
  growing art horticulture
  pear chayote
  pod hull, peasecod
  poison abrin
  sponge loofa(h)
  stunted scrub
  variety bean, beet, corn, okra, squash, tomato, cabbage, lettuce, rhubarb, spinach, cucumber, eggplant, artichoke
vegetation growth, plants, verdure
  floating sadd
  god Esus, Attis
vehement hot, eager, ardent, intense
vehicle
  armored half-track
  army jeep, tank
  child's pram, walker, scooter, tricycle
  covered sedan, caravan
  display/parade float
  snow plow, pung, sled
  two-wheeled gig, sulky, tonga
veil hide, mask, cloak, screen, shroud
  having a velate
  head caul
  in botany velum
  papal orale
vein bed, mood, seam, tenor, streak, vessel
  arrangement neuration
  enlarged varix
  fluid ic(h)or
  inflammation phlebitis
  leaf rib
  mine/mining lode, reef
  pert. to veinal, venous
  rich ore bonanza
  small venule
  throat jugular
veining marbling
veinstone gangue, matrix
velamen membrane, integument
velar palatal, guttural
veld(t) meadow, grassland
vellum parchment

velocipede ride, (bi, tri, quadri)cycle
velocity pace, rate, speed, rapidity
  instrument cinemograph
  measuring device tachometer,
    speedometer
velum membrane, soft palate
velvet cloth, drink, birodo (Jp.), fabric,
  profit, surplus
  -breast merganser
  fabriclike panne, velure
  knife trevet
vend hawk, sell, utter, market, peddle,
  publish
vendace whitefish
vendetta feud, rivalry, contention
vendor seller, butcher, peddler, supplier
  route walk
vendue sale, auction
veneer lac, coat, glaze, enamel, facing,
  surface
veneration awe, fear, homage, reverence
  of saints and angels dulia
venerida clam, mollusks, carpet shell
Venezuela, Venezuelan
  capital Caracas
  city Aroa, Coro, Barinas, San Juan,
    Valencia, San Carlos
  coin real, medio, bolivar
  dam Guri
  discoverer Christopher Columbus
  fiber erizo
  fish guppy
  god Tsuma
  Indian Timote
  language Pume, Spanish
  measure bag (wgt.), libra, milla, fanega
  patriot Simón Bolivar
  river Apure, Caura, Orinoco
  snake lora
  tree balata
vengeance
  god Erinys, Alastor
  goddess Ara, Ate, Nemesis
venial trivial, pardonable, insignificant
  opposite mortal
Venice, Venetian
  barge bucentaur

  beach Lido
  boat gondola
  boatman gondolier
  bridge Rialto
  canals Rii
  coin bezzo, ducat, sequin
  gondolier's song barcarole
  Little Venice Venezuela
  magistrate doge
  painter Titian, Bellini, Veronese
  river Brenta
  traveler Marco Polo
  Venice of the North Stockholm
venin poison, venene, venine
venireman juror
venison deer meat
Venite psalm, canticle
vennel lane, alley, sewer
vent exit, flue, hole, outlet
  tailor's slit
  whale's blowhole, spiracle
ventage (finger) hole
venter womb, belly, abdomen
ventral sternal, abdominal
  opposite dorsal
ventriloquist's medium dummy, puppet
Venus planet, Vesper
  as morning star Lucifer
  beloved Adonis
  flytrap plant, dionaea
  girdle cestus
  island Melos
  mother Dione
  planet Vesper
  poet. Hesperus
  son Cupid
  tree sacred to myrtle
verandah porch, loggia, piazza, balcony,
  portico
  Southern gallery
verb action
  as a noun gerund
  auxiliary had, has, may, was, will, might,
    shall, would
  form tense
  suffix le, ire, ise, esce
  table paradigm

taken from rhematic
tense aorist
verbal oral, spoken
  attack tirade, diatribe, harangue
  thrust dig (sl.)
  word for word literal, verbatim
verbiage talk, diction, verbosity, wordiness
verboten tabu, taboo, forbidden
verdant raw, fresh, green, innocent
Verdi, Guiseppe composer
  character Amneris, Radames
  opera Aida, Otello, Traviata, Rigoletto
verdigris rust, patina, aerugo
verdin bird, titmouse
verdun river Meuse
verecund shy, modest, bashful
verein society, organization
verger gardener, official, sacristan
Vergil see Virgil
veridical real, actual, genuine, accurate,
  truthful, veracious
verily yea, amen, parde, certes, indeed, really
verjuice liquor, acidity, sourness
vermiform long, thin, slender, wormlike
  process appendix
vermillion red, color, pigment, scarlet,
  cinnabar
vermin lice, mice, rats, filth, rodents
Vermont see also Quick Reference List
  city Barre, Montpelier
  county Essex, Orange, Addison,
    Bennington
  mountain range Taconic
vernal mild, warm, fresh, young, youthful,
  springlike
Verne, Jules author
  character Nemo
  submarine Nautilus
verneuk cheat, swindle
veronal barbital
verrel ferrule
verruca wart
versant slope
versate turn, revolve
versatile handy, flexile, variable, adaptable
verse line, poem, rune, meter, stanza,
  revolve, stichos

accented arsis
Bible text
foot iamb
form sonnet, couplet
half line hemistich
maker poet, meterist
pert. to poetic
set to music lyric(s)
stress ictus
verset prelude
verso vo
  opposite recto, obverse
versus vs., con, against
vert green
vertebra axis, bone, spondy
  body centrum
  comb. form spondyl(o)
  top atlas
vertebrae spine
vertebral bone coccyx, sacrum
vertebrate ray, fish, mammal, reptile,
  amphibian
  class aves (birds)
  division somite
  feathered bird
vertex top, apex, summit
verticil whorl
vertiginate twirl, whirl, vitiginous
vertigo megrim, staggers, dizziness
Vertumnus
  wife Pomona
vervet monkey
very so, too, real, tres (Fr.), molto (It.), quite
  comb. form eri
  new red-hot
  well first-rate
vesica vessel, bladder
vesicate blister
vesicle sac, cell, cyst, bulla, cavity
  air aerocyst
vespa wasp
Vesper star, Venus, Hesperus
vespertilione bat
vessel cask, duct, craft, airship, utensil
  anatomical vein, artery
  comb. form vaso
  drinking flask, stein

having more than one vascular
  oil cruet
  sacred ama, pyx
  wooden skeel, piggin
vesta match, taper, lighter
Vesta Hestia
vestal nun, pure, chaste, virgin
  virgin tuccia
vestiture garb, dress
vestment gown, robe, dress, garment
  clerical alb, cope, amice, fanon, miter
  pert. to vestiary
Vesuvian fusee, match, volcanic
Vesuvius volcano
  city destroyed by Pompeii,
    Herculaneum
vetch ers, tare, weed, fetch
veteran old, vet, trouper, seasoned,
  experienced
  of battles warhorse
veterinarian leech, doctor, farrier
vetiver bena, grass, cuscus
veto cancel, forbid, overrule
  sl. nix, kibosh
vettura couch, carriage
veuve bird, whydah
vex irk, tew, cark, gall, miff, rile, roil, nettle,
  acerbate
vexed sorry, grieved
vexillum web, flag, banner
via way, road, passage
viaduct bridge, trestle
vial ampul, phial, caster, vessel
viand dish, fare, food, edible
  choice cake
viaticum money, supplies, Eucharist
viator traveler, wayfarer
Viaud
  pen name Loti
vibration wag, quiver, thrill, tremor,
  tremolo, undulation
  check damp, mute
  point without node
vibrissa whiskers
vicar proxy, deputy, priest
  assistant curate
  of Christ pope

Vicar of Wakefield
  author Oliver Goldsmith
vice sin, fault, taint, defect
  president see also Quick Reference List;
    veep, veepee
  versa conversely
vicenary number twenty
viceroy nabob, exarch, satrap, butterfly
  wife vicereine
vicinity area, region, nearness, proximity,
  neighborhood
vicious lewd, mean, vile, faulty, unruly,
  depraved, modicious, profligate
  act outrage
vicissitude change, mutation, variation,
  difficulty, alternation, interchange
victim dupe, goat, prey, stooge, sucker, quarry
  accident casualty
  list toll
victor captor, winner, champion, unbeaten,
  conqueror, vanquisher, prizewinner
  fish aku
Victoria queen, empress, carriage, waterlily
Victory
  author Joseph Conrad
  heroine Lena
victory win, success, triumph, conquest,
  supremacy
  celebration epinician
  crown bay, laurel, anadem
  easy runaway
  goddess Nike, Athena
  kind rout, barely, landslide
  memorial arch, spoils, trophy
  ruinous Pyrrhic
  symbol palm, laurel
victualler sutler, caterer, innkeeper
videlicet viz, namely
Vienna Wien
  palace Schonbrunn
  park Prater
  Woods composer Strauss
Vietnam (North)
  capital Hanoi
  coin dong
  gulf Tonkin
  native meo

Vietnam (South)
  capital Saigon
  coin piastre
  guerrillas Vietcong
  river Mekong
Vietnam (Unified)
  capital Hanoi
view aim, goal, scene, slant, survey, opinion
  extended panorama
  mental envision
  obstruct hide, conceal
  open to bare
viewing instrument (tele)scope, spyglass, binoculars, fieldglass
vigil eve, wake, watch, service
vigilant person Argus
vigilantes posse
vigneron winegrower (Fr.)
vignettist artist, author, writer, painter
vigor dash, snap, force, energy
  drain sap, enervate
  loss sag, fail, pine, decline
  pinnacle heyday
  with great amain
Viking rover, pirate, Norseman, Scandinavian
  famous Eric, Olaf, Rollo
  poet Skald
vilayet eyalet, region, division
  subdivision sanjak
villa aldea, dacha (Rus.), house, estate
Villa, Pancho leader, Mexican, revolutionist
villain churl, felon, knave, rogue, scoundrel
  fictional Iago, Legree
  movie heavy
  myth. ogre, giant, dragon
  nemesis hero
villatic rural, rustic
villein serf, churl, cottar, cotter, tenant, cottier
Villon, Francois poet
vim zip, force, spirit, vitality, enthusiasm
vimen shoot
vin wine
vina instrument
vinaceous fruit grape
vinaigrette box, sauce, bottle

vinca myrtle, periwinkle
vincible beatable, conquerable
vinculum tie, band, bond, brace, union
vindication excuse, apology
vine hop, odal, betel, creeper, wisteria
  coil tendril
  comb. form viti
  covered ivied, lianaed
  fruit-bearing grape, cupseed
  parasite aphis
  twining bine
  woody smilax
vinegar acid, eisel, alegar
  bottle cruet, castor
  change to acetify
  dregs mother
  pert. to acetic
  pickling marinade
  spice tarragon
vinegarroon scorpion
vineyard cru (Fr.), clos
  protector Priapus
vinous winy
vintage crop, model, yield, choice
vintner dealer, merchant
  assistant taster, gourmet
viol gigue, rebec(k), sarinda
viola alto, (de) gamba, pansy, violet
Viola
  brother Sebastian
violate rape, break, defoul, infract, desecrate
  trust rat (sl.), betray
violation
  sentence structure anacoluthon
violent acute, fiery, rabid, stormy, intense
  anger fury
  blow bash
  contact crash, impact, collision
violet mauve, blaver, flavor, purple
  blue indigo
  perfume irone
  root orrisroot
  tip butterfly
violin kit, fiddle
  border purfling
  bow arco, (knob) nut

city Cremona
forerunner rebec
part peg, hole, neck, scroll, string, eclisse
rare Amati, Strad, Guarnerius
-shaped waisted
small kit
stroke upbow
violinist (first) concertmaster
   comic Jack Benny
   fabled Nero
   famous Auer, Elman, Ricci, Stern, Ysaye, Kreisler, Heifetz, Menuhin, Perlman
VIP big shot, notable, celebrity, very important person
viper asp, adder, snake, fer-de-lance
   genus Echis
   horned cerastes
virago randy, scold, beldam(e), randie, termagant
virelay poem, verse
vireo redeye, grasset, greenlet, songbird
virgate twiggy
Virgil
   birthplace Mantua
   character Amata, Damon, Corydon
   family name Maro
   friend Maecenas
   hero Aeneas
   language Latin
   queen Dido
   work epic, Aeneid
virgin new, girl, lass, pure, chaste, damsel, modest
   queen Elizabeth
   the Mary
   unblemished camilla
   vestal Rhea
virginal pure, spinet, virgin, maidenly, harpsichord
Virginia see also Quick Reference List
   aristocrats FFV
   capital Richmond
   creeper ivy
   dam Kerr
   dance reel
   mountain Cedar, Alleghany, Blueridge
   pine loblolly

quail bobwhite
   settlement Jamestown, Williamsburg
Virgin Island
   discoverer Christopher Columbus
   coin bit, franc
Virgin Mary
   flower marigold
   image Pieta
   mother Anne
virgin's-bower clematis
Virgo virgin, constellation
   star spica
viridian pigment
viridity youth, greenness
virl ferrule
virtu curio, rarity, antique, bibelot, excellence
virtue merit, bounty, quality, chastity, excellence
   cardinal hope, faith, charity, justice, prudence, temperance
   paragon saint
virtuoso expert, savant, aesthete, connoisseur
vis force, power, rigor, visual, strength
   -à-vis seat, sofa, facing, opposite, face-to-face
visage face, look, image, aspect
viscera guts, bowels, organs, entrails
viscount peer, deputy, sheriff
   heir master
vise dial, clamp
   part jaw, lever, screw
Vishnu the Preserver
   bearer Garuda
   consort Sri, Lakshmi
   incarnation Rama, Krishna
   serpent Naga
visible evident, obvious
   to naked eye obvious, macroscopic, perceptible
Visigoth Teuton
   king Alaric
vision dream, fancy, image, sight
   comb. form opto
   defect myopia, astigmatism
   double diplopia
   illusory mirage

instrument retina
lacking purblind
pert. to ocular, visual, optical
scope scan
visionary fey, airy, laputan, idealist, imaginary
pert. to Quixote, quixotic
visit stay, haunt, sojourn, inspection
kind social, official, professional
short call, drop by/in
visne hood, jury, neighbor
vison mink
vista view, scene, outlook, prospect
Vistula River Wisla (Polish)
tributary Bug, San
vita life
Vita Nuova
author Dante Alighieri
vital basic, fatal, deadly, viable, essential
fluid sap, blood, lymph
organ lung, heart, liver
principle soul
statistics age, race, size, gender, measurements
vitalize animate
vitals viscera
vitellus yolk
vitrics glassware
vitrify bake, glaze
vitrine showcase
vitriol acid, sory, caustic
vitta ribbon, headband
vittle food
vituline animal calf
viva cheer, acclaim
voce orally
vivandiér sutler, provisioner
vivarium box, zoo, hothouse
vive brisk, lively
-le roi
vivify revive, enliven, quicken, sharpen, brighten
vivres (Fr.) foodstuff, provisions
vixen nag, scold, shrew, woman, she fox
viz to wit, namely, videlicet
vizard mask, guise, visor
vizcacha rodent

Vladimir, Illich Ulianov Lenin
vocabulary argot, slang, words, diction, lexicon
of a lexical
vocabulist lexicographer
vocal oral, sung, vowel, unwritten
composition song
cords larynx
solo aria (mus.)
vocalist alto, basso, tenor, singer, baritone, soprano, coloratura
vocalization melismatics
vocation call(ing), trade, business, occupation, inclination
voe bay, creek, inlet
vogie vain, merry, proud
vogue cut, fad, ton, mode, style
in stylish, au courant (Fr.), prevailing
voice say, vox, emit, wish, utter
box larynx
handicap lisp, stutter
loss anaudia, aphonia
loud foghorn, stentorian, megalophonic
natural singing dipetto
part glottis
pert. to vocal, phonetic
practice solfeggio
principle cantus
quality timbre
quiet sotto
stop affricate
stress arsis
voiced said, sonant, vibrant
stop media
voiceless mum, mute, surd, flated, silent
sound sign cedilla
voices, for all tutti
void free, null, egest, empty, vacuum
of infinite space inane
voilà (Fr.) lo, see, look, behold, there it is
voile ninon, fabric
voiture (Fr.) auto, wagon, carriage
volary cage, flock, aviary, flight
volatile airy, bird, lively, gaseous
volatilize vaporize, evaporate
volcano
activity belching, eruption

ash tuff
cinder scoria
crater maar
earth trass
kind active, dormant
matter aa, oo, lava, tufa
mud salse
opening mouth, crater, fumarole
slag cinder, scoria
steam stufa
well-known Apo, Etna, Fuji, Taal, Asama, Pelee, Shasta, Mauna Loa, Vesuvius, Mt. St. Helens
vole mouse, craber, rodent
Volga Rha
figure boatman
tributary Kama
volk folk, nation, people
volplane coast, glide
Volpone
character Mosca
Volsunga Saga
dragon Fafnir
dwarf nibelung
hero Sigurd, Siegfried
king Atli
Voltaire
character Pangloss
estate Ferney
novel Zadig, Candide
true name Francois-Marie Arouet
voluble glib, wordy, fluent, talkative, loquacious
volume book, bulk, mass, space, cubage, strength
large tome
measure stereometer
of sound unit decibel
Volund
brother Egil(l)
voluntary free(ly), music, elective, intentional
volunteer offer, enlist, proffer
opposite draftee, slacker
volute turn, whorl
vomica pus, cavity
vomit puke, spew, reject, disgorge

act emesis
effort retch
voodoo obi, obeah, fetish, sorcerer
charm mojo
deity zombie
vorago gulf, abyss
vortex apex, eddy, gyre, whirl
votary fan, nun, monk, zealot, devotee
vote poll, elect, grant, assign, choice, choose, declare
counting/survey poll
group bloc
kind proxy, straw, voice, secret, write-in ballot
of assent aye, nod, yea, placet
of dissent nay
receptacle situla(e), ballot box
right to suffrage, franchise
solicitation lobby
voter poller, balloter, constituent
body electorate
illegal repeater, underage
vouch aver, pray, assure, attest, bestow, certify, confirm, guarantee
voucher chit, debenture, credential
vouchsafe give, allow, deign, grant, beteem, permit, concede
voussoir wedge, keystone
projection ear
voust boast
vow bind, oath, wish, swear, pledge, promise
dedicated by votive
taken nun, monk, votary, witness, celibate
vowel vocal, letter
contraction crasis, diphthong, syneresis
mark breve, tilde, umlaut, dieresis, circumflex
omission aphesis
slurring elision
sound dental, labial, palatal
unaspirated lene
vox voice
voyage trip, travel, journey, passage
one who takes sailor, boatman, trapper, traveler
pleasure cruise
voyeur Peeping Tom

vraic seaweed
vrouw (Dut.) frau, frow, woman, housewife
vs. versus
vug, vugh cavity, hollow
Vulcan (black)smith, Hephaestus
  consort Maia, Venus
  epithet Mulciber
  son Cacus
  workshop Etna
vulcanite rubber, ebonite
vulcanize cure (rubber)
vulgar lewd, crude, gross, randy, common, obscene, indecent, plebeian
Vulgate
  author/translator Jerome
vulnerable liable, exposed, defenseless
  point Achilles heel
Vulpecula little fox, constellation
vulpine foxy, artful, clever, cunning, alopecoid
vult mien, aspect, expression
vulture arend, griph(e), urubu, atrata, condor, buzzard, lammergeier
  food carrion
  genus Gyps
  hawklike caracara
vum vow

W

W waw
  in chemistry tungsten
  old English wen
waag grivet, monkey
Wabash River
  city Terre Haute
  tributary Tippecanoe
wabeno shaman
wachna cod
wad cram, lump, dossil, pledget
  of paper money roll
Wadai Museum Maba
wadding material hemp, kapok, cotton
waddy beat, cane, club, cowboy
wadi, wady oasis, river, ravine, channel

wading bird ibis, crane, flamingo
wadset pawn, pledge
wafer disk, snap, cracker
  container pix, pyx
waff flap, gust, odor, paltry
waffie tramp, vagrant
wagang death, departure
wage pay, utu, hire, incur, salary, stipend
  boost raise, increase
  deduct from dock
  insurance chomage
wagger dog, pipit
waggery jest, joke, foolery
waggly unsteady
Wagner, Richard
  father-in-law Franz Liszt
  wife Cosima
Wagnerian earth goddess Erda
wagon cart, dray, trailer, tumbrel
  ammunition caisson
  baggage fourgon
  driver carter
  horse poler
  Oriental araba
  police paddy, Black Maria
  prairie schooner
  track rut
  yoke inspan
wagoner auriga
wagon-lit sleeper
wagonload fother
wagtail bird, lark, pipit
wah panda
wahine wife, woman
wahoo elm, fish, peto, nonsense
Wailing Wall
  custom prayer, lamentation
  site Jerusalem
wain cart, fetch, wagon, convey
wainscot lining, ceiling, partition
waist blouse, bodice
  circumference girth
  of dress taille
waistcoat vest, benjy, gilet, fecket, jerkin
  unlined singlet
waiting line cue, queue
waka canoe

Wakashan Nootka
Walden
  author Henry David Thoreau
Waldensian Leonist
Wales Cymru, Cambria
  capital Cardiff
  city Swansea
  dog corgi
  emblem leek
  mus. instr. pibcorn
  patron saint David
  poet Dylan Thomas
  poet. name Cambria
walk hike, hoof, plod, stoa, alley, tramp, tread, trudge
  a beat patrol
  about ambulate
  beach esplanade
  covered stoa, arcade
  inability abasia
  kind limp, strut, waddle
  on stilts trampolio
  to and fro pace
walking ambulant, gradient
  adapted for gressorial
  like a bear plantigrade
  meter pedometer
  papers dismissal
  shoes balmorals
  stick cane, staff, malacca
walk out strike
walk out on desert, abandon
wall fence, barrier, parapet
  band cordon
  border dado
  bracket sconce
  dividing septum
  -ed town burg
  end anta
  -eyed fish dory, pike
  garden haha
  lizard gecko
  opening bay, scuttle
  pert. to mural
  sea mole, pier
walla(h) (India) agent, owner, fellow, servant
wallaba tree apa

wallaby kangaroo
wallflower heartsease
wallowish flat, insipid
wallpaper measure bolt, roll
wally fine, robust, sturdy, first-rate
walnut tree, wood, bannut
  skin zest
Walpurgis Night revelers witches
walrus seal, seacow, tusker
  female cow
  herd pod
  male bull
  order bruta
  tooth tusk
walt unsteady
waltz king Strauss
wambly faint, shaky, nauseous
wame belly, abdomen
wampish swing, fluctuate
wampum money
wamus jacket, doublet, cardigan
wand baton, pointer, scepter
  -shaped virgate
wanderer vag, Arab, hobo, waif, nomad, truant, pilgrim
  religious palmer
wandering erratic, vagrant, odyssey
  aimlessly gad, stray, traipse
  beggar rogue
  student/minstrel goliard
  tribe Gypsy
wandering Jew ivy, plant, zebrina
wanderoo langur, monkey, macaque
wandle agile, lithe, supple
wane ebb, lack, abate, peter, dwindle, diminish
  opposite wax
wang king, ruler, prince
wanga charm, spell, voodoo
wanhap mishap, misfortune
wanigan ark, house, trunk
wanion curse, plague, vengeance
wanted man outlaw, escapee, lamster, lamister, desperado
wanton lewd, tart, willful, unchaste
  destroyer vandal
wantwit fool

wanty tie, rope, girth
wapiti elk, deer, stag
war strife, conflict
  acquisitions spoils
  agreement truce, cartel
  cause casus belli
  dance pyrrhic
  games maneuvers
  god Tyr, Ares, Irra, Mars
  holy jehad, jihad, crusade
  pert. to martial
War and Peace
  author Lev Nikolayevich Tolstoi, Tolstoy
  heroine Natasha
warbird aviator, tanager
warbler wren, pipit, thrush, songster, beccafico, trochilus
ward
  part precinct
  politician heeler
  pert. to pupillary
  off fend, avert
wardship custody, guardianship
warehouse depot, etape, store, bodega
  candles chandlery
  fee storage
  platform pallet
  weapons arsenal
war hawk jingo
warhead
  missile payload
war horse steed, leader, charger, veteran, partisan
warkloom tool, utensil
warm heat, ardent, passionate
  baths/springs thermae
  compress stupe
warmonger jingo, militarist
warmth élan, zeal, ardor
  increasing calescent
  pert. to thermal
warning omen, alarm, knell, caveat
  in law caveat
  signal hiss, siren, tocsin
warp abb, hit, bias, expel, deform, pervert
  thread for loom stamen
warragal dingo, horse, warrigal

warrant order, plevin, voucher, guarantee
  convict's mittimus
  officer bosun
warren hutch, rabbitry, tenement
warrior toa, impi, jingo, singh, soldier
  arena gladiator
  female Amazon
  Trojan Hector, Agenor
warship carrier, cruiser, flattop, frigate, destroyer
  boat on dinghy, launch
  deck, lowest orlop
  fleet armada
  pert. to naval
  prison brig
  tower turret
warts, covered with verrucose
wase pad, wisp, bundle
wash pan, silt, bathe, clean, drift, scour, launder
  away erode, purge
  out fail, elute, flush
  up finish, discard
washbowl, church lavabo
washer rove, clove
washing bathing, ablution, lavation
  board dolly
  chemical eluate
  out (organ) lavage
Washington, Booker T. educator
Washington, D.C. (see also Quick Reference List) U.S. Capital
  museum Freer, Corcoran, National, Hirschhorn, Smithsonian
  original planner Pierre-Charles L'Enfant
Washington State see also Quick Reference List
  fort Lewis
  volcano Rainier
  wind chinook
wasp digger, hornet, yellow jacket
  genus Sphex
  nest vespiary
wassail lark, orgy, drink, revel, carouse
Wasserman
  test subject syphilis

waste ruin, ocean, desert, fritter, leftover
  allowance tret
  away rot, decay, emaciate
  drain sewer
  glass cullet
  metal slag, dross
  product dregs, runoff
wasting tabes, cachexia
wat temple, monastery
watch eye, tend, vigil, sentry, timepiece
  chain fob
  covering crystal
  duty vigil, patrol
  maker horologist
  men (myth.) Argus, Talos, Heimdall
  part case, dial, stem, stud, detent, pallet, spring
  sl. ticker, turnip
  time horologe
watchdog guardian
  Hel's Garm(r)
  underworld Cerberus
watchtower garret, beacon, bantayan
watchworks movement
  arrangement caliper
water aqua, dilute, irrigate
  baptismal laver
  bearer, astronomy Aquarius
  carrier bird albatross
  channel canal, flume, gully, sluice
  chestnut ling, caltrap
  clock clepsydra
  comb. form hydr(o)
  conduit aqueduct
  corral crawl
  cress mustard, potherb
  excursion cruise
  fairy nix
  gum tupelo
  hen coot
  ice sherbet
  jug ewer, olla
  nymph naiad, oceanid
  of aqueous
  raising device pump, noria, tabut
  science hydrology
  snake moccasin

source, power white coal
sports aquatics
spring lymph
storage tank, cistern, reservoir
tube hose
vessel lota
without dry, arid, desert, drought, parched
watercress brooklime, speedwell
watered moire, irrigated
waterfowl duck, loon, diver, goose
Watergate judge Sirica
watertight box caisson, cofferdam
waters
  primeval Apsu
waterwheel noria, sakia
watery thin, soggy, serous
  discharge rheum
  grave sea
wattle beat, flog, twig, cooba, fence, acacia, lappet
waugh weak, stale, insipid
Waugh, Evelyn novelist
wave flap, surf, crimp, marcel, flutter
  comb. form ondo
  large swell, roller, decuman
  little ripple
  tidal bore, eagre
  to and fro wag, flap
  top crest, whitecap
wavering sound tremolo, vibrato
wawl, waul howl, squall
wax cere, grow, cerumen, paraffin
  artist Tussaud
  comb. form cer(o)
  covered with cerated
  match vesta
  myrtle bayberry
  pert. to ceral
  source bee, carnauba
  used on skis klister
waxbill astrild
waxwing cedarbird
waxy substance cutin, suberin
way mode, road, habit, street, method
  give yield
  of walking/running gait

open pioneer
out exit, egress
-station town tank town, whistle stop
waybill manifest
waymark ahu, arrow, milestone
weaken sap, flag, dilute
  morally vitiate
  spirit demoralize
weakfish acoupa, totuava
weakling puler, sissy, softie
weakness defect, fetish, liking, frailty
  bodily/organic atony
weal mark, pomp, ridge, choice, stripe, wealth
wealth dhan, goods, assets, riches, opulence
  comb. form pluto
  god Plutus
  income from usance
  person of Midas, nabob, Croesus, magnate, plutocrat, millionaire
weanie baby
weaponry ordnance
weapons (sl.) hardware
wearisome boring, tedious, toilsome
  grow bore, pall
Weary Willie hobo, tramp, vagrant, shirker, feather bedder
weasand trachea, windpipe, esophagus
weasel cane, vare, sable, stoat, ermine, ferret, informer (sl.)
  cat linsang
  -like musteline
weather sky, season, climate, survive
  indicator barometer
  item moisture, pressure, temperature
  satellite Tiros
  study meteorology
weathercock fane, vane
weaverbird baya, taha
weaver's tool loom, reed, sley, shuttle
weaving
  frame loom, cylinder
  goddess Ergane
  material reed, yarn, fiber, wicker
web net(work), snare, tissue
  feather's vexillum

-footed/toed palmate
-like membrane tela
pert. to retiary
webbing binding
Weber, Carl Maria von
  opera Oberon
wedding splice, marriage, nuptials
  canopy chupa, huppah
  proclamation banns
wedge jam, key, shim, cleat, cotter
  -shaped sphenoid, cuneiform
Wednesday
  god Odin
  source Woden
  special Ash
weed rid, band, dock, loco, milk, cockle, dandelion
  killer herbicide
  mourning crape, weeder
  noxious tare
  poison(ous) ivy, loco, darnel, hemlock
  roadside dogfennel
  sl. cigar, tobacco
  tool hoe, spud
week hebdomad
weekday feria
weeks (two) fortnight
weel pit, cave
ween hope, fancy, think, expect
weeping goddess Niobe
  philosopher Heraclitus
weet wet, wit, know
weevil kis, lota, borer, beetle
  larva grugru
  wing cover shard
weft web, film, yarn, shoot
weighing machine scale, trone, steelyard
weight load, value, burden, stress
  allowance tare, tret
  balloon's/stabilizer ballast
  diamond carat
  for wool tod
  leaden plumb
  -lifting machine crane, loader, elevator
  pert. to baric

science metrology
sl. heft
weir dam, bank, garth, levee, barrier
wejack pekan, weasel
weka bird, rail
welding
  gas acetylene
  material rod, solder, thermit
welfare dole, sele, weal, prosperity
  goddess Salus
welkin sky, heaven
well fit, hale, spring, expertly
  bred genteel
  comb. form bene
  feeling euphoria
  grounded informed
  lining stean, steen
  made affabrous
  nigh almost, nearly
  pit sump
  prefix eu
  -to-do (sl.) loaded
  versed erudite
  worn trite, overused
Welland city, canal, river
wellaway woe, alas, regret
wellhead source, spring, fountain
Wellington, Arthur Wellesley
  soubriquet Old Nosy, Iron Duke
wellspring fountainhead
Welsh, Welshman Celt(ic), Taffy, cymric,
  Cambrian; see also Wales
  cheese dish rabbit, rarebit
  dog corgi
  god of sea Dylan
  onion cibol
  sl. cheat, default, swindle
wem flaw, scar, spot, stain
wen cyst, mole, talpa, tumor
Wend Slav, Sorb
Wendy
  brother John, Michael
  dog Nana
wenzel jack, knave, Wenceslaus
werewolf loup-garou (Fr.)
wergild cro, eric, money

Wesley, John
  follower Methodist
Wessex King Ine, Ini
West frontier, Occident
Western treaty alliance NATO
West Indies
  bird tody, courlan, limpkin
  coin pistareen
  fish pega, testar, bacalao
  lizard arbalo, galliwasp
  magic obi
  music calypso
  patois gumbo
  pert. to Antillean
  shrub anil, cascarilla
  tree balata, bonace, calaba
  volcano Pelee
  white man buckra
Westminster
  clock Big Ben
  landmark Abbey
  rite coronation
  street Whitehall
West Point
  island Iona
  mascot mule
  student cadet, plebe
West Virginia see Quick Reference List
west wind zephyr
  of the favonian
wet
  all (sl.) wrong, mistaken
  blanket killjoy, spoilsport
  comb. form hygro
  flax ret
  one's whistle drink, imbibe
  plaster painting fresco
weta insect
wetbird chaffinch
whale whip, thrash, finback, cetacean
  Arctic/tusked narwhal
  biggest blue
  constellation Cetus
  cry fall
  dolphin orca
  fat blubber

female cow
food brit
male bull
Melville's Moby Dick
pert. to cetic
school gam, pod
skin muktuk
sound mew, bark, squeal, whine
spear harpoon
sperm cachalot
tail part fluke
young calf
whaling huge, whopping
　cask rier, cardel
　profit lay
　ship whaler, Pequod
whammy jinx, evil eye
whample blow, stroke
whangee cane, bamboo
wharf dock, pier, quai, quay
　fish cunner
　space quayage
　worker stevedore
whatnot stand, cabinet, etagere
whaup fuss, curlew, outcry
wheal mark, stripe, postule
wheat
　beer weiss
　cracked/hulled groats
　duck widgeon, baldpate
　ground meal, flour
　husk bran, corn (Eur.), durum, spelt, cereal
　louse aphid
　meal semolina
　smut bunt, colbrand
wheatbird lark
wheatear bird, chickell, gorsehatch
wheel disc, helm, pivot, pulley, rotate, bicycle (sl.)
　center hub, nave
　horse poler
　-like trochal
　little caster
　part cam, hob, hub, rim, axle, tire, felly, spoke
　-shaped rotate, rotiform

spindle axle, arbor
tooth sprocket
water noria
wheezy breather asthmatic
whelk acne, snail, pimple
whemmel upset, tumble, confusion
when as, time, while, moment, whereas
where whither
whereas since, while
wherefrom whence
whereness ubiety
wherret box, hit, slap
wherry boat, barge, scull, vehicle
whether if
whewl cry, howl, whine
whey of milk serum
which who, that, whom
which was to be shown QED
whicker neigh, whinny
whid fib, lie, wold, frisk
whiffet dog, puff, whippersnapper
whig jog, whey, beverage
Whig
　opposite Tory
　poet Og, Shadwell
while as, yet, until, albeit, occupy
whilly gall, cajole
whilom once, formerly, erstwhile
whinchat gorsechat
whinnock whimper
whinyard sword
whip flay, flog, lash, flail, whale, scourge
　biblical scorpion
　leather knout, kurbash
　riding crop, quirt
whipcord catgut
whippersnapper squirt, upstart, whiffet
whippoorwill goatsucker
　feathers vibrissa
whirlbone kneepan, patella
whirling man dervish
　on toes pirouette
whirlpool eddy, vortex, maelstrom
whirlwind oe, cyclone, tornado, dust devil, maelstrom
whisht hush, silence
whiskers beard, sideburns

cat's vibrissa
chin goatee
side muttonchops
whiskey rye, corn, drink, liquor, poteen, rotgut, scotch, busthead, moonshine
maker distiller
punch facer
whiskin bowl
whist game, hush, mute, cards
declaration misere
dummy mort
hand tenace
whistle hiss, pipe, toot, siren, warble
-duck goldeneye
-pig woodchuck
-wing goldeneye
whit jot, atom, doit, iota, speck
white pale, ashen, milky, snowy
alkali soda ash
animal albino
ant anai, termite
cedar arborvitae
cliffs' site Dover
clouds cerri
comb. form leuk(o)
crow vulture
eye songbird
feather fear, cowardice
fish cisco, atinga, beluga
flag surrender
friar Alsatian, Carmelite
gentian feverroot
gum eucalyptus
horse nettle trompillo
House designer Hoban
jade alabaster
lead cerussite
magic theurgy
man buckra
monk Cistercian
mule gin, moonshine
nun smew
plantain pussytoes
poplar abele, aspen
pudding sausage
Rose house York
sl. fair, honest

Sunday Whitsunday, Pentecost
turning albescant
whale beluga
whitebelly grouse, pigeon
whiteboy pet, favorite
whitewash blanch, defeat, parget, cover-up
whiteweed daisy
whitewing sail, sweeper
whiting fish, chalk
whitlow sore, felon
whitster bleacher
whitten rowan
Whitman, Walt(er) poet
Whitney, Eli cotton-gin inventor
Whitsunday Pentecost
Whitsuntide pinxter, pinkster, whit week
whittling refuse chips, shavings
who quo (Lat.), wer (Ger.), wha (Scot.)
who goes there qui va la, challenge
whole toto, uncut, entire, intact
comb. form holo
number integer
wholesale gross, extensive
opposite retail
wholly quite, algates, totally, entirely
comb. form toto
whooper swan
whorl spiral, verticil
fingerprint ridge
whyo robber, footpad
wicked city Sodom, Babylon, Gomorrah
wicker twig, osier, withe
basket core, hamper, pannier
cradle bassinet
hut jacal
wickiup hut, shelter
widdrim fury, madness, confusion
widdy rope, noose, halter, widow
widespread prevalent
disease epidemic
fear panic
widgeon duck, fool, goose, simpleton
genus Mareca
widow widdy, relict, widder (sl.)
-hood viduage
in cards skat
monkey titi

   right dower
   suicide suttee
wife bride, spouse, helpmate
   bequest to dos
   common-law mistress
   dowry dot
   knight's dame
   pert. to uxorial
wig rug (sl.), gizz, caxon, jasey, peruke, spencer
wigwag signal, message
wild gaga, fierce, savage, stormy, primitive, licentious
   apple crab, creeper
   ass onager
   banana pawpaw
   Bill Hickok
   carrot hilltrot, Queen Anne's lace
   cattle banteng
   cry evoe, shriek, screech
   dog dingo
   Duck author Henrik Ibsen
   goat ibex
   goose greylag, Jacobite
   guess stab
   hog boar
   horse bronco, mustang
   life game
   plum sloe
   revelry orgy
   sage claru
   state of being ferity
wildebeest gnu
wildfowl duck, goose, quail, pheasant, partridge
   flight skein
wildlife preserve wetland, sanctuary
Wilkes Island Ashi
will power, desire, volition
   addition to codicil
   exercise of the volition
   handwritten holograph
   having made a testate
   having no intestate
   power, loss of abulia
Willard, Jess boxing champion
Willard, Frances temperance leader

William the Conqueror
   burial place Caen
William II
   home Doorn (exile)
William Tell
   canton Uri
   composer Gioacchino Rossini
   hero Egil
willies creeps, jitters, nervousness
Willkie, Wendell presidential candidate
   dream one world
willow iva, itea, osier, salix, sallow
   basket prickle
   herb rosebay
   of the salicaceous
   shoot wand
   wren chiffchaff
willy trap, basket, willow
Wilson's thrush Veery
Wimbledon
   event tennis
   location England
wimick cry
wimple bend, fold, turn, veil, curve, ripple
win pot, earn, reach, attain, defeat, entice, obtain, succeed, overcome
   all tricks slam, thirteen
   back recover
   over persuade
wince crab, reel, start, flinch, recoil
Winchester city, rifle
wind gale, hint, blast, duster
   away from alee
   comb. form anemo
   dry foehn
   east eurus
   equatorial trade
   god Adda, Vayu, Eolus
   Indian Ocean monsoon
   myth. Sansar
   north aquilo, boreas
   of the salicaceous
   science anemology
   side away from lee
   side toward weather
   shoot wand, sucker
   south auster

warm foehn
west zephyr, favonian
winder pear warden
windflower anemone
winding staircase caracole
windmill fighter Don Quixote
  part sail, vane
  pump gin
window
  bay oriel, picture
  dressing trim
  frame casement
  part grill(e), jamb(e), pane, sash, sill,
    lintel, grating
  pert. to fenestral
  trellised lattice
Windward Island Grenada
Windy City Chicago
wine
  bottle magnum, decanter, jeroboam
  comb. form bini, oeno
  date vintage
  distillate brandy, cognac
  dry sec, brut
  flavor mull
  fragrance bouquet
  god Bacchus
  of vinic, vinous
  Rhine hock, moselle
  sauterne yquem
  study oenology
wine and dine fete
wineskin askos
wing pinna, pennon
  comb. form ptero
  cover shard, elytrum
  feather pinion
  in anatomy ala
  length span
  of building ell, annex, alette
  pert. to alar
  -shaped alar(y), aliform
  without apteral, apterous
    bird emu, kiwi, ratite, apteryx
winged alar, flew, alate, pennate, feathered
  being amor, angel, seraph(im)
  figure Icarus

  goddess Nike
  fruit samara
  hat petasos
  hat/sandals wearer Hermes, Mercury
  heraldry aile
  horse Pegasus
  monster (myth.) harpy
  staff caduceus
  two dipteral
  without apteral
wingless locust weta
winks, forty nap, doze
winner reaper, victor
  long shot/surprise sleeper
Winnie the Pooh
  author A.A. Milne
  character Owl, Roo, Piglet, Tigger,
    Christopher Robin
winning
  lottery combination tern
winnings (sl.) velvet
winter season, hibernate
  cap toque, tuque
  pert. to brumal, hiemal, hibernal
  solstice festival saturnalia
winterbloom azalea
wintergreen pipsissewa
winy drunken, intoxicated
wire
  brush card
  coil/spiral spring
  cutting tool pliers
  lightbulb filament
  measure mil, stone
wire-puller snake, intriguer, puppeteer
wirework filigree
wireworm myriapod, millipede
wis deem, know, suppose
Wisconsin see also Quick Reference List
  state animal badger
  state fish musky, moskellunge
wisdom lore, learning, sapience
  god Nebo, Ganesa
  goddess Minerva
  symbol owl
  universal pansophy
wisdom tooth molar

wise deep, sage, brainy, erudite, learned, informed
   adviser mentor
   and pithy gnomic
   infinitely omniscient
   men, biblical magi
   saying saw, adage, maxim
   sl. fresh, savvy
wiseacre dunce, wisenheimer
wish
   mood of expression optative
wishbone furculum
wisht eerie, dismal, uncanny
wishy-washy pale, weak, trashy, watery
wist know
wistaria bush, fuji, violet
wit wag, mind, irony, sense, wisdom, drollery
   lively esprit (Fr.)
   lowest form pun
   sting barb
witch hag, hex, baba, siren, wizard, hellcat, sorceress
   cat grimalkin
   city Salem
   folklore Lilith
   Homer's Circe
   male warlock
   Shakespeare's Duessa
witchcraft cunning, sorcery, sortilege
   goddess Obeah, Hecate
witches' broom hexenbesen (Ger.)
witch hazel tree, hornbeam, astringent
with con (It.), cum (Lat.), mit (Ger.), avec (Fr.), near, along, among
   cruel tendencies sadistic
   force (mus.) con brio
   prefix col, com, cyn, pro, syn
withering away tabescent
within ben, inner, inside
   comb. form ent(o), eso
   prefix intra
without sans, sine, bereft, lacking, outside
   comb. form ecto
   feet apod
   life azoic

   prefix se, ect
   sound mute, silent
   this hoc, sine
witness see, attest, observe, testify, onlooker
   perjured strawman
   place in court stand
witticism gag, (bon) mot, pun, jest, joke, quip, sally, wisecrack
wittol fool, cuckold
Witt's planetoid Eros
witty droll, funny, salty, jocose, sparkling
   exchange repartee
   poem epigram
   reply sally, retort
wivern dragon, wyvern
wizard of Menlo Thomas Edison
woad dye, pastel, mustard
Woden Odin, Othin
woe
   tale jeremiad, lamentation
wolaba kangaroo
wold (Ger.) lea, weld, plain, woods
wolf lupus, philanderer
   female bitch
   male dog
   pert. to lupine
   young whelp
Wolfe, Nero fiction detective
wolfhound alan, borzoi
wolfsbane aconite, monkshood
Wolsey
   birthplace Ipswich
wolverine carcajou
   genus Gulo
woman
   bad-tempered bitch, shrew, vixen
   beautiful doll, belle, siren, Venus
   Brit. sl. bird
   chaste vestal, virgin
   childless nullifara
   comb. form gyn
   dowdy frump
   fairest Helen
   graceful sylph
   hater misogynist
   homosexual lesbian

killing femicide
unmarried old maid, spinster
origin Adam's rib
popular belle
shameless Jezebel
sl. babe, broad, skirt
spy Mata Hari
wombat marsupial
won win, live, abide, dwell
wonder boy prodigy
wonder of the world Pharos, Colossus,
  pyramids
wong field, meadow
wonky off, shaky, wobbly, tottering
wood grove, forest, lumber, timber
  alcohol methanol
  anemone thimbleweed
  bits kindling
  block nog, sprag
  charred bray
  comb. form hyl(o), xyl(o), lign(o), ligni
  cutter saw, ripsaw, chainsaw
  eater anay, termite
  flat piece splat
  groove chamfer
  hard elm, oak, ebony, maple, locust,
    hickory, mahogany
  inlaid buhl
  knot knar
  layer veneer
  light balsa
  measure cord, foot
  of xyloid, ligneous
  pussy skunk
  stork ibis
  strip slat, batten
woodbine ivy, honeysuckle
woodchuck marmot, groundhog
wooded sylvan
  area weald, boondocks
  hill holt
wooden dull, stiff, stolid
  bench settle
  bowl kitty, mazer
  bucket cannikin
  limb peg leg
  shoe clog, geta, sabot, patten

woodland
  burned brulee
  clearing glade
  deity Pan, faun, Diana, satyr, Silenus
  landscape boscage
woodpecker flicker, popinjay,
    sapsucker
  genus Yunx, Picus
  type hairy, imperial, pileated
woods forest
  love of nemophily
  pert. to sylvan, nemoral
woody bosky, xyloid, ligneous
  fiber bast, hemp, xylem
woof abb, cloth, fabric, filling
wool pile, alpaca, angora, fleece
  bearing laniferous
  blemish mote
  cluster nep
  comb. form lani
  covered with lanate, floccose
  dryer fugal
  fiber noil, pile, sliver
  goat's cashmere
  lock tag
  measure heer
  particles down
  sheep merino
  spinning machine throstle
  twisted rove
  weight tod
woolen cloth jersey, melton, tartan,
    doeskin, worsted
woolfell pelt
woolly-haired people Ulotrichi
word talk, parole, pledge, remark
  action verb
  appropriate mot juste
  battle logomachy
  change metaplasm
  final amen, ultimatum
  four-letter tetragram
  hard to pronounce jawbreaker
  long (sl.) mouthful
  of mouth oral
  of opposite meaning antonym
  of similar meaning synonym

same pronunciation, different meaning homonym, homophone
same spelling, different meaning heteronym, homograph
symbol logogram
word-for-word exactly, verbatim, literally
word of God Logos
word puzzle rebus, anagram, charade, acrostic, crossword, cryptogram
wordy prolix, verbose
work job, labor, effort
amount load
at ply
avoid shirk
bag kit
book manual
box etui, (tool) kit
hard toil, labor, sweat
life career
of wonder miracle
pants Levis
suitable metier
trainee apprentice
worker employe(e), laborer
agricultural Okie, peon, farmer, hired hand
coal mine collier
skilled artisan, craftsman
transient hobo, floater
white-collar clerk
works books, oeuvres (Fr.)
world earth, realm, cosmos, universe
bearer Atlas
out of this outre
pert. to mundane, temporal, terrestrial
wide global, ecumenic, universal
worm bob, ess, grub, crawl, creep, wretch, nematode
bloodsucking leech
comb. form vermi
feeler palp(us)
flat fluke, trematode
genus Nereis
larva maggot, caterpillar
out extract
round ascarid
sand nemertean

sea sao
-shaped vermiform
worn jaded, tired, shabby, tattered
by friction attrite
clothes rags
out seedy, spent, fatigued, exhausted
worricow devil, bugaboo
worse pejority
worship
comb. form latry
of all gods pantheism
of idols idolism
of saints hagiolatry
of stars sabaism
pert. to liturgic
system cult, fetish
wort herb, fleabane
worth merit, price, value, deserving
having asset, desirable
of little trifle
worthless
fellow bum, idler
ideas bilge
scrap ort
thing chip, tripe, rubbish
wound cut, gore, harm, pain, stab, grief, sting, insult, trauma, lacerate
in heraldry vuln
woven
double two-ply
with raised design broche
wowf wild, crazed
wowser prude, puritanical
wrap cover, mantle, swathe, pelisse
around sarong, loin cloth
in burial cloth cere
snugly tuck
up enfold, envelop
wrapper fardel, galabeah
wrasse ballan, cunner, fishes
wreath lei, anadem, garland
bridal spirea
heraldry torse
victor's crown, laurel
wreckage jetsam, flotsam
wrestling
hold (head)lock, (half) nelson, scissors

Oriental sumo
score fall
throw hipe
Wright, Wilbur/Orville airplane
  inventors
wrinkled crepey, rugate
  without smooth, erugate
wristbone carpal(e), trapezoid
writ breve, process, warrant, document
  of execution outre
  to serve in court venire, summons,
    subpoena
writer author, scribe, amanuensis
  inferior hack
  play dramatist
  verse poet, rhymer
writing
  comb. form log(ue)
  mark character
  pretentious kitsch
  secret code, cipher
  senseless balderdash
  sentimental slush
writings literature
  collection papers
  unpublished remains
wrong evil, abuse, sinful, wicked, immoral,
  erroneous, incorrect
  act misdeed
  civil tort
  name misnomer
  prefix mal, mis
wryneck (snake)bird, Ioxia, woodpecker,
  torticollis
  genus Jynx
Wurttemberg
  city Ulm, Stuttgart
  measure imi
  river Danube
Wuthering Heights
  author Emily Bronte
Wycliffe disciple Hus(s), Lollard
wynd haw, lane, alley, close, court
Wyoming see also Quick Reference List
  cavern Shoshone
  mountain Moran, Teton
wyvern dragon

X

X ten, mark, signature
  Gr. xi
  letter ex
  marker, usually illiterate
  marks the spot
  -shaped ex
Xanadu
  country China
  river Alph
  ruler khan
xanthic yellow
Xanthippe scold, shrew, nagger,
  termagent
  husband Socrates
xanthous yellow, Mongolian
Xavier, Francis Sp. Jesuit saint
xebec boat, ship, vessel
  common users commerce, corsairs
xema gull
xenagogue guide
xenagogy guidebook
xenicus bush, wren
xenium gift, present
xeno alien, guest, strange
  as prefix foreign, strange
xenodochy hospitality
xenogamy fertilization
xenon Xe, element
Xenophanean eleatic
Xenophon
  teacher Socrates
  work Anabasis
Xeres wine, Jerez, sherry
  bridge site Abydos
xerophilous plant cactus, xerophyte
  animal camel
xerotic dry, sec
xerus squirrel
Xerxes I
  parents Atossa, Darius
  wife Esther, Vashti
Xhosa, Xosa Bantu, tribe, language
xiphoid ensiform, sword-shaped

xiphosuran arachnid, king crab, horseshoe crab
X-ray
  inventor Wilhelm Roentgen
  measuring device quantimeter
  science rontgenology, roentgenology
  source target
  type grenzray
X-shaped cruciate
Xtian Christian
Xuthus
  consort Creusa
  son Dorus, Achaeus
xylan pentosan
xylem wood, hadrome
xylo, comb. form wood
xylograph print, engraving, impression (on wood)
xyloid woody, ligneous
xylonite celluloid
xylophone saron, gender, marimba, gambang, gamelan, sticcado, gigelira
xylotomous insect anay, termite
xyrid iris
xyst walk, xystum, xystus, portico
xyster (bone) scraper
xystos, xystus stoa, porch, portico, terrace

Y

Y wye
  in mathematics ordinate
  men Elis
yabber talk, jabber, chatter, language
yabbi wolf, dasyure (Austral. and Tasmanian)
yacht boat, race, craft, sonder
  club president commodore
  flag burgee
  racing sonderclass
  sail spinnaker
  tender dinghy
Yadkin Pee Dee River
yaff yap, bark, yelp
yaffle armful, handful, woodpecker

yager bird, hunter, jaeger, rifleman
yahoo lout, brute, savage, bumpkin
  creator Jonathan Swift
Yahwe(h) God, Jehovah
yak ox, zobo, sarlak, buffalo
  crossbred yakalo, yakattalo
  found in Tibet
yakamik trumpeter
yaki cayman
yakka work, labor
yaksha god, jinn, ogre, angel, demon, dryad, fairy, gnome, spirit
Yakut/Yakutsk River Lena
Yale Eli, lock, university
  bowl sound boola-boola
  Mr. Elihu Root
Yalta
  native Crimean
yam hoi, ube, ubi, tuqui, igname, boniata, cush-cush, sweet potato
Yamashita, Tomoyuki Jp. general
  sobriquet Tiger
yamen office, mansion, residence, headquarters
  resident mandarin, official
yammadji native, blackfellow
yamp tuber
yang cry, honk (like a wild goose)
  kin dulcimer
  opposite yin
yang-kin dulcimer
Yangtze River city Wuhu, Nanking
yank jerk, pull, hoick
Yank, Yankee American, Northerner
  bump pothole
  doodle Prince Rupert
yannigan scrub
yap apt, cur, bark, fool, yelp, mouth, active, bumpkin
  sl. rowdy, hoodlum, greenhorn
Yap Island money fei, stone
yapp binding
yard(s) area, staff, stick, enclosure
  5 1/2 rod
  600 heer
  16th nail
  220 furlong

yardland virgate
yare well, agile, eager, lively, prompt, prepared
yarm wail, whine, scream
yarn abb, eis, tale, crewel, genappe
  ball clew
  count typp
  holder cop
  reel pirn
  spindle hasp
  waste thrum
yarr spuvrey
yarrow herb, milfoil
yashmak veil
yataghan knife, saber
yaud jade, mare
yauld mare, sharp, healthy
yaupon holly, cassena
  use tea
yaw turn, veer, tumor, lesion, deviate
yawp bay, yap, call, bawl, complain
yaws pian, frambesia
  cause spirochete
yclept named, known (as), called
yeanling kid, lamb, newborn
year age, time, annum, annus (Lat.)
  book annal, almanac
  divisions fourth trimester (calendar), half semester (academic), third trimester (academic)
  types leap, lunar, solar, fiscal, calendar, bissextile
Yearling colt, leveret
  author Marjorie Kinnan Rawlings
  boy Jody
yeast bee, rise, froth, ferment
  brewer's barm
  enzyme zymase
yegg thug, thief, beggar, burglar
yellow mean, sere, blake, fallow, cowardly
  alloy brass
  copper ore chalcopyrite
  jacket wasp, eucalypt
  mustard charlock
  pigment etiolin, orpiment
  star sneezeweed
yellow race Mongol, Chinese, Mongolian

Yellow River Hwang Ho
yeme care, heed, regard, observe
Yemen Arab, Arabian, country
  capital Sanaa
  seaport Mocha, Mukha
  seat of government Taiz
  sect Zaidi
  town Sana, Damar
yenite livaite
yeoman clerk, farmer, retainer, assistant
  -ly sturdy, faithful
  of guard exon
yes yea(h), yep, agree
  Fr. oui
  Ger. ja
  man sycophant
  opposite no, nope, uh-uh
  Russ. da
  Sp. and It. sí
yeso gypsum
yeti monster, snowman
yew tree, conifer
  genus Taxus
  fruit cone, berry
Yiddish Jewish, language
  authority maven
  pray daven
  synagogue shul
yill ale
Ymir giant
  slayer Ve, Odin, Vili
yin one, dark, feminine, negative
yird earth (Scot.)
yirr growl, snarl
yogi fakir, swami, yogin, ascetic
yoke wed, join, pair, team, pillory, harness
  bar skey (S. Afr.)
  comb. form zygo
yoked joined, conjugate
yokel oaf, clod, rube, rustic, hayseed, gullible
yoking bout, contest
yolk essence, vitellus, inner core
yolkless alecithal
yore eld, formerly, long ago
Yorkshire
  district Otley, Selby

river Ure
town Leeds
young fry, tyro, junior, tender, offspring
  animal cub, pup, joey, chick, kitten, tadpole
  branch shoot
  hare leveret
  herring brit
  kangaroo joey
  squab piper
younker knight, nobleman
youth bud, minor, hoyden, adolescent, adolescence
  goddess Hebe
  myth. Etana, Adonis, Apollo, Icarus
  shelter hostel
yowl, yowt cry, wail, yell
yperite mustard gas
  used in battle Ypres
Yucatan
  city Merida
  drink balach
  people Maya, Mayan
  tree yaxche
yucca flat, lily, pita, palma, bear grass, adam's needle
  fiber isote
  -like plant sotol
Yugoslavia (former)
  brandy rakia, slivovitz
  capital Belgrade
  city Agram, Pirot, Zagreb, Belgrade, Sarajevo
  coin para, dinar
  commune Pec, Stip, Veles
  island Rab, Vis, Cres, Solta
  measure akov, khvat, palaze, dan oranja
  monarch Broz, Tito, Peter
  people Serb, Croat, Slovens
  region Banat(e), Bosnia, Serbia
  river Sava, Drina, Danube, Vardar
  weight oka, dramm, tovar, wagon, satlijk
Yukon
  capital Whitehorse
  mountain peak Logan

region Klondike
town Dawson
yummy tasty, delicious, delectable
Yum-Yum
  consort Nankipoo

Z

Z zee
Zabbai Israelite
  father Bebai
  son Baruch
Zabud
  father Nathan
zac goat, ibex
zacate hay, grass, forage
Zacch(a)eus pure, innocent
Zaccur
  father Imri, Asaph, Jaaziah, Mattaniah
  son Hanan
Zacharias
  father Barachias
  son John, Josep
  wife Elisabeth
zachun oil, bito
zadok just, righteous
Zadoke
  daughter Jerusha
  father Baana, Immer, Ahitub, Meraioth
  grandson Jotham
  son Ahimaaz
Zagreb(ab) city in Yugoslavia
Zagreus Dionysus
zaguan gate, entrance, entranceway
Zaire
  former name Congo, Belgian Congo
  animal okapi
  capital Kinshasa
  lake Tumba
  official language French
  people Bantu, Pygmy, Hamitic, Nilotic, Sudanese
  river Uele, Congo, Zaire, Aruwimi
zakuska whet, antipasto, appetizer, hors d'oeuvre

Zalmunna
  slayer Gideon
Zambales (Malay)
  capital Iba
  language Tino
Zambia Northern Rhodesia
  capital Lusaka
  monetary unit kwacha
  national park Luanga Valley
Zamboanga chief city of Mindanao
Zamindar
  chief/overseer mirdha, mirdaha
zampogna bagpipe, panpipe
zanja arrow, canal, ditch, gully, arroyo
zany, zanni dolt, clown, dotty, buffoon,
  simpleton, merry-andrew
Zanzibar island Pemba
  sultan sayid
Zarathustra see Zoroaster
zarf stand, cupholder
zati monkey, macaque
Zauberflote composer Wolfgang Mozart
zeal fire, ardor, hurrah, passion
Zealand
  city Copenhagen
Zealand Island
  fiord isse
zealot bug, bigot, friend, devotee
zealous avid, eager, ardent, earnest
Zebedee
  son John, James
  wife Salome
zebra dauw
  extinct quagga
  wood araroba, nakedwood, marblewood
Zebulun
  brother Levi, Judah, Simeon
  father Jacob
  mother Leah
  son Elon, Sered, Jahleel
zecchin(o) coin, sequin
Zechariah
  child Abi, John, Abijah, Uzziah
  father Elam, Bebai, Hosah, Jonathan
  grandson Hezekiah
  slayer Jehoram
  wife Elizabeth

Zedekiah
  brother Jehoahaz
  father Josiah, Hananiah, Jeconiah,
    Maaseiah
  mother Hamutal
Zen
  founder Bodhidharma
  master roshi
zenana harem, seraglio
  factotum eunuch
  resident odalisk(que), concubine
Zeno
  follower cynic, stoic
  philosophy stoicism
Zephaniah
  father Maaseiah
  son Josiah
Zephi, Zepho
  father Eliphaz
  grandfather Esau
zephyr aura, wind, breeze
Zerah
  brother Perez
  father Reuel
  grandfather Esau
  mother Tamar
  son Jobab
Zerbino
  beloved Isabella
  friend Orlando
  sister Ginevra
  slayer Mandricardo
Zeruah
  husband Nebat
  son Jeroboam
Zeruiah
  brother David
  sister Abigail
  son Joab, Asahel, Abishai
zest brio, tang, gusto, piquancy
  -ful racy, sapid, pungent
Zetes
  brother Calais
  father Boreas
  mother Orithyia
  slayer Hercules
zetetic seeker, doubter, skeptic

Zethus
  brother Amphion
  father Zeus, Jupiter
  mother Antiope
Zeus Jupiter
  attendant Nike
  beloved Io, Leda, Europa
  breastplate (A)egis
  brother Hades, Poseidon
  changed her to stone Niobe
  daughter Ate, Hebe, Kore, Irene,
    Athena(e), Artemis, Astraea, Despoina,
    Aphrodite, Persephone, Perephassa,
    Proserpina
  disguise bull, swan
  Egyptian's ammon
  epithet soter, ammon, Alastor
  festival nemean
  gift to Minos talos
  lover Juno, Leda, Aegle, Ceres,
    Aegina, Alceme, Europa, Latona,
    Themis, Antiope, Demeter, Callisto,
    Eorynome
  messenger Iris, Hermes
  monster killed by Typhoeus
  nurse goat, Cynosura
  oracle Dodona
  parent Rhea, Cronus, Kronos
  punishment to mankind Pandora
  sister Hera
  son Gad, Ares, Arcas, Argus, Minos,
    Aeacus, Apollo, Hermes, Tityus,
    Amphion, Dardano, Perseus,
    Dionysos(sus), Heracles, Herakies,
    Hercules, Sarpedon, Tantalus,
    Hephaestus
  surname Alastor
  victim Idas
  wife Hera, Danae, Metis, Semele
ziara, ziarat tomb, shrine
Zichri
  father Asaph, Shimei, Jeroham
  son Joel, Eliezer, Amasiah, Elishaphat
  victim Maaseiah
zigzag turn, weave, chevron
Zillah
  daughter Naamah

  husband Lamech
  son Tubal-cain
Zilpah
  son Gad, Asher
  husband Jacob
zimarra cloak, cassock, soutane
zimb bug, fly, insect
Zimbabwe
  capital Harare
  former name Rhodesia
Zimran
  father Abraham
  mother Keturah
Zimri
  father Zerah
  grandfather Judah
  victim Elah
zinc metal, spelter, adamine, element,
    tutenag
  alloy bidri, oroide, tombak(ach)
  blend sphalerite
  carbonate calamine, smithsonite
  ingots spelter
  ore blende
  oxide tutty
  silicate calamine
  symbol Zn
zingara(o) gypsy
zingel fish, perch
Zion hill, Jews, heaven
Zionism founder Theodor Herzl
Zionist
  Am. Szold
  Eng. Zangwill
  Ger. Nordau
  Israeli Buber, Weizman
Zipangu Japan, Cipango
  namer of Marco Polo
Zipporah
  father Reuel, Jethro
  husband Moses
  son Eliezer, Gershorn
zippy keen, spry, agile, intense
zircon jargon
  variety starlite, hyacinth
zither
  Chinese kin

featured in movie The Third Man
Jp. koto
Ziza
  father Rehoboam
  mother Maacah
zizany weed, tares, cockle
zizith fringes, tassles
zloty money of Poland
Zoan tanis
Zobeide
  sister Amina
zodiac circle, girdle
zoetic alive, vital, animated
Zohar
  father Simeon
  son Ephron
Zoheth
  father Ishi
Zola, Emile
  defender of Alfred Dreyfus
  work Nana, Verite, J'accuse
zombi(e) snake, python, cocktail
  subject corpse
zone area, belt, cincture
  geological succession assise
  marked by zonate
zonked high, tight, stoned
zooid coral, hydranth, polypite
zoologist
  Am. Hyatt, Kinsey, Osborn, Ditmars, Merriam
  Brit. Darwin, Huxley, Medawar, Lankester
  Dut. Swammerdam
  Fr. Cuvier
  Ger. Haeckel, Spemann
  Norwegian Nansen

S. Afr. Broom
Swedish Linnaeus
zoom chandelle
zoophyte coral, sponge, retepore
zoril(a) weasel, polecat, mariput
Zoroaster Zarathustra
  birthplace Azerbaijan
  demon Deva
  evil spirit Ahriman
  supreme deity Ormazd
  teaching Humata
  trian yema, Parsi, gheber
  works (Zend) Avesta
zucchetto calotte, skullcap
zug canton (Swiss)
zuisin duck, widgeon, baldplate
zules rook
Zulu Rantu, island, Kaffir, Matabele
  capital Eshowe
  headman Induna
  language Bantu
  native (Philippines) Muslim, Moro, Badjao
  spear assagai, assegai
  warriors impi
Zur
  brother Kish
  daughter Cozbi
  father Jeiel
zwieback bread, toast, biscuit
zygodactl bird parrot
zygoma bone
zygote oocyst, oosperm
zymase enzyme
zymogen activating substance kinase
zymone gluten
zythepsary brewer

Quick
Reference
List

FOREIGN ALPHABETS

Greek	Hebrew	Arabic
alpha	aleph	alif
beta	beth	ba
gamma	gimel	ta
delta	daleth	tha
epsilon	he	jim
zeta	vav	ha
eta	zayin	kha
theta	cheth	dal
iota	teth	dhal
kappa	yodh	ra
lambda	kaph	zay
mu	lamedh	sin
nu	mem	shin
xi	nun	sad
omicron	samekh	dad
pi	ayin	ta
rho	pe	za
sigma	sadie	ayn
tau	koph	ghayn
upsilon	resh	fa
phi	shin	gaf
chi	sin	kaf
psi	tav	lam
omega		mim
		nun
		hah
		waw
		ya

FOREIGN TERMS

Days of the Week	French	German	Italian	Spanish
Sunday	dimanche	Sonntag	domenica	domingo
Monday	lundi	Montag	lunedi	lunes
Tuesday	mardi	Dienstag	martedi	martes
Wednesday	mercredi	Mittwoch	mercoledi	miercoles
Thursday	jeudi	Donnerstag	giovedi	jueves
Friday	vendredi	Freitag	venerdi	viernes
Saturday	samedi	Soonabend	sabato	sabado

Months	French	German	Italian	Spanish
January	janvier	Januar	gennaio	enero
February	fevrier	Februar	febbraio	febrero
March	mars	Marz	marzo	marzo
April	avril	April	aprile	abril
May	mai	Mai	maggio	mayo
June	juin	Juni	giugno	junio
July	juillet	Juli	luglio	julio
August	aout	August	agosto	agosto
September	septembre	September	settembre	se(p)tiembre
October	octobre	Oktober	ottobre	octubre
November	novembre	November	novembre	noviembre
December	decembre	Dezember	dicembre	diciembre

Numbers	French	German	Italian	Spanish
1	un	eins	uno	uno
2	deux	zwei	due	dos
3	trois	drei	tre	tres
4	quatre	vier	quattro	cuatro
5	cinq	funf	cinque	cinco
6	six	sechs	sei	seis
7	sept	sieben	sette	siete
8	huit	acht	otto	ocho
9	neuf	neun	nove	nueve
10	dix	zehn	dieci	diez
20	vingt	zwanzig	venti	veinte
30	trente	dreissig	trenta	treinta
40	quarante	vierzig	quaranta	cuarenta
50	cinquante	funfzig	cinquanta	cincuenta
60	soixante	sechzig	sessanta	sesenta
70	soixante-dix	siebzig	settanta	setenta
80	quatre-vingt	achtzig	ottanta	ochenta
90	quatre-vingt dix	neunzig	novanta	noventa
100	cent	hundert	cento	cien
1000	mille	tausend	mille	mil

JEWISH CALENDAR

Tishrei
Cheshvan
Kislev
Tevet
Shevat
Adar or Veadar
Nissan
Iyar
Sivan
Tammuz
Ab or Av
Elul

JEWISH HOLIDAYS

Rosh Hashana, Rosh Hashona
Yom Kippur
Succos, Sukkos, Sukkoth
Shemini Atzereth
Simhath Torah
Chanukah, Hanukkah
Purim
Pesah, Pesach, Passover
Lag b'Omer
Shevouth
Tishah b'Ab or bov

NATIVE TRIBES

ALASKA Aleut, Sitka

ALEUTIAN Attu

ALGONQUIN Abnaki, Arapaho, Blackfoot, Cheyenne, Cree, Delaware, Fox, Illinois, Lenape, Massachuset, Miami, Micmac, Mohican, Montagnais, Ojibway, Ottawa, Piegan, Sac, Sauk, Shawnee, Sokoki, Wea

AMAZON Apcoa, Mua

NORTH AMERICA Abenaki, Abnaki, Aht, Algonquin, Amerind, Apache, Apalachee, Apalachi, Arapaho, Bank, Caddo, Cherokee, Chickasaw, Chippewa, Choctaw, Comanche, Coree, Cree, Creek, Dakota, Dene, Erie, Hitchiti, Hopi, Huron, Ioni, Iowa, Iroquois, Kania, Kansa, Kansas, Kaw, Keres, Keresan, Kickapoo, Kiowa, Lenape, Miami, Mohave, Mojave, Muskhogean, Narraganset, Navaho, Navajo, Nootka, Omaha, Oneida, Onondaga, Osage, Oto, Otoe, Ottawa, Paiute, Pawnee, Pima, Piute, Pokonchi, Red, Redman, Redskin, Sac, Sagamore, Sambos, Seminole, Seneca, Shoshone, Sioux, Siwash, Tana, Taos, Tinne, Ute, Winnebago, Yuma, Zuni

APACHE Lipan

ARAWAK Araua, Campa, Guana, Ineri

ARIKARA Ree

ARIZONA Apache, Hano, Hopi, Moki, Moqui, Navaho, Navajo, Pima, Tewa, Yuma

ATHAPASCAN Apache, Dene, Hoopa, Hupa, Lipan, Navaho, Navajo, Taku, Tinne, Tinneh

AYMARA Colla

BOLIVIA Aymara, Chiriguano, Cholo, Ite, Iten, Leca, Mojo, Moxo, Uran, Uro, Uru

BRAZIL Acroa, Andoa, Araua, Bravo, Came, Carib, Diau, Ge, Guana, Maku, Mura, Puri, Puru, Siusi, Tariana, Tupi, Yao, Zaparo

BRITISH COLUMBIA Gitksan

CADDOAN Adai, Andarko, Arikara, Arikaree, Bidai, Caddo, Eyeish, Hainai, Ioni, Machitoch, Pawnee, Ree, Waco

CALGARY Sarsi

CALIFORNIA Hupa, Koso, Maidu, Mono, Nozi, Pomo, Salina, Seri, Tatu, Yana, Yanan

CANADA	Aht, Athabasca, Athabascan, Cree, Dene, Niska, Sanetch, Sarcee, Taku, Tinne, Tinneh
CARIB	Trio, Yao
CARIBAN	Akawais, Aparais, Arara, Arecunas, Bakairis, Caribs, Chaymas, Cumanagotos, Macusis, Maquiritares, Oyanas, Tamanacos, Trios, Woyaways, Yaos, Yauapery
CAROLINA	Catawba
CHACO	Toba
CHILE	Auca
COLORADO	Ute
COLUMBIA	Boro, Choco, Duit, Muso, Muzo, Tama, Tapa
COPEHAN	Wintun
COSTA RICA	Boto, Voto
COWICHANS	Nanaimo
DAKOTAS	Arikara, Mandan, Ree, Santee, Sioux, Teton
DELAWARE	Lenape
ECUADOR	Andoa, Ardan, Cara
ESKIMO	Aleut, Atka
FLORIDA	Calusa
FUEGIAN	Alikuluf, Ona, Yahgan
GREAT LAKES	Erie, Huron
GUATEMALA	Chol, Itza, Ixil, Ixli, Kiche, Mam, Maya, Pipil, Ulva, Voto
HONDURAS	Paya
HOPI	Moki, Moqui
INDIANA	Miami, Wea
IOWA	Fox, Sac, Sauk
IROQUOIS	Cayuga, Erie, Hochelaga, Huron, Mohawk, Oneida, Seneca, Wyandot
JALISCO	Cora
KERESAN	Acoma, Sia
KUSAN	Coos
LESSER ANTILLES	Ineri
MANITOBA	Cree

MAYAN Chol, Mam

MEXICO Aztec, Chol, Cora, Mam, Maya, Mixe, Otomi, Pima, Pime, Seri, Seria, Teca, Teco, Toltec, Wabi

MIAMI Wea

MISSISSIPPI Biloxi, Tiou

MISSOURI Osage

MONTANA Crow, Hohe

MUSKOHEGAN Choctaw, Creek, Hitchiti, Seminole, Yamasi

NEBRASKA Kiowa, Omaha, Otoe

NEVADA Digger, Paiute

NEW MEXICO Acoma, Keres, Pecos, Piro, Sia, Tano, Taos, Tewa, Zuni

NEW YORK Erie, Oneida, Seneca, Tuscarora

NICARAGUA Mixe, Rama, Ulva

NORTH CAROLINA Buffalo, Coree

NORTHWEST Cree

OKLAHOMA Caddo, Cherokee, Choctaw, Creek, Kansa, Kiowa, Loup, Osage, Oto, Otoe, Pawnee, Ponca, Quapaw

OREGON Chinook, Coos, Kusan, Modoc

ORINOCO VALLEY Guahiribo

PANAMA Cueva, Cuna, Guaymi, Guaymie

PANAMINT Koso

PARAGUAY Guayaqui

PARU RIVER Araquaju

PAYAGUAS Agas

PEBAN Yagua

PERU Ande, Anti, Aymara, Boros, Campa, Cana, Carib, Chanca, Chimu, Cholo, Colan, Inca, Inka, Jibaro, Jiyaro, Kechua, Lama, Lamano, Panos, Peba, Pesa, Piba, Piroc, Quechau, Quichu, Yunca, Yuru

PERU (South) Cana, Chanca, Colla

PIMAN Cora, Jova, Mayo, Opata, Pima, Xova, Yaki, Yaqui

PLATTE RIVER Pawnee

PLAINS Cree, Crow, Kiowa, Osage, Pawnee, Ponca, Teton

PUEBLO	Hopi, Keres, Moki, Moqui, Piro, Tano, Taos, Zuni
QUAPAW	Ozark
QUECHUAN	Inca
RIO GRANDE	Tano, Tao
SACRAMENTO VALLEY	Yana
SALISHAN	Atnah, Lummi, Tulalip
SHOSHONE	Comanche, Hopi, Koso, Moki, Mono, Moque, Otoe, Paiute, Piute, Uinta, Utah, Ute
SIOUX	Biloxi, Catawba, Crow, Dakota, Hidata, Iowa, Kansa, Kaw, Mandan, Omaha, Osage, Oto, Otoe, Ponca, Saponi, Tutelo
SONORA	Jova, Pimi, Seri
SOUTH AMERICA	Arawak, Aztec, Carib, Ges, Inca, Ineri, Lule, Moxo, Ona, Pano, Piro, Toba, Yao
SOUTH CAROLINA	Catawba
TACANAN	Cavina
TANOAN	Tewa
TAPUYAN	Acroa, Ge, Ges, Ghes
TEXAS	Lipan
TIERRA DEL FUEGO	Agni, Ona
TLINGIT	Auk, Sitka
TUPIAN	Anta
UCHEAN	Uchee, Yuchi
UTAH	Paiute, Piute, Ute
VANCOUVER ISLAND	Aht, Ehatisaht
VENEZUELA	Carib, Guarauno, Timote, Timotex
VIRGINIA	Algonquin, Powhatan
WAKASHAN	Nootka
WASHINGTON	Aht, Callam, Hoh, Lummi, Makah
WESTERN	Kaw, Seri
WISCONSIN	Sac

WYOMING	Crow, Kiowa
XINGU RIVER	Aneto
YUCATAN	Maya
YUKIAN	Huchnom, Tatu, Wappo, Yuki
YUKON	Taku
YUNCAN	Chimu
ZUNI LAND	Cibola

BIRTH FLOWERS AND STONES

Month	Flower	Stone
January	carnation	garnet
February	primrose	amethyst
March	violet	aquamarine, bloodstone, jasper
April	daisy	diamond, sapphire
May	lily of the valley	emerald
June	rose	agate, alexandrite, pearl
July	sweet pea	ruby
August	gladiolus	peridot, sardonyx
September	aster	chrysolite, sapphire
October	dahlia	opal, tourmaline
November	chrysanthemum	topaz
December	poinsettia	turquoise, zircon

ZODIAC SIGNS

Zodiac	Symbol	Planet	Element
Aries	The Ram	Mars	fire
Taurus	The Bull	Venus	earth
Gemini	The Twins	Mercury	air
Cancer	The Crab	Moon	water
Leo	The Lion	Sun	fire
Virgo	The Virgin	Mercury	earth
Libra	The Scales	Venus	air
Scorpio	The Scorpion	Mars	water
Sagittarius	The Archer	Jupiter	fire
Capricorn	The Goat	Saturn	earth
Aquarius	The Water Carrier	Uranus	air
Pisces	The Fishes	Neptune	water

PRESIDENTS OF THE UNITED STATES

President First Lady	Vice President	Secretary of State
1. George Washington Martha Dandridge Custis	John Adams	Jefferson, Randolph, Pickering
2. John Adams Abigail Smith	Thomas Jefferson	Pickering, Marshall
3. Thomas Jefferson Martha Wayles Skelton	Aaron Burr George Clinton	Madison

4. James Madison
    Dorothy (Dolly)
    Payne Todd
	George Clinton
	Elbridge Gerry
		Smith, Monroe

5. James Monroe Elizabeth Kortwright	Daniel D. Tompkins	John Quincy Adams
6. John Quincy Adams Louisa Catherine Johnson	John C. Calhoun	Clay
7. Andrew Jackson Rachel Donelson Robards	John C. Calhoun, Martin Van Buren	Van Buren, Livingston, McLane, Forsyth
8. Martin Van Buren Hannah Hoes	Richard M. Johnson	Forsyth
9. William Henry Harrison Anna Symmes	John Tyler	Daniel Webster

10. John Tyler
    Letitia Christian,
    Julia Gardiner
	—	Webster, Upshur,
		Calhoun

11. James Knox Polk Sarah Childress	George M. Dallas	Calhoun, Buchanan
12. Zachary Taylor Margaret Smith	Millard Fillmore	Buchanan, Clayton

13. Millard Fillmore
    Abigail Powers,
    Caroline Carmichael
    McIntosh
	—	Clayton, Webster,
		Everett

14. Franklin Pierce Jane Means Appleton	William R. King	Marcy
15. James Buchanan	John C. Breckinridge	Marcy, Cass, Black
16. Abraham Lincoln Mary Todd	Hannibal Hamlin, Andrew Johnson	Black, Seward
17. Andrew Johnson Eliza McCardle	—	Seward, Washburne
18. Ulysses Simpson Grant Julia Dent	Schuyler Colfax Henry Wilson	Washburne, Fish
19. Rutherford Birchard Hayes Lucy Ware Webb	William A. Wheeler	Fish, Evarts

President First Lady	Vice President	Secretary of State
20. James Abram Garfield Lucretia Rudolph	Chester A. Arthur	Evarts, Blaine
21. Chester Alan Arthur Ellen Lewis Herndon	—	Blaine, Frelinghuysen
22. Grover Cleveland Frances Folsom	Thomas A. Hendricks	Frelinghuysen, Bayard

23. Benjamin Harrison
   Caroline Lavinia Scott,
   Mary Scott Lord
   Dimmock
	Levi P. Morton	Bayard, Blaine,
		Foster

24. Grover Cleveland Frances Folsom	Adlai E. Stevenson	Gresham, Olney
25. William McKinley Ida Saxton	Garret A. Hobart, Theodore Roosevelt	Olney, Sherman, Day, Hay

26. Theodore Roosevelt
   Alice Hathaway Lee,
   Edith Kermit Carow
	Charles W. Fairbanks	Hay, Root, Bacon

27. William Howard Taft Helen Herron	James S. Sherman	Bacon, Knox

28. Woodrow Wilson
   Ellen Louise Axon,
   Edith Bolling Galt
	Thomas R. Marshall	Knox, Bryan, Lansing,
		Colby

29. Warren Gamaliel Harding Florence Kling De Wolfe	Calvin Coolidge	Hughes
30. Calvin Coolidge Grace Anna Goodhue	Charles G. Dawes	Hughes, Kellogg
31. Herbert Clark Hoover Lou Henry	Charles Curtis	Kellogg, Stimson
32. Franklin Delano Roosevelt Anna Eleanor Roosevelt	John Nance Garner, Henry A. Wallace, Harry S. Truman	Hull, Stettinius

33. Harry S. Truman
   Elizabeth (Bess)
     Virginia Wallace
	Alben W. Barkley	Stettinius, Byrnes,
		Marshall, Acheson

34. Dwight David Eisenhower Mamie Geneva Dowd	Richard M. Nixon	Dulles, Herter
35. John Fitzgerald Kennedy Jacqueline Lee Bouvier	Lyndon B. Johnson	Rusk

36. Lyndon Baines Johnson
   Claudia (Lady Bird)
   Alta Taylor
	Hubert H. Humphrey	Rusk

President First Lady	Vice President	Secretary of State
37. Richard Milhous Nixon Thelma Patricia Ryan	Spiro Agnew Gerald R. Ford	Rogers, Kissinger
38. Gerald Rudolph Ford Elizabeth (Betty) Bloomer Warren	Nelson A. Rockefeller	Kissinger
39. Jimmy (James Earl) Carter Rosalynn Smith	Walter F. Mondale	Vance
40. Ronald Wilson Reagan Nancy Davis	George H. Bush	Haig, Shultz
41. George Herbert Walker Bush Barbara Pierce	J. Danforth Quayle	Baker
42. William Jefferson Clinton Hillary Rodham	Albert Gore Jr.	Christopher

THIRTEEN ORIGINAL STATES

State	Date of Admission
Delaware	December 7, 1787
Pennsylvania	December 12, 1787
New Jersey	December 18, 1787
Georgia	January 2, 1788
Connecticut	January 9, 1788
Massachusetts	February 6, 1788
Maryland	April 28, 1788
South Carolina	May 23, 1788
New Hampshire	June 21, 1788
Virginia	June 25, 1788
New York	July 26, 1788
North Carolina	November 21, 1789
Rhode Island	May 29, 1790

STATE FACTS

ALABAMA
Capital	Montgomery
Nicknames	Cotton State, Heart of Dixie, Yellowhammer State
Motto	We Dare Defend Our Rights
Flower	Camellia
Tree	Southern pine
Bird	Yellowhammer

ALASKA
Capital	Juneau
Nickname	The Last Frontier
Motto	North to the Future
Flower	Forget-me-not
Tree	Sitka spruce
Bird	Willow ptarmigan

ARIZONA
Capital	Phoenix
Nicknames	Apache, Grand Canyon State, Sunset Land
Motto	God Enriches (Ditat Deus)
Flower	Saguaro (giant cactus)
Tree	Palo verde
Bird	Cactus wren

ARKANSAS
Capital	Little Rock
Nicknames	Bear State, Bowie State, Land of Opportunity, Wonder
Motto	(Let) The People Rule (Regnat Populus)
Flower	Apple blossom
Tree	Shortleaf pine
Bird	Mockingbird

CALIFORNIA
Capital	Sacramento
Nickname	Golden State
Motto	(Eureka) I Have Found It
Flower	Golden poppy
Tree	Redwood
Bird	Valley quail

COLORADO
Capital	Denver
Nicknames	Centennial State, Rover State
Motto	Nothing without Providence (Nil Sine Numine)
Flower	Blue columbine
Tree	Colorado blue spruce
Bird	Lark bunting

CONNECTICUT
Capital	Hartford
Nicknames	Blue Law State, Constitution State, Nutmeg State
Motto	He Who Transplanted, Sustains (Qui Transtulit, Sustinet)
Flower	Mountain laurel
Tree	White ak
Bird	American robin

DELAWARE
Capital	Dover
Nicknames	Blue Hen State, Diamond State, First State
Motto	Liberty and Independence
Flower	Peach blossom
Tree	American holly
Bird	Blue hen chicken

DISTRICT OF COLUMBIA
Nickname	Capital City
Motto	Justice to All (Justita Omnibus)
Flower	American Beauty rose
Tree	Scarlet oak
Bird	Wood thrush

FLORIDA
Capital	Tallahassee
Nickname	Sunshine State
Motto	In God We Trust
Flower	Orange blossom
Tree	Sabal palm
Bird	Mockingbird

GEORGIA
Capital	Atlanta
Nicknames	Empire State of the South, Peach State
Motto	Wisdom, Justice, Moderation
Flower	Cherokee rose
Tree	Live oak
Bird	Brown thrasher

HAWAII
Capital	Honolulu
Nickname	Aloha State
Motto	The Life of the Land Is Perpetuated In Righteousness
Flower	Hibiscus
Tree	Kukui (candlenut)
Bird	Nene (Hawaiian goose)

IDAHO
Capital	Boise
Nicknames	Gem State, Potato State
Motto	It Is Forever (Esto Perpetua)
Flower	Lewis mock orange (syringa)
Tree	Western white pine
Bird	Mountain bluebird

ILLINOIS
Capital	Springfield
Nicknames	The Inland Empire, Land of Lincoln, Prairie State
Motto	State Sovereignty, National Union
Flower	Native violet
Tree	Burl oak
Bird	Cardinal

INDIANA
Capital	Indianapolis
Nickname	Hoosier State
Motto	Crossroads of America
Flower	Peony
Tree	Tulip (yellow poplar)
Bird	Cardinal

IOWA
Capital	Des Moines
Nickname	Hawkeye State
Motto	Our Liberties We Prize, and Our Rights We Will Maintain
Flower	Wild rose
Tree	Oak
Bird	Eastern goldfinch

KANSAS
Capital	Topeka
Nicknames	Jayhawker State, Sunflower State
Motto	To the Stars through Difficulties (Ad Astra per Aspera)
Flower	Sunflower
Tree	Cottonwood
Bird	Western meadow lark

KENTUCKY
Capital	Frankfort
Nickname	Blue Grass State
Motto	United We Stand, Divided We Fall
Flower	Goldenrod
Tree	Tulip poplar
Bird	Cardinal

LOUISIANA
Capital	Baton Rouge
Nicknames	Creole State, Pelican State, Sugar State
Motto	Union, Justice and Confidence
Flower	Magnolia
Tree	Bald cypress
Bird	Brown pelican

MAINE
Capital	Augusta
Nickname	Pine Tree State
Motto	I Guide (Dirigo)
Flower	White pinecone, tassel
Tree	White pine
Bird	Chickadee

MARYLAND
Capital	Annapolis
Nicknames	Free State, Old Line State
Mottos	Manly Deeds, Womanly Words (Fatti Maschi, Parole Femina); With the Shield of Thy Good Will (Scuto Bonae, Volintatis Tuae Coronasti Nos)
Flower	Blackeyed Susan
Tree	White oak
Bird	Baltimore oriole

MASSACHUSETTS
Capital	Boston
Nicknames	Bay State, Old Colony State
Motto	By the Sword We Seek Peace But Peace Only Under Liberty (Ense Petit Placidam Sub Libertate Quietem)
Flower	Mayflower
Tree	American elm
Bird	Chickadee

MICHIGAN
Capital	Lansing
Nicknames	Great Lake State, Wolverine State
Motto	If You Seek a Pleasant Peninsula, Look About You (Si Quaerie Peninsulam Anoenam Circumspice)
Flower	Apple blossom
Tree	White poplar
Bird	Robin

MINNESOTA
Capital	St. Paul
Nicknames	Gopher State, North Star State
Motto	The Star of the North (L'Etoile du Nord)
Flower	Pink and white lady's-slipper
Tree	Red (Norway) pine
Bird	Common loon

MISSISSIPPI
Capital	Jackson
Nickname	Magnolia State
Motto	By Valor and Arms (Virtute et Armis)
Flower	Magnolia
Tree	Magnolia
Bird	Mockingbird

MISSOURI
Capital	Jefferson City
Nickname	Show Me State
Motto	Let the Warfare of the People Be the Supreme Law (Salus Populi Suprema Lex Esto)
Flower	Hawthorn
Tree	Flowering dogwood
Bird	Eastern bluebird

MONTANA
Capital	Helena
Nicknames	Bonanza State, Mountain State, The Big Sky Country, Treasure State
Motto	Gold and Silver (Oro y Plata)
Flower	Bitterroot
Tree	Ponderosa pine
Bird	Western meadowlark

NEBRASKA
Capital	Lincoln
Nicknames	Antelope Blackwater State, Beef State, Cornhusker State
Motto	Equality Before the Law
Flower	Goldenrod
Tree	American elm
Bird	Western meadowlark

NEVADA
Capital	Carson City
Nicknames	Battle Born State, Sagebrush State, Silver State
Motto	All for Our Country
Flower	Sagebrush
Tree	Single-leaf piñon
Bird	Mountain bluebird

NEW HAMPSHIRE

Capital	Concord
Nickname	Granite State
Motto	Live Free or Die
Flower	Purple lilac
Tree	Paper (white) birch
Bird	Purple finch

NEW JERSEY

Capital	Trenton
Nickname	Garden State
Motto	Liberty and Prosperity
Flower	Purple violet
Tree	Red oak
Bird	Eastern goldfinch

NEW MEXICO

Capital	Santa Fe
Nickname	Land of Enchantment
Motto	It Grows as It Goes (Crescit Eundo)
Flower	Yucca
Tree	Pinon (nut pine)
Bird	Roadrunner

NEW YORK

Capital	Albany
Nickname	Empire State
Motto	Ever Upward (Excelsior)
Flower	Rose
Tree	Sugar maple
Bird	Bluebird

NORTH CAROLINA

Capital	Raleigh
Nicknames	Old North State, Tar Heel State
Motto	To Be, Rather than To Seem (Esse Quam Videri)
Flower	Dogwood
Tree	Pine
Bird	Cardinal

NORTH DAKOTA
Capital	Bismarck
Nicknames	Flickertail State, Sioux State
Motto	Liberty and Union, Now and Forever, One and Inseparable
Flower	Wild prairie rose
Tree	American elm
Bird	Western meadowlark

OHIO
Capital	Columbus
Nickname	Buckeye State
Motto	With God All Things Are Possible
Flower	Scarlet carnation
Tree	Buckeye
Bird	Cardinal

OKLAHOMA
Capital	Oklahoma City
Nickname	Sooner State
Motto	Labor Conquers All Things (Labor Omnia Vincit)
Flower	Mistletoe
Tree	Redbud
Bird	Scissortailed flycatcher

OREGON
Capital	Salem
Nickname	Beaver State
Motto	The Union
Flower	Oregon grape
Tree	Douglas fir
Bird	Western meadowlark

PENNSYLVANIA
Capital	Harrisburg
Nickname	Keystone State
Motto	Virtue, Liberty and Independence
Flower	Mountain laurel
Tree	Hemlock
Bird	Ruffed grouse

RHODE ISLAND
Capital	Providence
Nicknames	Little Rhody, Ocean State
Motto	Hope
Flower	Violet
Tree	Red maple
Bird	Rhode Island red (hen)

SOUTH CAROLINA
Capital	Columbia
Nickname	Palmetto State
Mottos	Prepared In Mind and Resources (Animis Opibusque Parati); While I Breathe I Hope (Dum Spiro, Spero)
Flower	Yellow jessamine
Tree	Palmetto
Bird	Carolina wren

SOUTH DAKOTA
Capital	Pierre
Nicknames	Blizzard State, Coyote State, Sunshine State
Motto	Under God the People Rule
Flower	Pasqueflower
Tree	Black Hills spruce
Bird	Ringnecked pheasant

TENNESSEE
Capital	Nashville
Nicknames	Big Bend State, Volunteer State
Mottos	Agriculture and Commerce; America At Its Best
Flower	Iris
Tree	Tulip poplar
Bird	Mockingbird

TEXAS
Capital	Austin
Nickname	Lone Star State
Motto	Friendship
Flower	Bluebonnet
Tree	Pecan
Bird	Mockingbird

UTAH
Capital	Salt Lake City
Nickname	Beehive State
Motto	Industry
Flower	Sego lily
Tree	Blue spruce
Bird	Seagull (California seagull)

VERMONT
Capital	Montpelier
Nickname	Green Mountain State
Motto	Freedom and Unity
Flower	Red clover
Tree	Sugar maple
Bird	Hermit thrush

VIRGINIA
Capital	Richmond
Nickname	Old Dominion State
Motto	Thus Ever to Tyrants (Sic Semper Tyrannis)
Flower	Flowering American dogwood
Tree	Flowering American dogwood
Bird	Cardinal

WASHINGTON
Capital	Olympia
Nickname	Evergreen State
Motto	By and By (Alki)
Flower	Western rhododendron
Tree	Western hemlock
Bird	Willow goldfinch

WEST VIRGINIA
Capital	Charleston
Nicknames	Mountain State, Panhandle State,
Motto	Mountaineers Are Always Free (Montani Semper Liberi)
Flower	Big rosebay rhododendron
Tree	Sugar Maple
Bird	Cardinal

WISCONSIN
Capital	Madison
Nickname	Badger State
Motto	Forward
Flower	Butterfly wood violet
Tree	Sugar maple
Bird	Robin

WYOMING
Capital	Cheyenne
Nickname	Equality State
Motto	Equal Rights
Flower	Indian paintbrush
Tree	Cottonwood
Bird	Western meadowlark

ACADEMY AWARDS

1927-1928
Best actor	Emil Jannings (*The Way of All Flesh*)
Best actress	Janet Gaynor (*Seventh Heaven*)
Best director	Frank Borzage (*Seventh Heaven*)
Best picture	*Wings*

1928-1929
Best actor	Warner Baxter (*In Old Arizona*)
Best actress	Mary Pickford (*Coquette*)
Best director	Frank Lloyd (*The Divine Lady*)
Best picture	*Broadway Melody*

1929-1930
Best actor	George Arliss (*Disraeli*)
Best actress	Norma Shearer (*The Divorcee*)
Best director	Lewis Milestone (*All Quiet on the Western Front*)
Best picture	*All Quiet on the Western Front*

1930-1931
Best actor	Lionel Barrymore (*A Free Soul*)
Best actress	Marie Dressler (*Min and Bill*)
Best director	Norman Taurog (*Skippy*)
Best picture	*Cimarron*

1931-1932
Best actor	Frederic March (*Dr. Jekyll and Mr. Hyde*)
	Wallace Beery (*The Champ*)
Best actress	Helen Hayes (*The Sins of Madelon Claudet*)
Best director	Frank Borzage (*Bad Girl*)
Best picture	*Grand Hotel*

1932-1933
Best actor	Charles Laughton (*The Private Life of Henry VIII*)
Best actress	Katharine Hepburn (*Morning Glory*)
Best director	Frank Lloyd (*Cavalcade*)
Best picture	*Cavalcade*

1934
Best actor	Clark Gable (*It Happened One Night*)
Best actress	Claudette Colbert (*It Happened One Night*)
Best director	Frank Capra (*It Happened One Night*)
Best picture	*It Happened One Night*

1935
Best actor	Victor McLaglen (*The Informer*)
Best actress	Bette Davis (*Dangerous*)
Best director	John Ford (*The Informer*)
Best picture	*Mutiny on the Bounty*

1936

Best actor	Paul Muni (*The Story of Louis Pasteur*)
Best actress	Luise Rainer (*The Great Ziegfeld*)
Best director	Frank Capra (*Mr. Deeds Goes to Town*)
Best picture	*The Great Ziegfeld*

1937

Best actor	Spencer Tracey (*Captains Courageous*)
Best actress	Louis Rainer (*The Good Earth*)
Best director	Leo McCarey (*The Awful Truth*)
Best picture	*The Life of Emile Zola*

1938

Best actor	Spencer Tracey (*Boys Town*)
Best actress	Bette Davis (*Jezebel*)
Best director	Frank Capra (*You Can't Take it with You*)
Best picture	*You Can't Take it with You*

1939

Best actor	Robert Donat (*Goodbye, Mr. Chips*)
Best actress	Vivien Leigh (*Gone with the Wind*)
Best director	Victor Fleming (*Gone with the Wind*)
Best picture	*Gone with the Wind*

1940

Best actor	James Stewart (*The Philadelphia Story*)
Best actress	Ginger Rogers (*Kitty Foyle*)
Best director	John Ford (*The Grapes of Wrath*)
Best picture	*Rebecca*

1941

Best actor	Gary Cooper (*Sergeant York*)
Best actress	Joan Fontaine (*Suspicion*)
Best director	John Ford (*How Green Was My Valley*)
Best picture	*How Green Was My Valley*

1942

Best actor	James Cagney (*Yankee Doodle Dandy*)
Best actress	Greer Garson (*Mrs. Miniver*)
Best director	William Wyler (*Mrs. Miniver*)
Best picture	*Mrs. Miniver*

1943

Best actor	Paul Lucas (*Watch on the Rhine*)
Best actress	Jennifer Jones (*The Song of Bernadette*)
Best director	Michael Curtiz (*Casablanca*)
Best picture	*Casablanca*

1944

Best actor	Bing Crosby (*Going My Way*)
Best actress	Ingrid Bergman (*Gaslight*)
Best director	Leo McCarey (*Going My Way*)
Best picture	*Going My Way*

1945

Best actor	Ray Milland (*The Lost Weekend*)
Best actress	Joan Crawford (*Mildred Pierce*)
Best director	Billy Wilder (*The Lost Weekend*)
Best picture	*The Lost Weekend*

1946

Best actor	Frederic March (*The Best Years of Our Lives*)
Best actress	Olivia de Havilland (*To Each His Own*)
Best director	William Wyler (*The Best Years of Our Lives*)
Best picture	*The Best Years of Our Lives*

1947

Best actor	Ronald Coleman (*A Double Life*)
Best actress	Loretta Young (*The Farmer's Daughter*)
Best director	Elia Kazan (*Gentlemen's Agreement*)
Best picture	*Gentlemen's Agreement*

1948

Best actor	Laurence Olivier (*Hamlet*)
Best actress	Jane Wyman (*Johnny Belinda*)
Best director	John Huston (*Treasure of the Sierra Madre*)
Best picture	*Hamlet*

1949

Best actor	Broderick Crawford (*All the King's Men*)
Best actress	Olivia de Havilland (*The Heiress*)
Best director	Joseph L. Mankiewicz (*A Letter to Three Wives*)
Best picture	*All the King's Men*

1950

Best actor	Jose Ferrer (*Cyrano de Bergerac*)
Best actress	Judy Holliday (*Born Yesterday*)
Best director	Joseph L. Mankiewicz (*All about Eve*)
Best picture	*All about Eve*

1951

Best actor	Humphrey Bogart (*The African Queen*)
Best actress	Vivien Leigh (*A Streetcar Named Desire*)
Best director	George Stevens (*A Place in the Sun*)
Best picture	*An American in Paris*

1952

Best actor	Gary Cooper (*High Noon*)
Best actress	Shirley Booth (*Come Back, Little Sheba*)
Best director	John Ford (*The Quiet Man*)
Best picture	*The Greatest Show on Earth*

1953

Best actor	William Holden (*Stalag 17*)
Best actress	Audrey Hepburn (*Roman Holliday*)
Best director	Fred Zinnemann (*From Here to Eternity*)
Best picture	*From Here to Eternity*

1954

Best actor	Marlon Brando (*On the Waterfront*)
Best actress	Grace Kelly (*The Country Girl*)
Best director	Elia Kazan (*On the Waterfront*)
Best picture	*On the Waterfront*

1955

Best actor	Ernest Borgnine (*Marty*)
Best actress	Anna Magnani (*The Rose Tattoo*)
Best director	Delbert Mann (*Marty*)
Best picture	*Marty*

1956

Best actor	Yul Brynner (*The King and I*)
Best actress	Ingrid Bergman (*Anastasia*)
Best director	George Stevens (*Giant*)
Best picture	*Around the World in Eighty Days*

1957

Best actor	Alec Guinness (*The Bridge on the River Kwai*)
Best actress	Joanne Woodward (*The Three Faces of Eve*)
Best director	David Lean (*The Bridge on the River Kwai*)
Best picture	*The Bridge on the River Kwai*

1958

Best actor	David Niven (*Separate Tables*)
Best actress	Susan Hayward (*I Want to Live*)
Best director	Vincente Minnelli (*Gigi*)
Best picture	*Gigi*

1959

Best actor	Charlton Heston (*BenHur*)
Best actress	Simone Signoret (*Room at the Top*)
Best director	William Wyler (*BenHur*)
Best picture	*BenHur*

1960
Best actor	Burt Lancaster (*Elmer Gantry*)
Best actress	Elizabeth Taylor (*Butterfield 8*)
Best director	Billy Wilder (*The Apartment*)
Best picture	*The Apartment*

1961
Best actor	Maximillian Schell (*Judgement at Nuremberg*)
Best actress	Sophia Loren (*Two Women*)
Best director	Jerome Robbins, Robert Wise (*West Side Story*)
Best picture	*West Side Story*

1962
Best actor	Gregory Peck (*To Kill a Mockingbird*)
Best actress	Anne Bancroft (*The Miracle Workers*)
Best director	David Lean (*Lawrence of Arabia*)
Best picture	*Lawrence of Arabia*

1963
Best actor	Sidney Poitier (*Lilies of the Field*)
Best actress	Patricia Neal (*Hud*)
Best director	Tony Richardson (*Tom Jones*)
Best picture	*Tom Jones*

1964
Best actor	Rex Harrison (*My Fair Lady*)
Best actress	Julie Andrews (*Mary Poppins*)
Best director	George Cukor (*My Fair Lady*)
Best picture	*My Fair Lady*

1965
Best actor	Lee Marvin (*Cat Ballou*)
Best actress	Julie Christie (*Darling*)
Best director	Robert Wise (*The Sound of Music*)
Best picture	*The Sound of Music*

1966
Best actor	Paul Scofield (*A Man for All Seasons*)
Best actress	Elizabeth Taylor (*Who's Afraid of Virginia Woolf?*)
Best director	Fred Zinnemann (*A Man for All Seasons*)
Best picture	*A Man for All Seasons*

1967
Best actor	Rod Steiger (*In the Heat of the Night*)
Best actress	Katharine Hepburn (*Guess Who's Coming to Dinner*)
Best director	Mike Nichols (*The Graduate*)
Best picture	*In the Heat of the Night*

1968

Best actor	Cliff Robertson (*Charly*)
Best actress	Katharine Hepburn (*The Lion in Winter*)
	Barbra Streisand (*Funny Girl*)
Best director	Sir Carol Reed (*Oliver!*)
Best picture	*Oliver!*

1969

Best actor	John Wayne (*True Grit*)
Best actress	Maggie Smith (*The Prime of Miss Jean Brodie*)
Best director	John Schlesinger (*Midnight Cowboy*)
Best picture	*Midnight Cowboy*

1970

Best actor	George C. Scott (*Patton*)
Best actress	Glenda Jackson (*Women in Love*)
Best director	Franklin Schaffner, Frank McCarthy (*Patton*)
Best picture	*Patton*

1971

Best actor	Gene Hackman (*The French Connection*)
Best actress	Jane Fonda (*Klute*)
Best director	William Friedkin (*The French Connection*)
Best picture	*The French Connection*

1972

Best actor	Marlon Brando (*The Godfather*)
Best actress	Liza Minnelli (*Cabaret*)
Best director	Bob Fosse (*Cabaret*)
Best picture	*The Godfather*

1973

Best actor	Jack Lemmon (*Save the Tiger*)
Best actress	Glenda Jackson (*A Touch of Class*)
Best director	George Roy Hill (*The Sting*)
Best picture	*The Sting*

1974

Best actor	Art Carney (*The Tomato*)
Best actress	Ellen Burstyn (*Alice Doesn't Live Here Anymore*)
Best director	Francis Ford Coppola (*The Godfather, Part II*)
Best picture	*The Godfather, Part II*

1975

Best actor	Jack Nicholson (*One Flew over the Cuckoo's Nest*)
Best actress	Louise Fletcher (*One Flew over the Cuckoo's Nest*)
Best director	Milos Forman (*One Flew over the Cuckoo's Nest*)
Best picture	*One Flew over the Cuckoo's Nest*

1976

Best actor	Peter Finch (*Network*)
Best actress	Faye Dunaway (*Network*)
Best director	John G. Avildsen (*Rocky*)
Best picture	*Rocky*

1977

Best actor	Richard Dreyfuss (*The Goodbye Girl*)
Best actress	Diane Keaton (*Annie Hall*)
Best director	Woody Allen (*Annie Hall*)
Best picture	*Annie Hall*

1978

Best actor	Jon Voight (*Coming Home*)
Best actress	Jane Fonda (*Coming Home*)
Best director	Michael Cimino (*The Deer Hunter*)
Best picture	*The Deer Hunter*

1979

Best actor	Dustin Hoffman (*Kramer vs. Kramer*)
Best actress	Sally Field (*Norma Rae*)
Best director	Robert Benton (*Kramer vs. Kramer*)
Best picture	*Kramer vs. Kramer*

1980

Best actor	Robert De Niro (*Raging Bull*)
Best actress	Sissy Spacek (*Coal Miner's Daughter*)
Best director	Robert Redford (*Ordinary People*)
Best picture	*Ordinary People*

1981

Best actor	Henry Fonda (*On Golden Pond*)
Best actress	Katharine Hepburn (*On Golden Pond*)
Best director	Warren Beatty (*Reds*)
Best picture	*Chariots of Fire*

1982

Best actor	Ben Kingsley (*Gandhi*)
Best actress	Meryl Streep (*Sophie's Choice*)
Best director	Richard Attenborough (*Gandhi*)
Best picture	*Gandhi*

1983

Best actor	Robert Duvall (*Tender Mercies*)
Best actress	Shirley MacLaine (*Terms of Endearment*)
Best director	James L. Brooks (*Terms of Endearment*)
Best picture	*Terms of Endearment*

1984

Best actor	F. Murray Abraham (*Amadeus*)
Best actress	Sally Field (*Places in the Heart*)
Best director	Milos Forman (*Amadeus*)
Best picture	*Amadeus*

1985

Best actor	William Hurt (*Kiss of the Spider Woman*)
Best actress	Geraldine Page (*The Trip to Bountiful*)
Best director	Sydney Pollack (*Out of Africa*)
Best picture	*Out of Africa*

1986

Best actor	Paul Newman (*The Color of Money*)
Best actress	Marlee Matlin (*Children of a Lesser God*)
Best director	Oliver Stone (*Platoon*)
Best picture	*Platoon*

1987

Best actor	Michael Douglas (*Wall Street*)
Best actress	Cher (*Moonstruck*)
Best director	Bernardo Bertolucci (*The Last Emperor*)
Best picture	*The Last Emperor*

1988

Best actor	Dustin Hoffman (*Rain Man*)
Best actress	Jodie Foster (*The Accused*)
Best director	Barry Levinson (*Rain Man*)
Best picture	*Rain Man*

1989

Best actor	Daniel Day-Lewis (*My Left Foot*)
Best actress	Jessica Tandy (*Driving Miss Daisy*)
Best director	Oliver Stone (*Born on the Fourth of July*)
Best picture	*Driving Miss Daisy*

1990

Best actor	Jeremy Irons (*Reversal of Fortune*)
Best actress	Kathy Bates (*Misery*)
Best director	Kevin Costner (*Dances with Wolves*)
Best picture	*Dances with Wolves*

1991

Best actor	Anthony Hopkins (*The Silence of the Lambs*)
Best actress	Jodie Foster (*The Silence of the Lambs*)
Best director	Jonathan Demme (*The Silence of the Lambs*)
Best picture	*The Silence of the Lambs*

1992

Best actor	Al Pacino (*Scent of a Woman*)
Best actress	Emma Thompson (*Howard's End*)
Best director	Clint Eastwood (*Unforgiven*)
Best picture	*Unforgiven*

1993

Best actor	Tom Hanks (*Philadelphia*)
Best actress	Holly Hunter (*The Piano*)
Best director	Steven Spielberg (*Schindler's List*)
Best picture	*Schindler's List*

NOBEL PEACE PRIZE

Year	Awarded to
1901	Henri Dunant (Switzerland)
	Frederick Passy (France)
1902	Elie Ducommun, Albert Gobat (Switzerland)
1903	Sir William R. Cremer (England)
1904	Institut de Droit International (Belgium)
1905	Bertha von Suttner (Austria)
1906	Theodore Roosevelt (U.S.)
1907	Ernesto T. Moneta (Italy)
	Louis Renault (France)
1908	Klas P. Arnoldson (Sweden)
	Frederik Bajer (Denmark)
1909	Auguste M.F. Beernaert (Belgium)
	Baron Paul H.B.B. d'Estournelles de Constant de Rebecque (France)
1910	Buereau International Permanent de la Paix (Switzerland)
1911	Tobias M.C. Asser (Holland)
	Alfred H. Fried (Austria)
1912	Elihu Root (U.S.)
1913	Henri La Fontaine (Belgium)
1915	No award
1916	No award
1917	International Red Cross
1919	Woodrow Wilson (U.S.)
1920	Léon Bourgeois (France)
1921	Karl H. Branting (Sweden)
	Christian L. Lange (Norway)
1922	Fridtjof Nansen (Norway)
1923	No award
1924	No award
1925	Sir Austen Chamberlain (England)
	Charles G. Dawes (U.S.)
1926	Aristide Briand (France)
	Gustav Stresemann (Germany)

Year	Awarded to
1927	Ferdinand Buisson (France)
	Ludwig Quidde (Germany)
1928	No award
1929	Frank B. Kellogg (U.S.)
1930	Lars O.J. Söderblom (Sweden)
1931	Jane Addams
	Nicholas M. Butler (U.S.)
1932	No award
1933	Sir Norman Angell (England)
1934	Arthur Henderson (England)
1935	Karl von Ossietzky (Germany)
1936	Carlos de S. Lamas (Argentina)
1937	Lord Cecil of Chelwood (England)
1938	Office International Nansen pour les Réfugiés (Switzerland)
1939	No award
1944	International Red Cross
1945	Cordell Hull (U.S.)
1946	Emily G. Balch
	John R. Mott (U.S.)
1947	American Friends Service Committee (U.S.)
	British Society of Friends' Service Council (England)
1948	No award
1949	Lord John Boyd Orr (Scotland)
1950	Ralph J. Bunche (U.S.)
1951	Léon Jouhaux (France)
1952	Albert Schweitzer (French Equatorial Africa)
1953	George C. Marshall (U.S.)
1954	Office of U.N. High Commissioner for Refugees
1955	No award
1956	No award
1957	Lester B. Pearson (Canada)
1958	Rev. Dominique Georges Henri Pire (Belgium)
1959	Philip John Noel-Baker (England)
1960	Albert John Luthuli (South Africa)
1961	Dag Hammarskjöld (Sweden)
1962	Linus Pauling (U.S.)
1963	Intl. Comm. of Red Cross; League of Red Cross Societies (Geneva)
1964	Rev. Dr. Martin Luther King, Jr. (U.S.)
1965	UNICEF (United Nations Children's Fund)
1966	No award
1967	No award
1968	René Cassin (France)
1969	International Labor Organization
1970	Norman E. Borlaug (U.S.)
1971	Willy Brandt (West Germany)
1972	No award

Year	Awarded to
1973	Henry A. Kissinger (U.S.)
	Le Duc Tho (North Vietnam)
1974	Eisaku Sato (Japan)
	Sean MacBride (Ireland)
1975	Andrei D. Sakharov (U.S.S.R)
1976	Mairead Corrigan, Betty Williams (Northern Ireland)
1977	Amnesty International
1978	Menachem Begin (Israel)
	Anwar el-Sadat (Egypt)
1979	Mother Teresa of Calcutta (India)
1980	Adolfo Pérez Esquival (Argentina)
1981	Office of the United Nations High Commissioner for Refugees
1982	Alva Myrdal (Sweden)
	Alfonso García Robles (Mexico)
1983	Lech Walesa (Poland)
1984	Bishop Desmond Tutu (South Africa)
1985	International Physicians for the Prevention of Nuclear War
1986	Elie Wiesel (U.S.)
1987	Oscar Arias Sánchez (Costa Rica)
1988	U.N. Peacekeeping Forces
1989	Dalai Lama (Tibet)
1990	Mikhael S. Gorbachev (U.S.S.R.)
1991	Daw Aung San Suu Kyi (Myanmar)
1992	Rigoberta Menchú (Guatemala)
1993	Nelson Mandela, Frederik Willem de Klerk (South Africa)

NOBEL PRIZE FOR LITERATURE

Year	Awarded to
1901	René F.A. Sully Prudhomme (France)
1902	Theodor Mommsen (Germany)
1903	Björnstjerne Björnson (Norway)
1904	Frédéric Mistral (France)
	José Echegaray (Spain)
1905	Henryk Sienkiewicz (Poland)
1906	Giosuè Carducci (Italy)
1907	Rudyard Kipling (England)
1908	Rudolph Eucken (Germany)
1909	Selma Lagerlöff (Sweden)
1910	Paul von Heyse (Germany)
1911	Maurice Maeterlinck (Belgium)
1912	Gerhart Hauptmann (Germany)
1913	Rabindranath Tagore (India)
1915	Romain Rolland (France)
1916	Verner von Heidenstam (Sweden)

Year	Awarded to
1917	Karl Gjellerup (Denmark)
	Henrik Pontoppidan (Denmark)
1919	Carl Spitteler (Switzerland)
1920	Knut Hamsun (Norway)
1921	Anatole France (France)
1922	Jacinto Benavente (Spain)
1923	William B. Yeats (Ireland)
1924	Wladyslaw Reymont (Poland)
1925	George Bernard Shaw (Ireland)
1926	Grazia Deledda (Italy)
1927	Henri Bergson (France)
1928	Sigrid Undset (Norway)
1929	Thomas Mann (Germany)
1930	Sinclair Lewis (U.S.)
1931	Erik A. Karlfeldt (Sweden)
1932	John Galsworthy (England)
1933	Ivan G. Bunin (Russia)
1934	Luigi Pirandello (Italy)
1935	No award
1936	Eugene O'Neill (U.S.)
1937	Roger Martin du Gard (France)
1938	Pearl S. Buck (U.S.)
1939	Frans Eemil Sillanpää (Finland)
1944	Johannes V. Jensen (Denmark)
1945	Gabriela Mistral (Chile)
1946	Hermann Hesse (Switzerland)
1947	André Gide (France)
1948	Thomas Stearns Eliot (England)
1949	William Faulkner (U.S.)
1950	Bertrand Russell (England)
1951	Pär Lagerkvist (Sweden)
1952	Francois Mauriac (France)
1953	Sir Winston Churchill (England)
1954	Ernest Hemingway (United States)
1955	Halldór Kiljan Laxness (Iceland)
1956	Juan Ramón Jiménez (Spain)
1957	Albert Camus (France)
1958	Boris Pasternak (U.S.S.R.)
1959	Salvatore Quasimodo (Italy)
1960	St.-John Perse (Alexis St.-Léger Léger) (France)
1961	Ivo Andric (Yugoslavia)
1962	John Steinbeck (U.S.)
1963	Giorgios Seferis (Seferiades) (Greece)
1964	Jean-Paul Sartre (France)
1965	Mikhail Sholokhov (U.S.S.R.)

Year	Awarded to
1966	Shmuel Yosef Agnon (Israel)
	Nelly Sachs (Sweden)
1967	Miguel Angel Asturias (Guatemala)
1968	Yasunari Kawabata (Japan)
1969	Samuel Beckett (Ireland)
1970	Aleksandr Solzhenitsyn (U.S.S.R.)
1971	Pablo Neruda (Chile)
1972	Heinrich Böll (Germany)
1973	Patrick White (Australia)
1974	Eyvind Johnson, Harry Martinson (Sweden)
1975	Eugenio Montale (Italy)
1976	Saul Bellow (U.S.)
1977	Vincente Aleixandre (Spain)
1978	Isaac Bashevis Singer (U.S.)
1979	Odysseus Elytis (Greece)
1980	Czeslaw Milosz (U.S.)
1981	Elias Canetti (Bulgaria)
1982	Gabriel García Márquez (Colombia)
1983	William Golding (England)
1984	Jaroslav Seifert (Czechoslavakia)
1985	Claude Simon (France)
1986	Wole Soyinka (Nigeria)
1987	Joseph Brodsky (U.S.)
1988	Naguib Mahfouz (Egypt)
1989	Camilo José Cela (Spain)
1990	Octavio Paz (Mexico)
1991	Nadine Gordimer (South Africa)
1992	Derek Walcott (Trinidad)
1993	Toni Morrison (U.S.)

OLYMPIC GAMES

Summer Games

Year	Location	Year	Location
1896	Athens, Greece		
1900	Paris, France	1956	Melbourne, Australia
1904	St. Louis, Missouri	1960	Rome, Italy
1908	London, England	1964	Tokyo, Japan
1912	Stockholm, Sweden	1968	Mexico City, Mexico
1920	Antwerp, Belgium	1972	Munich, West Germany
1924	Paris, France	1976	Montreal, Canada
1928	Amsterdam, The Netherlands	1980	Moscow, USSR
1932	Los Angeles, California	1984	Los Angeles, California
1936	Berlin, Germany	1988	Seoul, South Korea
1948	London, England	1992	Barcelona, Spain
1952	Helsinki, Finland	1996	Atlanta, Georgia

Winter Games

Year	Location	Year	Location
1924	Chamonix, France	1968	Grenoble, France
1928	St. Moritz, Switzerland	1972	Sapporo, Japan
1932	Lake Placid, New York	1976	Innsbruck, Austria
1936	Garmisch-Partenkirchen, Germany	1980	Lake Placid, New York
1948	St. Moritz, Switzerland	1984	Sarajevo, Yugoslavia
1952	Oslo, Norway	1988	Calgary, Canada
1956	Cortina, Italy	1992	Albertville, France
1960	Squaw Valley, California	1994	Lillehammer, Norway
1964	Innsbruck, Austria		

THE SUPER BOWL

	Year	Winner	Loser
I	1967	Green Bay Packers (N.F.L.)	Kansas City Chiefs (A.F.L.)
II	1968	Green Bay Packers (N.F.L.)	Oakland Raiders (A.F.L.)
III	1969	New York Jets (A.F.L.)	Baltimore Colts (N.F.L.)
IV	1970	Kansas City Chiefs (A.F.L.)	Minnesota Vikings (N.F.L.)
V	1971	Baltimore Colts (A.F.C)	Dallas Cowboys (N.F.C.)
VI	1972	Dallas Cowboys (N.F.C.)	Miami Dolphins (A.F.C.)
VII	1973	Miami Dolphins (A.F.C.)	Washington Redskins (N.F.C.)
VIII	1974	Miami Dolphins (A.F.C.)	Minnesota Vikings (N.F.C.)
IX	1975	Pittsburgh Steelers (A.F.C.)	Minnesota Vikings (N.F.C.)
X	1976	Pittsburgh Steelers (A.F.C.)	Dallas Cowboys (N.F.C.)
XI	1977	Oakland Raiders (A.F.C.)	Minnesota Vikings (N.F.C.)
XII	1978	Dallas Cowboys (N.F.C.)	Denver Broncos (A.F.C.)
XIII	1979	Pittsburgh Steelers (A.F.C.)	Dallas Cowboys (N.F.C.)
XIV	1980	Pittsburgh Steelers (A.F.C.)	Los Angeles Rams (N.F.C.)
XV	1981	Oakland Raiders (A.F.C.)	Philadelphia Eagles (N.F.C.)
XVI	1982	San Francisco 49ers (N.F.C.)	Cincinnati Bengals (A.F.C.)
XVII	1983	Washington Redskins (N.F.C.)	Miami Dolphins (A.F.C.)
XVIII	1984	Los Angeles Raiders (A.F.C.)	Washington Redskins (N.F.C.)
XIX	1985	San Francisco 49ers (N.F.C.)	Miami Dolphins (A.F.C.)
XX	1986	Chicago Bears (N.F.C.)	New England Patriots (A.F.C.)
XXII	1987	New York Giants (N.F.C.)	Denver Broncos (A.F.C.)
XXII	1988	Washington Redskins (N.F.C.)	Denver Broncos (A.F.C.)
XXIII	1989	San Francisco 49ers (N.F.C.)	Cincinnati Bengals (A.F.C.)
XXIV	1990	San Francisco 49ers (N.F.C.)	Denver Broncos (A.F.C.)
XXV	1991	New York Giants (N.F.C.)	Buffalo Bills (A.F.C.)
XXVI	1992	Washington Redskins (N.F.C.)	Buffalo Bills (A.F.C.)
XXVII	1993	Dallas Cowboys (N.F.C.)	Buffalo Bills (A.F.C.)
XXVIII	1994	Dallas Cowboys (N.F.C.)	Buffalo Bills (A.F.C.)

NATIONAL BASKETBALL ASSOCIATION CHAMPIONSHIPS

Year	Winner	Loser
1947	Philadelphia Warriors (E.)	Chicago Stags (W.)
1948	Baltimore Bullets (W.)	Philadelphia Warriors (E.)
1949	Minneapolis Lakers (W.)	Washington Capitols (E.)
1950	Minneapolis Lakers (W.)	Syracuse Nationals (E.)
1951	Rochester Royals (W.)	New York Knickerbockers (E.)
1952	Minneapolis Lakers (W.)	New York Knickerbockers (E.)
1953	Minneapolis Lakers (W.)	New York Knickerbockers (E.)
1954	Minneapolis Lakers (W.)	Syracuse Nationals (E.)
1955	Syracuse Nationals (E.)	Fort Wayne Pistons (W.)
1956	Philadelphia Warriors (E.)	Fort Wayne Pistons (W.)
1957	Boston Celtics (E.)	St. Louis Hawks (W.)
1958	St. Louis Hawks (W.)	Boston Celtics (E.)
1959	Boston Celtics (E.)	Minneapolis Lakers (W.)
1960	Boston Celtics (E.)	St. Louis Hawks (W.)
1961	Boston Celtics (E.)	St. Louis Hawks (W.)
1962	Boston Celtics (E.)	Los Angeles Lakers (W.)
1963	Boston Celtics (E.)	Los Angeles Lakers (W.)
1964	Boston Celtics (E.)	San Francisco Warriors (W.)
1965	Boston Celtics (E.)	Los Angeles Lakers (W.)
1966	Boston Celtics (E.)	Los Angeles Lakers (W.)
1967	Philadelphia 76ers (E.)	San Francisco Warriors (W.)
1968	Boston Celtics (E.)	Los Angeles Lakers (W.)
1969	Boston Celtics (E.)	Los Angeles Lakers (W.)
1970	New York Knickerbockers (E.)	Los Angeles Lakers (W.)
1971	Milwaukee Bucks (W.)	Baltimore Bullets (E.)
1972	Los Angeles Lakers (W.)	New York Knickerbockers (E.)
1973	New York Knickerbockers (E.)	Los Angeles Lakers (W.)
1974	Boston Celtics (E.)	Milwaukee Bucks (W.)
1975	Golden State Warriors (W.)	Washington Bullets (E.)
1976	Boston Celtics (E.)	Phoenix Suns (W.)
1977	Portland Trail Blazers (W.)	Philadelphia 76ers (E.)
1978	Washington Bullets (E.)	Seattle Supersonics (W.)
1979	Seattle Supersonics (W.)	Washington Bullets (E.)
1980	Los Angeles Lakers (W.)	Philadelphia 76ers (E.)
1981	Boston Celtics (E.)	Houston Rockets (W.)
1982	Los Angeles Lakers (W.)	Philadelphia 76ers (E.)
1983	Philadelphia 76ers (E.)	Los Angeles Lakers (W.)
1984	Boston Celtics (E.)	Los Angeles Lakers (W.)
1985	Los Angeles lakers (W.)	Boston Celtics (E.)
1986	Boston Celtics (E.)	Houston Rockets (W.)
1987	Los Angeles Lakers (W.)	Boston Celtics (E.)
1988	Los Angeles Lakers (W.)	Detroit Pistons (E.)
1989	Detroit Pistons (E.)	Los Angeles Lakers (W.)
1990	Detroit Pistons (E.)	Portland Trail Blazers (W.)

Year	Winners	Losers
1991	Chicago Bulls (E.)	Los Angeles Lakers (W.)
1992	Chicago Bulls (E.)	Portland Trail Blazers (W.)
1993	Chicago Bulls (E.)	Portland Trail Blazers (W.)
1994	Houston Rockets (W.)	New York Knickerbockers (E.)

WORLD SERIES

Year	Winner	Loser
1903	Boston Red Sox (A.L.)	Pittsburgh Pirates (N.L.)
1904	No Series	
1905	New York Giants (N.L.)	Philadelphia Athletics (A.L.)
1906	Chicago White Sox (A.L.)	Chicago Cubs (N.L.)
1907	Chicago Cubs (N.L.)	Detroit Tigers (A.L.)
1908	Chicago Cubs (N.L.)	Detroit Tigers (A.L.)
1909	Pittsburgh Pirates (N.L.)	Detroit Tigers (A.L.)
1910	Philadelphia Athletics (A.L.)	New York Giants (N.L.)
1911	Philadelphia Athletics (A.L.)	New York Giants (N.L.)
1912	Boston Red Sox (A.L.)	New York Giants (N.L.)
1913	Philadelphia Athletics (A.L.)	New York Giants (N.L.)
1914	Boston Braves (N.L.)	Philadelphia Athletics (A.L.)
1915	Boston Red Sox (A.L.)	Philadelphia Phillies (N.L.)
1916	Boston Red Sox (A.L.)	Brooklyn Dodgers (N.L.)
1917	Chicago White Sox (A.L.)	New York Giants (N.L.)
1918	Boston Red Sox (A.L.)	Chicago Cubs (N.L.)
1919	Cincinnati Reds (N.L.)	Chicago White Sox (A.L.)
1920	Cleveland Indians (A.L.)	Brooklyn Dodgers (N.L.)
1921	New York Giants (N.L.)	New York Yankees (A.L.)
1922	New York Giants (N.L.)	New York Yankees (A.L.)
1923	New York Yankees (A.L.)	New York Giants (N.L.)
1924	Washington Senators (A.L.)	New York Giants (N.L.)
1925	Pittsburgh Pirates (N.L.)	Washington Senators (A.L.)
1926	St. Louis Cardinals (N.L.)	New York Yankees (A.L.)
1927	New York Yankees (A.L.)	Pittsburgh Pirates (N.L.)
1928	New York Yankees (A.L.)	St. Louis Cardinals (N.L.)
1929	Philadelphia Athletics (N.L.)	Chicago Cubs (N.L.)
1930	Philadelphia Athletics (A.L.)	St. Louis Cardinals (N.L.)
1931	St. Louis Cardinals (N.L.)	Philadelphia Athletics (A.L.)
1932	New York Yankees (A.L.)	Chicago Cubs (N.L.)
1933	New York Giants (N.L.)	Washington Senators (A.L.)
1934	St. Louis Cardinals (N.L.)	Detroit Tigers (A.L.)
1935	Detroit Tigers (A.L.)	Chicago Cubs (N.L.)
1936	New York Yankees (A.L.)	New York Giants (N.L.)
1937	New York Yankees (A.L.)	New York Giants (N.L.)
1938	New York Yankees (A.L.)	Chicago Cubs (N.L.)
1939	New York Yankees (A.L.)	Cincinnati Reds (N.L.)

Year	Winner	Loser
1940	Cincinnati Reds (N.L.)	Detroit Tigers (A.L.)
1941	New York Yankees (A.L.)	Brooklyn Dodgers (N.L.)
1942	St. Louis Cardinals (N.L.)	New York Yankees (A.L.)
1943	New York Yankees (A.L.)	St. Louis Cardinals (N.L.)
1944	St. Louis Cardinals (N.L.)	St. Louis Browns (A.L.)
1945	Detroit Tigers (A.L.)	Chicago Cubs (N.L.)
1946	St. Louis Cardinals (N.L.)	Boston Red Sox (A.L.)
1947	New York Yankees (A.L.)	Brooklyn Dodgers (N.L.)
1948	Cleveland Indians (A.L.)	Boston Braves (N.L.)
1949	New York Yankees (A.L.)	Brooklyn Dodgers (N.L.)
1950	New York Yankees (A.L.)	Philadelphia Phillies (N.L.)
1951	New York Yankees (A.L.)	New York Giants (N.L.)
1952	New York Yankees (A.L.)	Brooklyn Dodgers (N.L.)
1953	New York Yankees (A.L.)	Brooklyn Dodgers (N.L.)
1954	New York Giants (N.L.)	Cleveland Indians (A.L.)
1955	Brooklyn Dodgers (N.L.)	New York Yankees (A.L.)
1956	New York Yankees (A.L.)	Brooklyn Dodgers (N.L.)
1957	Milwaukee Braves (N.L.)	New York Yankees (A.L.)
1958	New York Yankees (A.L.)	Milwaukee Braves (N.L.)
1959	Los Angeles Dodgers (N.L.)	Chicago White Sox (A.L.)
1960	Pittsburgh Pirates (N.L.)	New York Yankees (A.L.)
1961	New York Yankees (A.L.)	Cincinnati Reds (N.L.)
1962	New York Yankees (A.L.)	San Francisco Giants (N.L.)
1963	Los Angeles Dodgers (N.L.)	New York Yankees (A.L.)
1964	St. Louis Cardinals (N.L.)	New York Yankees (A.L.)
1965	Los Angeles Dodgers (N.L.)	Minnesota Twins (N.L.)
1966	Baltimore Orioles (A.L.)	Los Angeles Dodgers (N.L.)
1967	St. Louis Cardinals (N.L.)	Boston Red Sox (A.L.)
1968	Detroit Tigers (A.L.)	St. Louis Cardinals (N.L.)
1969	New York Mets (N.L.)	Baltimore Orioles (A.L.)
1970	Baltimore Orioles (A.L.)	Cincinnati Reds (N.L.)
1971	Pittsburgh Pirates (N.L.)	Baltimore Orioles (A.L.)
1972	Oakland Athletics (A.L.)	Cincinnati Reds (N.L.)
1973	Oakland Athletics (A.L.)	New York Mets (N.L.)
1974	Oakland Athletics (A.L.)	Los Angeles Dodgers (N.L.)
1975	Cincinnati Reds (N.L.)	Boston Red Sox (A.L.)
1976	Cincinnati Reds (N.L.)	New York Yankees (A.L.)
1977	New York Yankees (A.L.)	Los Angeles Dodgers (N.L.)
1978	New York Yankees (A.L.)	Los Angeles Dodgers (N.L.)
1979	Pittsburgh Pirates (N.L.)	Baltimore Orioles (A.L.)
1980	Philadelphia Phillies (N.L.)	Kansas City Royals (A.L.)
1981	Los Angeles Dodgers (N.L.)	New York Yankees (A.L.)
1982	St. Louis Cardinals (N.L.)	Milwaukee Brewers (A.L.)
1983	Baltimore Orioles (A.L.)	Philadelphia Phillies (N.L.)
1984	Detroit Tigers (A.L.)	San Diego Padres (N.L.)

Year	Winner	Loser
1985	Kansas City Royals (A.L.)	St. Louis Cardinals (N.L.)
1986	New York Mets (N.L.)	Boston Red Sox (A.L.)
1987	Minnesota Twins (A.L.)	St. Louis Cardinals (N.L.)
1988	Los Angeles Dodgers (N.L.)	Oakland Athletics (A.L.)
1989	Oakland Athletics (A.L.)	San Francisco Giants (N.L.)
1990	Cincinnati Reds (N.L.)	Oakland Athletics (A.L.)
1991	Minnesota Twins (A.L.)	Atlanta Braves (N.L.)
1992	Toronto Blue Jays (A.L.)	Atlanta Braves (N.L.)
1993	Toronto Blue Jays (A.L.)	Philadelphia Phillies (N.L.)